T0305333

THE THIN EDGE OF INNOVATION

THE THIN EDGE
OF INNOVATION

METRO VANCOUVER'S
EVOLVING ECONOMY

Roger Hayter, Jerry Patchell,
and Kevin Rees

UBCPress · Vancouver

© UBC Press 2025

All rights reserved. No part of this publication may be reproduced, stored in a retrieval system, or transmitted, in any form or by any means, without prior written permission of the publisher, or, in Canada, in the case of photocopying or other reprographic copying, a licence from Access Copyright, www.accesscopyright.ca.

Originally printed in Canada
Print and bound by CPI Group (UK) Ltd, Croydon, CR0 4YY.

UBC Press is a Benetech Global Certified Accessible™ publisher. The epub version of this book meets stringent accessibility standards, ensuring it is available to people with diverse needs.

___

Library and Archives Canada Cataloguing in Publication

Title: The thin edge of innovation : Metro Vancouver's evolving economy / Roger Hayter, Jerry Patchell, and Kevin Rees.
Names: Hayter, Roger, 1947- author | Patchell, Jerry, author | Rees, Kevin (Economic geographer), author.
Description: Includes bibliographical references and index.
Identifiers: Canadiana (print) 20240519493 | Canadiana (ebook) 20240521544 | ISBN 9780774869928 (hardcover) | ISBN 9780774869942 (PDF) | ISBN 9780774869959 (EPUB)
Subjects: LCSH: Economic development—British Columbia—Vancouver—Case studies. | LCSH: Technological innovations—Economic aspects—British Columbia—Vancouver—Case studies. | LCSH: Entrepreneurship—British Columbia—Vancouver—Case studies. | LCSH: Industries—British Columbia—Vancouver—Case studies. | LCSH: Small business—British Columbia—Vancouver—Case studies. | LCSH: Diversification in industry—British Columbia—Vancouver—Case studies. | LCSH: International business enterprises—British Columbia—Vancouver—Case studies. | LCSH: Vancouver (B.C.)—Economic conditions. | LCGFT: Case studies.
Classification: LCC HC118.V35 H39 2025 | DDC 338.09711/33—dc23

___

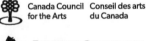

UBC Press gratefully acknowledges the financial support for our publishing program of the Government of Canada, the Canada Council for the Arts, and the British Columbia Arts Council.

This book has been published with the help of a grant from the Canadian Federation for the Humanities and Social Sciences, through the Scholarly Book Awards, using funds provided by the Social Sciences and Humanities Research Council of Canada.

UBC Press is situated on the traditional, ancestral, and unceded territory of the xʷməθkʷəy̓əm (Musqueam) people. This land has always been a place of learning for the xʷməθkʷəy̓əm, who have passed on their culture, history, and traditions for millennia, from one generation to the next.

UBC Press
The University of British Columbia
www.ubcpress.ca

For our families

Contents

Figures and Tables

Figures

Tables

Acknowledgments

This book began as a (Hayter) retirement project sparked by an interest in the origins and evolution of innovative businesses in changing the global face of Metropolitan Vancouver from its resource-driven industrial past toward a more knowledge-based, creative future. As the scope of this grappling became more evident, Jerry and Kevin, former Simon Fraser University (SFU) graduate students, happily and thankfully agreed to participate to make this book possible. In a general sense, our book reflects economic geography's long-standing focus on what distinguishes local economies and makes them tick in an increasingly interdependent world. Indeed, we readily acknowledge debts to much insightful research that has sought to unravel the anatomies and challenges of urban and regional restructuring from manufacturing and resource specialisms towards more innovative, often service sector activities. However networked, and notwithstanding forces of standardization, local difference is an essential feature of the global mosaic of uneven development. As one contribution to this end we offer this book.

To say the least, our research has benefited from interviews and class visits to individual businesses and the help they generously provided, and by access to a plethora of newspaper and magazine articles that have provided much information on our case studies. Prior to submission, early drafts were also aided by advice from David Edgington, Klaus Edenhoffer, and Jacquie Hayter, while John Ng of SFU's Geography Department provided tireless support in drawing (and redrawing) the maps and figures in this book, his long-standing support kindly continuing in my retirement. At UBC Press, from when he saw our first proposal, James MacNevin became an enthusiastic supporter of our project, and we happily acknowledge his championship and advice. Two referees offered considerable encouragement and much constructive commentary and we are grateful for their insights. Once in production, Meagan Dyer's help in guiding us through a lengthy, challenging process has been much appreciated.

Financial support is essential, and in this regard we readily acknowledge the crucial help of a grant from the Federation for the Humanities and Social Sciences through the Scholarly Book Awards program, using funds provided by the Social Sciences and Humanities Research Council of Canada.

Finally, this book is dedicated to our family and friends. We can't mention them all, but at SFU, Len Evenden and Bill Bailey (1950–2005) were wonderful, supportive colleagues *and* mentors to us all and deserve special mention. We all enjoy a rich family life in which Kevin would like to tip his hat to his Dad, David Rees, while Jerry's acknowledgments to Suzy, Jack, and Max can also be found in his recently published opus on South China's industrialization (*China's Greater Bay Area*, Routledge, 2024), a much bigger economic geography than this study. As for me, Jacquie is our bedrock, and our lives greatly enlivened by daughters Alison (Frank), Lynn (Rob), and Megan (Gary) and their families, not least through the ongoing excitement and hope offered by Kiera, Caylee, Phelan, Matthias, Lily, Lauren, and Clark.

Roger Hayter
Calgary, May 2024

THE **THIN** EDGE OF INNOVATION

Introduction

Metro Vancouver's Post-Industrial Transformation toward an Innovation Economy

Innovation is the complete process of taking new ideas and devising new or improved products and services. It comes in all stages of the production of goods and services, from the first vision, design, development, production, sale, and usage.[1]

Over the past two generations, Metro Vancouver has striven to build a new "postindustrial" economy that embraces creative and innovative activities, most obviously the so-called high-tech sector. Such a transformation is readily discerned but still evolving and vulnerable, high tech not as transparently dominant in the local economy as resource activities, especially forestry, once were. For 100 years, commodity forestry was the principal engine of economic development in Vancouver and surrounding communities, providing the region with its industrial identity, substantively expressed in terms of employment, exports, diversification, and wealth and profoundly shaping its emerging metropolitan status in British Columbia and globally. Then forestry started to decline in the 1980s, and, although still contributing to government tax coffers, jobs, and trade, that decline left a large hole in Metro Vancouver's economy and global roles. Has this hole been replaced? In particular, what are the nature and extent to which postindustrial Metro Vancouver has based its economic development on innovation and creativity? Has it achieved that capacity already? If so, then what are the foundations of its innovation capacities, especially in relation to the key high-tech sector? Its high-tech firms have embarked on aerospace, electronics, software engineering, fuel cells, film and game animation, carbon sequestration, and many other specializations, but how broad and/or how deep is this sector? Has innovation reached out to other sectors that contribute to Metro Vancouver's postindustrial identity? Most importantly, has Metro Vancouver developed an innovation economy that complements contemporary patterns of globalization in ways that maintain and enhance its lifestyles and creates so-called high-road jobs that generate and spread the wealth in the economy in a sustainable way? Can all this be accomplished when, although it has an enviable living environment, Metro Vancouver sits on the periphery of national, continental, and global economies? In this book, we seek to address these local development questions, and we come up with some mixed answers. Our primary theme is innovation because it is the accepted answer to maintaining a constantly evolving economy.

Yet, as the basis for development strategies touted around the world, (business) innovation is a multi-faceted, even problematic, imperative, beginning with its conventional starting point definition as new commercial uses of products qua goods or as services, processes, marketing methods, or organizational attributes.[2] Moreover, processes of innovation are incredibly varied in terms of motivation, organization, time horizon, and impact.[3] Innovation can be supply or demand driven; organized by individual inventors, R&D teams, and/or networks of participants in both private and public sectors; time horizons can be incredibly long and replete with financial and technological uncertainties; and outcomes can range from paradigmatic changes – exerting pervasive effects throughout the economy – to small, incremental improvements in productivity. Innovation also requires investment decisions that access talent pools, and if becoming cumulative the first initiatives in particular places are hard to predict or design. In much of this book, we seek to reveal these origins and the subsequent makeup of Metro Vancouver's emerging innovation economy.

The Evolution of Metro Vancouver's Innovation Economy

This book offers an evolutionary economic geography of Metro Vancouver's innovation economy through an analysis of the signature activities redefining its global role through research, development, and/or design (RD&D) initiatives. Our starting thesis is that this evolution has been led principally by locally based entrepreneurial initiatives. That is, the region's innovation economy has been driven from the "bottom up" rather than from the "top down" by government policies or dominant corporations. This reliance on entrepreneurialism is Metro Vancouver's way of dealing with its peripheral location and lack of depth in new industries. From an activity perspective, the entrepreneurially inspired search for a new globally defining innovation economy in Metro Vancouver is most obviously indicated by the so-called high-tech sector, but it is further evident in other parts of the economy, not least in attempts to rejuvenate forestry and by various lifestyle initiatives. Although gathering much recent momentum, the collective nature and scope of these activities are problematic and not fully understood.

High tech's entrepreneurial stimulus can be traced to the 1960s and the formation of several local companies, led by Glenayre and MacDonald Dettwiler and Associates (MDA). As the most notable and enduring business marker of Metro Vancouver's innovation economy, MDA started in 1969 as a spinoff by two University of British Columbia (UBC) professors who expressed a need for Metro Vancouver to diversify its economy to supply jobs for their graduate engineers.[4] MDA subsequently became a Canadian high-tech symbol with its world-leading development of the Canadarm for NASA and is still a vibrant company in Metro Vancouver's innovation economy. Yet a broader high-tech economy remains a work in progress. The sector remained limited in scope until the 1990s, when it became officially recognized, its growth started to be recorded,[5] and studies of specific high-tech clusters were conducted, especially in relation to telecommunications, life sciences or biotechnology, and new media.[6] Similarly, the rejuvenation of the forestry sector around value-added initiatives, such as engineered wood, and the formation of innovative lifestyle businesses (especially in apparel and restaurant chains) has occurred mainly since the 1990s and been driven by local entrepreneurial companies. This growth of high-tech, lifestyle, and even rejuvenated forestry companies has also been strongly service sector oriented, supported by some prototype and custom-made manufacturing but with large-scale manufacturing located elsewhere.

Admittedly, if innovation is becoming an increasingly important force driving Metro Vancouver's economy, according to conventional metrics, such as per capita R&D employment or patent counts, then the region's innovativeness is not particularly distinguished, within Canada or globally. Most saliently, the region lacks the corporate depth for long-term R&D. Metro Vancouver's entrepreneurial innovation has arisen from basic research, intuition, experience, insight, and some response to local demand. Yet that innovation is often incremental, and many firms seek to apply and design technologies and ideas – large and small – developed elsewhere in novel ways. Moreover, most are not committed to controlling an entire production system, and if, as the epigraph to this introduction notes, innovation "comes in all stages of the production of goods and services" then Metro Vancouver firms tend to specialize in one or a few of these stages. The flipside of the remarkable number of innovative firms generated in recent decades is that most of them have remained small and are distributed across many different activities. Only a few have become relatively high-profile ("big firms locally"), and rarely if ever have they grown to the status of giants or even (larger) mid-sized "core" firms. Along the way, many notable companies have failed, such as Glenayre, or been acquired, such as MDA. Although Metro Vancouver is a successful entrepreneurial story, it seems to confront a conundrum of arrested development; development has occurred but without achieving large-scale dominant industries and firms.

Explaining this conundrum is complicated because the spawning and growth of local firms have stimulated greater participation by universities and government policies. In addition, industry organizations and financial services have co-evolved into an increasingly sophisticated array of institutional supports or "architectures" for innovation. Moreover, entrepreneurial firms have sent signals to multinational corporations (MNCs) not only of the availability of acquisition targets but also of Metro Vancouver's expanding talent pool. Together these factors are shaping the nature and extent of Metro Vancouver's innovative milieu and the potential for stronger industry clusters. However, whether the region is solving its seemingly arrested development by using innovation and entrepreneurial diversity as a foundation for long-term cumulative causation remains in question.

In this book, we wish to flesh out the conundrum confronting Metro Vancouver – the strengths and weaknesses of its innovation and its local elaboration. The successes depend on a diversity of high-tech, lifestyle, and rejuvenated forestry activities that draw their innovativeness from the vitality of entrepreneurial firms. The constant generation of these firms is required not only for innovation and diversity per se but also because their capacity to scale up (thus far) has been limited. To make this argument, we emphasize the actual behaviour of entrepreneurial firms, their origins and growth, especially that of relatively high-profile companies, their connections to MNCs, and their implications for a wider institutional architecture, especially within Metro Vancouver. In terms of style, the study seeks to elucidate Metro Vancouver's search for an innovation economy in a readily accessible way that hopefully informs interests beyond those of specialists.

An Integrated Approach

Metro Vancouver's innovation economy might be relatively small, but it is remarkably diverse and complex; this "place-based" study addresses this complexity with an integrative, synthetic analysis. This approach complements previous individual case study clusters, for example of life sciences, by focusing on business behaviour across high-tech, forestry, and lifestyle activities, to provide a broader picture of the region's innovation economy. Analytically, the study is informed by multiple, established, and related concepts drawn from evolutionary qua institutional literatures in business, economics, and economic geography and directed toward understanding the particular global-local dynamics shaping Metro Vancouver's innovation economy. In particular, we fully appreciate our intellectual debt to a multidisciplinary literature on innovation, especially in the Schumpeterian tradition of creative destruction, for which Dan Breznitz's recently acclaimed study provides an exemplar for a wider audience.[7]

As a brief synopsis of this tradition, we note that evolutionary economic theories emphasize the interdependent development of various economic and social factors over the long run. Within this evolution, innovation is particularly important and occurs in a multi-faceted and systemic manner drawing together science, technology, business, and governmental and nongovernmental institutions into regional and national innovation systems.[8] Innovation-based models of industry evolution and changing business organization have been part of this thrust.[9] Adding geographic perspective, locational analyses of innovative activities have sought to understand both their agglomeration and clustering tendencies in place and their global connections across space. They are integrated into regional innovation systems when further incorporating place-based public institutions, industry associations, universities, and cultural contexts.[10] The understanding of local geographies has been enriched by explanations that highlight the leading role of creative or knowledge-driven cities in driving contemporary postindustrial pathways of development.[11] Within evolutionary economic geography, the study of such trajectories by "adaptive" cities is a related focus that provides a specific springboard for this case study of Metro Vancouver, of how this particular place and innovative behaviour interact with one another.[12]

Underlying discussions of the wide-ranging adaptive trajectories of postindustrial cities is a visceral concern: how does a region substantively pursue so-called high-road rather than "low-road" development (see Figure I.1).[13]

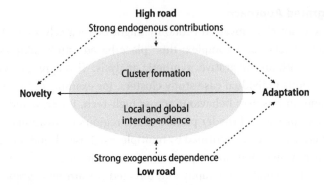

FIGURE I.1 This figure shows that knowledge-based clusters feature novel goods and adaptations that involve both local and global connections. Clusters that originate from local sources are considered a high-road form of development, and those originating from external sources are considered a low-road form of development.

For the former, innovation, talent, and creativity, especially when stimulated entrepreneurially, are widely deemed vital to local development that enhances regional competitiveness, productivity, and per capita income and that can address social goals related to equity and environment. In this scenario, local, innovative entrepreneurship offers key roles to create, endogenously, distinctive, sustainable specialties that can be scaled up and organically deepen locally supportive institutional architecture, all the while underlain by local roots, interests, and understandings. Metro Vancouver is potentially on such a path toward a high-performing, resilient local economy. But this path is not guaranteed; it can change and coexist with – even be challenged by – low-road alternatives. Although Metro Vancouver has not been associated with the classic low road of attracting low-wage "destructive" competition through routinized branch plant operations, a substantial share of its high-tech employees are paid less than their counterparts south of the border. Moreover, the region has been enthusiastic about "place-selling" strategies with little thought for self-generating growth momentum, regional competitiveness, or more social concerns.[14] It might be churlish to describe Metro Vancouver's global promotion of its real estate assets and tourism as low road, but these trajectories are limited in value-added, income-generation, and human-development potential and as a basis for improved productivity. Moreover, money laundering, often organized via casinos before entering real estate (and other) markets, has become contentious, not least for abetting house price inflation and drug pushing, imposing a (low-road) cost-of-living penalty, and failing to attract talent to Metro Vancouver.[15] For the region, ultimately, the most interesting question regarding the evolution of its innovation economy is the extent to which it reflects a high road to local development.

The purpose of this introduction is to provide context for understanding Metro Vancouver's innovation economy and to emphasize that innovation shapes and is shaped by the peculiarities of place. That shaping often occurs in unpredictable ways, at least until momentum is achieved (or lost). The analysis is especially stimulated by pleas for more investigations of the genesis and evolution of innovative private sector firms "to ultimately understand what creates sustainable competitive advantage" in particular places.[16] Our study essentially seeks to appreciate Metro Vancouver's new innovation economy as a "local model" resulting from the distinctive global-local interactions forged by the dynamics of local entrepreneurship within an urban context in which metropolitanism has been built upon an enduring peripherality of geography and political economy.[17] Given Metro Vancouver's population in 2022 of 2.6 million, this appreciation is boosted by recognition of the dynamic role of "intermediate cities," with populations between 300,000 and 5 million and often located in peripheral regions.[18] Compared with megacities, which have been the prime focus of study, these cities, especially in advanced countries, have grown faster and experienced higher rates of innovation-driven productivity growth in recent decades. These cities offer both agglomeration economies and high levels of livability. The signs are promising for Metro Vancouver.

In the rest of this introduction, first we outline Metro Vancouver's growing service sector orientation and the decline of its forest commodity dependence. Then we note the (potential) high road toward innovative development, especially as led by high tech. And then we review this emergence through a global-local lens that links the broad trends of postindustrial transformations with the key distinctive characteristics of Metro Vancouver.[19]

The Resource Export-Urbanization Shift in Development
As David Ley's prescient analysis revealed, the stirrings of change toward postindustrialism and a service-dominated economy within Metro Vancouver were evident by the early 1970s.[20] To be sure, services, manufacturing, and resource activities are highly interdependent, locally and globally, but in a direct job- and wealth-producing sense service jobs have long dominated Metro Vancouver, albeit much stimulated by resource-driven wealth. The strength of that resource-services dependency might have made Metro Vancouver's search to replace an old resource-manufacturing-driven economy

with other independent sources of value generation more problematic. Awareness of the challenges facing such a transformation took root following the deep-seated recessionary crisis of 1981–85 and its termination in the optimism of Expo 86. These events were a critical, turbulent watershed that marked the beginning of the secular decline in forest commodity production and supporting activities (although not for the region's commodity-trading functions). The recession immediately sparked (high-road) thinking on whether rejuvenation should involve innovation-based renewal of forest industries or diversification into innovation-led high tech, then largely portrayed as alternative options. Meanwhile, Expo 86 kick-started two other divergent (and partially low-road) trajectories toward a new, postindustrial economy by placing Metro Vancouver in the eye of global tourists and property developers. In practice, as the old forest industries declined, within a service-dominated economy, all of these trends have occurred to some degree.

Forestry's Big Export Shoes

From the end of the nineteenth century, Vancouver grew as an industrial city, in tandem with the development of British Columbia's hinterland, around resource processing, control, and trading functions.[21] Entry into Confederation (1871), arrival of the Canadian Pacific Railway (CPR, 1887), and opening of the Panama Canal (1914), along with immigrant populations and entrepreneurs, spurred development of the city's resource and export-led growth. The city was the gateway to the province's wide-ranging resource wealth of mining, energy, and fishing, but the forest sector especially thrived as a dominating force throughout Vancouver and adjacent communities. Commodity sawmilling, making dimensional lumber, became the iconic core of the region's industrial identity. It was the engine of growth and had a concomitant influence on society and politics, with the BC forestry sector reaching peak momentum during the 1950s and 1960s. However, the 1970s and 1980s brought repeated crises, not least in large-scale sawmilling and related commodity wood processing. Throughout Metro Vancouver, these activities became undermined by obsolescence, competition from elsewhere, and technological change. In tandem, driven by escalating concern over the forests' ecological and spiritual values, conflicts became widespread throughout the province, and environmental stakeholders welcomed large-scale forestry industry's relentless decline.[22] In the following decades, sawmills and their contribution to development receded from Metro Vancouver's consciousness. Yet the opportunities and dilemmas that arose in commodity forestry's wake remain.

During the post–Second World War boom decades, forestry's dominance in Metro Vancouver's (industrial) economy remained evident until the recession of the 1980s. As one study noted, the metropolitan area's manufacturing base in the 1960s was relatively large but "deceptively narrow" and centred on large-scale wood-processing mills supplying standardized commodity outputs – activities that accounted for 35 percent of the region's manufacturing jobs that provided over 20 percent of its total employment.[23] Despite that narrowness, forestry processing helped to stimulate a wide range of linked activities, especially backwardly linked supplier connections in other forms of secondary manufacturing (machinery, transportation equipment, and metal fabricating) as well as in producer services (managerial, finance, legal, engineering, consulting, R&D). Often summarized with respect to "Fordist" characteristics, the main wood-processing mills were export-oriented, "landscape dominants,"[24] featuring relatively well-paid union jobs in support of standardized, large-volume outputs typically part of large, integrated corporations with head offices in downtown Vancouver.

Emblematic of Metro Vancouver's industrial evolution, as Canada's largest forest products corporation, MacMillan Bloedel (MB) opened its new, architecturally acclaimed head office on Georgia Street in 1968, with its flared footings reflecting an old-growth forest and at the time the tallest building in Vancouver. As the control centre of MB's global operations, the office had over 1,200 employees at its peak and was part of a cluster of related head offices. But the forest industry was about to become more volatile and the 1970s featured two sharp recessions stimulated by global energy crises. Still, Metro Vancouver's forestry activities continued to "bounce back" from downturns, culminating in 1979 and 1980 as record years for production, employment, and profitability. However, in a remarkably abrupt change in fortune, the recession that lasted from 1981 to 1985 provoked significant permanent downsizing and an immediate loss of over 30,000 forestry jobs in Metro Vancouver, with unemployment rates increasing from 6.7 percent to 14.7 percent.[25] As a turning point for forest commodity production in the region, this recession marked the beginning of its secular decline, which continued to unfold over the next two decades (see Chapter 1). By 2018, the old wood-processing mills (plywood and particleboard as well as sawmills) were gone, replaced by shopping malls, residential developments, and commercial uses. MB's head office is still there, renamed the Arthur Erickson Building in 2021, but MB is not, and neither are its managerial jobs.[26] New service companies are now occupying the office spaces.

The Rise of the Service Economy

The service sector's domination of Metro Vancouver's economy is readily
acknowledged, as is its highly varied nature, embracing wide-ranging activities that serve individual consumers (consumer services), businesses (producer services), and governments (public sector services).[27] In the Canadian
census, following international conventions, services are distinguished from
a goods-producing sector and further disaggregated into particular industry groups (see Table I.1).

Clearly, by 1970, the majority of jobs in Metro Vancouver were already
overwhelmingly in services, a dependence that has deepened since then,
while goods-producing jobs, especially in manufacturing, have declined
further, at least relatively. Overall, Metro Vancouver recorded impressive
growth, its population increasing from 1,077,480 to 2,551,000 and its
employment increasing more than threefold from 416,200 to 1,474,000

TABLE I.1 Employment by industry: Metro Vancouver, 1971, 2001, 2019,
and British Columbia, 2019 ('000s)

Industry	Metro Vancouver			British Columbia
	1971	*2001*	*2019*	*2019*
Construction	32.0	54.2	123.4	236.6
Manufacturing	78.8	104.2	96.2	165.7
Total goods	124.8	176.3	240.3	485.6
Trade (retail/wholesale)	85.7	165.6	230.5	389.2
Transportation and warehousing	50.0	67.1	88.4	140.8
Finance, insurance, real estate	28.2	77.2	113.9	158.9
Professional scientific and technical	n/a	95.9	154.8	223.7
Business, building, and support	18.2	42.3	69.3	112.3
Education	27.1	71.8	104.0	178.7
Health care and social assistance	30.3	96.1	160.6	312.6
Information, culture, and recreation	n/a	65.4	88.5	131.5
Accommodation and food	22.3	85.3	103.4	191.2
Public administration	22.3	41.8	51.6	116.0
Other	7.2	52.9	68.6	118.8
Total services	291.3	861.2	1,233.7	2,073.4
TOTAL	416.1	1,037.5	1,474.0	2,559.0

Sources: 2001 and 2019 data from Statistics Canada, Table 14-10-0098-01, "Employment by Industry,
Annual Census (× 1,000)," https://doi.org/10.25318/1410009801-eng. For 1971 data, see Census of
Canada, 1971, "Labour Force By Industry," https://publications.gc.ca/site/eng/9.845602/publications.html.

TABLE I.2 Metro Vancouver GDP by sector, 2017 (%)

Sector	GDP
Finance, insurance, and real estate	31
Construction	9
Manufacturing	8
Professional, scientific, and technical services	8
Transportation and warehousing	7
Retail trade	6
Wholesale trade	6
Health care and social assistance	6
Education services	5
Information and cultural industries	4
Public administration	4
Accommodation and food services	3
Other services	2

Source: City of Vancouver, "Economic Structure of Vancouver: GDP of Metro Vancouver, Fact Sheet #1.5," Vancouver Economic Commission, Figure 1, nd, 1. A map showing 2021 data is available from the same source, but uses slightly different categories to the above.

between 1971 and 2019. During this period, the service sector increased its share of total metropolitan area employment from 70.0 percent in 1971 to 83.0 percent and 83.7 percent, respectively, in 2001 and 2019. Once the industrial heartbeat of Metro Vancouver, manufacturing employment increased slightly until 2001 before declining absolutely as well as relatively, providing just 6.5 percent of metropolitan employment in 2019. That the goods-producing sector as a whole accounted for 16.3 percent of employment in 2019 reflected the doubling in size of construction jobs since 1971.

These broad trends are reinforced by GDP calculations. In 2017, for example, when Metro Vancouver's GDP amounted to $135.6 billion, or 61 percent of British Columbia's GDP ($239.2 billion) and the third largest metropolitan region in Canada, service sector contributions amounted to 83 percent of the total. Furthermore, GDP data confirm the decline of manufacturing and construction activities within Metro Vancouver's goods-producing sector, their combined GDP contributions dropping from 18 percent to 12 percent between 1987 and 2017. In contrast, finance, insurance, and real estate accounted for almost one-third of the region's GDP in 2017.

Moreover, services not only dominate employment and GDP but also are making, perhaps to a surprising degree, increasingly important contributions in replacing wood products as the export foundation of Metro Vancouver's (and British Columbia's) economy. As Metro Vancouver (and British Columbia) have grown, exports or – as they often have been labelled – "basic" activities might have become a less strong "autonomous" predictor of overall growth compared with when the economy was smaller,[28] but they remain essential to its well-being in terms of jobs, income generation, and global roles. The rise of services in this regard is an important trend. Indeed, service exports have climbed dramatically, and by 2018 services provided $32.5 billion or fully 46 percent of total exports ($74.2 billion), about 13 percent of provincial GDP ($246 billion).[29] BC service exports have also become greater than service imports and represent a higher proportion of GDP than in other provinces. It is reasonable to assume from the jobs and GDP data that most of those exports (70 percent or more) originate in Metro Vancouver. In 2018, transportation (gateway) services, tourism, and professional services were the most important categories (61 percent of service exports), and film and TV, education, and a category called "technology" provided 21 percent of service exports. However, although resource exports have declined relatively (and the province has been a net importer of goods since 2007), forestry (especially lumber), energy (especially coal), mining (e.g., copper), and agriculture still provided the overall leading (provincial) export industries in 2018 (and have since); forest revenues remain important to the provincial government even as they decline, and many service exports are resource related.[30]

Metro Vancouver is vital in leading British Columbia away from this dependence towards more innovative activities, as high-road approaches prescribe. However, this challenge is not only about adding new services but about integrating an entrepreneurial culture into a highly structured industry-union culture. It has also occurred in tandem with government policies enthusiastic for place-selling approaches to local development.

Place-Selling Strategies

Expo 86 provided a much-needed immediate stimulus to the local economy and to government and business enthusiasm for promoting Metro Vancouver's attractiveness as a tourist destination and property market. The fair attracted tourists from around the world, and its success helped encourage the initiation of a cruise ship industry, the rejuvenation of the adjacent Coal Harbour, the building of the nearby "world-class" Whistler ski resort, and its hosting of the Winter Olympics in 2010.[31] Tourists and visitors, including conference attendees, to Metro Vancouver have become important to its economy, adding to its amenity levels for all to enjoy, and providing jobs, especially in accommodation, food, and recreational activities. However, many tourism jobs are low waged, seasonal, and inherently labour intensive, and it is difficult to amplify productivity through capital deepening and scale effects. Despite sophisticated service offerings and high incomes for owners and managers of tourism activities, such jobs generally provide workers with low incomes that reflect a low-road form of development.

More controversially, Expo 86 put Metro Vancouver on the maps of global property developers, especially in Asia, with the "transformational" purchase in 1998 of Expo lands as one block to Li Ka-shing of Hong Kong. This purchase of one of North America's prime waterfront sites was made at the relatively modest price of $320 million, further discounted by the province's agreement to invest $145 million for property remediation.[32] Moreover, this deal helped to encourage a virtually uncontrolled (unregulated) flood of investment in housing stock, initially largely from Hong Kong, within a federally directed business investment immigration scheme, and after 2000 by a crescendo of investments from mainland China. Indeed, the increased penetration of foreign capital from Asia into Metro Vancouver property markets in recent decades has helped to commodify and globalize the region's housing.[33] Admittedly, housing market pressures have been pushed by increasing demands from a rising population and a land supply naturally restricted by mountains and the ocean and institutionally restricted by the US border and the Agricultural Land Reserve (greenbelt). Even so, the degree to which accommodation has become unaffordable in Metro Vancouver has been heightened by foreign capital that left much housing empty or occupied by nontaxpayers, increased levels of house flipping, and involved purchases motivated to seek safe havens, spread risks, sanitize illicit funds via money laundering, and/or gain profit rather than more basic reasons of shelter for local residents. As a result, strong inflationary tendencies in housing prices (and rents) have led to a significant affordability problem that has "decoupled" house prices from wages for many residents, threatening the region's self-styled livability characterization.[34] Paradoxically, as legacies of Expo 86, rapidly inflating house prices and low-wage labour in tourism-related activities stand in contradiction to aspirations to improve regional well-being.

To be sure, real estate and construction represent significant benefits to Metro Vancouver's economy, adding to government tax revenues and supporting an increasing number of well-paid jobs that require wide-ranging design and technical expertise within building companies and among professional services such as architecture, engineering, law, real estate, planning, and so on. These contributions readily complement a high road of local development. Yet finance, insurance, and real estate, along with construction, became unusually important in Metro Vancouver's economy, increasing their combined share of the region's GDP from 32 percent in 1987 to 40 percent in 2017, their growth faster than the other thirteen sectors shown (see Table I.2). For critics, however, land sell-offs, a not-well-thought-out investor immigration program, and a ("blind-eye") regulatory disregard for illegal financing have cast dark shadows over real estate and related activities. They argue, starting with billions of dollars from Hong Kong alone in the 1990s, and with increasing momentum until 2017, that provincial (and federal) governments became complicit in a "growth machine" organized by real estate developers in the global commodification of Metro Vancouver's housing market.[35] Indeed, "the Vancouver model" of money laundering from illicit sources in China via gambling in local casinos and its "cleaning" through house purchases has been well cited.[36] In effect, house sales became an export activity increasingly unaffordable to local residents even as it contributed to provincial government revenues.[37] Indeed, there is recognition that a decoupled housing market threatens Metro Vancouver's livability brand (and high-road hopes).[38] Conversely, a greater commitment to a high-road innovation economy, well expressed by but not limited to high tech, is seen as a way to address such problems.

Innovation for a High Road
Although the struggle to find a development foundation for Metro Vancouver might have veered onto the wealth offered by the low road of tourism and house sales, the resource industries' legacy simultaneously created an urban foundation for innovative and creative activities. They evolved organically at first but have been nurtured by Metro Vancouver's wealth, ambience, culture, and co-evolving institutions.

High Tech
High-tech activities are central to Metro Vancouver's aspirations as an innovation economy, with local roots that can be traced to the 1960s with the emergence of Glenayre Electronics (1963), Sierra Wireless (1966), and MDA (1969), along with the even earlier pioneering efforts of Donald Hings (see Case Study I.1). These firms anticipated the locally based entrepreneurial origins of high tech in Metro Vancouver including important roles of Burnaby and Richmond as well as for Vancouver itself. Meanwhile, Lenkurt

CASE STUDY I.1   Donald Hings: British Columbia's Inspirational
High-Tech Pioneer

In 2001, Donald Hings (1907–2004) of Burnaby received the Order of Canada in recognition of his role as inventor and innovator, notably his pioneering work in the 1930s and 1940s on the "C-58 wireless set," more popularly referred to as the "walkie-talkie." Hings was three when he came to Canada with his mother, first settling in Lethbridge, Alberta, before moving to New Westminster, British Columbia. With only a few years of formal education, Hings became a self-taught pioneer in electronics, producing fifty-five patents, including for an aircraft landing system, the klystron magnetometer survey system, the thermionic vacuum tube, and an electronic piano in addition to the walkie-talkie. It originated in his work on a "bush radio" for a mining company in the 1930s, with the first fully operational walkie-talkie developed in 1937 while Hings was living in the remote community of Rossland in the BC Interior. Subsequently, at the government's invitation in 1939, Hings developed this model in Ottawa with support from the National Research Council. His "revolutionary" walkie-talkie design was durable, simple, and versatile, and it allowed for two-way "talk-based" (rather than code-based) communication among troops in battlefield conditions while filtering out noise and preventing eavesdropping. Over 18,000 units were shipped from a Toronto manufacturing plant to Europe to support the Allied war effort, with Hings refusing any royalty payments. He received the Order of the British Empire in 1946 and soon after returned to British Columbia, where he established his home and business, Electronic Laboratories of Canada Ltd., on Capital Hill, North Burnaby, creating a mini complex of "towers, radar sheds, electronic shops and laboratories" as well as employee housing that formed a "hilltop community of scientists," which remained in operation until the mid-1980s.

Subsequently, Donald Hings mentored his grandson, Guy Cramer, on "innovation" and together they formed Hyperstealth Biotechnology Corp in 1989 to develop hyperbaric chambers and sophisticated forms of camouflage (an established Cramer interest), designs of which have been exported to over 50 countries. Hyperstealth operated in Moli Energy's old facility (see Case Study 2.1) until recently before relocating to Cramer's Maple Ridge home.

Sources: C. Hanson, "Walkie-Talkie Design Had Origins in the Bush," *Vancouver Sun,* August 17, 2001, B1, B7; T. Hawthorn, "Tinkerer Invented the Walkie-Talkie," *Globe and Mail,* April 7, 2004, http://www.radioalumni.ca/z_1937_walkie_talkie.htm. G. McIntyre, "Hidden Gem: Maple Ridge Firm Supplies Camouflage Worldwide," *Vancouver Sun,* January 9, 2024, https://vancouversun.com/news/local-news/hidden-gem-maple-ridge-firm-supplies-camouflage-worldwide.

Electronics (Burnaby, 1949), a Californian-based manufacturing subsidiary, foreshadowed the later arrival of foreign direct investment (FDI) in the sector.[39] Overall, however, high-tech growth remained tiny in scale until after Expo 86.

Indeed, the initial government reports that documented high tech in British Columbia began only in the mid-1990s.[40] Then the first statistical profile of the BC high-tech sector emphasized its growth for the 1988–95 period, albeit from small beginnings. As the report notes, in this period, high-tech GDP, employment, exports, and number of establishments all grew substantially faster than provincial averages: GDP in the BC high-tech sector more than doubled, from $1,083 million to $2,415 million; revenues increased from $2,048 million to $5,114 million, with exports increasing from 40 percent to 47 percent of these revenues; employment increased from 27,240 to 41,130; and the number of establishments expanded from 4,448 to 5,116 (see Table I.3). Since then, the BC government and other industry analysts with increasing frequency – BC tech reports are now annual – have documented the size and scope of the high-tech sector and invariably attest to its rapid growth. As these reports indicate, from 2006 to 2018, high-tech GDP, revenues, and jobs in manufacturing and services have grown substantially beyond 1995 levels (see Table I.4). The sector's export performance has grown in tandem with export sales ratios above 20 percent since 2006, and the United States has been the dominant export market complemented by sales around the globe (see Table I.5). In summary, high tech's share of provincial GDP increased from 1.8 percent in 1988 to 2.6 percent in 1995, almost 6 percent in 2009, and 6.5 percent in 2016, and in 2018 it contributed 6.4 percent of total exports.[41]

Not without ambiguity, high tech's definition in these reports is derivative and seemingly tautologous, namely as "those that produce high-tech [manufactured and services] goods."[42] In practice, the BC government and other authorities conceive of high tech broadly as industries that embrace new activities indicative of a knowledge-based innovative economy, driven by research, development, design, and other sources of creativity. Although businesses in life sciences, electronics, and renewable energy employ contingents of highly educated scientists and engineers in R&D programs and are the high-tech bellwethers, the so-called cultural and new media industries that draw from softer skills and experiences for creative inspiration are also designated as high tech. In this regard, the acronym RD&D rather than just R&D is a better designation for BC high tech, although the latter is still the more conventional label. R&D expenditures in the province grew from

TABLE I.3 British Columbia's high-tech activities, 1988–95: Selected characteristics

Sector	GDP ($ million)		Revenues ($ million)		Employment	
	1988	1995	1988	1995	1988	1995
Manufacturing	266	628	620	1,193	7,100	8,600
Service	817	1,787	1,428	3,921	20,150	32,530
Total high tech	1,083	2,415	2,048	5,114	27,240	41,130
Total BC economy	61,148	94,118	11,561	14,516	1,167,800	1,402,600

Note: GDP is estimated at factor cost.
Source: BC Stats, The British Columbia High Technology Sector, 1996, joint project of BC Stats, Ministry of Finance and Corporate Relations, and Science and Technology Branch, Information, Science and Technology Agency, prepared by J. Lawrance, S. Miller, M. Monkman, and J. Plant; selected information from Tables 2, 3, and 4 (24–26).

TABLE I.4 British Columbia's high-tech activities in the manufacturing and service sectors, 2006–16

Sector	GDP ($ billion)			Revenues ($ billion)			Employment		
	2006	2016	2019	2006	2016	2019	2006	2016	2019
Manufacturing	1.3	1.6	1.8	2.7	4.3	4.5	15,480	14,360	17,380
Service	9.7	12.9	16.6	14.4	24.5	30.4	70,300	92,070	113,840
Total	11.0	14.6	18.0	17.1	28.9	34.7	85,878	106,430	131,220

Note: GDP is estimated in constant dollar prices.

Sources: BC Stats, Profile of the British Columbia High Technology Sector 2017 Edition (Victoria: Prepared for Ministry of Jobs, Recovery and Innovation, 2017, by Dan Schrier); selected information from Tables A1 (12), A2 (18), 7 (52), and 10 (55); BC Stats, Profile of the British Columbia High Technology Sector 2020 Edition (Victoria: Prepared for Ministry of Jobs, Recovery and Innovation, 2021, by Dan Schrier); selected information from Tables A1 (8), A2 (13), 7 (45), and 10 (48).

TABLE I.5 Estimated geographic distribution of British Columbia's
high-tech exports, 2006–19 ($ billion)

Destination	2006	2016	2019
United States	2.2 (69%)	3.3 (56%)	4.5 (58.9%)
European Union	0.4 (12%)	0.8 (13%)	0.9 (12.2%)
Pacific Rim	0.4 (11%)	0.8 (14%)	1.0 (13.4%)
Other	0.2 (7%)	0.9 (15%)	1.2 (15.4%)
Total exports	3.2	5.9	7.6
Total revenues	14.6	28.9	34.9

Note: BC Stats provides data on exports of high-tech manufactured goods to the above regions, and
their shares in this regard are used to estimate the overall distribution of high-tech exports, including
services.
Sources: BC Stats, *Profile of the British Columbia High Technology Sector 2017 Edition* (Victoria: Prepared
for Ministry of Jobs, Recovery and Innovation, 2017, by Dan Schrier); selected information from Tables
A4 (30), A5 (33), 27 (71), and 48 (93); BC Stats, *Profile of the British Columbia High Technology Sector
2020 Edition* (Victoria: Prepared for Ministry of Jobs, Recovery and Innovation, 2021, by Dan Schrier);
selected information from Tables A4 (24), A6 (27), 27 (65), and 50 (89).

$2.2 billion in 2004 to $3.2 billion in 2014 and to $4.2 billion in 2017, when
business contributed 57 percent ($2.4 billion) of the total (universities ac-
counting for most of the rest).[43] Even so, Telus, as the largest of the business
spenders, only ranked fourteenth in Canada, and there are high-tech firms
that do not engage in long-term, substantive R&D, with design activities
more prevalent.

Given its growth momentum in recent decades, four key characteristics
of the BC high-tech sector are consistently highlighted in reports and can
be summarized: its concentration in Metro Vancouver, service emphasis,
diversified nature, and local entrepreneurialism. First, in terms of geographic distribution, initial estimates by BC Stats that Metro Vancouver
accounted for about 67 percent of high-tech activity in the province in
1995 have been verified and perhaps are conservative.[44] Subsequently,
PricewaterhouseCoopers (PwC) pioneered a direct sampling and mapping
of high-tech businesses throughout British Columbia and produced several
"techmaps" that indicated a deepening concentration of technology companies in Vancouver from 46 percent in 2003 to 54 percent in 2012 while
further recognizing Burnaby and Richmond as important inner-suburban
centres.[45] Overall, 82 percent of the 1,383 companies surveyed for the 2012
"techmap" were in Metro Vancouver. If adjacent areas such as Victoria and
Squamish are included, then this share would increase.

Second, on all indicators, service sector activities dominate high tech; in 1995, they accounted for 74 percent of employment and GDP and 77 percent of revenue, by 2016 they accounted for 89.0 percent, 86 percent and 86.5 percent, respectively, of high-tech GDP, revenues and employment, and similar levels of dominance or even higher (for GDP) in 2019 (see Tables I.3 and I.4). This domination highlights Metro Vancouver's transformation from an industrial to a postindustrial city in which manufacturing is restricted to prototype, custom-made, and specialized equipment functions.

Third, within Metro Vancouver, high tech has been remarkably diversified across multiple activities and is well illustrated by the range of innovative-driven product mixes pursued by the leading local firms (see Chapter 2) or controlled by MNCs (see Chapter 3). This diversity is not easy to classify, and the five to seven categories employed by BC Stats or KPMG are highly aggregated and contain much internal variation; indeed, PwC's 2003 and 2012 surveys of high-tech activities were allocated into twelve different clusters (see Chapter 4).[46] However classified, Metro Vancouver high tech comprises a remarkable range of activities in aerospace, computer hardware, software development in multiple business services, green energy and clean tech, electronics, artificial intelligence, biotechnology, film and TV productions, video games, and more. This diversification is a significant distinctive feature. The iconic Silicon Valley, for example, is over ten times larger in industrial scale but overwhelmingly focused on consumer and enterprise information technology.[47]

Fourth, in Metro Vancouver high tech, more so than elsewhere, the population pyramid of firms is strongly weighted to small, entrepreneurial firms. Thus, the number of high-tech businesses in British Columbia increased from 5,116 to almost 11,000 between 1995 and 2018, when 80 percent of the firms employed fewer than 10 and over 95 percent employed fewer than 100, with only 220 firms employing more than 100.[48] Furthermore, according to KPMG, whereas just 50 employees are needed to be in the 10 percent of high-tech companies in British Columbia, the Canadian average is 100 employees, and California, Germany, and Israel, respectively, require 500, 150+, and 200+ employees to join this category. The increasing levels of FDI in Metro Vancouver's high-tech industries, including the world's largest MNCs, so far have not changed this characteristic. Although several local firms have become relatively large, beyond conventional definitions of small and medium-sized firms (SMEs), none has become a global giant or even a big mid-sized firm, and among this group there have been failures and acquisitions by MNCs, and subindustries have experienced decline.[49] In comparison with other high-tech areas, Metro Vancouver, for better or worse, is highly fragmented by sector, dependent on SMEs, and, with a caveat regarding Telus, lacks dominant lead firms.

In summary, as of 2019, even as its profile has increased, high tech remains a modest (direct) component of Metro Vancouver's economy. Per capita R&D investments and patent counts also lag national and appropriate global averages.[50] If Metro Vancouver was assumed to have 75 percent of British Columbia's high-tech employment of 123,710 in 2018 (131,220 in 2019), then the resulting total of 92,376 jobs (98,415 in 2019) amounted to about 6.3 percent (6.6 percent in 2019) of its economy, roughly congruent with its share of the region's GDP. In terms of jobs, GDP, or exports, high tech is similarly about 6–8 percent of the region's economy. Yet, in comparison with the forest sector, high tech has become – at least since 2012 – as large in employment terms, and its growth more than compensated for the loss of commodity manufacturing jobs. Furthermore, even though not export oriented, it does serve global markets and has attracted much FDI.[51] High-tech activities have also stimulated a supporting institutional architecture involving government policy, financing, associations, and universities. As a high-road approach, high tech has added growth and productivity to the economy, with potential for further growth; its wage levels are higher than the local average, if lower than other high-tech centres, and it might help to close the gap between income and housing affordability. High tech, with its overall emphasis on clean service jobs and efforts to develop renewable energy as part of its diversified portfolio, is also acknowledged, if often uncritically, in support of Metro Vancouver's green aspirations. Moreover, the region's search for a globally competitive innovation economy is not restricted to high tech.

The Innovation Economy beyond High Tech

Beyond (new) high tech, innovation has stimulated globally distinct competitive advantages in Metro Vancouver's economy in mature industries, including through forest sector rejuvenation and emergence of new consumer-driven lifestyle activities.[52] In these industries, innovation has typically been incremental, design centred, and market driven, with some investment in formal RD&D programs. In the forest sector, the recession in the 1980s sparked a chorus of pleas for innovation to overcome obsolescence, even as rationalization and cost cutting then dominated industry behaviour. With gathering momentum, however, since the 1990s, innovation has helped to restructure Metro Vancouver's forest-related activities, especially through new entrants in equipment manufacturing, engineering, and other services, a reorganization of industry R&D, and an array of value-added operations, often involving small firms. Indeed, Metro Vancouver has been a pioneering (R&D-driven) hub of provincial expansions of engineered wood introduced commercially at Expo 86, even if its potential has been appreciated only within the past decade or so. Similarly, after much debate, forest sector R&D across Canada was reorganized in 2007 through the establishment of FPInnovations, a private, nonprofit organization with a major research centre in Metro Vancouver. FPInnovations mainly serves the provincial forest sector through new technologies and state-of-the-art advice while moving beyond its traditional sector and regional mandates.[53] These initiatives collectively support pleas for a knowledge-based forest sector economy.[54]

In Metro Vancouver's evolution to postindustrialism, changing patterns of consumption have helped to spark new demand-driven initiatives that complement as well as contrast with high tech. Indeed, one lively assessment of Metro Vancouver's postindustrial identity as West Coast "cool" and "laid-back" features not only new high-tech activities but also various lifestyle-related initiatives that range from distinctive restaurant chains to clothing design companies.[55] In these activities, entrepreneurs started locally and then expanded their brands through exports and investments across Canada and sometimes throughout North America and globally. Lululemon, Arc'teryx, Mountain Equipment Co-op, Aritzia, and Fluevog headline the apparel ventures, and other innovative examples ranging from mountain bikes to beer brewing can be cited. Essentially, these lifestyle ventures have spun out of traditional (low-tech) industries (clothing, brewing) based on design-led innovation. As in high tech, the local jobs created by these initiatives are primarily in services, with any local manufacturing involving small batch or niche production or prototype creation and large-scale manufacturing of these innovations occurring primarily elsewhere (see Chapter 7). Exceptionally, Lululemon has become a global and very large mid-sized company.[56]

The Global Context of Metro Vancouver's Innovation Economy

As a local model of development, Metro Vancouver's transformation to an innovation economy is both a distinctive and a shared experience. From this perspective, Metro Vancouver's evolution as part of broader trends – such as deindustrialization, globalization, and shifts toward knowledge-driven service economies – is largely grounded by its peripherality and the contingent performances of its endogenously inspired entrepreneurs, themselves globally connected to R&D, markets, finance, and ownership.[57]

Local Transformation as Shared Experience

Within the context of widespread deindustrialization, globalization, and restructuring, the rise of innovation-driven knowledge and creative economies has become a central theme in postindustrial cities' search for growth, adaptability, and resilience. The downsizing of Metro Vancouver's resource industries during the 1980s, for example, was part of the "deindustrialization" and massive loss of manufacturing jobs that occurred in cities throughout the historic manufacturing belts of Europe and North America.[58] In tandem, Metro Vancouver, as elsewhere, experienced an intensification of globalization processes that increasingly opened national and local economies to exogenous sources of change, including with respect to the shift of global export-oriented manufacturing capacity to emerging economies, especially in Asia.[59] From an evolutionary perspective, the restructuring of the technological and organizational foundations of global and local economies has been summarized as the transformation of "creative destruction" from Fordism to an information and communication technology (ICT) paradigm.[60] In this view, the signature characteristics of Fordist production systems, standardized mass production, unionism, and energy intensity were becoming increasingly obsolete. As models of replacement, micro-electronics and flexible manufacturing were the driving forces of ICT, generating novel industries and rejuvenating established Fordist industries by improving their productivity through more flexible, diverse forms of organization and employment, often in new economic spaces. The contemporary transformation of Metro Vancouver's economy has been interpreted along these lines, including the recognition that mass production, whether in resource industries or in secondary manufacturing, is cheaper elsewhere.[61] Metro Vancouver has had to jump on the innovation bandwagon or be left behind.

Vital to economic growth since ancient times, innovation and the application of new knowledge have spurred several waves of industrialization over the past 250 years, becoming an increasingly intense mantra for development over the past half century. Local development policies emphasizing innovation imperatives are now widespread.[62] Attempted clonings of Silicon Valley – through regional innovation systems or entrepreneurial ecosystems – have been prevalent strategies in this regard, albeit with varying degrees of success.[63] With high tech as the most significant marker,

contemporary postindustrial transformations toward knowledge-based local economies around the globe, including in Metro Vancouver, are distinguished by six key (related) trends: (1) a deepening of knowledge-based production functions, (2) the enhanced role of universities in national and
regional innovation systems, (3) the creation of new activities as sources of
employment, (4) the organization of local high-tech clusters that are also
part of global innovation systems, (5) the rise of specialized financing, and
(6) a search for sustained competitiveness that increasingly has engaged
environmental imperatives.

First, the transformation toward postindustrial cities has become driven
increasingly by innovation, the development and application of various
forms of knowledge, and ongoing commitments to learning as inputs within
production functions. Indeed, the imperatives of innovation, creativity, and
problem solving are pervasive throughout the economy and not restricted
to formal RD&D or to professional white-collar groups. In turn, these imperatives have required a sea change in attitudes toward local competitiveness among postindustrial cities that emphasize (local) knowledge creation
and thinking skills rather than reliance on repetitive physical, administrative, or service labour.

Second, the growth of knowledge- and learning-intensive activities has
been associated with an evolution in the nature of regional or local innovation systems. These systems typically evolved as specialized components
of national counterparts, formally since the end of the nineteenth century,
centred on the activities and networks of a "triple helix" of corporate, government, and university (and hybrid forms of) RD&D, which both supplemented and supplanted dependence on individual business innovators.[64]
For industrial cities, private sector corporate R&D was typically the major
driving force orchestrating innovation. However, for postindustrial cities,
universities have become more proactive within the triple helix, engaging
more fully in applied and generative technological transfer activities, in
addition to their traditionally important roles of teaching and basic research.[65] The increasingly sophisticated knowledge required in RD&D processes, the policy imperatives attached to innovation, and the income to be
acquired from licensing, patenting, and so on have supported this trend. In
the United States and globally, the Bayh-Dole Act of 1980, which granted
universities patenting and licensing rights for innovations funded by the federal government, was an important milestone. Again, the well-recognized
close association between Stanford University and the firms of Silicon Valley
has been the exemplar of university-industry technology transfer for other

regions around the world to follow. Indeed, a significantly enhanced role for "entrepreneurial universities" that more fully engage with innovation and its commercialization, including in peripheral regions where business-led innovation traditionally has been under-represented, is a widespread trend, even if university claims in this regard can be exaggerated.[66] Nevertheless, university roles in regional innovation systems have been widely expanded, including in Metro Vancouver, where the University of British Columbia and Simon Fraser University (SFU) have ramped up their industry liaison and entrepreneurship programs since the 1980s. Indeed, their increased participation in local innovation systems is associated with changing roles in postindustrial urban and regional transformation: from support systems to established industrial specialties, such as forestry, to becoming proactive sources of high-tech diversification.

Third, at the forefront of postindustrial transformation are technologies and products (goods and services) that did not exist prior to 1970 or 1980, and these new activities enable, indeed compel, competitive innovation. Many directly feature new information and communication (electronic and computer-related) products and processes, and the new digital technologies are widely used in other applications, including advances in biotechnologies, health sciences, and energy-related activities intended to reduce environmental impacts. These new activities have highlighted the importance of innovation to competitiveness and injected into local economies new skills, businesses, and employee relations as well as forms of RD&D. The increasing reference to RD&D, rather than just R&D, reflects the growing importance of design activities that typically involve computer assisted design and manufacture (CAD-CAM) techniques and are focused on technology transfer to (industrial and individual) consumers. Moreover, within advanced high-cost economies a focus on R&D and technology creation has been associated with declines in manufacturing's importance. Even Silicon Valley has witnessed a substantial restructuring along these lines with the mass production of semiconductors largely relocated to lower-wage regions in Asia and the rural United States in recent decades. As noted, manufacturing in Metro Vancouver has similarly declined.

Fourth, the geographies of postindustrial transformations broadly share, even if they vary locally, the clustering or agglomeration of activities that, as Metro Vancouver's experience demonstrates, are both complemented and threatened by processes of globalization. The mutual benefits that arise from local interdependencies are conventionally defined as agglomeration or external economies of scale and scope and further disaggregated as localization and urbanization economies of scale.[67] The former emphasize the development of talented labour pools, information sharing, supplier networks, and associations in support of *related* activities, whereas the latter primarily reflect the advantages provided to all businesses by the development of urban infrastructure (transportation, housing, etc.), amenities, and educational systems. Innovative and creative activities in general are predicated to a considerable degree on where talented entrepreneurs and labour forces wish to live, typically places that already provide or have the potential to provide high levels of amenities (educational, social, recreational) in safe, welcoming spaces (urbanization economies scale), and where job prospects and satisfaction in wide-ranging, high-income occupations that feature mutually expanding information exchanges and job opportunities are plentiful (localization economies). From these perspectives, the growth of innovative activities in Metro Vancouver reflects the location preferences of talent and its global ranking as a desirable place to live.[68] Hitherto, agglomeration diseconomies such as growing congestion and inflated house prices have not (yet) undermined this ranking.

For innovative activities, proximity is a powerful force facilitating information exchanges and networking within clusters. However, specialized inputs might not be locally available and require access from more distant places. In this regard, localization economies developed in particular places that become more accessible to firms located elsewhere shift from being "immobile," available only to local adjacent firms, to being "mobile," external economies that can be accessed globally.[69] Indeed, the globalization of "spatial information systems" linking high-tech clusters around the world through various forms of information exchange and expertise suggests that mobile external economies have become more important, including as a source of entrepreneurial spinoffs and venture capital.[70] In the case of Metro Vancouver, key high-tech initiatives often have depended on accessing crucial inputs from elsewhere, such as venture capital and specialized research activities, not available locally. That is, globalization has complemented local clustering for Metro Vancouver's distinctive experiences of postindustrial transformation.

Fifth, a growing commitment to innovation has required specialized forms of financing and incentives. Financing is necessary for aspiring entrepreneurs to fund initial capital and human resources expenses to develop technologies and products in their early stages and to support various stages of development so that a start-up can scale up. This financing must accept risk and be selective in choosing viable companies. Usually, investors also provide guidance for management, networking, and further development. Such financing comes in various forms, directly from venture capitalists, angel investors, and initial public offerings (IPOs) and indirectly through incubators and other means of providing facilities and managerial guidance. Coupled with finance are the incentives of payouts to the entrepreneurs, whether through buyouts by other firms or through IPOs. Scientific recognition, fame, and other incentives might help to spur on an innovation system, but financial payouts are the most high powered. Although Vancouver once was infamous for the risk taking in its mining-based stock market, it has had to construct a new system of institutions and organizations to support the financial needs of its innovation efforts and to rely on external funding and expertise.

And sixth, as climate warming and biodiversity degradation have become global problems, locally generated policy responses that enhance environmental as well as economic values have received increasing priority, including widely at urban scales.[71] Metro Vancouver, the birthplace of Greenpeace in 1971, has been part of these efforts. Its environmental opposition to resource corporations and industries grew rapidly, becoming especially strident since the 1980s. Policy efforts to promote a green economy in Metro Vancouver have been slower to develop, however, and in the past decade or so they have been associated loosely with support for high tech, as indicated by Vancouver's proposal in 2010 for a green economy. Indeed, this plea itself was stimulated by the emergence of local, environmentally motivated businesses, led by Ballard (see Chapter 2). A notable facet of Metro Vancouver's development dynamics is that environmental politics fervently have sought the demise of the resource commodities while supporting a new innovation economy to foster its postindustrial development.[72]

Entrepreneurialism and Peripherality as Defining Local Attributes

For Metro Vancouver, the nature of its expanding innovation economy, in the first instance, directly reflects its entrepreneurial foundations. Here as elsewhere, these foundations both shape and are shaped by extant development, often in ways that are hard to predict, serving both to reinforce and to redirect local trajectories.[73] Conventionally, this unpredictability has been captured in terms of Marshallian or Jacobs effects on local urban diversification. According to the Marshallian viewpoint, new firms reflect the impacts of localization economies and serve cumulatively to add to established industrial specializations and/or to elaborate them in closely related backwardly and forwardly linked activities. Alternatively, so-called Jacobs-style (urbanization) externalities generate new firms that might have little to do with existing specialties but represent completely different trajectories rooted in the diversity of the backgrounds, interests, and networks of growing, dynamic, urban populations.[74] For Metro Vancouver, its industrial identity in resource-based, especially forestry-related, activities can be interpreted readily along the lines of Marshallian agglomeration economies and linked activities. In contrast, formation of the pioneering high-tech firms in the 1960s such as MDA, Glenayre, Sierra Systems Group, or Hings's Electronic Laboratories represented new economic trajectories that reflect Jacobs's viewpoint, further reinforced by the continued strong role of local entrepreneurs in the diversification of the region's high-tech endeavours. In general, local innovative firms serve to retain local control, commitments, and direction of local transformation, and they help to embed supportive local institutional architectures. The proliferation of local firms also builds up local labour pools and talent that can stimulate spinoff developments, raise possibilities for their own growth as core firms, and attract MNCs from elsewhere looking to diversify geographically sources of innovation and forms of knowledge. Yet Marshallian and Jacobs effects are not always easy to distinguish; the extent and nature of relatedness of new activities to existing activities can vary substantially, and there is the question of when a new trajectory becomes an established one. Nevertheless, the regional diversification literature strongly suggests that expanding through forms of related variety is more likely to succeed in the long run than isolated separate trajectories.[75]

The entrepreneurial initiatives driving Metro Vancouver's innovation economy are necessarily contextualized by a particular form of urbanization in which a dominant narrative of metropolitanism is shaped by an enduring peripherality of geography and political economy. Even as Canada's dynamic third largest metropole, Metro Vancouver remains defined as a "city on the edge" in socio-economic (as well as geological) terms, located near the end of the world's time zones, at the margin of British Columbia, Canada, the North American Pacific Coast, and the Pacific Rim region.[76] Certainly, the region's core status in controlling, processing, supplying, and transporting the rich and varied resources of its hinterland has long defined British Columbia's space economy and provided the (economic) basis for its emergence as a metropolitan city-region by the 1960s.[77] Since then, and especially since Expo 86, metropolitanism and postindustrialism have deepened as Metro

Vancouver has increasingly embraced services and the knowledge economy.[78] In tandem, contacts around the Pacific Rim are increasingly evident. As a sea and air hub, Metro Vancouver offers important advantages in accessing Asia Pacific and becoming part of its extraordinary dynamism while offering adjacency to key US Pacific seaboard cities. Regarding the latter, Metro Vancouver is in the same time zone and only a short flight to any of San Diego, Los Angeles, San Francisco and Silicon Valley, Portland, and Seattle. Proposals for a Cascadia region linking Washington, Oregon, and British Columbia reflect growing functional ties within the Pacific Northwest. In terms of global rankings of cities, in addition to its high ranking in terms of livability,[79] Vancouver has become recognized for its knowledge-based local development.[80] The idea of Vancouverism as a planning model further captures the sense of metropolitanism and influence on the global stage.[81]

Even so, Metro Vancouver remains peripheral in geographic, economic, and political spaces. For local businesses, the immediate provincial market encompasses a noteworthy but relatively small market of 4 million people, with Canada's population of 39.3 million people (2021) largely located far away in other provinces. If Canada's strong federal structure is partly a response to the challenges of governance in a geographically huge country, then British Columbia (among other provinces) is peripheral to Canada's heartland of Ontario and Quebec and the centre of "national" policies and priorities. For both British Columbia and Metro Vancouver, these policies, when applicable, are a "sharing exercise" requiring mediation with federal bureaucracies on scope, funding, and regulations. In practice, geographic distances, a deeply divided heartland, and strong provincial governments have contributed to highly regionalized Canadian markets. Moreover, Canada itself is peripheral within North America, overwhelmingly dependent on the United States for both markets and supply sources, rendering Metro Vancouver doubly peripheral and its economy (like those of other Canadian centres) pulled strongly southward, always countering eastern integration into the national economy. In relation, Metro Vancouver (and British Columbia) have shared national tendencies in terms of openness toward the forces of globalization, including with respect to FDI, long dominated by the United States, helping to reinforce north-south connections. In this regard, more so than other Canadian cities and regions, Metro Vancouver is strongly connected with the major US Pacific Coast cities but without implications for changing the locus of decision-making power in the latter. Meanwhile, connections in Asia Pacific might be burgeoning, but they are far away geographically and with different political, regulatory, and usually more powerful economies and political regimes. For Metro Vancouver, peripherality implies both challenges and opportunities for an innovation economy.

Conclusion

As a postindustrial city-region, Metro Vancouver is certainly not a quintessential periphery,[82] but it is peripheral, and this peripherality has shaped its innovation economy. With private sector R&D limited, and an industrial economy dominated by mature industries preoccupied with processing efficiencies of standardized commodities, the rise of an innovation-driven knowledge economy more or less started from scratch. This development was dependent on the emergence of individual scattered, small-scale pioneering efforts in advanced technologies and products and their stimulus, gradual at first, to a more rapid accumulation of endogenous technological capabilities by a growing pool of entrepreneurs and the building of supportive infrastructure. Simultaneously, peripherality has also meant necessarily a strong reliance on exogenous access to markets, expertise, finance, and manufacturing capability. Peripheries require external contacts in all phases of innovation, "from the first vision to ... usage," an imperative readily apparent in Metro Vancouver. An important challenge facing its innovation economy is balancing the pros and cons of greater self-reliance with the pros and cons of connections elsewhere. The former enhance local multipliers, "buzz," and other impacts, but too much can lead to parochiality and institutional inertia, while the latter provides vital inputs and markets not available locally but can lead to excessive dependency and foreign control.[83]

Metro Vancouver clearly has much potential to elaborate its innovation economy in which local actors play proactive global roles. Indeed, its bottom-up, entrepreneurially dominated, innovative diversification illustrates a high-road approach to local development that enhances high-income, globally distinctive forms of competitiveness and sustainable specialties with deep local roots that can engage proactively in global value chains. Moreover, Metro Vancouver is a high-amenity location attractive to entrepreneurial initiatives and required talent. Still, questions can be raised regarding the region's entrepreneurialism about whether it is too diversified, whether it is ineffective in generating local core companies that can grow to expand employment, and whether the attraction to FDI will be reinforcing or dampening. Furthermore, the emphasis on "place-selling" strategies by the provincial and local governments in recent decades, though generating wealth and employment, have raised housing costs and congestion, both problematic for the high road of an innovation economy. Whether Metro Vancouver's hybrid forms of local development can shift more emphatically toward high-road options remains to be seen.

In the remainder of this book, we focus on the evolutionary geography of businesses, along with their institutional networking, that contribute to Metro Vancouver's global identity as an innovation economy. High tech is central to this contemplation because of its newness, dynamism, relative size, and potential to promote local development. In addition, providing bookends to the high-tech analyses, we explore distinctive innovation-led developments rejuvenating the forestry sector and promoting lifestyle business specialties within Metro Vancouver. Emphasizing the proactive role of local entrepreneurialism, we pay particular attention to local businesses that have scaled up and become higher profile. Certainly, as is documented, FDI has become an increasing force in high-tech and lifestyle activities (arguably less so in rejuvenated forestry), and foreign ownership has become an important attribute of the contemplation of future trajectories. Yet, with caveats aside, FDI in innovative activities has been attracted largely to the region by the emergence of a large pool of local companies, a growing talent pool, and growing local markets – features that FDI can be said to be reinforcing. In the final chapter, we reflect on the overall implications of Metro Vancouver's innovation economy as a local innovation model, its development prospects, and its role as an innovative city. The high road is possible but can be arrested and become part of hybrid trajectories of greater or lesser importance.

1
Rethinking Forestry's Roles in Value and Innovation

As a quintessential expression of Canadian economic history, Vancouver and surrounding communities developed around the export of "staples" or resource commodities, with ever-strengthening ties with the provincial hinterland.[1] Indeed, through the twentieth century, Metro Vancouver's development served the exploitation of a remarkable array of staples within the agricultural and fishing, mining and energy, and forestry sectors. Forestry was nevertheless pre-eminent, widely supposed in its heyday to account for fifty cents of every dollar made in British Columbia, and vital to Metro Vancouver's economy and identity.[2] Even in the 1970s, as Metro Vancouver transformed toward a postindustrial, service- and knowledge-based economy, a diversified, integrated cluster of forestry-related activities remained important. In fact, 1979 was a record year of forestry, employment, profit, investment, and export.[3] Large-scale lumber, plywood, and particleboard mills (and one pulp and paper mill) remained in operation throughout Metro Vancouver, virtually all unionized and organized by a substantial downtown head office complex. In turn, these activities helped to stimulate a plethora of "backwardly" linked activities in equipment and parts manufacturing; R&D operations and various sophisticated business services, including "world-class" engineering companies; some "forwardly" linked activities serving local markets, especially in paper conversion (e.g., fine paper, tissue paper, boxes) and secondary wood manufacturing (e.g., doors); and the region's role as the major provincial trans-shipment node for provincial forest product exports. Bearing in mind the additional contributions of this cluster to tax revenues ("fiscal linkages") and consumer demands ("final demand linkages"), Metro Vancouver epitomized the idea of local economic development as a process of Marshallian diversification around staple exports.[4]

In 1979–80, incipient trends toward postindustrial Metro Vancouver stood side by side with an industrial identity at its zenith. However, this co-existence of old and new was about to change, provoked by the unusually long, severe recession between 1981 and 1985 that signalled the beginning of permanent structural changes in the BC forest economy rather than the cyclical recessionary responses of previous decades.[5] These changes were especially apparent at first in Metro Vancouver and subsequently spread throughout the province, where they continue to undermine the old metropolitan-hinterland ties. Then, however, amid widespread social protest, how the provincial economy and especially the metropolitan economy might restructure and escape crisis was not clear.[6] The suggestion of a high-tech-led innovation economy, for example, was met with skepticism. Meanwhile, if Clark Binkley's plea for a "knowledge-based forest sector" raised legitimate innovation-based hopes for its rejuvenation rooted in established assets, expertise, and identity, and the richness of hinterland resources, its implementation has been difficult.[7] Overall, Metro Vancouver became the epicentre of the tensions between the sunsetting and rejuvenating forces in forestry; the virtual closing down of its once large-scale, iconic sawmills, along with much diminished corporate head offices and other supporting activities, have been offset, at least partially, by the growth of small, entrepreneurial firms, some innovation to achieve higher-value outputs, and a reconfiguration of the sector's RD&D (and innovation) system.

Metro Vancouver's transformation away from a corporate commodity model and toward an entrepreneurial value-added model of forestry is both evident and problematic, in effect a case of arrested development. Clearly, large sawmills (and other commodity wood-processing operations) are literally gone, closed and replaced by other (postindustrial) uses. Meanwhile, a proliferation of value-adding SMEs has emerged in the province, principally in Metro Vancouver and environs.[8] In support, with applause from environmental organizations, successive provincial governments have released timber supplies from corporate licences to SMEs, encouraged their value-added operations, and specifically helped engineered wood use through building code changes.[9] In addition, FPInnovations, a national private but nonprofit organization, was formed in 2007 with significant presence in

Metro Vancouver as the main R&D organization to serve forest sector restructuring.[10] Yet these trends have taken decades to unfold, through the decisions of individual firms and organizations rather than from any overall strategy, and the legacies of old policies and attitudes have remained. Across British Columbia, exports of commodity lumber and raw logs, investments in pelletized wood, and the opening in 2004 of the world's biggest "super-sized" sawmill, a precursor to several similar investments, are all seen as the antithesis of an innovative value-added strategy.[11] Meanwhile, within Metro Vancouver, the "new" FPInnovations was established by the amalgamation of three existing laboratories, with existing programs continuing even as new ones have been introduced. Moreover, rethinking forestry has been mired in conflicts caused by environmental, Indigenous, and American trade politics motivated collectively against large-scale industrial forestry, but by very different goals, creating a challenging if not chaotic forest policy environment.[12] Furthermore, support for SMEs too often is rationalized by criticism of corporate concentration that conflates value-added in forestry with SMEs, ignoring the drive for value existing in all organizations, large and small, and how this imperative relies on realizing scale economies, not least in R&D, and innovation. Unfortunately, R&D budgets in forestry have declined, arguably not helped by the uncertainties generated by forestry conflicts and declining overall harvest levels. If positive contributions toward a new innovation economy can be discerned, whether or not the potential for a "knowledge-based forest sector" has been fully appreciated, is another matter.

In this chapter, we describe and assess the shift toward a new and more innovative forestry economy within Metro Vancouver, noting the role played by entrepreneurial initiatives. This assessment necessarily involves recognizing the decline of old activities as well as the emergence of new ones. The remainder of the chapter is in three main parts. First, we refer to a resource cycle model of industry evolution as a prelude to changing population and production dynamics in the BC forest industries since 1980, especially within Metro Vancouver, where the loss of large-scale operations and control centres has occurred alongside the rise of SMEs. Second, we discuss the rise of the engineered wood "cluster" of diverse activities and their application to tall wood buildings as an illustration of the emergence of an innovative forestry-based value chain within Metro Vancouver. Third, we examine the implications of these trends for Metro Vancouver's "local" innovation system, as anchored by FPInnovations, particularly with respect to RD&D and technology transfer activities.

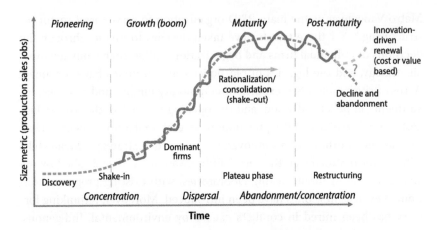

FIGURE 1.1 This figure shows a hypothetical resource cycle model and has an S-shaped curve, with pioneering growth slow at first, then becoming rapid before levelling off and declining. In this model, as firms grow, they become increasingly large scale and more geographically dispersed. In decline, rationalization and restructuring are the main features. The fluctuations around the long-term trend represent short-term business fluctuations.

Metro Vancouver's Forest Industries: Sunsetting with a New Dawn?

A resource cycle model that idealizes long-run (resource) industry evolution in a region in the life cycle terms of birth, growth, maturity, and old age, and possibly rejuvenation (rebirth), provides context for understanding Metro Vancouver's role in exploiting British Columbia's forestry staple (see Figure 1.1).[13]

As an overarching, long-run perspective on the boom-and-bust character of resource industries, the model anticipates that early stages are organized by small, entrepreneurial firms concentrated in particular centres, followed by rapid growth toward maturity that becomes dominated by large corporations able to realize productivity advantages through firm-level and factory-level economies of scale, often by dispersing new investments. With depleting resources in quantity, quality, and accessibility, post-maturity features downsizing, closure, and collapse, with the possibility of rejuvenation arising from innovation and/or policy changes.

In the BC case, in the late decades of the nineteenth century, the arrival of the CPR in Vancouver in 1884 stimulated the rapid growth of forest industries organized by an influx (shake-in) of entrepreneurial investments, admittedly associated with much speculation and exploitation.[14] Indeed, these latter concerns led to a Royal Commission on Forestry, and the subsequent Forest Act of 1912 imposed limits on further resource allocations. The 1920s and 1930s were volatile times for provincial forestry, but its Metro Vancouver–dominated entrepreneurial base remained in place. Crucially, following another Royal Commission, the Forest Act Amendment in 1947 provided a decisive turning point in the industry's evolution, establishing the basis of corporate-dominated ("Fordist") growth by opening up British Columbia's forests in the form of extremely large-scale timber tenures to corporations willing to make large-scale investments in forest operations throughout the province.[15] In practice, this policy was consistent with Canada's embrace of free trade, especially the idea of "continentalism," which cast the country as a resource supplier to US industrial demands[16] and was further justified for its potential to deliver sustainable stable growth. Indeed, over the next several decades throughout British Columbia, there was a remarkably rapid and relatively stable growth of forest product commodities centred on major investments in greenfield pulp and paper mills and large-scale wood processing, mainly organized by large horizontally and vertically owned corporations, many foreign owned.[17]

As the province's decision making, RD&D, business services, labour relations, and export trading centre, Metro Vancouver benefited greatly from the diffusion of forestry growth around the province while its established wood-processing operations also expanded. The growth, stability, and environmental credentials of corporate forestry, however, became increasingly exposed during the 1970s and were laid bare by the recession in the 1980s. As the production profile of British Columbia's sawmill output between 1946 and 2018 reveals, steady stable growth was replaced by considerable volatility, levelling off, and permanent decline (see Figure 1.2).[18] The main caveat to these trends involved a severe pine beetle epidemic in the early 2000s that led the government to allow increased harvesting rates before declining production was re-established.

For industry, the recession in the 1980s exposed its declining competitiveness arising from unsustainable harvesting practices rooted in a traditional pattern of exploitation, starting with the highest-quality, most accessible resources before moving on to more marginal supplies in support of increasingly large-scale operations.[19] The sustainability claims of the corporate model had relied for too long on misplaced assumptions about the strength of "natural" renewal, while deeming old growth as potentially "decadent" timber, and had failed to appreciate fully the implications of increasing scale economies on timber demand. Across British Columbia,

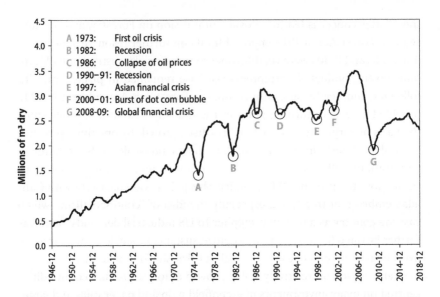

FIGURE 1.2 This figure shows the evolution of sawmill production in British Columbia between 1946 and 2018. Until 1970, growth was rapid and stable. During the 1970s and 1980s, growth became much more volatile and began to level off. Since 2004, sawmill production has declined. | Data from Statistics Canada. Original by Klaus Edenhoffer and Roger Hayter, redrawn by UBC Press.

emerging problems regarding the availability and cost of "first"- or "old"-growth timber supplies were documented in the 1970s and expressed in 1981 by the provincial government's first announcement of a "fall down" in harvesting levels, just as recessionary conditions took hold.[20] These timber supply constraints were most evident in the coastal region, where industry had first developed on a large scale, with important implications for Metro Vancouver, where sawmills, plywood mills, and other wood-processing activities also faced problems of technological obsolescence.

Demise of Large-Scale Wood Processing since 1980

Metro Vancouver's signature sawmill and related wood-processing activities were mainly established in the first part of the twentieth century. During the post–Second World War boom years, these mills were progressively expanded, typically to serve export markets, and, as part of industry-wide trends, increasingly supplied pulp and paper mills with "waste" wood chips and sawdust as fibre and energy sources.[21] Indeed, despite their age, these large-scale operations remained profitable for some time through economies of scale and integration, the advantages of using old (already depreciated) capital infrastructure and equipment, and access to established labour pools and global markets. However, in contrast to new mills in the interior, the higher costs of increasingly distant wood fibre supplies, and of land and labour, combined with more frictional labour relations, by the 1970s existing operations in Metro Vancouver were approaching obsolescence. In addition, within Metro Vancouver, modernization was becoming prohibitively expensive, inappropriate for a dynamic, rapidly urbanizing, and high-amenity environment. The recession in the 1980s starkly exposed these problems, stimulating the downsizing and ultimately the closure of large-scale wood processing in Metro Vancouver. In the past, hundreds of sawmills had been closed throughout British Columbia, but they had been small operations. Since 1980, downsizing has featured large-scale mills, first and foremost in Metro Vancouver (see Table 1.1). Subsequently, mill closures became widespread in the provincial interior, further reducing the rationale for head office and related functions in Metro Vancouver. The

TABLE 1.1 Closures of selected large-scale sawmills in Metro Vancouver since 1980

Location/sawmill	Notes
Coquitlam: Fraser Mills Sawmill	Opened in 1889 and evolved as a diversified lumber, plywood veneer complex. Employed 1,100 in 1980, 600 by 1984. After 1950, part of Crown Zellerbach Canada (becoming Crown Forest).* Acquired by Fletcher Challenge* (1983) and then Interfor. On closure in 2001, 500 laid off.
Maple Ridge: Hammond Cedar sawmill	Opened in 1908. Over 450 jobs by 1970 and 475 in 1980. After 1950, part of British Columbia Forest Products. Acquired by Fletcher Challenge* in 1987 and then by Interfor (previously Whonnock Industries). When closed in 2019, 147 jobs lost.
New Westminster: Shook Mills (lumber pieces for box manufacture)	Opened in 1918. Employed 200 in 1980. Part of MacMillan Bloedel after 1962. Acquired in 1999 by Weyerhaeuser* and then by Western Forest Products. Closed in 2007 with estimated loss of jobs around 100-150.
New Westminster: Rayonier Sawmill (from 1950s)	Opened in 1890s, part of Rayonier,* acquired by Western Forest Products in 1980 when employment was 250 (200 MMBF capacity). On closure in 2007, 284 jobs lost.
New Westminster: Sawmill	Part of MacMillan Bloedel. Employment of 196 in 1980. Acquired by Weyerhaeuser* in 1999 and closed in 2006–07.

▶

Location/sawmill	Notes
New Westminster: Queensborough sawmill	Opened in 1891 (200 MMBF). Estimated employment of 225 in 1980, part of Whonnock Industries since 1967. Acquired by Interfor in 1988. On closure in 2007–08, 110 jobs lost.
North Vancouver: L&L Lumber	Part of L&K Lumber. Employment of 200 in 1980. Closed in 1985.
Port Moody: Flavelle Sawmill	Opened in 1905. In 1964 and 1980, employment of 300. Part of Weldwood.* Acquired by Interfor in 1995, closed in 1998, reopened by Mill and Timber, and acquired by Aspen Planers of Merritt, BC. On closure in 2020, 70 employees laid off.
Richmond: Sawmill (and veneer mill)	Part of Crown Zellerbach Canada.* Employment of 145 in 1980 lost on closure in 1984.
Surrey: Surrey Sawmill	Part of Weldwood* after 1964. Estimated employment in 1980 of 200. Closed in 1987.
Vancouver: Eburne Sawmill	Opened in 1910, acquired in 1940 by Canfor. Employment in 1980 of 430. On closure in 1998, 220 jobs lost.
Vancouver: Canadian White Pine Sawmill	Opened in 1926, replacing mill built in 1910. Employment of 740 in 1980, reduced to 400 in 1984. Part of MacMillan Bloedel and acquired by Weyerhaeuser in 1999. On closure in 2002, 400 jobs lost (and another 90 in adjacent particle board mill).
Vancouver: Marpole Sawmill (large log focus)	Opened in 1930s–40s. Employment in 1980 of 225. Doman acquired mill from Rayonier* in 1980. Closed during Doman's creditor proceedings. Loss of estimated 200 jobs on closure in 2002–03.
Vancouver: Silvertree Division Sawmill	Opened in 1948 as Silvertree (replacing small older mill built in 1930s). Employment of 250 in 1980. Acquired by Rayonier* in 1967, then by Doman, becoming Western Forest Products in 2005. On closure in 2005, 151 jobs lost.
Vancouver: Vancouver sawmill	Leased by British Columbia Forest Products, acquired by Fletcher Challenge* in 1987. Employment in 1980 of 250, in 1988 of 175. Acquired by Interfor. Probably closed in 2000s.

Notes: * US owned; British Columbia Forest Products was partially US owned. Most firms listed above were big, fully integrated, forest product operations. Large scale means annual capacity was at least 100 MMBF (million board feet per year), usually much more. Sawmill names often changed with ownership changes.
Source: Hayter's research files.

consolidation of lumber production in a few larger "super" sawmills has oc-curred in the provincial interior, but even they have started to close down.[22]

In Metro Vancouver, since the (turning point of the) recession in the 1980s, the downsizing and ultimately closure of large-scale wood-processing mills – including sawmills, plywood, veneer, particleboard, and shingle and shake operations – has been relentless. MacMillan Bloedel, for example, closed its Vancouver plywood mill in 1982, with a loss of 400 jobs, and down-sized its Canadian White Pine Sawmill (740 employees in 1980) and adja-cent particle board mill on the Vancouver-Burnaby border, both closing in 1999. As other examples, the once "biggest sawmill in the world," Fraser Mills in Coquitlam, saw its employment reduced from 1,100 to 600 be-tween 1980 and 1984, with permanent closure following in 2001–02. New Westminster's last big sawmill closed in 2007 and North Vancouver's in 1985. Overall, between 1980 and 2008, seventeen large sawmills in Metro Vancouver were permanently closed, and by 2008 only four large mills were known to have survived, three in Surrey and Delta and just one in Vancouver. In virtually all cases, downsizing and temporary closures preceded final closures. Similarly, Metro Vancouver has lost its big plywood, shingle and shake, and veneer operations.[23] In the provincial interior, large sawmills have continued to close, with fewer if ever-bigger ones surviving, along with the downsizing of export-oriented pulp and paper.[24] The job losses have also been largely unionized, and in 2004 the once powerful Canadian branch of the International Wood Workers of America (independent from its US parent in 1987) was absorbed by the International Steel Workers Union.[25] Furthermore, mill closures have been replaced by postindustrial land uses; Canadian White Pine is now part of the "River District" residen-tial development, plans for the former massive Fraser Mills site are for a mixed Granville Island–type development, and Silvertree's vacant land be-came a bus parking lot for Metro Vancouver's transportation authority (Translink), with proposals for a riverside park.[26]

In tandem with the decline of large commodity mills, Metro Vancouver's head office roles and employment in forestry began to unravel in the reces-sionary context of the early 1980s.[27] MacMillan Bloedel, as the leading BC and Metro Vancouver–centred forest corporation, led this decline. Along with its rationalization of numerous wood-processing facilities in Metro Vancouver, MB downsized its head office from 1,200 to 560 while selling the building in 1982 for $60 million, along with its foreign assets, as part of its survival strategy. Exceptionally within British Columbia, MB initiated vari-ous innovative, higher-value forms of product differentiation in its lumber and pulp and paper mills, as illustrations of "flexible mass production," although they, too, occurred mostly within the context of substantial employment downsizing. However, MB sold its new engineered-wood (Parallam) factory, the result of globally leading R&D, to a US rival in 1984 (as will be discussed later). Subsequently, MB's acquisition in 1999 and the breakup of its operations, including the closure of its head office and R&D laboratory, confirmed the end of corporate forestry's dominance in Metro Vancouver's economy.[28] Admittedly, transformation toward a new, more innovative knowledge-based forest economy has depended in part on the collapse of the old, large-scale operations. While they remained dominant, why was change needed? Indeed, rethinking toward more innovative production has been challenging. For management, established technological capabilities and innovation priorities have been focused largely on increasing the efficiency of commodity production, and investments in R&D limited, MB apart. Meanwhile, during Fordism large forestry corporations had co-evolved with strong unions organized around highly structured internal labour markets based on principles of seniority, job demarcation and grievance procedures within cumulative collective bargains that were similarly not especially conducive to promoting innovativeness, or to the creation of spinoff companies. Nevertheless, a shift toward a new, more innovative trajectory can be detected, if not strongly, stimulated in part by a shake-in of SMEs and their value-adding roles.

An Expanding SME Population

Although estimates vary, forestry-based, secondary manufacturing SMEs in British Columbia have expanded considerably since the early 1980s, with Metro Vancouver (and environs) the main concentration. A provincial government–sponsored study in 1992 reviewed several studies, including from Statistics Canada, that variously estimated between 415 and 524 secondary wood-processing firms operating between 1982 and 1991 that increased employment from just over 6,180 to 8,190 in this period. The firms were typically small, in 1991 averaging 21 employees and less than $3 million in sales.[29] Subsequently, for the next two decades after 1991, secondary wood- and paper-processing firms grew further, probably reaching a peak employment of about 12,000 in 700–800 plants by 2012. As indicated in one relatively comprehensive study, based on data voluntarily provided by firms in trade directories, between 1980 and 2008, recorded that secondary wood-processing plants increased from 275 to 477 and paper-conversion mills from 53 to 71, with the former doubling their job total and the latter

TABLE 1.2 Forest product plants and employment in British Columbia by commodity type, 1980 and 2008

	Plant number		Employment		Coastal share of plants (%)	
	1980	2008	1980	2008	1980	2008
Large sawmills	96	47	25,775	10,052	35.1	23.5
Medium sawmills	90	50	7,131	3,796	58.2	65.8
Small sawmills	124	92	1,251	1,141	42.8	55.9
Large board mills	13	10	5,506	12,191	54.5	1.0
Value-added wood	194	362	3,681	8,680	67.9	66.0
Pulp and paper	22	19	18,022	8,155	58.3	40.9
Value-added paper	36	54	1,203	1,673	94.3	90.1
Total	609	679	64,609	36,849	–	–

Note: The coastal region of British Columbia includes Vancouver Island, with forestry towns such as Crofton, Chemainus, and Port Alberni, Powell River on the Sunshine Coast, as well as Metro Vancouver.

Source: R. Hayter and K. Edenhoffer, "Shakeouts, Shakeins and Industry Population Dynamics: British Columbia's Forest Industries 1980–2008," *Growth and Change* 47 (2016): 497–519.

increasing theirs by over 40 percent, the two combining for 10,313 employees by 2008 (see Table 1.2).

This study confirms the small size of these activities; for example, wood SMEs averaged about 19 and 24 jobs in 1980 and 2008, respectively, still much smaller than large sawmills even following their continued automation. The study also captures the idea of a shake-in, proposed as at least a 30 percent increase in firm or mill numbers over a "lengthy" period of time, for value-added firms (and a corresponding shake-out of large and medium-sized sawmills).[30] Although the SME population of value-added firms exhibits a high turnover, between 1980 and 2008, entry rates were higher than exit rates.[31] For example, within wood processing, this study identified 103 SME survivors throughout the study period, while 172 closures were offset by a shake-in of 374 new entrants. Such a large turnover of predominantly small operations reflects their relative ease of entry and exit, with small fixed costs of start-up still facing the challenges of reaching the minimum efficient scale to survive. Overall, the shake-ins of plants in secondary wood processing and paper converting, respectively, amounted to 73.5 percent and 34.0 percent increases in the study period. Meanwhile, the shake-out of large sawmills featured a high exit rate with scarcely any new entrants.

To a significant degree, the growth in secondary forest manufacturing SMEs has been concentrated in the coastal region – 66 percent in wood and 90 percent in paper value-added in 2008, and especially Metro Vancouver, with the rapidly urbanizing Okanagan region increasingly important (see Table 1.2). Secondary plants now constitute more than half of the forest industry totals, and most are owner managed, a trend supporting the view of the emergence of a new dual structure of the BC forest economy that contrasts the diverse entrepreneurial activities in small-scale plants in Metro Vancouver with corporately organized, large-scale production in the provincial interior.[32] For the former, Metro Vancouver offers locational advantages in terms of accessibility to a diverse range of markets and wood fibre sources, and various agglomeration economies. However, increasing land and labour costs, perhaps a surprising lack of skilled labour, and preferences among young people for other occupations are likely to limit and even reduce growth, especially in the inner city and suburbs.[33]

SMEs Are Diverse, and Innovation Is Limited

SME-dominated secondary forestry manufacturing in Metro Vancouver is extremely diverse. Treated lumber, engineered wood products, finished building products, prefabricated houses and components, posts, remanufactured wood, log-frame homes, mouldings, pallets, flooring, fencing, architectural millwork, furniture, cabinetry, art, and semi-finished goods are all part of the mix of conventionally recognized activities. Individual operations also vary considerably in organizational and production characteristics, including with respect to the extent of their value-added contributions. Even within categories, there is much variation, as illustrated with reference to a study of six "remanufacturing" activities in 1991 (see Table 1.3).

Although all were small (from eleven to fifty-four employees), four of the firms (A–D) were locally owned, single-plant operations, one was a branch plant of a large, established forestry giant (E), and one (F) acted as a broker between suppliers and consumers with no operations of its own. The latter two had access to timber tenures, whereas the others purchased fibre on open markets. These firms can be differentiated further by product diversity, range of fibre species used, employee relations (including flexibility features and employment of nonunion labour), access to markets around the world, and extent of value added to wood inputs. In case E, a specialized branch plant of a giant firm producing one particular product (from formerly "waste" wood) generated the highest value of $1,800 per 1,000 board feet, clearly rooted in its ability to realize economies of scale in a specialized

TABLE 1.3 Remanufacturing case studies in Metro Vancouver: Production characteristics, 1991

Firm type (Employees) / (Value per unit)	Product / Functions / Supply inputs	Species mix	Main markets	Labour flexibility
A Isolated (40) ($1,000)	Windows, door parts, panelling, siding / Mostly in-house, 15% subcontracted	35% hemlock, 25% red cedar, 23% Douglas fir	25% United States, 25% Europe, 13% Japan, 15% Canada, 10% local	Skilled job rotation / Training
B Contractor (15) ($900)	Windows, door parts, panelling, decking / 50–60% subcontracted, high-value work	48% SPF, 12% hemlock, 35% red cedar	40% United States, 9% Europe, 12% Japan, 7% local	Unskilled job rotation
C Capacity contractor (11) ($800)	Initial log breakdown, decking, siding	100% red cedar	95% United States, 1% local	Strong job demarcation / limited training
D Specialty contractor (54) ($1,500)	High-quality drying, moulding, packaging, door parts, siding, fencing / 60% subcontracted	50% red cedar, 50% yellow cedar	50% Canada, 45% United States	Skilled job rotation / training
E Branch plant (24) ($1,800)	Laminated finger stock for windows / In-house, high volume	90% hemlock	55% Europe, 40% Japan, 2% local	Unionized with job rotation / training
F Branch organizer ($1,000)	Windows, door parts, sauna blanks / All work subcontracted	75% hemlock	80% Europe, 7% local	n/a

Source: K. Rees and R. Hayter, "Flexible Specialization, Uncertainty and the Firm: Enterprise Strategies and Structures in the Wood Remanufacturing Industry of the Vancouver Metropolitan Area, British Columbia," *Canadian Geographer* 40 (1996): 203–19.

product. The specialty subcontractor D, a supplier of high-quality components to house builders, also exhibited a high value per unit of fibre use at
$1,500 per 1,000 board feet, whereas the others yielded much lower values.
As the highest value-added firms, D and E nevertheless differed in their
component supplier systems, the former relying on external sources and the
latter relying on internal sources. Regardless of value-added variations, however, all firms had developed significant export markets, particularly to rich
countries in the European Union, Japan, and the United States.[34] Although
a small, dated sample, this information illustrates the highly varied wood
value-added contributions among SMEs, many of which serve small markets that do not permit significant economies of scale, often fail, and cannot
be assumed to generate more value per unit fibre than big operations.

Moreover, two relatively recent and large surveys of SMEs in British
Columbia seriously question their environmental performance and innovation. In the first, forty-one SMEs (sales between $0.5 million and $30 million) were surveyed in Metro Vancouver and environs in 2010 with respect
to their environmental awareness, use of environmentally certified wood,
and adoption of pollution-reducing measures. The results were disappointing. Only five had taken "comprehensive" measures to reduce waste, and
just six considered themselves knowledgeable about environmental certification. Its cost, the bureaucracy involved, a lack of awareness, and consumer
uninterest were the main factors in limiting – and dropping – the use of
certified wood.[35] In addition, none of the sample firms could be labelled as a
"green green" or "ecopreneurial" firm established with the main goal to enhance sustainability. The second, larger-scale survey (123 respondents from
373 contacted) of wood sector SMEs across British Columbia focused on
tendencies to create new products and forms of business organization, such
as the adoption of certification in the chain of custody arrangements.[36]
Overall, this study similarly deemed innovativeness to be limited, reinforcing the characterization of the BC wood industry as low tech and technologically conservative, including with respect to SMEs. Indeed, for such
SMEs, formal R&D is scarcely a possibility, patenting activity extremely low,
and networking with R&D agencies limited. Despite a rhetoric of value-
adding, innovative, and sustainable SMEs, the reality seems to be different.
Admittedly, exceptions can be found. Greenhus, for example, is a tiny firm
that has invested in R&D, in cooperation with FPInnovations, to patent and
produce innovative products that meet its intention to become a so-called
ecopreneurial firm that develops environmentally sustainable products (see
Case Study 1.1).

CASE STUDY 1.1 **Greenhus**

Greenhus is an innovative, ecopreneurial firm that conducts R&D and designs and patents sustainable products through the use of minimal wood fibre inputs obtained from certified sources without using harmful coatings or glues. Since 2010, it has developed a patented family of corrugated plywood products, led by Corelam, that are custom designed, based on key local collaborations, and produced on a purpose-built press in Vancouver. Christian Blyt, the company's founder and an Emily Carr faculty member, developed his products with technical help from FPInnovations and the Acoustic and Noise Control Lab in UBC's Mechanical Engineering Department, with financial aid from British Columbia's Business Innovation Partnership. As new forms of walls, ceiling panels, and furniture, Corelam and related products are lightweight, durable, and easy to transport, and they have distinct acoustic, sustainability, and flexibility properties. Corelam products were originally developed by Blyt at Aalto University, Finland, and perfected in Vancouver, where he says "having access to FPInnovations' suite of lab equipment and expertise greatly shortened my product development time. Working with our design engineer, their knowledge was transferred to us" to create a "revolutionary" press design and manufacturing process to produce uniform products. These products are easy to move for "urban nomads" and provide gift ("moi") items, and they include ceiling and wall panels with "remarkable" acoustic properties, such as Soundframe, and a range of stylish ("Scandi–West Coast") furnishings (coat racks, side tables, stools, doors, etc). Greenhus is also exceptional in the extent of its collaboration with FPInnovations.

Sources: FPInnovations, "Product Development Helps Corelam Commercialize Novel Panel Product," *FPInnovations Newsletter* 27 (2013): 1; L. Lau, "Green Living: Studio Corelam Crafts Flexible Furniture for Urban Nomads," *Georgia Strait,* May 24, 2017, https://www.straight.com/life/914016/green-living-studio-corelam-crafts-flexible-furniture--urban-nomads.

Certainly, innovation does occur among wood-based SMEs, if not typically. For example, a targeted survey of eight relatively large wood-processing SMEs (four in Metro Vancouver), selected for their innovative capacities, revealed the importance of design activities and associated technical flexibilities, including by applications of CAD-CAM techniques, to provide customized modifications.[37] In this regard, (modern) engineered woods are especially noteworthy. Engineered woods are relatively high value, formal R&D has been important in their evolution, their innovation has been strongly design oriented, and their use has become acceptable in tall building. Their potential for local development and sustainable buildings is frequently touted, including by the provincial government.[38]

Toward an Engineered Wood Design Cluster: Supplying Tall Wood Buildings

Engineered wood products, also called mass timber and composite wood, comprise numerous products made from different manufacturing processes and can be defined as "value-added wood products that are made by bonding lumber, veneers, strands or fibres together, usually with glue."[39] According to this definition, plywood and oriented strand boards (OSB), the latter growing rapidly in British Columbia from the late 1960s, represent established forms of (mass-produced) engineered wood used in sheathing. However, newer forms of engineered wood – such as glulam, cross-laminated timber (CLT), laminated veneer lumber, parallel strand lumber, laminated strand lumber, oriented strand lumber, and dowel laminated timber – are currently emphasized as innovative building materials for individual homes and, most spectacularly, in (increasingly) tall wood buildings that can address economic, environmental, and aesthetic expectations. Engineered woods have uniform technical properties, comparable to steel or concrete, can be used for structural or interior design purposes, are fire resistant, can be flexibly manufactured according to desired sizes and shapes for construction and aesthetic purposes, and offer carbon-neutral footprints. Their use in high-rises, beyond four stories, in turn has required changes in regulations and architectural attitudes rooted in fire hazards and structural limitations of traditional wood components.

Within Metro Vancouver and British Columbia, these developments first focused on parallel strand lumber, specifically Parallam, and subsequently on CLT and glulam products, the former R&D driven, coming out of MB's corporate R&D program, the latter involving newer entrepreneurial initiatives based on imported technology. As a globally pioneering venture, MB developed Parallam at its Burnaby R&D laboratory in the 1970s and 1980s in an R&D program ($15 million over fifteen years) as a patented structural timber. Parallam is made by bonding together under pressure thin strands of wood typically four to eight feet long, involving little waste of materials and was first manufactured in a new factory located on Annacis Island, Delta, that supplied beams for Vancouver Expo in 1986. By then, as part of its recessionary-induced restructuring, MB had sold the plant to Trus Joist

(US) in 1984, subsequently acquired by Weyerhaeuser, employing about 121.[40] Further expansion of engineered woods, however, took some time and was led by the Penticton-based Structurlam, a firm that began in 1962 as Greyback. Later, the firm initiated small-scale production of glulam beams in which solid boards are bonded ("glued") together in parallel fashion to form load-bearing joists. It became Structurlam in the late 1990s and, following its takeover in 2007 by the Aldera group, a Vancouver-based development company, licensed CLT technology from Europe in 2011.[41] As of 2018, Structurlam was one of only two CLT manufacturers in Canada, with employment of about 225 in two factories when it was bought by the California-based KingFish Group, an investment advisory firm.[42] The production of engineered woods is sophisticated, conducted in computerized, design-driven factories able to manufacture products of differing dimensions according to customer needs. For example, Structurlam's projects "begin in the company's CADD (computer-aided design and drafting) studio. There, drafters transform architect or engineer specifications into 3D models to execute the manufacturing process. A host of robotic machines then glue, join and press the wood and cut the panels or beams to size. Some final components are added by hand."[43] Such an operation illustrates the economies of scale and scope associated with flexible mass production not within the reach of most small firms; indeed, as a (large) SME, Structurlam's growth nevertheless depended on its acquisition by the Aldera group and support from the BC government, and it is now part of a large California-based company. Other smaller firms manufacturing engineered wood typically focus on local, residential sales.[44]

In practice, the emergence and acceptance of engineered woods as structural materials comparable to steel and concrete have become most evident in their "revolutionary" use in "tall" buildings over the past decade. This potential and its implications for local development are well illustrated by the new Brock Commons residence at UBC.

The Brock Commons Project

On completion in 2017, Brock Commons was reputedly the largest tall wood building in North America, its eighteen storeys reaching a height of 53.4 metres. Strictly speaking, it is a hybrid building since the engineered wood structures are complemented by the use of steel and other metals for the roof. Nevertheless, the building was fundamentally designed around the use of an extraordinary quantity of wood (2,233 cubic metres), principally CLT and Parallam. Indeed, the use of these prefabricated structures allowed

FIGURE 1.3 This figure identifies the main agencies involved in the design and building of Brock Commons, a pioneering tall wood residence at UBC that exemplifies the use and potential of engineered wood.

the residence to be erected in just sixty-six days, months ahead of schedule. Although direct building costs might have been a little high compared with the use of conventional materials, savings were realized through a faster rate of construction, with prefabricated building components arriving on site. Environmental and aesthetic benefits were also achieved. Given prior technological breakthroughs in engineered woods, the evolution of Brock Commons and its local development implications depended, first, on the creation of a new cluster of specialized, interacting, mainly locally based actors, including architects who appreciated their potential, and, second, on changes in building regulations.

The design, planning, and completion of the project took over four years and required innovative problem-solving contributions and coordination among diversified sources of expertise, including architects, engineers, 3D modellers, construction companies, university-based managers, and developers (see Figure 1.3).[45] Much of this expertise was located in Metro Vancouver. Thus, the UBC Properties Trust's project team, the lead structural engineers (Fast and Epp), and architects of record (Acton Ostry) are based in Vancouver. Similarly based in Metro Vancouver, Cadmakers (Burnaby), GHL Consulting, RDH Building Services, FPInnovations, Urban One, Seagate Structures (Surrey), and Whitewater Concrete (Coquitlam) informed the design team. These organizations provided wide-ranging expertise and services ranging from 3D modelling, fire science and building design inputs, forest sector–based R&D capabilities, project management, and construction capabilities, including an engineered wood specialist construction company. The main engineered wood suppliers to Brock Commons were Weyerhaeuser's (originally MB's) pioneering Delta plant that manufactured Parallam and Structurlam's Penticton plant that manufactured CLT and had been acquired by the Vancouver-based Aldera group to promote engineered wood use. In addition, the local design team was complemented by three Alberta-based companies, including Read, Jones and Christoffersen Consulting from Calgary, one of the two review teams for the project, and Stantec, a large Edmonton-based MNC that specializes in building design and consulting, including LEED (Leadership in Energy and Environmental Design) systems. Trotter and Morton of Calgary was another member of the design team, with expertise in the life cycles of building projects from land clearance to maintenance after building. Two Austrian companies, with expertise in engineered woods, were also involved, one providing architectural advice and the other part of the review team.

The Brock Commons project further depended on input from the federal and provincial governments in terms of regulatory approval and various forms of support, reflecting their growing appreciation of the environmental potential of engineered woods in building construction. Indeed, this project contributed to building code changes, and to reducing cultural resistance to the use of wood in large buildings, traditionally rooted in concerns about fire and other hazards such as earthquakes. In 2013, Natural Resources Canada announced financial support ($5 million in total) for demonstration projects through its Tall Wood Building Demonstration Initiative. Brock Commons was one of two projects (the other a residential building in Quebec) that received funds deemed "indispensable in bridging the innovation funding gap in the preliminary, design, approval and construction phase."[46] With the end of this initiative in 2017, the federal budget provided $39.8 million to support a four-year Green Construction through Wood Program to facilitate further use of mass timbers in tall building construction.

BC governments have progressively encouraged tall wood buildings, including specific support for Structurlam. Thus, in 2012, the provincial government changed the height restrictions on wood buildings from four to six storeys and, although scaled down from initial plans, funded ($25 million) the 29.5-metre-tall Wood Innovation and Design Centre in Prince George. This Centre was completed in 2014, providing a showcase for engineered wood designed by a Vancouver-based architect and with CLT supplied by Structurlam. British Columbia was also the first province to accept the twelve-storey building code limit for wood buildings in 2019, which might be increased further, and announced in 2020 that all new public buildings up to this size were to be thus constructed. In the case of Brock Commons, given existing restrictions of six storeys, site-specific negotiations were required among the project team, UBC's chief building official, and the British Columbia Building and Safety Standards Branch, and there were reviews by third-party engineers and expert panels, dealing respectively with structural and safety concerns, the panels comprising architects, engineers, fire and building code officials, building scientists, advanced wood construction research organizations, and UBC engineering and building science faculty. Fast and Epp, the project's engineers, also conducted reviews. Moreover, the green building credentials of Brock Commons are underlined by its meeting LEED gold certification. In fact, its environmental benefits are impressive, with estimated savings in material use of 2,432 tonnes, and the carbon savings equivalent to removing 511 cars off the road for a year. Also, its main timber supplier, Structurlam, obtained Sustainable Forestry Initiative chain of custody certification in 2017, and Parallam uses "waste" wood materials.

Brock Commons, among other initiatives, has been an important stimulus to the development of an engineered wood cluster as part of Metro Vancouver's innovation economy. The various agencies involved in designing and building Brock Commons have added to a growing pool of expertise in Metro Vancouver, enhanced by resolving the technological and organizational challenges posed by the project, including how to adopt 3D technologies by architects and designers, link 3D designs to computerized manufacturing, and develop advances in the engineering of steel connectors to fasten wood beams.[47] These and other lessons learned have added to the expertise of Metro Vancouver architects, engineers, building specialists of various kinds, real estate companies, consultants, FPInnovations, and wood designers. In turn, this expertise has led to exports; for example, the architects involved in the Wood Innovation and Design Centre in Prince George and Brock Commons in Vancouver have bid successfully on contracts for tall wood buildings elsewhere, as have FPInnovations and Cadmakers; Seagate has witnessed considerable growth in the United States for tall office buildings that it services from an office in Bellingham, Washington; and KTC Engineering, opened in 1990 in Surrey as a relatively small firm with about forty employees, has become a globally recognized designer and builder of engineered wood plants (see Case Study 1.2). Indeed, globally, the potential for tall wood buildings is becoming increasingly apparent.[48] Within Canada, university-based research contributions to this potential continue, while a recent federal government–sponsored study has articulated the practice and promise of engineered woods qua mass timber in British Columbia's forest sector.[49]

Restructuring the Forestry RD&D System in Metro Vancouver

The growth of large-scale, export-oriented forest product commodities across British Columbia was complemented by an RD&D and innovation system centred in Metro Vancouver that reached its zenith around 1980. Indeed, the structural crisis in commodity production in the early 1980s simultaneously challenged its supportive R&D activities. After all, big corporations and their harvesting and manufacturing operations were the major financial contributors to and recipients of technology development centred on processing cost efficiencies. In tandem, pleas for the forest economy to become more value oriented, innovative, and sensitive to SMEs, within a broader context of forest policy emphasizing nonindustrial priorities, have encouraged a rethinking and restructuring of forestry's RD&D organization and related technology transfer activities.[50] Three main organizational features of this rethinking, all centred in Metro Vancouver, can be discerned: first, the virtual collapse of in-house RD&D; second, the consolidation in 2007 of several associations and cooperative forestry RD&D agencies as FPInnovations; and, third, changes in the mix of businesses providing technology services and equipment to forestry. In practice, this evolution has been piecemeal, not directed by any overall plan, and it has involved both closures and rationalizations as well as the emergence of new actors and mandates, with several of the latter having roots in the acquisition of established operations. The innovation system, as it was in 1980, provides a prelude to appreciate these trends.

The Forestry RD&D (Innovation) System, circa 1980

At its peak in 1980, Metro Vancouver's forest commodity–driven RD&D (then labelled simply R&D) and related technology-transfer activities comprised a number of private, public, and hybrid R&D laboratories, supplemented by numerous engineering companies and equipment (machinery, capital goods) manufacturers, especially in logging and wood processing (see Figure 1.4).[51] At the time, formal R&D was provided principally by Forintek (100 employees) in sawmilling, Feric (12 employees) in logging, and the Council of Forest Industries (COFIs) plywood laboratory (10 employees); UBC's forest faculty and other secondary educational institutions; and two in-house (corporate) R&D laboratories, notably MB's laboratory in

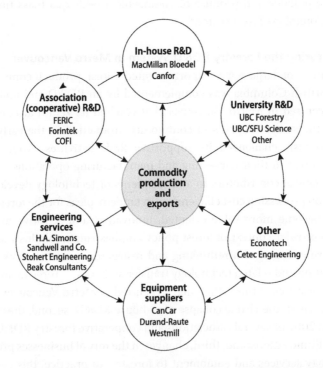

FIGURE 1.4 This figure identifies the main institutions comprising British Columbia's forest sector innovation system in 1980. Most operations were located in Metro Vancouver and principally supplied technological expertise in support of large-scale commodity production.

Burnaby, which employed over 100 professionals, Canada's largest. These R&D agencies were supplemented by a large, vibrant community of consulting engineers led by H A Simon's International and Sandwell's, the former with over 2,200 employees worldwide (1,200 in Vancouver), the latter with over 1,000 employees in 1979. There were also at least thirty equipment manufacturing firms serving the resource sector then, most with fewer than fifty employees, with CanCar's 400-plus employees the largest. Other small R&D companies can be mentioned, such as the Richmond-based Econotec, established in 1971 as a spinoff from a large-scale, albeit short-lived, R&D laboratory established in Prince Rupert in the 1960s, and Vancouver's Cetec Engineering.[52]

This cluster of activities contributed excellent problem-solving capabilities and important inputs to Metro Vancouver's industrial economy, generally devoted to increasing the efficiencies of industrial forest commodity operations within British Columbia's distinctive operating conditions. The cluster especially embraced the design and technological choices involved in the construction of new, large-scale facilities, such as sawmills, plywood mills, and pulp and paper mills, in remote locations, and the operation, maintenance, and modernization of operations throughout the forestry value chain, including with respect to transportation logistics. From logging to distribution, the reduction of costs was the paramount concern in support of a commodity culture, with emerging environmental initiatives mainly restricted to "end-of-the-pipe solutions."[53] MB's in-house group that engaged in product development, such as Parallam and value-added paper, was exceptional, and the closure of its laboratory in 1997 essentially marked the end of in-house forestry R&D in Metro Vancouver.[54] Engineering companies and equipment suppliers exported their expertise in services and goods, complementing forest commodity exports, but secondary manufacturing of cabinets, doors, window frames, boxes, and tissue paper was limited, mainly supplying local and regional markets. However, in R&D employment and patenting, Metro Vancouver's (and British Columbia's) performance lagged well behind that of other leading forestry regions, especially regarding industry efforts, with design scarcely mentioned.[55]

In recent decades, as corporate R&D has virtually disappeared, this innovation system has been further changed by the creation of FPInnovations and new engineering consulting companies and equipment manufacturers. The once dominant H.A. Simons was acquired by even bigger MNCs, first AMEC (UK) and then Wood (US) in 2017, leaving its Vancouver office with about 235 employees. The other engineering consulting giant of 1980,

Sandwell, was acquired by Ausenco (Australia) in 2008. In addition, Noram Engineering and KTC engineering, both located in Surrey, established in 1988 and 1983, respectively, have emerged as rapidly growing innovative companies serving the forest sector, the former with 400 employees (see Case Study 1.2). Fast and Epp is another noteworthy new engineering company, established in 1989 in Vancouver, that has grown rapidly and featured in the Brock Commons project (see Figure 1.3). Although foreign ownership has increased, engineering consulting services have remained important to the local forest sector innovation system, complemented by the growth of numerous environmental and cultural impact assessment companies and by the long-established Econotech, that since its establishment in Metro Vancouver as a corporate R&D spinoff in 1971, has specialized in environmental impact (and other) services. In the case of equipment suppliers, the loss of established companies in Metro Vancouver has been somewhat offset by a few new arrivals. CanCar, which once employed over 400, was first acquired in 1983 by Kockums (Sweden) and in 1996 by the (US) State of Washington-based USNR, which retains a facility in Richmond. Optimal Machinery is another surviving spinoff of CanCar. Although new machinery manufacturers are rare, Westmills is an important plywood machinery component manufacturer established in Abbotsford (adjacent to Metro Vancouver) in 1975. Indeed, these three firms have designed and developed patented products that, in the case of Westmill, occurred in association with support from FPInnovations (and its predecessors).[56]

FPInnovations: Toward More Collaborative RD&D

FPInnovations was established by the consolidation of three existing national R&D organizations, namely Paprican, Forintek, and Feric, respectively serving the pulp and paper, wood-processing, and wood-harvesting sectors. Planned and effectively operated as "industry association" laboratories serving the collective needs of industry members, even as government funding remained important, Feric and Forintek started operations in separate locations in Metro Vancouver in the 1970s following the "privatization" of two long-standing government laboratories (in Ottawa and Vancouver). In Metro Vancouver, the consolidation of R&D activities within FPInnovations on the UBC campus was reinforced when a Paprican West laboratory was added (Montreal being the original and main centre of Paprican's activities). Although Montreal remains its national head office location, FPInnovations maintains a significant presence in Metro Vancouver, probably accounting for about 40 percent of the organization's budget and employment that amounted nationally in 2018 to $72.5 million, and about 500 jobs, respectively, both totals representing a substantial decline from its early years, beginning in 2007. Although its governance is somewhat ambiguous, FPInnovations has distanced itself from a forest industry "association" label, moving toward a more collaborative endeavour ("hub") between public and private interests and sources of funding that might be seen as a quasi-autonomous form of public-private partnership (P3).[57] Although its activities are focused on the BC forest sector, FPInnovations has also diversified somewhat beyond this mandate, functionally and geographically.

As the dominant RD&D supplier to forestry in Metro Vancouver, FPInnovations displays key features that can be usefully summarized.[58] Its formation in 2007 entailed a concentration of activities on the UBC campus via the consolidation of previously separately run laboratories of Feric, Forintek, and Paprican West, with their respective R&D foci on logging, wood processing, and pulp and paper. With other R&D operations closing, including MB's laboratory in 1997 and the Council of Forest Industries North Vancouver "association" plywood laboratory (ten employees), FPInnovations instantly became the overwhelmingly dominant forest sector RD&D operation in Metro Vancouver (as well as in Canada), with about 200 employees and its (estimated) share of the national budget of (roughly) about $30 million in 2018. Meanwhile, in-house, private sector R&D has all but disappeared, limited to the ten employees (2018) or so at Canfor's New Westminster laboratory, focused primarily on pulp and paper efficiencies. FPInnovations sees itself as a collaborative hub providing (integrated) technological support to diverse industry and nonindustry stakeholders in Canada's (and British Columbia's) largely publicly owned forests. Its membership and funding are drawn from multiple public and private sector sources. Although no one organization or type of organization is dominant, within British Columbia FPInnovations' full-time members in 2018 were principally forest industry organizations clustered within Metro Vancouver, including the head offices of corporations controlling operations throughout the province (see Figure 1.5).[59]

As a somewhat autonomous (P3), nonprofit initiative, FPInnovations collaboratively engages in highly diverse applied, development, technology transfer, and facilitative activities, particularly but not exclusively throughout the forestry value chain. Its activities are organized around teams often involving external members. These roles involve both long-term programs

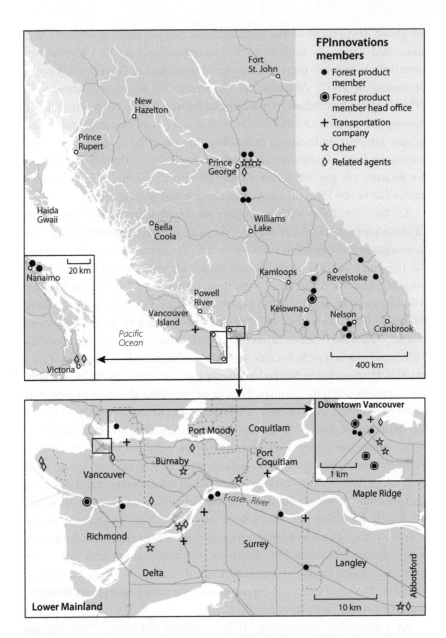

FIGURE 1.5 This map shows the locations in British Columbia and the types of activities of the members supporting FPInnovations. Most members, but not all, are forest product manufacturers. | Data from FPInnovations' Annual Report, 2018; redrawn by Eric Lienberger.

(five years or more) and short-term problem-solving services, seminars, and webinars to communicate expertise of various kinds, cooperation in technology transfer, and provision of fee-based, contracted services to non-members as well as members. As with its predecessor organizations, FPInnovations is an important supplier of expertise throughout the BC hinterland through its own programs, such as the development of Fitnir Analyzers for pulp mills developed as a multinational collaboration and spun off as a local company.[60] Furthermore, FPInnovations' mandate has broadened to embrace environmental and social as well as economic goals, to provide support to SMEs, Indigenous Peoples, and nonforest-industry partners, and to involve collaborative projects outside Canada.

FPInnovations' Diversified Hinterland Connections and Beyond

Within British Columbia, FPInnovations has initiated programs to engage with SMEs and Indigenous Peoples, the former with lower membership fees, new priorities beyond its traditional focus on large-scale forestry (see Figure 1.6). As FPInnovations' summary reports indicate, much of its support for SMEs features trouble-shooting exercises and providing expert advice, often involving on-site visits of a few days or a month that can be quickly implemented. Typically, the (few) SMEs that have sought assistance from FPInnovations were motivated to learn new knowledge consistent with their strategic plans and to be leaders in specific market niches. The kind of support supplied to Greenhus is atypical (see Case Study 1.1). Interestingly, though much of FPInnovations' support for SMEs has been to reduce cost and waste, including advice on lean management and technological expertise, design activities have also been supported, involving contact with design consultants, market analyses, prototype assistance, the provision of testing processes, and introductions to architectural and engineering services. Meanwhile, FPInnovations' services for Indigenous Peoples were introduced in its 2007 Indigenous Forestry Program in British Columbia, which has since supported over fifty Indigenous businesses through custom-based, on-site advice and technical support for appropriate forestry practices and fledgling business development, for example regarding log export operations and small sawmills. FPInnovations also encourages the incorporation of Indigenous designs in wood products, for example through the Opening Doors Exhibition that began in 2015 (and

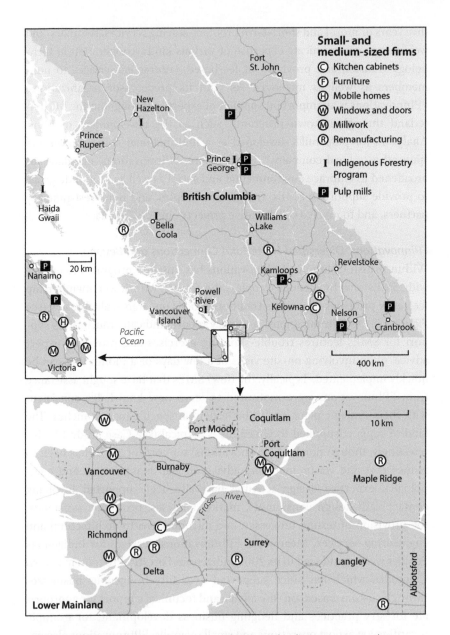

FIGURE 1.6 This map shows the location of SMEs and Indigenous groups that FPInnovations has supported and pulp mills that have adopted Fitnir technology developed by FPInnovations. | Data from FPInnovations reports, 2019; redrawn by Eric Leinberger.

has continued since) in Vancouver. That exhibition is a collaboration involving the Freda Design School of Northwest Coast Art, Emily Carr University of Art and Design, aboriginal artists and other partners including FPInnovations, which provides CAD-CAM and related technical assistance in door design.

Moreover, FPInnovations is increasingly proactive in contributing to global R&D collaborations, in effect exporting and reinforcing Metro Vancouver's technological expertise in forestry, and the roles played by engineering companies and equipment suppliers, such as KTC, Noram (see Case Study 1.2), USNR, and Optimal Machinery, along with the subsidiaries of engineering companies, such as Wood. In addition, globally, FPInnovations has developed increasingly important connections, with various public and private sector actors extending its predecessors' focus on serving forest businesses in Canada.[61] These global connections are spatially diverse and often embrace other peripheries, such as Alabama, the South Island of New Zealand, and Brazil. With respect to business collaborations, this trend is indicated in FPInnovations' licensing agreements with foreign companies, including as part of joint venture R&D projects with domestic companies, that have focused on Europe and South America in pulp and paper projects. Similarly, with respect to wood products FPInnovations obtained, in 2015, the North American rights to the patented post-tensioning technology for building systems developed by the New Zealand–based Structural Timber Innovation Company and Prestressed Timber, along with access to their future research in this field, which also involves co-investigators at the University of Canterbury. This technology will increase the attractiveness of mid-rise and tall wood buildings, especially in seismic and high-wind zones. Beyond these business connections, FPInnovations has established global collaborations with technical institutes and universities, including the French-based Centre technique du papier (CTP) and Institut technologique FCBA; the former is researching cellulose bio-based applications in nontraditional markets, and the latter is looking to collaborate on tall wood buildings and wood building recycling issues. With respect to university contacts, in 2016 FPInnovations signed a five-year agreement with Auburn University, through its Alabama Center for Paper and Bioresource Engineering, to form a partnership to help deliver FPInnovations' near-neutral brightening technology to local mills and to export FPInnovations' technology there. Joint

CASE STUDY 1.2 **Two Recent Locally Based Innovative Supplier Firms
Serving Metro Vancouver's Forest Sector**

Noram Engineering, established in 1988 in Vancouver by George Cook and
John Rae, and KTC (KTC Engineering since 2005) established in 1990 in Surrey
by John Karnik, are two new, innovative, design-intensive companies that contribute to Metro Vancouver's innovation economy in resource engineering and
manufacturing.

In 2020, Noram employed 170 engineers, technologists, and tradespeople. In
addition to its Vancouver head office, Noram has a manufacturing facility in
Delta and offices in Burnaby and Sweden, and it is organized around six business groups including pulp and paper and a strong emphasis on environmental imperatives. Noram specializes in development, commercialization, and
supply of leading-edge proprietary chemical processes and environmental
technologies, typically sold in the form of equipment and engineering pack-
ages implemented by the end users' engineering and construction contractors.
For example, Noram offers VERTREAT, an activated sludge process that produces
reuse-quality effluent from industrial and municipal waste streams, and VERTAD,
an aerobic digestion process that produces pathogen-free Class A biosolids.
Efficient oxygen transfer results in half the operating cost of conventional systems, and, with less than 20 percent of the land requirements, these systems
apply widely. Expanding beyond its initial focus on commodity chemicals, Noram
has achieved global leadership in nitration process technologies, with proprietary technology and equipment providing over 50 percent of the world's nitro-
benzene, an intermediate feedstock in the synthesis of polyurethane polymers.

research is also planned, and a 2018 agreement between FPInnovations
and its PIT research (transportation) group, and Auburn University and the
(US) National Center for Asphalt Technology is contributing technical services to road transportation issues. In formal terms, FPInnovations is moving beyond a localized external economy serving forestry businesses within
British Columbia (and Canada) to become a mobile external economy
whose expertise is developed and shared outside Canada and even outside
forestry. As such, it has become an autonomous growth-generating partici-
pant in Metro Vancouver's innovation economy.

Noram has further developed innovations in the sulfuric acid and electrochemical fields and become active in the biological wastewater treatment industry with the acquisition of Deep Shaft Technologies in 1998. Noram has collaborated with FPInnovations to create Lignoforce (replacing fossil fuel–based adhesives in wood product manufacture) and (also with Eco-tec of Ontario) in commercializing in 2015 a precipitator dust purification system (PDP) now used in mills in North and South America and Japan.

In the case of Surrey-based KTC Engineering, John Karnik developed engineering services for the engineered wood industry, in particular designing and building OSB manufacturing plants. Since then, KTC has designed many OSB plants throughout North America. In addition, in 2005, KTC Drevoprojekt in the Czech Republic was established to serve the forest industry there, and in 2006 KTC Tilby was formed to supply the biofibre industry with a separation process that processes sugar cane and sweet sorghum into various bioproducts. The firm also built a plant to process agricultural fibres into nonwoven natural fibre insulation, and KTC Panelboard serves the engineered wood and panel industry. The firm has completed 650 projects, including twenty-four new mills in North America, Europe, and Asia. It employs about forty people and has annual sales from $10 to $15 million.

Sources: "Noram Engineering and Constructors Ltd: Putting Process Innovation on the Fast Track to Commercialization," Innovate, https://innovationsoftheworld.com/noram-engineering-and-construction-putting-process-innovation-on-the-fast-track-to-commercialization; OSB and Engineering Wood History – KTC Engineering, www.panelboard.net>history.asp.

Conclusion

Within Metro Vancouver, forestry has moved substantially away from its commodity past to become a part of the region's knowledge-based, innovation economy. This restructuring and "rethinking" have been highly diverse and somewhat diffuse, rather than reflecting some overall master plan, and have featured wide-ranging entrepreneurial initiatives engaging hundreds of SMEs in numerous wood-processing and paper-converting activities, along with equipment suppliers and a range of business and engineering services. And a few new MNCs in engineering services have also arrived on the scene. Engineered wood has been part of this shift. In tandem, the sector's underlying RD&D (and innovation) system has been recalibrated around FPInnovations and is strongly focused on technology transfer and development activities in relation to market opportunities that are mainly incremental, adaptive, and design oriented. Formal RD&D laboratory programs and patenting exist but are not important compared with leading forestry regions.

Unfortunately, a comprehensive, knowledge-based approach to British Columbia's forest resource still seems to be a long way off. Corporate R&D has all but disappeared, FPInnovations' (national) budget has declined substantially, much less in 2018 (and 2021) than in 2010, and long-term, experimental R&D programs that (elsewhere), for example, have explored "see-through" wood stronger than glass, wood fibre for auto and plane parts, rigid lignin for bumpers, and paper as a plastic substitute, do not appear to have been given much consideration in Metro Vancouver.[62] Even as BC government policy has shifted decisively in recent decades to embrace non-industrial as well as industrial goals, science and innovation have continued to be seen as supportive backups but not pre-eminent activities. From the early 1900s to now, science and innovation policy has reflected the vision of a periphery, primarily to adapt technology originating elsewhere for local industrial use. In this regard, technological capabilities have been excellent, and have involved globally recognized achievements. Yet, investments in RD&D and innovation as an ongoing, cumulative source of competitive advantage for world-leading core companies (or to become a global leader in conservation best practices) has not been strongly evident in corporate strategies or as public policy ambition. However, the potential for British Columbia's huge – and largely publicly owned – forest estate to be a sustainable, nondepleting and job-creating resource surely depends on its participation in the knowledge economy with science and innovation activities established as priorities in support of clearly articulated multiple economic and noneconomic goals. Within Metro Vancouver, a network of agencies provides much potential in this regard and readily can help to cement core-periphery relations. Whether or not such potential can be enhanced remains a challenge; development has occurred, but it has been arrested. As a recent union report attests, industrial restructuring, including various policy initiatives, continues as an ad hoc, limited process and with public policy lacking a clear articulation of overall goals.[63]

2

Metro Vancouver High-Tech Firms in Arrested Transition?

The emergence of new industries in driving urbanization and local development often depends on entrepreneurial initiatives at their origins.[1] Although hard to predict in terms of timing and location, such initiatives are vital in the creation of some initial competitive advantage in places where similar and related firms concentrate, giving rise to processes of cumulative causation generating industrial specializations with global reach. Given the highly competitive nature of the global economy, these processes are not automatic, initial advantages can be lost in particular places, and alternative trajectories can be contemplated. Even so, as much literature has argued, high-road trajectories toward innovation-based economies in postindustrial cities and regions effectively are initiated by locally based entrepreneurial businesses.[2] Firms and regions shape one another, and such intimacies are especially well revealed by local entrepreneurs.[3] Innovative local entrepreneurs can offer distinct competitive advantages that draw from local experiences and resources yet require an awareness of local limitations and the ability to supplement local networks with global ones. For peripheral cities, the need for such contributions and abilities is particularly stark. Metro Vancouver is a fascinating case in point.

The outstanding feature, and dilemma, of the Metro Vancouver high-tech landscape are its capacity to generate a diversity of entrepreneurial start-ups without creating particularly large firms. In this chapter, we focus on the role of locally based entrepreneurial businesses in shaping the nature and dynamism of Metro Vancouver's high-tech sector and reflect on this apparent contradiction. As we noted in the introduction, MacDonald Dettwiler and Associates (MDA), Sierra Systems, Glenayre, and Electronic Laboratories of Canada were early markers from the 1960s, anticipating the influence of small and medium-sized firms (SMEs) as the sector gathered momentum following Expo 86. Indeed, over time, the population pyramid (size distribution) of firms comprising the BC high-tech sector has remained bottom heavy. As the number of high-tech businesses in British Columbia has increased, to almost 11,000 in 2018 (from 5,116 in 1995), 80 percent employed fewer than 10, and over 95 percent employed fewer than 100, with only 220 firms employing more than 100, and in 2020 just 22 employed more than 500.[4] Relatively few have expanded to become medium-sized firms, and even fewer larger still to become mid-sized firms, with only Telus (questionably) deserving anchor firm status.[5] Not incidentally, foreign-owned subsidiaries are part of this larger-sized segment (see Chapter 3).

In this chapter, we examine the origin, scope, and performance of high-tech firms in Metro Vancouver that began as locally owned, entrepreneurial businesses since the 1960s and subsequently expanded to become relatively large SMEs and larger (without ever becoming giant companies). Statistical definitions of SMEs vary, and in Canada and the United States, for example, small firms are considered to have fewer than 100 employees and medium-sized firms between 100 and 500 employees. In Europe (and most countries), the upper limit of SMEs is 250 employees.[6] In this chapter, our focus is on those locally originating (larger) SMEs that since the 1960s have reached 250 employees and/or generated sales of $50 million Canadian. Despite a flourishing in overall numbers and sectors, up to 2018–19, as a comprehensive if not complete list, just forty-four companies were thus identified and their origins and growth patterns examined in regard to general and particular characteristics. This information was derived from the authors' research, inspection of various publications, and stories in newspapers and business magazines of individual firms (see Appendix 1).[7]

If admittedly a small segment of the size-based population pyramid, these firms provide key indicators of high-tech's vitality, diversification, and future directions – and limits – in Metro Vancouver's innovation economy. These businesses can be summarized as "transitioning" in that they have grown successfully from local entrepreneurial origins to become SMEs and even bigger (without ever becoming giant). Their transitioning as independent organizations has evident limits, whether by choice, market forces, closure, or acquisition by giants. Nevertheless, through innovation-driven strategies that have led to new manufactured products and especially new producer services, these firms capture the diverse and dynamic expressions of entrepreneuralism that have shaped profoundly the Metro Vancouver high-tech landscape. Whether sourced from a (big) pool of small firms or as spinoffs from large organizations, the selected firms represent successful start-ups that have "scaled up" to become efficient, (mostly) profitable operations, moving past the "valley of death" in which initial (fixed, sunk, and variable) costs occur before any or sufficient revenues are generated.[8] In this regard, innovation is both a push and a pull factor of firm growth. Thus, firms are pushed to achieve a scale of operation (and revenue generation) to pay for the accumulated costs incurred by the innovation process, as well as ongoing operating costs, and they are stimulated (pulled) to expand further by the opportunities and markets opened up by innovation. Such transitioning, however, is fraught with vulnerabilities. Within high tech as a whole, start-ups can be undermined by technological and financial uncertainties, and, as across all industries, death (exit) rates among firms are invariably highest among new and tiny firms, a reflection of the manifold difficulties in seeking minimum efficient size (MES) when revenues (first) cover costs. The often considerable time needed for innovation processes to unfold adds to the challenges of scaling up by high-tech firms to reach the MES. Furthermore, even successfully commercialized innovations can experience short lives, whether for market size, technological, or competitive reasons, an occurrence that in turn pressures specialized, dependent SMEs to repeat their engagement with innovation and scaling-up processes.

In practice, the firms identified in this chapter have transitioned successfully as SMEs and beyond, at least for a time and to some degree, and constitute a particularly dynamic segment of the local high-tech economy. In the process, they have generated important knowledge-based, relatively high-income employment, along with various multiplier effects and external economies, and typically they have become global in scope with respect to exports and supplier relations. Moreover, these relatively high-profile firms contribute to Metro Vancouver's high-tech reputation, not least by signalling employment opportunities for talent around the world and stimulating interest among multinational corporations (MNCs). Indeed, as the principal acquisition attractants for foreign direct investment (FDI), their evolutionary dynamics help to reflect on an ongoing debate about the lack of "anchor" or "core" firms in the BC high-tech sector.

The remainder of the chapter is divided into four parts. First, to provide a comparative foundation for understanding the generation of Metro

Vancouver's high-tech businesses, we underscore that their pre-eminent need for innovation to be transformed into scalable products simultaneously requires increased organizational capabilities. Second, we discuss the selected forty-four relatively large, locally originating, high-tech firms in Metro Vancouver in terms of selected characteristics associated with their founding owners and entrepreneurs. Third, we summarize the diversity of the transitioning paths of these firms especially in relation to their product and market characteristics, including their global orientation through exports and investments. Using Ballard Power as both a distinctive and a representative company, in the fourth section we explore its transitioning from a local/global perspective, especially with respect to R&D commitments, exports, investments, and financing. The conclusions reflect on the issue of missing so-called anchor firms.

Contextualizing Metro Vancouver's High-Tech Entrepreneurial Firms

Local development is strengthened through a mix of firms of different sizes, and the population size distribution of firms provides a useful starting point for thinking about high-tech Metro Vancouver. The oft-noted classic polar distinction in this regard is between tiny, specialized, small firms operating in single locations and controlled by individual entrepreneurs and giant, hierarchical, MNCs with diverse, multi-plant operations, controlled by decentralized decision-making structures and globally integrated in various ways. A more nuanced, albeit still highly generalized "triad" summary of business segments and transitioning, recognizes distinctions among SMEs, large (mid-sized) firms, and giants (see Figure 2.1).[9] In this model, businesses are classified not only by their sizes but also in terms of varying decision-making routines, organizational structures, geographic and functional scope, and impacts. For local development, each business segment potentially offers distinctive contributions around the entrepreneurial pools of small firms and SMEs, the focused innovativeness of larger mid-sized firms, and the size, power, and scope of giant MNCs.

As this template model anticipates, in general terms, the evolution of firms from small to giant typically involves an increasing scale and geographic scope of activities alongside an increased scale and decentralization of decision making. In addition, reflecting valley of death and scaling up problems, exit (failure) rates are highest among new small firms. Given that in practice growth motivations are highly varied (and for many small firms do not exist beyond reaching the MES), this model underlines the

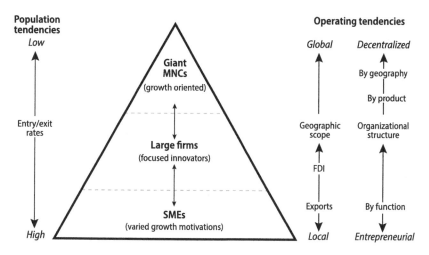

FIGURE 2.1 This model shows a population pyramid of firms comprising SME, large-firm, and giant-firm segments. With increased size, there are fewer firms, entry and exit rates become lower, their geographical scope becomes increasingly global, and decision-making structures become more decentralized.

importance of innovation (as a push and pull factor) for SMEs that wish to grow, including those becoming larger and mid-sized.

The significance of these innovation-driven, mid-sized firms has long been recognized in developing national and regional economies, and such firms have been labelled "hidden champions" and "*Mittelstand*" (Germany), "little giants" (United States), and "backbone firms" (Japan).[10] Moreover, these firms typically develop their specializations on a global scale, often enjoying dominant or important market shares in their specialities and supported by multinational operations. Indeed, such firms require both an expansive global demand and networks and pipelines to draw information.[11] These firms are not as big or diverse or as well known as giants, but their sizes can be impressive, with revenues in the billions of dollars and employment in the tens of thousands. In Canada, the lack of such firms has long been bemoaned, reflected in the old Science Council of Canada's pleas to promote "threshold firms."[12]

Meanwhile, growth-oriented, giant MNCs exploit substantial firm-, factory-, and product-level economies of scale and size, control multiple products in different stages of their life cycles, and their R&D and innovation comprise parts of their organizational capability and power. Over time, organizational capacities can supersede innovation per se as the core competency of these giants.

In effect, the scaling up of start-ups to SME or larger-size firms requires their product innovation capacity to co-evolve with numerous other attributes of business performance and governance, related for example to the nature of decision making, employee relations, supplier arrangements, and marketing. Admittedly, firm growth and increasing size cannot be assumed precisely to reflect changes in other indicators of firm performance (e.g., exports) or governance (e.g., nature of decision making). However, in practice, business segments are typically identified according to firm size, usually by revenues and/or employment.[13] Size itself is an important attribute and readily understood and comparatively appreciated, information on business revenue and employment tends to be more readily available than indicators of other business attributes, and firm size is widely accepted as a reasonable proxy for processes of segmentation. Indeed, the extent to which products can be scaled up within the markets that they serve defines the potential for a firm's local base to increase growth, efficiency, and value-added and high-road jobs. Even if products are relocated within export markets, key functions such as R&D, headquarters, and financing remain to sustain the local base with high-income jobs. This scalability-driven organizational morphology is crucial to understanding how Metro Vancouver start-ups can become global without becoming particularly large.

Within the context of the business segmentation model (see Figure 2.1), high-tech firms in Metro Vancouver as a whole are strongly concentrated in the SME segment and just beyond it as (small) mid-sized firms. All of the selected firms at the focus of this chapter have transitioned from small firms to SMEs and even larger firms, close to or beyond 250 employees and/or $50 million in revenues. These locally originating firms stand out in Metro Vancouver's high-tech sector in terms of their size, and they demonstrate innovation-driven growth dependent on market acceptance of a new product or service. To be sure, the many small firms at the base of Metro Vancouver's high-tech population pyramid generate important collective external economies and are vital to local dynamics in high tech (see Chapter 5), and individual firms that have not reached the size threshold of SMEs as defined here can have big local impacts. Moli Energy and Distinctive Software, for example, are two pioneering, innovative small firms whose influence continues to resonate long after their acquisitions (see Case Study 2.1). A brief sketch of these firms helps us to appreciate the varied nature of the (initial) transitioning challenges facing high-tech firms in Metro Vancouver.

The bottom-heavy population pyramid of high-tech firms in Metro Vancouver, more so than in other places, has been fuelled continually by new (locally owned entrepreneurial) entrants very small in scale. These firms face an immediate valley of death challenge to scale up (in time) to achieve the MES implying that a sufficient number of customers have been found to enable profitability, the required sources of financing have been accessed, employees have been hired and trained, a suitable location has been found, and a host of regulations has been met.[14] Although the MES is not easy to specify, varying among firms and types of activity, in Metro Vancouver relatively few local firms have exhibited desires and abilities to grow and transition much beyond being small firms, let alone SMEs or bigger companies. Indeed, this study was able to identify – for over a fifty-year period within a growing sector – just forty-four local high-tech firms that have become large SMEs or bigger companies; this is not that many, bearing in mind that several have failed and that others have been acquired by MNCs. Few of them have employed more than 1,000 people, entering the mid-sized firm segment, and only one company (now defunct) ever exceeded 4,500 jobs. Nevertheless, the forty-four identified companies have transitioned successfully on the basis of innovative strategies, at least for a while, to become relatively high-profile, locally based SMEs and small mid-sized firms. They offer key insights into the nature and challenge of transitioning high-tech firms in Metro Vancouver, beginning with their key characteristics at start up and their searches for the MES.

Origins: Metro Vancouver as High-Tech Seedbed

A striking characteristic of Metro Vancouver's emerging innovation economy has been as a high-tech seedbed for entrepreneurial initiatives. This role began slowly and gathered momentum especially after the 1980s, led principally by locally based founders with high levels of formal education and with little connection to the region's resource industry specialties. Rather, these entrepreneurs and owners represent agents of Jacobs-style urban diversification. From the beginning, entrepreneurial spinoffs from existing organizations, acting as "incubators," have been important in the creation of new high-tech businesses. In terms of the location of start-ups, Vancouver has been strongly complemented by other metropolitan municipalities, led by the inner suburbs of Burnaby, Richmond, and to some extent North Vancouver. Additionally, as is usual with the entrepreneurial foundations of new industries, the labour forces among Metro Vancouver's new,

CASE STUDY 2.1 **Small-Firm Innovative Pioneers:**
Moli Energy and Distinctive Software

Originating in Metro Vancouver, Moli Energy and Distinctive Software were two globally recognized innovators, respectively, in lithium battery production and video games, both of which were acquired by foreign interests even while relatively small (see Appendix 2). Their influence remains evident, however, even if in Moli's case it could have been greater. Their different stories add appreciation to the diverse nature of Metro Vancouver's high-tech economy.

Moli was founded in 1977 (in Burnaby) by Rudi Haering (Order of Canada in 1976), a professor of physics at UBC and partially funded by Tech Mining. Based on research at Haering's laboratory, Moly was formed to commercialize lithium batteries that offered a longer life than existing nickel-cadmium batteries. The first flagship product, the 2.2 volt Molicel, was not produced until 1984, when the company had 75 employees, and then manufactured to scale and marketed in 1988–89 in a factory located in Maple Ridge, when the company had 192 employees. Shortly after the company became public (1986). Molicel powered cellphones and laptops, mainly for large Japanese consumers such as NEC (Nippon Electric Company), and was the world's first company to produce lithium batteries commercially, with plans to make 20 million a year. Unfortunately, there were problems with lithium use, and when a Molicel battery caught fire in a Japanese cellphone in 1989 Moli's future was threatened. The BC government pulled its loan, forcing Moli into receivership, and almost immediately sold Moli's assets valued at $58 million and patents to Japanese interests for $5 million. The plant became somewhat moribund until acquired in 1998 by One-E Moli Energy, which

small, high-tech companies are largely nonunionized – and mainly have remained so (the film industry being exceptional in this regard).

Localness
The formation of the forty-four high-tech businesses in Metro Vancouver, the focus of this chapter, was dominated by founders already resident in the area, many of whom had been born there. The overwhelming majority of the thousands of new, small, high-tech firms started within Metro Vancouver in recent decades undoubtedly share this characteristic. New and small firms in various industry contexts tend to be locally owned and controlled by es-

subsequently developed a lithium-ion battery, with about 80 employees (see Appendix 2). Jeff Dahn, a graduate student of Haering's and Moli employee, became Canada's leading authority in the industry.

Distinctive Software was founded in 1982 by Dan Mattrick and Joe Sember as seventeen-year-old high school students in the basement of Mattrick's family home in Burnaby, with Mattrick acquiring control in 1984. They created a multi-level game called Evolution, the first Canadian computer game to enter production, and within a few years they had become the largest video game developer not owned by a console, developing a variety of games. As Metro Vancouver's pioneering video game firm, Distinctive Software received a couple of takeover offers that Mattrick rejected before selling to Electronic Arts (EA), reportedly for about $11 million, in a friendly, negotiated acquisition in 1991. At the time, Distinctive Software had between 60 and 75 employees, and EA Canada has since grown substantially to over 1,000 employees in Burnaby (see Appendix 2). Mattrick continued in EA as a senior executive until 2007, when he joined Microsoft. Distinctive Software and EA Canada comprised the base of a family tree of video game firms in Metro Vancouver numbering 170 in 2009.

Sources: E. Jarrett, "New Lessons from the Epic Story of Moli Energy, the Canadian Pioneer of Rechargeable Lithium Battery Technology," *Electric Autonomy Canada,* September 18, 2020, https://electricautonomy.ca/ev-supply-chain/batteries/2020-09-18/moli-energy-lithium-battery-technology; K. Blain, "Case: Vancouver's Video Game Family Tree," January 28, 2009, *Georgia Straight,* https://www.straight.com/article-198534/video-game-family-tree.

tablished residents, a fact long recognized by the so-called seedbed hypothesis in location studies, and such firms are key drivers of new industry life cycles.[15] Indeed, the tendency of new firms to be locally generated is economically rational since new firm founders can take advantage of their ("inherited") knowledge of local economic, political, and social conditions and their local understanding of access to markets, suppliers, financial resources, and even voluntary help. In more formal terms, such seedbed behaviour reduces the transaction costs of locating firms in new, unfamiliar places that would impose substantial costs and uncertainties in the search for information on appropriate locational conditions. New firm founders face many challenges in setting up their businesses without compounding them by locating those businesses in unfamiliar places. In practice, many new businesses begin in the homes of founders and thus avoid any explicit locational choices at that time. In this regard, John MacDonald's decision to start his new company, which became MDA, in his home basement (while still employed by UBC) is an illustrative low-cost, low-risk locational "choice" prior to finding a more permanent, larger, but still local space (in Richmond) that drew from already successful experimentation in business formation.

To be sure, migrants to Metro Vancouver, not only from British Columbia's hinterland but also from other parts of Canada and foreign countries, have made important contributions to creating the region's high-tech dynamics. These contributions began with the first companies started in the 1960s and 1970s; for example, among the first seven companies, three key founders were born in Manitoba, one in hinterland British Columbia, another in Ontario, and one each in Israel, Germany, and Switzerland (see Appendix 1). But all had lived and worked in Metro Vancouver prior to their involvement in their high-tech start-ups. Thus, Glenayre had begun in 1963 as a restructuring toward a modern electronics business of a long-established family firm owned by the Chisholms, plans that depended in practice on the key hiring of Klaus Deering. He had been born in Manitoba but, following his war service, had been living in Vancouver since 1946, first employed in his family's (logging) business (a rare resource connection). Also born in Manitoba, Grant Gisel had just moved to Vancouver, where he subsequently co-founded Sierra Systems in 1966 with two other local, established residents. Another Manitoban, Norman Dowds, had moved to Vancouver, where he joined BC Tel and, in 1979, became the leader of the firm's spinoff, the highly innovative MPR Teltech. As for John MacDonald, a co-founder of MDA, he had been born and raised in remote Prince Rupert but had moved to Vancouver as a (UBC) student, where he also became a professor years prior to establishing his company. Meanwhile, his co-founder, Vern Dettwiler, had been born in Switzerland but had moved to Vancouver as a young boy; he was a colleague of MacDonald's at UBC before MDA began. As perhaps Metro Vancouver's most famous early high-tech immigrant, Dan Gelbart arrived from Israel and first worked at MDA for several years before helping to start Mobile Data International (MDI, in 1978) and then Creo (in 1983). Fred Kaiser and Grace Borsari, immigrants from Germany and Switzerland, respectively, arrived just a few years before co-founding Alpha Technologies (Burnaby) in 1975, the former first working as an electrical engineer and the latter in photo labs in existing companies. Although they quickly moved many of Alpha Technologies' activities to Bellingham, Washington, the Burnaby location remained. As for Ballard Power (1979), as we will discuss later, its main founder, Geoffrey Ballard, was born in Ontario and arrived in Vancouver for a project before setting up his company.

Indeed, the origins of all forty-four selected companies are broadly similar, with founders knowledgeable of Metro Vancouver by birthright and schooling or at least becoming residents before establishing their companies. With respect to the most recent of these companies, for example, as Slack's driving force, Stewart Butterfield was born in a tiny community (a commune apparently) near Lund on the BC coast and graduated from the University of Victoria (later Cambridge) before moving to Vancouver. There he started, with varying success, various video game companies, eventually starting Slack (2013) along with other local residents, albeit born in the United States, United Kingdom, and Russia. As other recent examples, the two companies established in 2012, AbCellera Biologics and Bench, were led by founders who had graduated from UBC and were long-time local residents. iQmetrix varies from this pattern in that it was founded in 1999 by Christopher Krywulak in Regina, his place of birth (and schooling experience). Krywulak moved to Vancouver in 2009, where the head office of iQmetrix was established in 2010 (the Regina office has continued to operate). The norm is nevertheless for founders to establish their new companies where they are already living.

Education and Co-Founding

In Metro Vancouver's contemporary high-tech activities, local founders typically have gained high levels of formal education, specifically in universities, colleges, and various institutes, a characteristic widely reported among high-tech activities in general. There are exceptions to this trend among the selected forty-four firms: Christopher Krywulak and Alexander Fernandes left high school for workforce experience before starting, respectively, iQmetrix and (after other initiatives) Avigilon Corporation (2004), as did Ryan Holmes, a co-founder of Hootsuite Media (2009), and Klaus Deering, who became Glenayre's leader, and Kenneth Patrick, the founder of Avcorp are not postsecondary graduates.[16] Among other noted high-tech entrepreneurs, Dan Mattrick (see Case Study 2.1), Donald Hings (see Case Study I.1), and Phil Nuytten (see Case Study 4.1) were pioneering local innovators whose formal schooling stopped at high school. However, compared with the old industrial economy, when many manufacturing start-ups often involved skilled blue-collar labour, high-tech founders typically have gained postsecondary degrees and diplomas before establishing new companies. This trend, not without exception, reflects the growing importance of advanced, formal learning of accumulated knowledge, most obviously in the principles governing physical laws and human behaviour as preconditions for innovation.

In practice, the (formal) postsecondary education and training of the founders of transitioning companies are highly varied in terms of source, focus, and level. As expected, science engineering, medical, and computing educational backgrounds are particularly important, especially in the more R&D-intensive initiatives. At the same time, bearing in mind the many companies involved in innovation in business and social media services, the postsecondary focus of founders frequently has been in accounting and management studies, law, and even the social sciences and humanities. Regarding the latter, for example, Stewart Butterfield's Bachelor of Arts (University of Victoria, 1996) and Master of Arts (Cambridge University, 1998) degrees were in philosophy. The level of postsecondary education also varies, although some form of university graduation (BSc/BA, MSc/MA, PhD) dominates. Among the forty companies in which the founders' educational backgrounds are known, thirty-seven involved postsecondary education, and thirty-four had completed at least one university degree. In eleven companies, at least one founder had obtained a PhD (typically in the sciences and medicine), and several more have received honorary degrees for lifetime achievements, including Dan Gelbart, whose award in 2009 from UBC reflected his remarkable scientific and innovative achievements.[17] As expected, these high-level educational backgrounds are especially associated with the science- and technology-driven companies such as MDA, Ballard, Creo, the biotechs (Angiotech, Stemcell Technologies, Zymeworks, AbCellera Biologics), Westport Fuel Systems (originally Westport Innovations), and D-Wave Systems. In more business-service-oriented companies, such as Clio and Bench, specialized "professional" education in business and law is important, with most degrees at the BA/BSc level. Outside conventional university education, several co-founders, for example in Hootsuite and Bench, had attended the Vancouver Film School, which features a one-year intensive program.

As expected, transitioning company founders often obtained postsecondary education from within Metro Vancouver, led by UBC. Thus, for seventeen companies, at least one co-founder received a degree from UBC, and in five of those companies one of the co-founders received a PhD from

UBC. Four founders became professors at UBC after receiving their PhDs from elsewhere, and four founders, including John MacDonald, obtained their first degrees at UBC before obtaining their PhDs elsewhere and returning. Other local postsecondary institutions educating founders include Simon Fraser University (4), British Columbia Institute of Technology (1), Vancouver Film School (2), and Pitman Business School (1), and the nearby University of Victoria is also mentioned (2). At the same time, the founders of Metro Vancouver's transitioning companies gained postsecondary education from a wide range of institutions across Canada and elsewhere. Canadian postsecondary institutions, especially in the Prairies and Ontario, for example, educated founders of seventeen companies, including PhD-level talent in three cases. In addition, sixteen companies have founders who received postsecondary education from universities in the United States (9), United Kingdom (3), Germany (1), Israel (1), Russia (1), and Ukraine (1). This support includes PhD talent in seven of these companies.

Within Metro Vancouver, postsecondary institutions have been important to the development of high tech, places where local founders have received advanced, specialized knowledge upon which to build, while reinforcing the social power of localness not least through forming friendships and networking. The learning provided by postsecondary institutions also adds to the mobility of individuals, and the founders of high-tech companies in Metro Vancouver have benefited greatly from education elsewhere, where they were born or chose to go. In broad terms, according to the information on these (forty-four) companies, the postsecondary education achieved among all founders and co-founders has been roughly balanced between local and the nonlocal sources, with the latter perhaps being somewhat more important. Metro Vancouver has been a flourishing seedbed in which to cultivate highly varied educational backgrounds undertaken in a variety of locales.

A further notable start-up characteristic of high-tech firms in Metro Vancouver is the role played by co-founding. In fact, the majority of the forty-four firms studied were co-founded. Bearing in mind that PNI Digital Media's founders are unknown, as are several Xantrex founders, twenty-eight of the remaining forty-three companies were co-founded by two or more individuals. In addition, a couple of spinoff companies, namely MDI (1978) and MPR Teltech (1979), retained ties with their parent companies and were not individually founded and controlled in a conventional sense. Similarly, Glenayre was rooted in a co-owned family firm that wanted a change in strategic direction. In three other cases, co-ownership at start up involved close family relations, but in these cases each member had a distinct, formal role. Overall, among the twenty-eight co-founded firms, sixteen, five, and seven cases, respectively, comprised two, three, and four or five individuals.

As an important feature of high-tech start-ups among Metro Vancouver's transitioning firms, the rationale for co-founding relates to the sharing of complementary expertise, risks, and financial burdens and extending friendship ties. Along with a high level of educational attainment, the sharing of expertise in co-founding points to the challenging, uncertain nature of high-tech innovation. That is, entrepreneurial innovation in high tech is often multi-faceted and most obviously, if not always, expressed in science- and technology-intensive companies. Among early start-ups, for example, MDA combined MacDonald's engineering knowledge with Dettwiler's physics and computer science expertise; at Ballard, the three founders similarly complemented one another in terms of scientific background and expertise (with advanced degrees in environmental science, chemistry, and mechanical engineering), and Creo's start up combined Dan Gelbart's imaginative technological talents with Ken Spencer's science background (BSc in electrical engineering from UBC) and managerial knowledge (MBA from SFU). By all accounts, in these cases, the co-founders also had different but complementary personalities and developed strong friendships. Regarding the science- and technology-intensive start-ups in the biotechs, Quadra Logic Technologies (QLT,1981), Angiotech (1992), Zymeworks (2003), and AbCellera Biologics (2012), the co-founders had strong UBC connections (as undergrads, grads, and/or professors). In addition, Stemcell Technologies (1993) was founded by Allen Eaves while a UBC professor, and the company grew out of joint work with his wife while running the Terry Fox Foundation. Point Grey Research (1997) and D-Wave Systems (1999) are other science-intensive companies with multiple founders and UBC connections, the latter especially.

Tertiary educational institutions clearly have played important roles in bringing together founders of Metro Vancouver's transitioning high-tech companies. In some cases, founders have met each other at university before moving to Metro Vancouver, others have met in Vancouver with different university backgrounds, and local institutions have attracted both students and faculty members educated elsewhere. These varied post-secondary experiences have added to the sources of expertise in the region's innovative companies. Local universities have been incubators and contributed to so-called spinoff developments.

Sourcing from Spinoffs

Spinoffs occur when entrepreneurs leave one organization to start another, usually a relatively small firm. Indeed, among Metro Vancouver's high-tech population of firms as a whole, many spinoffs likely have been generated by other small firms, whether because the original firm failed, some employees wanted to start their own company, or existing owners desired a change in direction. As PricewaterhouseCoopers' Tech Map for 2012 reveals, the evolution of high-tech activities across British Columbia featured a dizzying array of "influences" that reflected the movement or spinoff of key people from one organization to create or manage a new firm.[18] Among the forty-four firms studied in this chapter, several of the founders had previous start-up (and small-firm) experiences, ranging from Ballard (1979) to Slack (2013) (see Appendix 1). High-tech entrepreneurship is often a trial-and-error process marked by failure and uncertainty and illustrated by Geoffrey Ballard's somewhat unusual peripatetic career that founded several companies before setting down roots in Burnaby with the establishment of Ballard Engineering (before becoming Ballard Power Systems, see later discussion). In addition, as noted above, postsecondary institutions led by UBC have been fecund incubators of the selected transitioning firms, plus many other much smaller initiatives. However, UBC (and SFU) did not begin to develop an explicit role to support business incubation until the 1980s (see Chapter 5). BC Hydro, a large, provincial, crown corporation that had acquired considerable engineering and computing expertise, has been another public sector source of high-tech spinoffs, including Westech Information Systems (1989), run by former employees of BC Hydro until its controversial privatization in 2003.[19]

Given that among businesses in high-tech Metro Vancouver spinoffs frequently occur, the incubating roles of MDA and Telus are well known.[20] Ken Spencer and Dan Gelbart, for example, were two high-level employees at MDA who left to form Creo, and Gelbart was instrumental in starting MDI, both ventures becoming successful. By the late 1990s, MDA had spun off another dozen or so smaller high-tech companies. In turn, these spinoffs have stimulated further spinoffs, as when Creo was virtually closed down after its acquisition by Kodak in 2005 and its former employees began several new high-tech companies in Metro Vancouver.[21] As another high-profile business spinoff, MPR Teltech is noteworthy (see Appendix 1). MPR began in 1979 as part of Microtel, then part of BC Tel (now Telus), and was located in Burnaby, becoming a relatively autonomous venture in 1987 but still affiliated with BC Tel. For some observers, MPR became an unrivalled incubator. Its employees created PMC (Pacific Microelectronics Centre) Sierra and several small local companies and sold proprietary technology that led to impressive commercial successes.[22] As other examples, Glenayre and Xantrex were unusual in that, respectively, they initially manufactured machinery and electrical power equipment, and their subsequent decisions to engage in high-tech activities were associated with hiring experienced leaders from other local high-tech firms who then shaped the innovation-driven, long-term directions of their companies. In these firms, the key entrepreneurs – Klaus Deering became especially well known at Glenayre as its "fourth" employee – were not the controlling founders, although they did become part owners.

In general, high-tech spinoffs in Metro Vancouver have been voluntary, "friendly," complementary initiatives, providing distinct goods and services that the incubating firms did not wish to supply themselves (and which might be customers). Creo, for example, pursued computer technologies in relation to the printing industry, and MDI's focus on mobile data systems differed from MDA's product market focus. Other MDA spinoffs were similarly complementary. Although such spinoffs added to local diversification and multiplier effects, others did not. For example, when Telus (as BC Tel) dissolved MPR in the late 1990s, many of its assets were acquired by companies such as Newbridge Networks, IBM Corporation, Northern Telecom, and Digital Access based outside British Columbia. BC Tel had no interest in upscaling MPR's innovations, and in pursuing manufacturing possibilities, and these innovations were sold to nonlocal companies. As one example, MPR licensed its new ATM technology to Newbridge (Ontario) in 1992 and then its entire ATM business unit. Subsequently, France's Alcatel acquired Newbridge in 2000 for US $7.1 billion, mainly attracted by the benefits of acquiring the ATM technology, and effectively drained it from Metro Vancouver as a matter of corporate policy.[23] High-tech spinoffs in Metro Vancouver have also been "involuntary," stimulated by the "shock" of downsizing or closure. Glenayre's and Creo's closures in 2001 and 2009, for example, have been noted in this regard, the latter encouraging new initiatives by Gelbart.

Locational Patterns within Metro Vancouver

The main decision-making and research centres of the selected transitioning firms are dispersed among the major municipalities of Metro Vancouver, although none is in the communities of North Vancouver and West Vancouver (see Figure 2.2).

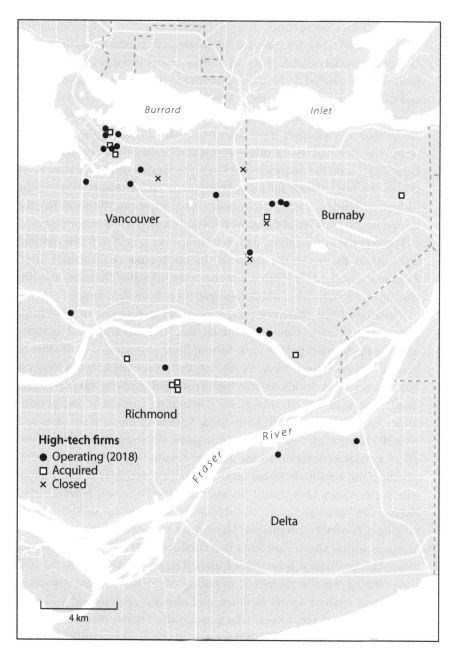

FIGURE 2.2 This map shows the main locations of the operations of relatively large entrepreneurial, high-tech firms in Metro Vancouver. Although many are located close to downtown Vancouver, others are dispersed among the inner suburbs, especially Burnaby and Richmond. They are listed in Appendix 1. | Cartography by Eric Leinberger.

A few firms have operated in several locations within Metro Vancouver; Burnaby-based Creo, for example, supplemented its major manufacturing facility on Annacis Island, Delta, with other offices in the region. Typically, however, the selected firms have concentrated their main decision-making and R&D operations in one place. Although these centres are relatively dispersed, modest intra-urban clustering tendencies are evident. About half are located in Vancouver itself, with two small clusters in the downtown peninsular area, and several others are located beyond these concentrations, especially toward the east, including Glenayre, located just on the Vancouver side of the border with Burnaby. Westport is farther south, close to the Richmond border. Among metropolitan municipalities, Burnaby has the second largest number of firms, with several clustered in a major commercial zone in the north-central part, with PMC-Sierra located to the east and three others located in the south on the north bank of the Fraser River. Richmond also hosts five firms, and the outer suburb of Delta has two, including Avcor Industries, which relocated there from Richmond.

These locational patterns express widely held preferences for these firms to locate their main control functions, head offices, and R&D facilities within a single metropolitan area. Several firms have located in or close to Vancouver's downtown business district, the traditional heart of business head offices. Such locations face high costs and property taxes but gain multiple accessibility advantages for commuting employees and person-to-person connections with co-located, high-level business services and related "strategic" decision-making functions. Vancouver's downtown also offers a ready connection to the airport; a wide range of entertainment, amenity, and routine business services; and a prestigious address, often with scenic views. Less central city and suburban locations, however, offer cheaper land costs and more available space, and they can still offer wide-ranging accessibility advantages. Many firms thus choose inner suburban locations within Metro Vancouver that combine R&D and head office functions. This preference is reinforced among larger firms that seek to offer wide-ranging, on-site amenities, including relaxation centres, day cares, indoor and outdoor sports facilities, and pleasant gardens and walks for their professional employees, who provide the human resource core of technology-based competitive advantages. In effect, within British Columbia, these firms reflect the clustering of high tech in Metro Vancouver, and within the region both clustering and dispersal are evident.

The significance of land costs and zoning regulations is especially evident if manufacturing activities are important. For example, Avcor, which builds components for aircraft, including for Boeing and Bombardier, relocated from Richmond to Delta to access low-cost land. In Creo's case, its printing machine manufacturing operations, now closed, were located on the long-established, industrially zoned Annacis Island in Delta. Within Vancouver and its inner suburbs, industrially zoned land has become increasingly scarce and too expensive to maintain manufacturing operations. Even if batch and custom-made manufacturing can be viable in Metro Vancouver, if the need for space is important, then a peripheral location is required.

Timing

In terms of origins, just three of the selected companies started in the 1960s and only seven before 1980. Indeed, when Dan Gelbart arrived from Israel in Vancouver in 1973, he joined MDA, as he noted, as one of only a couple of technology companies that were potentially interesting employers. Since 1980, however, as part of more rapid growth of the high-tech sector, thirty-seven of the identified companies were established (by 2013), with thirteen starting in the 1980s and a further twenty-four starting since 1990 (see Appendix 1). Prior to 1980, the relatively few origins of these companies reflect the vision and foresight of their founders at a time when the global role of Metro Vancouver's economy remained industrial. The crisis of the early 1980s, terminated by the excitement of Expo 86, opened debate about Metro Vancouver's economy and greater recognition of the potential of embracing innovation. That technological opportunities were rapidly changing and computer-driven capabilities were rapidly diffusing shaped this debate and behaviour. By the early 2000s, Metro Vancouver had become a fertile seedbed for high-tech growth, indicating the possibility of the self-generating momentum of an innovation economy.

Transitioning Trajectories: The Diversity of Product Market Specialties

After start up, the identified forty-four, locally originating, firms typically have transitioned around highly specialized core competencies stemming from original innovations. Collectively, these specialties are extremely diverse within Metro Vancouver's high-tech sector and include video games, film graphics, computers, pills, airplane parts, spaceship components, fuel cells, security systems, film production, and myriad forms of software that organize record keeping, customer relations, security, financing, and other aspects of organizational behaviour. The diversity of these enterprise specialties can be appreciated by reference to PwC's (2013) classification of high-tech firms in British Columbia that identified twenty-six of the forty-four firms listed in Appendix 1 and allocated them to nine different classes.[24] Thus, QLT, Stemcell, Angiotech, and Zymeworks clearly illustrate life science companies, all having been involved in innovating drugs, and the aerospace company Avcorp is readily associated with advanced manufacturing. As for other firms identified by PWC (2013), five are designated as software firms (Fincentric, Westech Information Systems, Mobile Data Solutions Inc. [MDSI], Pivotal, and Bench), and another eleven are classified as software firms combined with other categories, for example with digital media (MDA, Quartech, ACL Services (now Galvanize), Absolute Software, Crystal Decisions, and Hootsuite); electronics and peripherals (Creo); telecommunications and wireless (Sierra Wireless); advanced manufacturing (PMC-Sierra, D-Wave Systems); and mobile and web (Avigilon Corporation). Firms in Appendix 1 referenced in PWC's map of 2013 also illustrate the cloud integration (e.g., Quartech) and clean technology (e.g., Ballard and Westport) categories. The sixteen firms in Appendix 1 not part of PWC's (2013) survey mainly illustrate software, digital media, and services and analytics firms. However, categories such as software development and applications, digital media, electronics, and services and analytics do not intuitively indicate the type of product or service provided. In practice, how companies are classified inevitably involves judgment. For example, Ballard and Westport rightly can be seen as clean technology companies, or as energy companies (along with Xantrex), Creo can be cited as an advanced manufacturer (of custom-built printing machines), and Glenayre, although classified in services and analytics, achieved fame as a globally leading producer of pagers.

Product and Service Innovations

No matter how classified, many of Metro Vancouver's high-tech service activities are linked with manufacturing and not simply advanced manufacturing within the region. MDA is essentially a service sector company, but its signature innovation led to the (custom-made, extremely challenging) manufacturing of the space arm for NASA. Ballard is engaged primarily in R&D, although it is often extended to include prototype and custom-made manufacturing of stationary units and fuel systems incorporated into vehicles. Its sponsors undoubtedly hope for innovations that can be mass produced that almost certainly would be located outside British Columbia. Other firms provide services, including video game makers, incorporated into products produced elsewhere, often in China. Nevertheless, it remains useful to distinguish a tangible product or service orientation.

Thus, companies such as Glenayre, Sierra Systems, Creo, Ballard, and Westport have focused their RD&D on creating and prototyping new tangible products and technologies, with the inner suburbs of Burnaby and Richmond preferred sites for manufacturing (see Table 2.1). Before their closures, for example, Glenayre and Creo located their manufacturing in Burnaby. Xantrex similarly manufactured its power converters partly in Burnaby until 2007, when it consolidated manufacturing in its California locations (while strengthening its R&D in Burnaby). Ballard manufactures its fuel cells in Burnaby and globally by licensing to major customers. Similarly, Westport continues to manufacture in Richmond while expanding to the United States and China through joint venture partners, the former involving Cummins in Detroit. D-Wave's massively complex quantum computers are essentially custom-made products for a select few customers, and Seanix Technology, although downsized, still manufactured computers in Richmond in 2018.

Many of Metro Vancouver's high-tech transitioning firms operate solely within the service sector and have developed innovations that seek to improve organizational practices of the businesses that they serve (see Table 2.2). Examples include Absolute Software and Avigilon, which have focused on enhancing the security of businesses and households; Traction on Demand, which increases efficiencies in business-client interactions; Hootsuite Media, which has developed a widely used social media platform; Clio, which has specialized in providing software to organize all aspects of legal practice; and Visier, which provides software for improved workforce planning.

Given that the product-service distinction is blurred, Metro Vancouver favours a product-service, high-tech economy with some prototype manufacturing, as evident in companies such as Ballard, Xantrex, and Westport Innovations (now Westport Fuel Systems). Other companies seek to improve organizational efficiency or security and do so by developing software provided as part of a manufactured device, even if the device itself is rather standardized. Meanwhile, in Metro Vancouver, the leading life science companies are predominantly research-driven services, with large-scale manufacturing of their innovations in new products, as pills, drugs, or vaccines, conducted elsewhere. Furthermore, though the high-tech sector is highly varied in focus, even firms involved in similar activities appear largely to complement rather than rival one another, in effect illustrating strategies of related diversification. For example, the life science companies QLT, Stemcell Technologies, and Zymeworks all originated from UBC to innovate and commercialize new drugs in part to battle the (global) problem of

TABLE 2.1 Selected product innovations and achievements among Metro Vancouver high-tech firms

Company	Innovations and achievements
Glenayre Electronics	Developed world's first microprocessor-based radio telephone in 1977.
	Developed advanced radio telephone switch (with BC Tel) in 1982.
	Pioneered pager development in 1983, installing first pager systems in the United States (1985), China (1990), and Europe (1994).
	Became a world leader in developing new paging codes and the first to integrate paging and voice messaging and allow the transfer of 2,400 bits per second (mid-1990s).
	Company switches once activated 50 percent of the world's pages; manufactured in Vancouver but rendered obsolete by cellphones.
Sierra Systems Group	R&D on three continents created over 550 patents.
	Launched in 1997 the world's first cellular-embedded module and became the first to commercialize the world's smallest module, embedded software, embedded SIM (subscriber identity module card), open-source Linux-based embedded platform, most rugged industrial gateway, and 4G and LTE-PRO (Long term evolution in 4G plus speeds) embedded solutions, among others.
	By 2018, over 150 million devices embodied in products of diverse original equipment manufacturers (OEMs).
Creo	Developed core imaging technology in the 1980s, and three years of R&D led to the world's first optical data recorder (a large-scale data-recording system).
	Developed first large-format, postscript, image-setter engine.
	Refocused innovations in 1993 on automating the prepress phase of printing through computer-to-plate (CTP) technologies for the graphic arts industry.
	First to commercialize various product innovations, beginning with high-speed CTP in 1994 delivered to the United States and thermal CTP introduced in 1995.
	By 1999, most US printers used Creo products, and global sales were facilitated by arrangements with a German firm.
Ballard Power Systems	Secured over 2,000 patents in support of fuel cell technology that since 1989 have emphasized proton-exchange membrane (PEM) technology, primarily fed by hydrogen, an essentially inexhaustible resource.
	Between 1979 and 2019, spent over $1 billion in R&D, and its "clean energy" fuel cells have been incorporated into many different transportation modes, stationary power plants, and electricity for buildings.
	By 2019, 850 megawatts of PEM fuel cell products installed.
	Manufactures in Burnaby (and elsewhere), but will profitability be possible?

Westport Innovations (Westport Fuel Systems)	R&D-driven core technology involved using natural gas at high pressure in diesel engines, trademarked as high-pressure direct injection, Westport (HPDI), and the basis of Westport 15L technology. This technology reduced emissions of nitrous oxides and particulate matter without compromising performance characteristics of diesel engines. Commercialized in heavy-duty trucks in a joint venture with Cummins (Chicago) and other companies (in China and Sweden) with manufacturing capabilities. Related technologies have been developed to use clean fuels such as liquid natural gas, hydrogen, and biofuels for various transportation modes.
Xantrex	Developed expertise gradually, first in electronic equipment for testing and measurement purposes for industrial consumers. By 1998, developed advanced technology that interfaced power sources and users at small power levels (less than one megawatt), using proprietary software. After 1998, the company focused on making increasingly small, efficient, and reliable power converters with diverse applications for homes and small businesses as well as for big consumers. R&D-driven product development continued in 2001 and since then with an array of compact (cheap) power systems. Acquisition by MNCs reinforced its R&D in Burnaby, though manufacturing stopped there in 2007, and consolidated in California, with programmable products in San Diego and solar commercial products in Livermore.
Seanix Technology	Research, design, and manufacturing of complete PC systems have been done largely in Canada. Emphasis has been on best practice and quality control.
D-Wave	UBC research group in quantum computing, collaborating with several other universities, provided core expertise to set up the company in various locations in Vancouver before moving to Burnaby. The prototype built in 2007 and the first commercially available quantum computer built in 2011. In collaboration with NASA and other high-tech organizations, by 2017 four generations of D-Wave computing built and a fifth one introduced in in 2020. Offers rapid solutions to extremely large and complex problems. Computers are expensive and operate in highly specialized environments. Customers are limited to very large organizations such as NASA.

Sources: Authors' research files.

TABLE 2.2 Selected business service innovations and achievements among Metro Vancouver high-tech firms

Company	*Innovations and achievements*
Absolute Software	Developed and patented the CompuTrace software technology platform, a client-server architecture that includes the CompuTrace Agent.
	Sales are mainly of CompuTrace Theft Recovery software for monitoring, tracking, deterring, and recovering theft on computers.
	Developed the CompuTrace Asset Tracking and Universal Agent, which incorporates other services.
Avigilon	A global leader in providing security through video analytics. Whereas conventional surveillance techniques are used post-incident, video analytics seek to detect suspicious behaviour in real time, hopefully to prevent crimes from occurring.
	The company portfolio includes over 600 patent assets.
	Three R&D labs have been built, each specializing in different security technologies, in Vancouver, Boston, and Dallas (2015 AR).
Traction on Demand	The custom integration of several cloud-based technologies involves marketing automation, social media integration, a digital e-signature platform, plus customer relationship technology (CRM) software for overall management.
	TractionGuest is a cloud-based platform to replace paper-based lobby books for visitors, tours, etc.
Hootsuite Media	A social media management platform originally developed at Invoke Media in 2008 as a Twitter dashboard called Brightkit became the Hootsuite platform in 2009.
	There were 15 million users globally by 2017 (including 800 of *Fortune*'s top 1,000 companies).
Clio	Leading supplier of legal software to organize documentation, whether for individual lawyers, SMEs, or large legal firms.
	Most comprehensive, integrated management tools for all aspects of organizing legal work.
	Supplies 150,000 legal groups in ninety countries
	Developing beyond a support company to a "partner"-style company.
Visier	Developed cloud-based models for workforce planning, serving 140 firms in seventy-five countries.
	Developed two software solutions: Visier People and Visier Embedded Analytics.
	Created models for mid-sized and large companies.

Sources: Authors' research files.

cancer. Although these businesses are in the same field, they have differentiated themselves by developing and patenting drugs with different characteristics and by addressing other diseases. In clean energy, the innovative efforts of Ballard, Xantrex, Westport Innovations, and Alpha Technologies have developed along different lines: Ballard focuses on hydrogen fuel cells, Westport on diesel technology, Xantrex on small-scale alternative wind and solar technologies, and Alpha on telecommunications. In software development, companies such as Sierra Systems, Quartech, Fincentric, Microserve, Absolute Software, iQmetrix, Crystal Decisions, Pivotal, Avigilon, Hootsuite, Clio, and Bench provide a range of services that supports business in organizing data, customer relations, security systems, and internal communication systems. Absolute Software, ACL, and Avigilon, for example, focus on security services; Fincentric has specialized in serving the banking industry, especially credit unions; Westech Information Systems served BC Hydro and other utilities; iQmetric specializes in retail management solutions for the wireless industry; Clio provides legal services; and Bench focuses on bookkeeping services. Both MDA and Hootsuite, though software and digital media companies, serve totally different markets.

Typically, these firms are highly specialized in particular products or services, with diversification closely related to existing innovative strengths. In this regard, MDA was an exception for a while as it developed expertise along two distinct product market paths, serving, respectively, aerospace, especially space technology programs, and data requirements for resource and real estate markets through sophisticated data collection methodologies, including via satellite communication. It sold the latter interests, however. Indeed, the challenges facing transitioning firms are significant. Such transitioning requires continued attention to innovation processes and the enabling changes in organizational capacities, in terms of seeking funding, managing larger workforces, and accessing markets, not least exports, all the while becoming more global in operation and outlook. Among Metro Vancouver's high-tech firms, the need to sustain innovative behaviour can be challenging, even posing threats to survival. Innovations need to be reinforced, modified, complemented, and/or replaced, and the increasing sizes of firms typically, if not always, require that local connections across corporate functions be enriched by global ones. Ballard is a fascinating case study in this regard.[25]

Ballard's Long Winding Road

Ballard Power System's origin and evolution were driven by the vision of Geoffrey Ballard, its principal founder, to develop an alternative and

renewable energy technology to replace fossil fuels in transportation vehicles. As a high-profile member of Metro Vancouver's high-tech community,
Ballard is globally recognized for its pioneering efforts to develop clean
energy sources in transportation and other applications. As with most of the
forty-four high-tech companies examined here, its founder profoundly
shaped this growth, which continued after his departure. By 2019, Ballard
had achieved revenues of over $100 million and had over 900 employees,
mostly in Burnaby (800), with a few in Europe and China. Its evolution
since 1979 dramatically reveals the opportunities, costs, and uncertainties
of R&D-led innovation strategies, the concomitant need for governance
changes, and the increasing importance of global connections in support of
local operations and connections. Indeed, Ballard is one of Metro Vancouver's most research-intensive companies and the lead founder of an emerging clean energy cluster (see Chapter 5). Yet that Ballard has grown and
survived for so long without scarcely being profitable, and remains locally
controlled and headquartered in Burnaby without being (fully) acquired
by foreign interests, might be considered surprising. Its trajectory is both
distinctive and illustrative of broader dynamics.

From Small-Scale Origins to Volatile Growth

Ballard Power (as Ballard Research) was a small R&D-driven entrepreneurial operation with just thirteen employees ten years after its start-up in
1979. Its three principal co-founders provided sophisticated, complementary expertise, all committed to Geoffrey Ballard's long-standing ambition
to replace the internal combustion engine, initially by a focus on high-
energy lithium batteries.[26] This work had started in the United States, becoming centred in a new business venture in Arizona in the 1970s. While
there, Ballard was hired to help refurbish a small research submarine (the
Ben Franklin) in North Vancouver, where he formed Ultra-Energy, a company whose failure led to its immediate reincarnation as Ballard Research.
A lack of interest by the US military in lithium battery research further
encouraged Ballard and his colleagues to move permanently to Metro
Vancouver. Although Ballard Power might not be a classic example of seedbed formation – Ballard was born and raised in Ontario and moved to the
United States – he was interested in returning to Canada, and he had worked
for a few years in Metro Vancouver, making key business connections, before co-founding Ballard Power.

For a decade, the company remained small, with fluctuating and faltering
revenues derived from contracts and lithium battery–powered sources of

(mobile) power. Indeed, its future growth depended on a strategic shift in 1983 toward working on the new idea of low-cost polymer (hydrogen) fuel cells, or proton-exchange membrane cells, commonly called PEMs. Somewhat fortuitously, as the firm was looking for alternative options for energy development, Ballard became aware that Canada's Department of National Defence was offering funds for the development of PEMs. Without prior knowledge of work on fuel cells, the co-founders of Ballard gathered sufficient information to bid successfully for this project.[27] A decade later Ballard delivered its first fuel cell bus in Vancouver, in 1993, and the blueprint of its future strategy had been established.

Indeed, by the 1990s, organizational winds of change were evident at Ballard; financing, marketing, inter-firm relations, and human resource management were becoming more challenging. In response, Ballard became a public company with listings on the Toronto Stock Exchange in 1993 and NASDAQ in 1995, initiatives presaged by the hiring of Firoz Rasul, an "outsider" head-hunted from MDSI in 1988 as a joint partner for his marketing expertise (and engineering background), and he became CEO in 1999 (until 2004). The three original founders, not enamoured of the direction of organizational change, left the company in 1997 (Ballard), 1998 (Prater), and 1999 (Howard), and Ballard and Howard formed a new company (General Hydrogen) in Richmond in 1999.[28] In practice, the company's grappling with organizational metamorphosis reflected the growing importance of financing and marketing issues, its new status as a public company, which required full disclosure of operations with added responsibilities to shareholders, and a need for more decentralized decision making with company growth. In 2019, for example, Ballard's CEO was supported by four vice-presidents (finance, commerce, technology, and operations) and overseen by a nine-person board of directors. Even so, Ballard remained technology driven.

From its small-scale beginning, Ballard's growth became more evident since the 1990s, reporting sales of over US $100 million in 2019, five times larger than in 1994, a notable if not spectacular expansion (see Table 2.3). During this period, Ballard increasingly emphasized developing PEMs for use in heavy- and medium-duty transportation applications (trucks, buses, and rail engines). Overall, sales have comprised either contracted technological services provided to partners or customers or PEMs; in 2019, the latter were about one-third of sales. In large, long-distance vehicles, PEMS can be efficiently "stacked," but not so in cars, which can be supplied better with battery-based electric engines and better serviced by "plug-in" infrastructure.

TABLE 2.3 Ballard Power Systems: Revenues, R&D costs, and net income
(US$000), selected years 1994–2021

Year	Revenue	R&D cost	Revenue/ R&D ratio (%)	Income (loss)
1994	19,218	6,182	32.2	(5,211)
1996	25,784	15,445	59.9	(6,142)
2006	49,823	52,274	104.9	(181,137)
2009	46,722	26,628	57.0	3,258
2012	43,690	19,273	44.2	(42,385)
2015	56,463	16,206	28.1	(6,574)
2016	85,270	19,827	23.3	(21,687)
2017	121,288	25,002	20.6	(8,048)
2018	96,586	27,039	28.0	(27,323)
2019	105,723	26,928	25.5	(35,291)
2020	103,877	35,519	34.2	(49,469)
2021	104,505	62,162	59.5	(114,397)

Note: Revenues in 2021 comprised sales of fuel cells for heavy-duty vehicles (49.4 percent), material handling (7.8 percent), and backup power (7.9 percent), with 34.9 percent for technology support.
Sources: Ballard Power Systems, Annual Reports, selected years, 1994–2021.

Technologically intensive, Ballard has spent heavily on R&D in absolute or relative terms (see Table 2.3). By 2020, Ballard had spent over US $1 billion on R&D, one of the biggest global R&D spenders among global fuel cell companies,[29] and it had produced over 1,400 patents to protect its highly secretive Burnaby-centred operations. Its R&D cost to revenue ratio also has been remarkably high, in the twelve selected years shown, ranging from 20.6 percent to 104.9 percent.

Data permitting, other strong R&D performers among the forty-four selected firms in Metro Vancouver can be noted (see Table 2.4).[30] In general, the sales to R&D ratios of these nine firms vary from 6.4 percent to much higher and are mostly in recognized high-tech industries, including alternative energy development (Ballard, Westport Innovations), advanced electronic communications (Sierra Wireless, PMC-Sierra, MDA), and biotechnologies or life sciences (QLT, Stemcell Technologies, Zymeworks, AbCellera). In addition, Absolute Software and Avigilon represent innovative business service companies that incorporate new products in their sales. Creo was somewhat unusual (until its demise) in that its large R&D workforce (about 900) and investment (over US $100 million) supported its

TABLE 2.4 R&D costs and revenues for selected case study firms in selected years

Company	Year	Revenues ($000s)	R&D costs (ratio to revenue)
Sierra Wireless	2003	101.7	16.0 (15.7%)
	2013	441.9	73.1 (16.5%)
	1018	793.6 (US $)	93.7 (11.8%)
MDA	2004	751.4	116.6 (6.4%)
	2013	1,819.0	–
	2016	2,063.8	–
Creo	2003	578.0 (US $)	104.0 (18%)
PMC-Sierra	2003	297.3	120.5 (40.5%)
	2007	449.3	159.1 (35.4%)
	2013	508.0	211.0 (41.5%)
Absolute Software	2013	88.3	11.4 (12.9%)
	2018	93.6 (US $)	20.0 (21.4%)
QLT Norvelion Therapuetics*	2004	186.1	50.1 (26.9%)
	2013	No new sales	18.5
	2018	130.4 (US $)	38.8 (29.8%)
Westport Fuel Systems (formerly Westport Innovations)	2004	32.4	26.0
	2006	43.5	16.9
	2013	164.0 (US $)	91.1
	2018	270.3 (US $)**	30.6 (11.3%)
Avigilon	2011	60.0	3.1 (5.2%)
	2013	178.3	4.0 (gross) (6.7%)
	2015	369.4	11.8 (6.6%)
	2017	408.7	31.5 (gross) (8.5%)
Stemcell Technologies	2009	1.0	19.9 (-199%)
	2013	21.5	20.5 (95.3%)
	2017	5,777	5,000 (86.6%)
	2018	6,136	4,560 (74.6%)
Zymeworks	2014	14.01	10.5 (74.7%)
	2018	82.52	56.7 (68.7%)
AbCellera Biologics	2020	233.2	29.4 (12.6%)
	2021	375.2	62.1 (16.6%)

Notes: *Closed 2023. **Does not include data from Westport's joint venture with Cummins (CWI); the latter's revenues were US319.4m in 2018. Costs are in Canadian dollars unless otherwise indicated and are firm level with R&D costs largely, if not completely, spent in Metro Vancouver.
Sources: Annual reports of the selected companies and years plus authors' research files.

relatively large-scale manufacturing in Metro Vancouver, although the printing machines that it built incorporating its patented technology were highly specialized and custom made.

Bearing in mind that business R&D levels in Canada and British Columbia as a whole are not globally impressive, these companies stand out, even if their R&D investments have not necessarily guaranteed profitability. Indeed, for Ballard, revenues have been volatile, and operating losses have been routine and often substantial, with positive net income recorded only once, in 2009, among the twelve years shown (see Table 2.3). Although sales have fluctuated considerably, Ballard's share history particularly underlines its volatility: from 1995 to 2021, closing stock prices varied from $132.20 to $7.20, with an average price of $18.64 for the year ending March 2020.[31] After reaching a peak value of $210.80 in 2000, Ballard's shares actually dropped below $1 in 2012. Skepticism about investing in Ballard can be noted.[32] Yet its potential to contribute to a green economy is huge, and the company has attracted financing and customer support, often in tandem from MNCs and other large organizations from around the world.[33]

From Local to Global Financing

Ballard Power Systems illustrates well the funding challenge facing high-tech start-ups and their transitioning to larger organizations, with a "global" search for large-scale funding and markets replacing local sources and demands. For Ballard, this (joint) search was led by going public through IPOs and by partnership agreements and joint ventures with larger organizations and potential customers, with government research grants further sources of funding.

In the early years, prior to forming his company in Burnaby, Geoffrey Ballard reportedly used his savings and pension funds, plus further support from colleagues, to establish research facilities in Arizona. After moving to North Vancouver to work on the *Ben Franklin,* he received funds (and space) from the submarine's local owner (John Horton) for research on lithium batteries.[34] The firm's shift toward researching PEMs initially depended on contracts with Canada's Department of National Defence and by a loan of $1.3 million from Michael Brown, a well-known, Vancouver-based, venture capitalist. As losses mounted ($1 billion by 2011), Ballard's financial needs became acute, a concern that encouraged the hiring of Firoz Rasul and the initiation of IPOs on the Toronto Stock Exchange and NASDAQ in 1993 and 1995, respectively, with a stock-split share offering in 1998 and another soon following in 2000.[35] In practice, going public has been an important source of funding for seventeen of the forty-four transitioning firms examined in this chapter (see Appendix 1). Indeed, it has been argued, a major function of contemporary stock exchanges is to fund growing high-tech businesses rather than giants.[36] In this view, though giants such as Apple and Microsoft have little need for IPOs, rapidly emerging firms frequently seek funds by going public, the success of which sends positive signals to customers and investors alike while allowing the firm to grow.

But Ballard has needed more than the stock exchanges to meet its funding needs, not least because of collapsing share prices. In this regard, partnerships and joint ventures with customer organizations around the world have been vital. Two overlapping phases in these relations are evident. First, Ballard signed agreements with leading auto MNCs, beginning with General Motors (and the US Department of Energy) in 1991 to work jointly on fuel cells for passenger vehicles. In 1997, Ballard negotiated agreements with Daimler (Germany) and Ford to provide these companies, respectively, with 25 percent and 15 percent of its equity shares in return for an investment of $450 million. However, with fuel cell applications in cars seemingly a declining prospect, in 2008 Ballard divested its auto development division into a new private (Vancouver) company, Automotive Fuel Cell Corporation, which in 2009 became wholly owned by Daimler and Ford.[37] Meanwhile, General Motors had become a rival. Its relations with (European) auto companies continued, particularly through a research partnership with Volkswagen starting in 2013 that led to various contracts that provided the latter with intellectual property rights and engineering services in return for payments to Ballard in excess of $100 million. A collaboration with Audi was also signed in 2018. A second phase of partnerships, in line with its emphasis on heavy vehicles, began in 2016 when Ballard entered a strategic partnership with Zhongshan Broad-Ocean Motor Company and a joint venture with Guangdong Nation-Synergy Hydrogen Power Technology, two Chinese manufacturers. In 2018, a third Chinese-based strategic partnership involved Weichai's obtaining 19.9 percent of Ballard's shares for US $163 million. In these cases, foreign partners have provided capital, manufacturing capacity, and market access, and Ballard provides the technology. In addition, in 2020, Ballard partnered with Westport Fuel Systems (originally Westport Innovations; Appendix 1) and the latter's long-standing partner Cummins Diesel of Detroit in a joint venture to fund clean energy sources in heavy-duty trucks manufactured by Cummins.

For Ballard, the IPOs and these agreements have provided both funds and market opportunities without losing control of the company. Admittedly, the IPOs imposed new conditions on Ballard and created takeover possibilities, and partnerships with customers can entail the selling and licensing of proprietary information to rivals. But funding has been essential to Ballard's survival and evolved in tandem with the need to expand and globalize sales.[38]

From Local to Global Markets

As with most new small firms, in starting up Ballard Power Systems relied on local connections and markets, centred on the (failed) hope of developing a rechargeable lithium battery for use in the *Ben Franklin* renovation. Subsequently, Metro Vancouver was one of the two sites for its first two hydrogen bus demonstrations (the other being Chicago). However, Ballard's increasing R&D focus on hydrogen fuel cells has been linked overwhelmingly to finding global markets (see Table 2.5).

TABLE 2.5 Ballard's sales by major geographical market: Selected years, 2006–19

Market ($000s)	2019	2018	2014	2006
China	47,132	30,791		
Germany	30,604	28,685	17,484	19,567
United States	13,500	23,505	15,989	17,041
Belgium	5,408	3,531		
United Kingdom	2,794	1,431		
Japan	2,743	3,901	2,797	10,344
Denmark	1,701	1,889		
Canada	766	366	2,869	1,305
Norway	478	187		
Switzerland	359			
France	287	276		
Taiwan	216	287	23,495	
Netherlands	115	892		
Finland	65	196		
Spain	20	168		
India			1,229	
Others	139	479	4,858	1,566
Total	106,327	96,586	68,721	49,823

Note: The countries are listed from largest to smallest according to the 2019 rankings, with India inserted into the 2014 ranking.
Sources: Ballard Power Systems, Annual Report, 2019, D12 and Ballard 2008, 115.

By 2006, less than 3 percent of Ballard's revenues of almost $50 million were in Canada, and though 2008 and 2009 were high points for domestic sales they still amounted to only about 15–16 percent of overall revenues. Since then, domestic sales have become relatively minor (about 0.7 percent in 2019). In terms of export geography, Ballard's sales are widespread, but initially they were concentrated in a few rich countries, especially the United States, Germany, and to a lesser degree Japan, with exports subsequently increasing to the rapidly industrializing Taiwan. The United States and Germany, for example, provided over 75 percent of Ballard's sales in 2006 (with Japan accounting for much of the rest). Recently China has become its dominant market, accounting in 2019 for almost 46 percent of its $106 million in sales. As of 2019, for its joint venture with Weichai (51 percent ownership), Ballard (49 percent ownership) sends the critically important component called membrane electrode assemblies made in Burnaby to be incorporated into fuel cell stacks for buses, trucks, and forklifts in a Shandong factory, and Ballard exports fuel cell modules to another nearby factory in Zhongshan.[39]

In addition to its partnerships with MNCs, Ballard has further pursued FDI to help penetrate export markets, such as through the acquisitions of Dantherm Power (Denmark) in 2010 and Protonex Technology (United States) in 2017, and in 2016 Ballard signed a distribution agreement with Toyota Tsusho for fuel cell products in Japan. By 2021, with its fuel cells now in their eighth generation, Ballard had supplied vehicles that had travelled over 75 million kilometres, including 3,400 buses and commercial trucks deployed in over thirty countries, in some cases for over eight years of year-round operation. With its focus on heavy- and medium-duty applications, Ballard is also serving rail and marine markets, and in 2021, for example, it supplied six fuel cell modules to Canadian Pacific Railway to replace diesel-powered engines with hydrogen fuel cells, the first such initiative in North America.[40] For Westport, a related but differently focused clean energy company, its export focus is the United States, where its main joint venture partner is located.

If Ballard's almost complete reliance on exports is exceptional, as are its connections to China, then it highlights the importance of global markets to many of Metro Vancouver's transitioning high-tech firms.[41] For British Columbia, the average export sales ratio for the high-tech sector in 2018 was 22.5 percent, with the United States still dominating sales and the Asia Pacific region becoming more important (see Table I.5). The undoubtedly greater importance of export sales for the relatively large firms examined in this chapter is reflected in the number that have established a presence in "distant" markets, whether as affiliated sales office, manufacturing operation, joint venture, or licensing. Such connections help to provide local know-how and contacts and can help to address foreign ownership and security issues, advantages even more apparent when local partners are involved. At least twenty of the forty-four transitioning firms controlled offices in other parts of Canada, the United States, and elsewhere, ten established foreign links through some form of investment or licensing, and for firms acquired by MNCs the desire for better access to markets has been a motivation (see Chapter 3). Among recently established service companies, for example, the growth of Clio (2008), Hootsuite (2009), and Visior (2010) was supported by the rapid development of a network of offices around the world. These three firms combined had located twenty-five offices in Europe, Asia, and the United States as well as a few in eastern Canada. Partnerships, FDI, and licensing also tend to be market oriented, with exports concentrated in the same regions. These exports often are institutionalized in affiliated connections or at least in contracts of varying length closely controlled for proprietary information.[42] In terms of overall spatial patterns, although caveats can be noted, Metro Vancouver's transitioning high-tech firms have not used important markets across Canada as stepping stones to export commitments.[43]

Conclusion: Limits to the Transitioning of Local Firms

Metro Vancouver has become a fertile seedbed for high-tech innovation by myriad small firms in which immigrant residents, spinoffs, and other small firms have played important roles. This seedbed has helped to support Metro Vancouver's postindustrialism and new global roles through highly diversified exports of goods and (especially producer) services. Yet transitioning to larger firms, in which the challenge of transforming innovation into scalable products requires the scaling up of organizational capabilities, has been daunting. Among the forty-four transitioning firms that have become large SMEs or larger examined in this chapter, Creo (with more than 4,000 employees) and MDA (once reaching over 5,000 jobs globally) remain the biggest local employers, although Creo was virtually closed after its acquisition. A few others (Sierra Wireless, Creation Studios, Stemcell Technologies, Westport Innovations, Hootsuite) have supported from 1,400 to 2,500 jobs at some point prior to 2021, with sales to match, placing them in the lower reaches of mid-sized firms, but most are smaller.

In otherwise enthusiastic endorsements of high-tech growth in Metro Vancouver, concerns about the lack of core or anchor firms have been flagged.[44] Although these reports have not explicated the concerns, the dominant roles of Boeing and Microsoft in the nearby Seattle Metropolitan Area or Apple in Cupertino in Silicon Valley illustrate the massive impacts – in terms of direct employment, income levels, and indirect effects – that such giant firms can have on local development. Similarly, Germany's famous "mid-sized" (*Mittlestand*) firms, which can employ tens of thousands and have sales in excess of $100 million or even $1 billion, are often "big firms locally" and dominate the economies of smaller places.[45] In Metro Vancouver, however, there is little indication that such a transition will occur. Does it matter?

Several factors can be suggested to explain why there is a lack of locally originating core firms. First, the BC market for high-tech goods and services is relatively small and peripheral, and firm growth is quickly dependent on exports (and financing from elsewhere). Moreover, the Canadian market is fragmented, and its main potential is a long way from British Columbia. Exporting is a challenging process for Metro Vancouver's high-tech transitioning firms, however, often dependent on negotiating and partnering with distant, often larger customers or becoming part of MNCs.

Second, the dynamism of the selected companies has led to interest among foreign MNCs, which have acquired over one-third (sixteen) of them, in effect solving their challenge to scale up (Appendices 1 and 2). Even so, subsidiary status imposes local mandates and limits on local functions and in certain cases (Glenayre and Creo) has led to closure.

Third, significant technological and financial uncertainties facing successful innovations limit the sustained growth of Metro Vancouver's high-tech firms, especially when repeated innovations are necessary. Although Ballard has survived without being profitable, other companies (QLT, Angiotech, Seanix, MPR, and Aim Global Technologies) have found these difficulties insurmountable.

Fourth, the entrepreneurs driving Metro Vancouver's diversified high-tech structure have favoured difference and independence, with each firm organizing its own networks, rather than creating a large-scale, dominant presence in any one (or two) activities.

Fifth, the diversification of Metro Vancouver's high-tech economy has been reinforced by FDI (see Chapter 3) and by government policies, university contributions, and other services (see Chapter 5).

And sixth, in behavioural terms, beyond the need to reach the MES, the growth ambitions of firms reflect personal choices that include preferences for staying at "comfortable" or desired small scales of operation. For still others, realizing wealth by selling their companies to MNCs is a goal or, in Slack's case, a relocation to San Francisco.

Whether or not the lack of anchor companies matters to Metro Vancouver development is hard to say (see Chapter 7) and perhaps simply an academic question since such companies might never emerge. Yet Metro Vancouver's high-tech evolution has depended on ongoing entrepreneurship, itself uncertain and subject to change, not least by FDI, as we explore in the next chapter.

3
The Influence of FDI in Metro Vancouver High Tech

Foreign direct investment (FDI) to establish subsidiary or branch plant operations in Metro Vancouver's high-tech sector has gathered considerable momentum in recent decades.[1] The arrival of two global high-tech giants, Amazon in 2020 and Apple in 2021, and their plans to attract substantial workforces in two new high-rise office blocks in downtown Vancouver, mark particular milestones in the region's high-tech status.[2] With Meta (formerly Facebook before late 2021) and Microsoft already present, these US-based cloud giants highlight the increasing significance of FDI in Metro Vancouver's high-tech sector. These investments are both a tribute and a challenge to the local entrepreneurialism around which the tech sector was founded and evolved. FDI has contributed, not without incident, to the sector's global roles while redefining its potentials and constraints. In this chapter, we explore the evolution, nature, and implications of FDI for the development of Metro Vancouver's high-tech sector.

This evolution has gathered considerable momentum in recent decades. A few foreign companies participated in the sector's early development but had little long-lasting influence. However, a rising tide of FDI has been stimulated by the rapidly expanding pool of locally based entrepreneurial firms, signalling Metro Vancouver's growing high-tech prowess and the opportunities available to global investors. Thus, the arrival of multinational corporations (MNCs) became more frequent following the late 1980s, entering Vancouver's tech landscape through both the acquisition of local operations and the opening of new facilities. Both entry decisions have occurred across the diverse spectrum of activities that comprise Metro Vancouver's high tech.

The expansion of FDI in Metro Vancouver is both an old and a new story. Although FDI has long exercised a significant influence on the Canadian economy, including in British Columbia, in high tech it is distinct in terms of motivation compared with previous eras and sectors. Historically, across Canada, FDI focused considerably on the resource-based and secondary manufacturing sectors to serve local markets (e.g., autos in Ontario) or to provide crucial resource inputs (e.g., forest products in British Columbia) for global corporate operations.[3] Neither type of FDI did much to enhance technological capability in Canada, especially in terms of promoting globally leading innovation-based competitiveness. Indeed, at the time, albeit controversially, critics argued that FDI "truncated" such possibilities since MNCs concentrated vital R&D and new product development in their home countries.[4] In contrast, for high-tech FDI in Metro Vancouver (as across Canada), issues of technological capability and innovativeness are central to corporate motivations – and to local development aspirations. For high-tech FDI in Metro Vancouver, if access to local (domestic) markets is a consideration, then the local availability of innovative talent is clearly a priority and the region's primary drawing card.[5] In turn, the nature of and extent to which this talent is nurtured and expanded (or not) are vital for Metro Vancouver's innovation economy.

To be sure, among business and public policy–making circles in British Columbia (and Canada), the contributions of FDI to high-tech growth are widely acclaimed as sources of investment, financing, expertise, jobs, and access to markets. Such contributions are further appreciated for their multiplier and spillover effects that augment the generation of creativity in Metro Vancouver. Admittedly, concerns about a loss of sovereignty, local technological leadership, and the appropriation of intellectual property, along with the crowding out of local businesses, are occasionally voiced.[6] Such concerns are a reminder that FDI is not only "not free" but also changes the nature of business organization and decision making in the local economy. Suffice it to say that the roles of high-tech FDI in stimulating innovation and the quality of local talent pools in Metro Vancouver cannot be simply assumed. In general, the nature of the "strategic coupling" among MNCs and local actors (government, business, labour, and others) can shape significantly local roles in global production networks, especially with increasing levels of FDI, as is the case here.[7]

In this chapter, we explore the evolution and implications of FDI for Metro Vancouver high tech. We document key entry and post-entry characteristics of foreign-owned firms in Metro Vancouver to provide a "microbehavioural" perspective on the motivations, performance, and local impacts of FDI. This focus on individual cases reveals a range of implications and allows insights into the broader impacts of foreign ownership as it imposes new institutional framings and global connections, along with a loss of decision-making discretion, on local operations. Such contemplation raises interesting questions. Is Metro Vancouver's entrepreneurially driven high-tech sector being supplemented, challenged, or replaced by MNCs? Is FDI helping or hindering the search to be self-sustaining?

In the absence of official, ongoing data sources of foreign ownership in British Columbia, this discussion draws from information on high-tech FDI in Metro Vancouver gleaned from various sources, specifically for fifty-seven MNCs that entered the region between 1980 and 2018–19, a database that is strongly representative if not entirely complete (see Appendix 2).[8] In the first section of this chapter, we discuss the arrival of FDI, especially since 1980, in terms of its strategic motivations and selected entry characteristics (size of MNC, timing, geographic origin, mode of entry). In the second section, we explore the locational factors in Metro Vancouver high tech that favour FDI. And in the third section, we explore its roles in local development, specifically with respect to innovation and technology, vital in assessing implications for high- (or low-) road behaviour. Hopefully, at least the complexity of the pros and cons of FDI for local development can be appreciated.

High-Tech FDI: Entry Characteristics

As theories of internationalization of firms have long articulated, FDI typically evolves as an integrated component of wider corporate strategies and plans.[9] This integration is broadly classified conventionally as "vertical," in which branch plants, offices, and laboratories are functionally connected to parent company operations in terms of inputs or outputs, and/or as "horizontal" as branch plants extend existing parent company operations and expertise to new places.[10] These categories can be further divided, though in practice FDI can incorporate elements of both horizontal and vertical integration. Corporate and regional priorities, however, might or might not overlap. Broadly speaking, the local economic development implications of FDI depend on the size and role of branch facilities and subsidiaries and the nature of their integration with parent companies with respect to decision making, R&D, and operating linkages. Within high-tech industries, the extent to which FDI nurtures and reinforces local talent – whether as part of manufacturing, service, or R&D occupations – is a crucial issue. Innovative activities tend to be labour intensive, and especially talent intensive, and the attributes of talent form an important locational criterion for business. Even so, variations in the motives of high-tech FDI, and in the relationships between their foreign branch or subsidiary operations and parent companies, need to be recognized.[11]

FDI in high tech, as in other sectors, can seek to eliminate local rivals or simply exist to institutionalize local market connections. High-tech FDI can also value the distinctive nature of local expertise as an asset to be acquired while still providing it with the autonomy to flourish globally. In this latter context, knowledge-based exchanges between branch operations and parent companies are likely to be highly interactive rather than hierarchical and orchestrated from the top.[12] The local development benefits of FDI in a general sense are also most readily appreciated with respect to new site investments that stimulate construction activities, new jobs and income flows, and multiplier effects through (locally) linked activities in supply and marketing chains and from household expenditures by employees. In contrast, the local development implications that arise from foreign acquisitions of existing operations are less obvious, or more nuanced, except perhaps in rescues of otherwise failing endeavours. Even so, acquisitions can support new investments and provide the advantages of integration within established MNC-controlled global networks especially if the subsidiary can have its market expanded through the acquirer's global distribution system. Regardless of whether entry by FDI is by new investments or acquisitions, however, local development interests arguably are served best by subsidiaries that are relatively independent and provide important, specialized contributions to parent companies.

For Metro Vancouver, insights into the local development implications of FDI can be initiated by the nature and motivations underlying the entry characteristics of the fifty-seven MNCs identified as establishing high-tech operations in the region since 1980. The firms are described in some detail in Appendix 2, but a summary of their characteristics includes the following.

- They recently entered Metro Vancouver as established giants or large mid-sized companies (with one exception).
- They are highly diversified in terms of the high-tech activities that they support.

- Their home economies are geographically diversified even as the United States is dominant.
- The modes of entry are split between acquisitions and greenfield investments, with some emphasis on the former.

In general, MNC motivations for investing in Metro Vancouver are both old, typical of why firms seek international expansion, and new, shaped by their high-tech focus. Furthermore, the favourable public policy environment for such expansions needs to be underlined. In only one instance – regarding acquisitions of MDA – was there noteworthy policy opposition from one federal government, whose decision was reversed anyway by its successor (see Case Study 3.4). As for the BC government, it is hard to underestimate its enthusiasm for FDI in high tech, as signalled by its ditching in 1988 of Moli Energy, a pioneer in lithium battery commercialization, literally to give away its assets to Japanese interests (see Case Study 2.1).[13] In general, BC governments have been open-door enthusiasts of FDI.

Strategic Motivations

Overwhelmingly, MNC expansions in Metro Vancouver high tech have reflected strategies of horizontal integration and/or diversification: that is, adding activities similar or closely related to their existing product market expertise and further building their competitive advantages. As with most FDI, these horizontally expanding high-tech MNCs seek to build and coordinate globally integrated corporate systems across national boundaries that realize economies of scale and scope to meet growth objectives. The entry into Metro Vancouver of high-tech MNCs is further motivated by desires to increase their human resource potential to innovate. For Metro Vancouver, an important question arising from this motivation is the extent of its encouragement of creative branch facilities and subsidiaries to be relatively independent and/or have specialized roles within globally integrated corporate operations, for example compared with simply using local talent to perform tasks generated elsewhere. After all, investments that target the employment of innovative talent can suggest expectations of proactive creation and diffusion of place-based knowledge from below within interactive forms of information exchange. The extent to which these expectations are realized or not following entry is a key issue in assessing the role of FDI in Metro Vancouver's high-tech development.

As might be expected, among the MNCs investing in Metro Vancouver are the oligopolistic giants of high tech, such as IBM, Apple, Microsoft, and

Amazon. These giants have significant market shares in their home US market as well as around the world, dominate several related major market segments, perform a wide variety of functions themselves, and organize global value chains. Apple, for example, is a dominant presence in personal computers, phones, TVs, watches, and related products, and it is nominally a major manufacturer of its products, although mostly they are outsourced to contract manufacturers in China and elsewhere. Microsoft and Amazon also operate or outsource important manufacturing facilities (although Meta does not despite trying). These companies are massive and have tremendous market power and ability to bargain with local suppliers, labour, and governments. Indeed, these companies have revenues that match or exceed British Columbia's GDP, Amazon's worldwide employment is over 25 percent of British Columbia's total employment, and Apple's R&D budget of US $19 billion in 2019 was six times bigger than UBC's budget of CDN $2.6 billion in 2018 that supported a comprehensive program of higher education across all disciplines in a university of over 70,000 students.

Perhaps less well known or anticipated, many MNCs that enter Metro Vancouver high tech are better classified as large mid-size companies that are innovation driven and highly specialized and serve specific market segments, albeit on a global scale (see Figure 2.1). Such firms themselves can be substantial operations in terms of size and geographical scope. Nintendo, Electronic Arts, and Activision (now Activision Blizzard), for example, are highly specialized, innovative firms within the video game industry that generated revenues, respectively, of US $12 billion, $5.2 billion, and $5.1 billion in 2018 and have offices in several countries. Similarly, relatively large companies with specialized market foci include Delta Electronics (energy), Salesforce (business services), and Business Objects (business services), and smaller specialized companies with sales in the US $1–2 billion range include DNEG (films, until 2014 called Double Negative), Fortinet (security software), Tile (key finders), and Flir Systems (sensors).

There are exceptions to the characteristics noted above. Grammerly (language software), for example, is unusually small among this group of internationally expanding companies and unusual given its Ukrainian origins. In addition, the huge Taiwanese company that eventually acquired Moli's operations is distinctive in that it illustrates international expansion through conglomerate-style diversification – its focus on energy-saving batteries was a significant strategic and "experimental" departure since its activities focus primarily on heavy industries. That is, E-One Moli is not an integrated extension of parent company know-how but an attempt to begin a new high-tech path of growth for its parent. Even so, both E-One Moli and Grammerly, like the other MNCs, located in Metro Vancouver largely because its potential for innovation arises from the availability of local talent.

Timing

FDI in Metro Vancouver's embryonic high-tech activities had occurred sporadically through the twentieth century but became more significant in the 1980s. With respect to early entries, New York–based IBM quickly established offices in Canada in its early days, including one in Vancouver in 1921; however, that office involved sales and support facilities, and an active, creative role for IBM's subsidiary there did not occur until the late 1990s. Also in the 1920s, a controlling interest in BC Tel, now Telus, was acquired by GTE Corporation (US) and held until 1988 (see Case Study 4.2). During the Second World War, the Seattle-head-quartered Boeing Company built planes in Richmond to support the war effort, a prelude to using Richmond's, now Delta's, Avcorp as a component supplier (see Appendix 1). Boeing established its own offices in 2000 in Vancouver for air-routing expertise. In addition, the California-based firm Lenkurt Electronics established an operation in Burnaby in the 1950s and 1960s. With these caveats aside, the sustained arrival of high-tech FDI in Metro Vancouver as a creative presence has been relatively recent, effectively waiting for the establishment of a local entrepreneurial base. The gathering momentum FDI in Metro Vancouver for high tech can be readily appreciated through the arrival times of the fifty-seven MNCs (see Appendix 2). Only four cases between 1977 and 1989 are identified, and just seven more in the 1990s, but there were thirty-two cases between 2000 and 2021. Announcements from Amazon and Apple of major new offices, and expectations that they will become two of the largest high-tech employers in the region, reinforce this sense of recent FDI momentum.[14]

Nintendo, the first major foreign company to establish an office in Vancouver in this recent wave, arrived in 1983 and anticipated the growing video game industry in Metro Vancouver. Nintendo, however, did not become a major force in Vancouver and soon established offices in New York before deciding on Seattle as its major North American hub. Motorola and Raytheon had also located in Metro Vancouver in the late 1980s. Arguably, however, it was the arrival in 1991 of Electronic Arts (EA), the California-based video game company, that provided the greatest signal of the proliferation of FDI in Metro Vancouver's high-tech activities. The arrival of EA was accomplished by acquiring the pioneering, and locally born, Distinctive

Software (see Case Study 2.1). It was located in the new Discovery Park adjacent to the British Columbia Institute of Technology (BCIT) in Burnaby, and EA remains there as a major creative player in the region's video game industry.

With respect to MNCs' origins in their home countries, several were established before the Second World War as pioneering high-tech companies, such as the US-based IBM, Disney, Boeing, and Kodak, along with Japan's Fujitsu. In a couple of cases, high-tech activities were created from the restructuring of long-established activities. The Kyoto-based Nintendo, for example, had manufactured playing cards and toys since the late nineteenth century until its commitment to video game production in the 1970s, and France's Schneider Electric was built around steel processing and shipbuilding from the mid-nineteenth century before refocusing on electronics in the 1980s, including by acquiring Xantrex in Metro Vancouver.

However, the majority of MNCs investing in Metro Vancouver high tech are relatively new firms, created since 1969, with nineteen established after 1980, including Mark Zuckerberg's Facebook (2004, now Meta) and Jeff Bezos's Amazon (1994). Other major US-based internet companies that have invested recently in Metro Vancouver, including Apple, Microsoft, and Oracle, were founded in the 1970s, and, as the local marker of the proliferation of FDI in Metro Vancouver, EA was not formed until 1982. Moreover, as examples of much older companies, Nintendo and Schneider essentially reinvented themselves as high-tech companies in modern times. IBM, by the way, has restructured itself from the dominant, pioneering, high-tech, highly diversified giant with significant hardware manufacturing capabilities to the smaller, more focused, if still giant service company. As part of this restructuring, SAP, with its focus on enterprise software, started as a German-based spinoff from IBM that by 2019 had become a significant large firm, with revenues that year in excess of 24 billion euros and over 96,000 employees, serving over 400,000 customers in 180 countries in various industries. It now competes with the US-based Oracle, which also has a Metro Vancouver presence.

Diversity of Origins (Geographical and Industrial)

The high-tech MNCs entering Metro Vancouver, as expected, have been dominated by US-based companies, which account for forty-one or 72 percent of the total of *initial* (fifty-seven) arrivals (see Table 3.1). The other sixteen (28 percent) MNCs hail from various countries, including Japan,

TABLE 3.1 Entry characteristics of FDI in Metro Vancouver high tech

	1980–89	*1990–99*	*2000–09*	*2010–22/23*
Number (by acquisition)	4 (2)	7 (6)	14 (11)	32 (16)
US source (Pacific Coast)	2	7 (4)	7 (5)	25 (15)

Source: See Appendix 2.

Taiwan, Hong Kong, Germany, France, Sweden, the Netherlands, Italy, the United Kingdom, and the Ukraine (see Appendix 2). Some subsidiaries of MNCs themselves have been acquired, mostly by US-based MNCs, so that US-based control has somewhat increased in importance. Overall, FDI has been sourced in other long-industrialized countries, notably the United States, European countries, and Japan, and there are a few companies based in newly industrialized Asian countries, including Taiwan, South Korea, and Hong Kong. With respect to the US companies, though head offices are distributed throughout the country, there is a relative concentration of MNCs originating on the Pacific Coast, such as Amazon, Microsoft, Apple, and Boeing, amounting to twenty-three of the forty-one US companies entering Metro Vancouver. This concentration reflects both the importance of the Pacific Coast region as the location of the biggest high-tech centres in the United States and its geographical proximity to Metro Vancouver, conveniently located in the same time zone where operations can be readily coordinated.

Moreover, the geographical diversity of FDI sources in Metro Vancouver's high-tech activities is matched by their industrial diversity. FDI has not been clustered or specialized in specific high-tech segments but has reinforced the underlying diversification of Metro Vancouver high tech established by its entrepreneurial base. Thus, FDI is distributed among sectors such as video games, internet applications, aerospace, energy, telecommunications, information systems, film production, and a number of dedicated software applications for business services. That is, Metro Vancouver's highly diversified range of high-tech activities in turn has attracted a diversified range of FDI.

Mode of Entry

Both acquisition of local companies and establishment of new facilities have been important paths to entry for FDI in Metro Vancouver's high tech, with the former accounting for thirty-five (61 percent) of total arrivals. Both modes of entry largely reflect horizontal integration, principally in the form of related diversification strategies. That is, rather than simply duplicating their existing product mix, high-tech MNCs locating in Metro Vancouver often have sought market differentiation in related but distinct product lines, well illustrated by Electronic Arts' distinctive range of games designed in Burnaby (see Case Studies 3.1 and 3.2). For these MNCs, related diversification not only meets expansion-related goals but also serves to reduce the risks of relying on talent pools in their home locations and provides new sources of creative abilities potentially to help sustain innovative behaviour. In some cases, the MNCs entering Metro Vancouver have been acquired themselves. Germany's SAP, for example, acquired Business Objects of France and the operations that it controlled in Metro Vancouver. Similarly, Ericsson of Sweden became a somewhat indirect presence in Vancouver by acquiring Redback Networks of California, which had acquired another California company with a Vancouver office, and Abatis Systems of Burnaby. In one case, a reacquisition involved reversion to local control.

In most cases, entries by MNCs into Metro Vancouver's high tech by acquisition have featured local firms with a demonstrated record of creating and marketing innovations by entrepreneurs and their skilled workforces. Although their contributions to local development might not be as evident as entry via new site investments, and sometimes controversial, for MNCs entry by acquisition offers substantial advantages, especially by providing a relatively quick form of expansion, compared with building new facilities, and a ready-made workforce and talent pool with established local networks and an understanding of local conditions. By the late 1990s, BC tech firms also had become favoured acquisition targets for US firms because of the low value of the Canadian dollar in relation to the American dollar, rendering Canadian firms cheaper than American ones. At the same time, from the perspective of local firms, acquisitions have been welcomed widely as a source of funds and market access, as well as by realizing the profits of their sales. Acquisitions are rarely considered hostile. Opposition to the acquisition of MDA, for example, came primarily from the federal government, not from MDA itself, whose management was in favour of its takeover (see Case Study 4.4). Furthermore, as the experience of QLT reveals, finding a foreign partner to provide such benefits might not be straightforward and inevitably depends on local firms themselves offering key creative assets.

Investments in new facilities nevertheless have been an important method of entry (39 percent of the total), recently highlighted by the new research-based office complexes planned by Amazon and Apple. Other important entries achieved by building new dedicated facilities include Microsoft, Meta, Fortinet, and Moli. Indeed, and exceptionally, the latter two firms' Vancouver laboratories are their parent companies' central R&D operations. Other firms have moved into available office space. Whatever their mode of entry, all of these MNCs, regardless of geographic origin or nature of their business, have shared locational preferences for Metro Vancouver, much facilitated by Canada's and British Columbia's openness to FDI. Metro Vancouver has become a desirable location for high-tech investments by MNCs and the talent that they need.

Metro Vancouver: A Sticky Place for Mobile Talent

That highly educated or trained, creative, and experienced individuals are highly mobile geographically has long been recognized and well-illustrated by high-tech activities and places.[15] As a vital input to high-tech operations, talent has decisive effects on business location.[16] Indeed, places considered desirable by high-tech talent to live and work can become "sticky," attracting and encouraging businesses to remain locally committed. Although the sense of (local) desirability for high-tech talent is subjective and not easy to quantify, it is usually assessed by wide-ranging locational attributes or factors that relate to recreational and cultural amenities, the quality of public services such as education and health, political and legal stability and security, job prospects, housing quality, aesthetic considerations, and global connectivity. In recent decades, Metro Vancouver has been judged highly in these terms, a prized "livable region" and an "intermediate-sized" city that, even if peripheral, offers ready connections around the Pacific Rim, not least to the US West Coast, and within Canada its attractiveness is reinforced by a (relatively) benign climate. As a national newspaper article noted about Metro Vancouver, "tech is sticky. Sure it is not physically stuck to a resource like mining or forestry. But it is surprisingly difficult to pick up and move an established tech company – especially the creative part."[17]

In practice, Metro Vancouver's stickiness for high tech has evolved rapidly in recent decades, in tandem with its postindustrialism. When Dan Gelbart – a future co-founder of Creo (1983) – arrived in Metro Vancouver from Israel in 1970, he considered his choice of high-tech employment to be limited to just a couple of options, including the newly established MDA. Subsequently, local firms gradually built up a high-tech talent pool that in turn flagged increased interest from foreign firms, sparked especially by the acquisition by Electronic Arts of Distinctive Software in 1990 and its leadership role in the video game industry.[18] In effect, the locational preferences of high-tech MNCs for Metro Vancouver have been predicated on earlier developments led primarily by local firms that revealed high-tech potential, provided targets for acquisition, and contributed to an accumulating, sticky talent pool. MNCs have reinforced this process of accumulation, including by stimulating demands for local education and training programs and attracting migrants from elsewhere. In turn, an increasingly large talent pool facilitates further start-ups, widens career opportunities, increases networking possibilities, and generates niches for innovation while adding to increased population, income, taxes, and demands for services and amenities. For MNCs, "access" to talent is a widely cited reason for locating in Metro Vancouver (as elsewhere), in practice an umbrella term for multiple attributes related to an interrelated range of cost and noncost factors. As with assessing the desirability of places to live, assessing talent by firms in the context of choice of location involves a considerable degree of subjectivity.

Talent as a Multi-Attribute Locational Factor
In choosing to invest in Metro Vancouver, high-tech MNCs frequently have emphasized the attraction of the region's talent pool and its potential for expansion through internal sources (other firms, the education system) and from outside (through in-migration). However, the locational calculus of talent is not just about costs but also about considerations related to creativity, productivity, problem solving, availability, flexibility, cooperation, and commitment to ongoing learning. In practice, assessing locational (dis)-advantages of talent by high-tech business is judgmental and ultimately more about value creation than about cost.[19] Nevertheless, in Metro Vancouver (and British Columbia), it is well established that, though average high-tech wages are (slightly) higher than local (or Canadian) averages, they are lower, usually significantly so, compared with American levels. As BC Stats recently reported, even after purchasing power differences and exchange rates are considered, among American states only Mississippi and South Dakota offer their high-tech workers lower remuneration than similar workers in British Columbia.[20] For California and Washington State, BC Stats reported average (real) incomes over two times higher than those in British Columbia.[21] Indeed, this labour cost advantage for high-tech businesses in Metro Vancouver (if less so for its workforce) is recognized by MNCs – including the cloud giants Amazon, Apple, and Microsoft – and typically is highlighted in local promotional materials seeking to attract high-tech investment.[22] As Evan Duggan reinforces, "Vancouver's relatively low labour costs are one of the main attractants for enormous tech companies

like Amazon," bearing in mind that "salaries typically account for about 70 per cent" (of operating costs).[23] The low value of Canadian currency versus American currency further underlines this cost advantage, and publicly funded health and education services in Canada is another, if understated, cost-related locational advantage.

In addition to its cost, however, talent has to be available and offer MNCs the *specific* kinds of expertise that they seek. EA's acquisition of Distinctive Software, for example, evolved from both partners seeking each other out and recognizing close and complementary expertise in sports-based video games, reminiscent of a merger as much as an acquisition, with Don Mattrick as a co-founder of the latter becoming a leading executive in the former.[24] Other examples of specifically targeted acquisitions by giant MNCs are Boeing's purchase in 2000 of Aeroinfosystems of Richmond, with its expertise in flight routing; Schneider's acquisition of Xantrex's expertise in power electronics; and SAP's acquisition of Business Objects and of Crystal Decisions business software. Among mid-sized companies, Flir (US) and Sorin (Italy) are similar examples of acquisition-based related diversification, while Nintendo's diversification entry into Metro Vancouver seems to have been more of a stepping stone for plans to expand in the United States. Although it did not work out, Kodak's acquisition of Creo could have helped to restructure the former if Creo's talents had been recognized properly. These examples underscore the importance of horizontal integration as a motive for FDI.

Moreover, for many high-tech MNCs, including mid-sized firms, the attraction of Metro Vancouver is its potential for ready expansion. DNEG, for example, a British-based, major world producer of visual effects for the film industry, established its third overseas office, and its first in North America, in Vancouver in 2014. As its CEO, Matt Holben, noted, "part of the reason that we chose Vancouver is because there is a talent pool here already ... We're ... building out for a capacity for about 450-plus (employees)."[25] As for other locational advantages, he pointed to the availability of building spaces that DNEG could adapt to suit its particular needs in accessible locations within the city, noting that "the combination of Vancouver's top tech schools, talent pool and willingness by 'all levels of government' to help court visual effect companies have made the city a major draw for international firms like DNEG."[26]

Tile, founded in 2012 in Silicon Valley and reaching sales of US $100 million with 125 employees by 2016, exemplifies Metro Vancouver's ability to attract talent for a new, relatively small firm. Tile makes small, Bluetooth-enabled devices that consumers can place in wallets or attach to key chains to keep track of belongings, or the devices can be incorporated into consumer electronics such as headphones. Tile chose Metro Vancouver in 2019 as its first expansion outside its hometown of San Mateo to establish a new engineering hub.[27] On its entry into Vancouver, Tile anticipated building an office of twenty or so employees over the next eighteen months, with further growth possible. As a senior manager at its Silicon Valley headquarters stated, "being a tech company in the Bay area comes with a certain set of challenges these days, and one of those is competing for talent ... So, like a lot of other companies, we're looking to start a second engineering hub to help us accelerate our hiring and retention efforts."[28] For Tile, Canada is also an important growing market, and it had made a deal with the Herschel Supply Company of Vancouver, a backpack and accessories manufacturer that makes wallets fitted with Tile's devices. As a related example, Rivian, an emerging, California-based competitor to Tesla in electric vehicle production, opened its Vancouver office in 2020, in the words of its manager, to work on "digital experiences inside and outside of the Rivian vehicle ... [with a] significant portion of these applications ... [to be] developed here in Vancouver."[29] This manager especially emphasized – as a talent pool for Rivian – the roles of UBC, SFU, UVic, and BCIT and noted that his team of 100 or so employees as of 2021 would be involved in multiple roles, in relation not only to mobile and infotainment maps but also to fleet management and vehicle services.

Moreover, MNCs have recognized that the size of the area's talent pool has been well supported by immigration facilitated by the federal government's Global Skills Strategy and the BC government's nominee program. For example, when Tile sought to locate a new engineering hub "Canadian immigration policies also factored into looking beyond the U.S."[30] For Tile, Metro Vancouver has become a "magnet" for talent seeking firms that will continue to develop such talent. Similarly, in 2019, Microsoft increased its existing development staff of 300 to 700 while consolidating them in a new space in downtown Vancouver as an "international development centre" (its first such centre in North America but not globally). As a senior manager communicated, "we're recruiting from around the world and, from a candidate perspective, Vancouver is very desirable despite the high cost of living."[31] That desired employees need visas for immigration is generally not a problem in Canada, reinforcing the sense of Metro Vancouver as a global talent pool. In general, complementing its lower cost, the productivity and availability of Metro Vancouver's talent pool, that is increasingly reinforced by local universities and colleges and by supportive government policies, underlies the sense of the region's high-tech labour supply as a multi-attribute location factor.

The ability to coordinate Metro Vancouver's talent within global operations is another important consideration for MNCs, most obvious in the twenty-four Pacific Coast–based companies (59 percent of the American total) from the United States that have operations in Metro Vancouver, relatively close to their head office locations. For MNCs such as Microsoft, Amazon, Apple, Boeing, Fortinet, Tile, and Hollywood film producers, their Pacific Coast head offices and major operations are in the same time zone, readily accessible and integrated. As a Microsoft manager noted, the Vancouver subsidiary is "close to Microsoft's international headquarters in Seattle, although what really matters, for people collaborating on projects, is that it's in the same time zone."[32] For Microsoft, its enlarged commitment to Metro Vancouver recognizes its need for talent and for this location to develop as a distinctive base of innovation as part of related diversification. Similarly, Seattle-based Boeing engineers regularly visit Avcorp in Delta to discuss design developments. In addition, Los Angeles–based Hollywood, film producers routinely arrange short-term, even daily, visits to film sets and to clusters of video game designers in Vancouver, supported by easy local connections, including rapid transit, from the airport to the downtown core.

Admittedly, talented firms and workforces can relocate elsewhere, and innovative individuals and firms have left Metro Vancouver, especially for the United States, particularly the Pacific Coast states.[33] The film industry is a well-known example that sticky places compete with other sticky places for investment and talent, encouraging Metro Vancouver to offer substantial subsidies and tax breaks to help it maintain its competitiveness with other locations in Canada (especially Toronto and Montreal) and the United States. Even so, the core locational advantages for filming in Metro Vancouver are rooted in a highly productive, cooperative, and flexible workforce that, unusual for high tech, has been effectively organized by a strong union.[34] For the most part, Metro Vancouver's high-tech workforce, including in the video game industry closely connected to filmmaking, is nonunionized and highly flexible.[35] The region's film industry nevertheless demonstrates that unionization is not necessarily opposed to flexible work arrangements.

Metro Vancouver's desirability as a place to live and the stickiness of its high-tech talent have co-evolved but not without fissures or problems. The region's cost of living is extremely high, especially for housing, and a significant gap between income and investment for housing exists even for (most) high-tech talent. Possibly, increasing demand for talent will increase its price and reduce this gap, if not necessarily for everyone else. And, if high-tech incomes were to increase significantly, might not the region's attractiveness to high-tech investment decline? Will income disparities within the region widen? Meanwhile, we can note that MNCs often can out bid local firms for talent and provide affiliated career ladders for workers to leave for other sticky places. Moreover, since the region remains committed to growing rapidly, so-called urban diseconomies of scale are becoming ever more apparent, most obviously in housing costs but also in congestion and pressure on green spaces. Even as this growth is occurring more or less regardless of demand for talent, it is rendering Metro Vancouver's overall desirability more problematic (see Chapter 7). Suffice to say that hitherto FDI has helped to enhance the local talent pool even while raising implications for the region's long-run development, including with respect to high tech itself.

Local Development Implications
Although welcomed by policy makers within British Columbia (and Metro Vancouver) as a sign of success in high tech, FDI is not altruistic or driven primarily by local goals; rather, it is driven by the strategic objectives and plans of MNCs with respect to growth, profitability, market presence, and competitiveness. MNCs, for example, charge their subsidiaries for head office and R&D services, even if such payments are rarely published. More broadly, the sustained value of FDI to parent companies in high-tech sectors is rooted in the actual and potential contributions of creative employees (talent) in ensuring the viability of branch plant operations in serving the goals of MNCs as a whole. In this regard, the local stickiness of Metro Vancouver's growing talent pool challenges MNCs regarding its maintenance and enhancement, for example, by providing financing, marketing connections, and access to complementary expertise that in turn promote job- and income-creating local development.

Whether FDI is via new investments or acquisitions, local development interests, arguably, are best served by subsidiaries that are relatively independent and provide important, specialized, global contributions to parent companies. Some time ago, the Science Council of Canada urged such initiatives, labelled as "global product mandates."[36] For the Science Council, the idea of product mandating was proposed in the 1970s in the context of secondary manufacturing to offset the widespread tendency of branch plants to focus on mature products only for the Canadian market, without abilities to innovate, diversify, and export. Such operations were deemed to have limited potential for growth and likely to become increasingly non-competitive. As a solution, product mandates were proposed to allow foreign subsidiaries in secondary manufacturing to become more innovative and competitive by engagement in all of the functions – including R&D, manufacturing, and marketing on a global scale – for particular products for which they alone would be responsible within the parent company. Currently, Metro Vancouver is unlikely to be a viable location for large-scale manufacturing. Nevertheless, global mandates for RD&D activities are potentially significant for FDI to enhance such activities in Metro Vancouver, giving credence to overlaps between corporate and local development aspirations. In practice, such mandates are widely evident in Metro Vancouver. However, such plans have not always worked out as intended for either MNCs or local interests, and controversies over security have occurred. Indeed, though scarcely mentioned in a BC context, foreign ownership of high tech also raises questions about local sovereignty. Reflections on these themes add insights into the role of FDI in Metro Vancouver's high-tech sector.

Reinforcing Local Stickiness: The Global Mandating of Creativity

In Metro Vancouver's high-tech sector, locally distinctive mandating practices focus principally on RD&D or creative activities, and – apart from the possibilities of building prototypes and custom-based products – any resulting manufacturing is often located elsewhere, either in affiliated operations or contracted out by parent companies. In tandem, creative exports from Metro Vancouver subsidiaries occur in accord with the policies of parent companies, often by supplying affiliated or established contracting parties. Nevertheless, that local operations have autonomy in and responsibility for the creative processes of particular products is a major contribution to sustained local development, even if manufacturing activities are limited. Product mandates enhance the quality of local jobs and creativity while providing unique contributions for parent companies that do not compete with other company operations. These strategies both broaden the core advantages of parent companies and deepen the expertise of sticky local talent as it adds to local development.

An important key to understanding the benefits of FDI for local development in high tech is whether local innovativeness within subsidiaries is supported and given some form of global mandate. That MNCs that have entered Metro Vancouver through acquisitions typically have targeted specific complementary expertise potentially illustrates such tendencies. Electronic Arts,

CASE STUDY 3.1   **Acquired Foreign Subsidiaries Illustrating Globally
Mandated High-Tech Functions in Metro Vancouver**

Electronic Arts. Its acquisition in 1991 of Distinctive Software was as much a
merger of creative minds as an acquisition. In 1991, Distinctive Software was
Metro Vancouver's largest independent video game developer, with seventy-
five employees, led by Don Mattrick. Over a thirty-year period, EA has remained a central creative hub and at its peak employed over 1,300, although
there have been fluctuations. Several famous video games developed at
Burnaby include the NHL series (since 1991), the Fédération internationale de
football association's (FIFA's) Soccer series (since 1993), NBA Live series, and
Need for Speed series (1994–2000). EA is located in Burnaby's Discovery Park
in a facility built in 1998, further expanded in 2009 by amalgamating with a
studio from downtown Vancouver and again in 2020, when a major new expansion to its Burnaby location was announced. Mattrick relocated to the EA
head office in San Francisco, where he remained until 2007.

Schneider Electric. It acquired in 2008 part of Xantrex, a $250 million company
that developed power inverters and related products in the utilization of inter-
mittent renewable energy (RE) (especially solar power) sources with multiple
applications. A large MNC with 150,000 employees globally, Schneider reinforced Xantrex's activities to perform quality assurance testing with a new
$13 million lab opened in 2013 dedicated to its grid and solar inverting tech-
nologies, and Schneider supported its own solar business unit with a new
$14 million lab opened in 2014, also in Burnaby. (In 2019, Schneider acquired
McRea Electric of Vancouver and Victoria to provide electric systems for marine users.) In December 2018, Schneider sold the Xantrex part of its business
and its branded (mobile power) products to Mission Critical Electronics of
Huntington Beach, California. The latter has maintained Xantrex's operations
(including some manufacturing), which remain in Burnaby, having relocated
from Discovery Park in 1996, and Schneider continued its solar energy product design work (Burnaby and Richmond).

SAP. In 2008, SAP acquired Business Objects of France, which in 2003 had
acquired Crystal Services and its signature business service software of that
name. As the world's leader in business software and related services, with
130 offices around the world employing 74,000 people, SAP has expanded its

presence in Vancouver, with major R&D renovations in 2016 and 2018, costing $22 million, creating the SAP Canadian Centre of Excellence for Analytics, reputedly the largest software employer in British Columbia, with almost 1,200 employees.

Sorin. Sorin of Italy paid $27 million in 2003 to acquire Mitroflow Enterprises from the Swiss-based Sulzer Medica, which had first acquired Mitroflow, then located in Richmond, for more than $50 million in 1999. In that year, Mitroflow, started by Paul Geyer (UBC science grad) in 1991 with 9 employees, employed 125 people to develop and commercialize bovine tissue heart valves exported globally. Sorin's new (2004) Burnaby-based facility employed 150, including 15 in R&D and 113 in manufacturing, and it was subsequently expanded to employ 250. The Burnaby operation has a global mandate to design and manufacture tissue-based heart valves, and Sorin focuses on mechanical heart valves. Manufacturing in Burnaby is performed by a skilled female workforce that involves sewing together the components for heart valves. This operation was expanded in 2007 and exemplifies a classic form of global product mandate.

Boeing. In 2000, Boeing acquired Aeroinfo Systems in Richmond, a small private company founded in 1996 with fourteen employees with expertise in airline maintenance, and these employees were retained. In 2016, Boeing built a new R&D laboratory in downtown Vancouver to expand its software development activities to complement its Richmond lab. The latter employs 200, and the new lab will employ another 50 highly skilled software engineers and scientists. Both labs focus on supporting Boeing's global operations and the aviation industry in general by improving efficiency while seeking collaborations with local industries and universities.

Sources: Boeing, "Boeing Vancouver Labs Opens Its Door in Yaletown," news release, September 15, 2016, https://skiesmag.com/press-releases/boeing-vancouver-labs-opens-soors-yaletown/; K. Chan, "Electronic Arts Planning Major Expansion of Burnaby Office Campus," *Vancouver Urbanized,* August 24, 2020, https://dailyhive.com/vancouver/3700-gilmore-way-burnaby-electronic-arts-ea-campus; J. Lee, "SAP Unveils $11-Million Vancouver Office Reno," *Vancouver Sun,* April 12, 2016; C. Ritchie, "Xantrex Poised for Global Growth," *Strategy and Finance,* June–July, 2014, https://xantrex.com/wp-content/uploads/2022/05/IBI-2014-profile-Xantrex.pdf; S. Simpson, "Sorin Takes Hands-On Approach to Heart Valve Technology," *Vancouver Sun,* April 7, 2011.

Schneider, and SAP provide well-known examples of reinforcing innovative, relatively independent roles for their subsidiaries (see Case Study 3.1). Indeed, for Electronic Arts, its Burnaby facility arguably has been – and remains – its most important innovative centre for video games after forty years (by 2021). Meanwhile, Schneider helped to enlarge and modernize Xantrex, including by increasing its market potential and by building a new R&D laboratory in 2013. In the case of SAP, based in Germany, its acquisition in 2008 of the French-based Business Objects (plus some local companies), which previously had acquired a local company around 2003, led to a rejuvenation of the latter. As its managing director noted, "the impetus for investing in Vancouver wasn't sales, but the city's ability to create and attract talent ... SAP wants to stay here." Furthermore, the extensive renovations reconfigured about 20,000 square feet into collaborative workspaces for "unplanned collisions," according to a facilities manager, indicating further support for the expression of local creativity.[37] In addition, the local acquisitions made by Sorin, Boeing, Flir, Delta Electronics, Salesforce, and Mastercard have served similarly to maintain the vitality and specialties of Metro Vancouver acquisitions, as is likely the case with the US-based EnerSys recent (2019) acquisition of Burnaby's Alpha Technologies and its 500 (BC) employees.

With respect to MNCs entering Metro Vancouver in new or available office spaces, the implications for the development of some form of global mandate are similarly evident. Thus, the US high-tech giants – Amazon, Microsoft, Apple, IBM, Oracle, Facebook, and Raytheon Technologies, along with the smaller Fortinet – have located offices in Metro Vancouver to access local talent that, to varying degrees, provides specialized inputs to parent company operations (see Case Study 3.2).[38] In this regard, Fortinet is particularly unusual in that its Burnaby operation is its corporate hub for R&D activities and has been so since its formation in 2000.[39] In contrast, Facebook's operation, at least until 2018, was relatively small, with fluctuating employment levels and primarily a "testing of the waters" exercise that focused on training local workers for possible recruitment. The extent to which these specialties are conducted only in Metro Vancouver is hard to say, although Raytheon, IBM, Microsoft, and Amazon, and less so Oracle, have given their Vancouver-based operations strong complementary and relatively specialized roles in parent company activities. In the cases of Raytheon and Amazon, their respective R&D and tech hub offices are also associated with serving Canadian markets, and IBM's subsidiary, until its recent closure, predominantly served markets within and beyond Canada.

CASE STUDY 3.2 New Offices of Selected US-Controlled Foreign
Subsidiaries with "Globally" Mandated High-Tech
Functions in Metro Vancouver

Raytheon Technologies. This US-based MNC has several subsidiaries in Canada
and established its Richmond facility in 1989 with 150 employees. As a defence and security company, Raytheon is a major supplier to the Canadian
government as well as the American government. At Richmond, its core
activities are the design, development, and integration of major software
systems, especially for air traffic management. The Richmond operation has
developed the Canadian Automated Air Traffic System (CATTS) and the Military Automated Air Traffic System (MATTS) while supplying the Tracview system developed by the parent company and innovated commercially in 1989.
Richmond also offers next-generation products developed by the parent
company.

IBM. IBM Canada opened its new Pacific Development Centre in Burnaby in
1989 with about 280 employees. IBM itself underwent a corporate-wide restructuring starting in the 1990s, redefining itself from a highly integrated
manufacturing company producing computer hardware and backup services
to a highly sophisticated software specialist company serving the needs of
businesses in a wide range of industrial activities. The Pacific Development
Centre is a creative part of this new corporate vision serving the needs of
customers largely (96 percent) outside British Columbia, sometimes in
cooperation with IBM's global services. The Burnaby facility has developed
twenty-nine patents.

Microsoft. Starting in 2007, Microsoft, headquartered in the nearby Seattle
Metropolitan Area, leased several offices superseded by a major new office
in Vancouver that opened in 2016 as a Microsoft Development Centre, one of
twelve major development centres around the world and the only one in
Canada. This brought Microsoft's local employment to about 750. Close to
its Seattle-area head office, the new centre hosts senior leadership and
board meetings. The company's OneNote system (innovated in 2003) is a
focus of further applications in education. In addition, other distinct activities
centred in Vancouver relate to Skype, technology and news feeds for
Microsoft Network, applications of Microsoft Band (discontinued), the
HoloLens augmented reality system, and video games (e.g., *Gears of War*).

▶

Amazon. Starting in 2013, Amazon, headquartered in the nearby Seattle Metropolitan Area, leased office space in downtown Vancouver, employing over 100. Development work was based broadly on serving the company as a whole, and employment expanded to 1,000. In 2019, Amazon announced plans to lease new offices (on the former site of Vancouver's old post office) amounting to 1.1 million square feet and with the potential to house 7,000 employees in one of its two "tech hubs" (the other is in Toronto). This tech hub planned to open fully in 2023 and by December comprised 4,500 employees (more than in Toronto's tech hub). Development activities will focus on cloud computing, e-commerce and machine learning, media programming, and support for the company as a whole.

Oracle. With its head office in California, Oracle has several operations in Canada, including a relatively small office (Oracle labs) established in 2013 in downtown Vancouver employing 220. Many of its activities focus on contributions to the firm's RAPID project with aspects such as database and query processing, systems software, and networking, also performed in other global R&D centres of the company.

Fortinet. With its head office in California, in a highly unusual development, on its formation in 2000, Fortinet established its principal R&D "hub" in Burnaby, with a focus on high-performance security solutions. In 2017, the Burnaby facility was expanded from over 300 jobs to accommodate about 700 jobs (with 1,000 jobs in Canada as a whole). In early 2024, it announced plans to invest in Calgary. Fortinet has patented numerous products at its Burnaby hub, led by Fortiguard as its leading cybersecurity initiative sold around the world (320,000 customers by 2017). Much of its hiring has been local talent, with especially strong connections with SFU.

Sources: G. Shaw, "Microsoft Eyes Bright Future for Vancouver's Tech Sector," *Vancouver Sun,* May 1, 2014, https://vancouversun.com/business/technology/microsoft-eyes-big-things-for-vancouvers-tech-sector; T-Net, "Fortinet to Add 1,000 New Tech Jobs in Vancouver in New State of the Art Data Centre," *T-News,* September 12, 2017, https://brainstation.io/magazine/fortinet-announces-operations-expansion-in-burnaby; J. Ferreras, "Amazon Expands in Vancouver, Where Tech Workers Make over $50k Less than in Seattle: Data," *Global News,* April 30, 2018, https://globalnews.ca/news/4178326/amazon-vancouver-tech-workers-pay/; D. Dyck, "How Amazon's Plan to Expand Will Reshape Vancouver's Tech Scene," *Globe and Mail,* November 29, 2019, https://www.theglobeandmail.com/business/article-how-amazons-plan-to-expand-will-reshape-vancouvers-tech-scene/; E. Duggan, "Amazon to Take over Entire Former Canada Post Building in Downtown," *Vancouver Sun,* December 10, 2019, https://vancouversun.com/business/commercial-real-estate/commercial-real-estate-amazon-to-take-over-entire-former-canada-post-building; W. Johnson, "8 Global Tech Companies in Vancouver that We Should Be Talking About," *Venture,* September 5, 2019, https://dailyhive.com/vancouver/global-vancouver-tech-companies; C. Wilson, "Virtue of Being a Single Corporate Tenant: A Peek Inside Amazon's New Vancouver Office," *Times Colonist,* May 21, 2023, https://www.timescolonist.com/real-estate/virtue-of-being-a-single-corporate-tenant.

As for giant Asian MNCs that have entered Metro Vancouver by in-vesting in new facilities, as noted, E-One Moli Energy is an exceptional case by being its Taiwanese parent company's sole high-tech subsidiary, dependent on nurturing local talent. Since its acquisition in 1998, E-One Moli's battery production expanded for a while, until a facility was built in the United States. However, Maple Ridge retained its R&D functions and 100 jobs, and in late 2023 the firm announced a federal government sup-ported $1b plan to re-establish battery manufacturing in a new facility that will add 350 jobs.[40] As a recent arrival, the Japanese-based Fujitsu, an estab-lished high-tech giant, has chosen Metro Vancouver for its global head-quarters for development work on quantum computing and AI, an initiative seeking to take advantage of the area's established expertise in these fields.[41] Meanwhile, South Korea's giant Samsung has allocated specialized func-tions to its Metro Vancouver operations in mobile security applications that complement other corporate activities.[42]

Within the film industry, MNCs such as Disney and Sony have played important roles in building facilities and organizing Metro Vancouver–based productions and local talent. Attracted by the region's talent pool and tax regimes, Disney and Sony developed their local operations in the 1990s but remain relatively small and ultimately are controlled by Los Angeles head-quarters. Sony has the biggest presence through its Imageworks. Established in 1992 with just five employees, in 2010, Sony Imageworks opened a new production studio in Vancouver that by 2014 had expanded to over 700 em-ployees and had taken on (subsidiary) headquarter functions relocated from Culver, California (along with many of the latter's employees). Disney's operations began in 1995 and remain smaller.

Regardless of modes of entry, within parent company operations, the nature and extent of the specialized and distinctive mandating of high-tech subsidiaries within Metro Vancouver vary. There is a group of sub-sidiaries – most obviously represented by E-One Moli and Fortinet but also embracing Electronic Arts, Sorin, Xantrex, possibly IBM, and Fujitsu – that provides strongly independent, creative, and significant roles for parent companies. A larger group of subsidiaries is more closely integrated within the global networks of MNCs, such as Raytheon, Amazon, Microsoft, Oracle, Samsung, and on a smaller scale Double Negative and Boeing. There are still other subsidiaries, including giants such as Meta (Facebook) and Nintendo, only loosely connected locally in any important creative sense, with limited implications for local development.

In general, FDI has helped to sustain the growth of Metro Vancouver's high-tech activities, reinforcing the momentum of innovativeness. Yet increasing level of FDI has not led to the emergence of dominant core or anchor-type firms. As of 2018, for example, the local employment total of the several huge companies combined (Amazon, Apple, Microsoft, Meta, Raytheon, Oracle) was less than the loss of more than 4,000 jobs that occurred when Creo was downsized following its acquisition. As of 2018 (or 2020), the biggest high-tech companies to have operated in Metro Vancouver since 1970 remain Creo and MDA (plus Telus). However, since 2020, Amazon has grown rapidly, and the company claims that it employs (c. 2022) over 10,000 people in British Columbia, including almost half in its (new) Vancouver tech hub and many other offices in the metropolitan area and close by (see Case Study 3.2).[43] It also claims (in general, self-promoting terms) contributions to wages, taxes, and aid to small firms in marketing their products, providing financing, and offering incubator advice. With the new, adjacent Apple and Microsoft offices, Amazon is part of a cluster of high-profile activities in prestigious new buildings, helping both to redefine (and relocate) downtown Vancouver's corporate head office focus from resources to high tech and to change the governance structure of Metro Vancouver high tech from its entrepreneurial roots to subsidiary status, without involving individually dominant core companies. The increased levels of foreign control, however, are not without concerns.

The Darker Shadows of FDI: Does Sovereignty Matter?

Specific, albeit limited and rather civilized, controversies over the role of FDI in Metro Vancouver's high-tech sector have arisen from time to time, the most high profile being the acquisitions and subsequent rationalizations of Glenayre and Creo and the largely national debates that have occurred twice over whether or not MDA should be taken over by US companies. A brief discussion of these cases, in which the shifts to foreign ownership were not driven by local interests, helps point to the darker shadows of FDI for local development.

As a starting point, selected details of the acquisitions and rationalizations of Glenayre and Creo have been summarized to provide context for several general observations (see Case Study 3.3). First, both cases occurred as part of corporate-wide restructurings of parent companies that themselves were in financial trouble and looking to develop new strategies.

CASE STUDY 3.3 **The Glenayre and Creo Restructurings**

Glenayre Electronics was founded in 1963 as a machinery manufacturer and reorganized in 1969 under the leadership of Klaus Deering. After pioneering paging systems, Glenayre Electronics was acquired by another local firm, Trans-Canada Glass, owned by Tom and Alan Skidmore. With their focus on retailing, they sold in 1992 the manufacturing operations to the N-W Group of Portland before becoming part of Glenayre Technologies, initially headquartered in Charlotte, North Carolina, and then Atlanta, Georgia. In 2001, the Burnaby manufacturing operation was closed and consolidated in Quincy, Illinois, and R&D was consolidated in Atlanta. In practice, the pager market had become obsolete, overwhelmed by the rising cellphone business. Meanwhile, in Burnaby, the nonmanufacturing assets of Glenayre Electronics became Glentel (owned by the Skidmore brothers) and the core of a locally owned and rapidly growing retail business focusing on cellphones. In 2014, Glentel was acquired by Bell and Rogers, two Canadian telecom giants (rivals of Telus), and in 2018 it had over 2,000 employees across Canada. Although a retailer relying on parent companies for R&D, Glentel is often classified as a high-tech company in British Columbia. Reputedly, many professional employees laid off by Glenayre Electronics found jobs in other local high-tech companies.

In the case of Creo, "before Kodak got its hands on it, Creo was a jewel of BC's tech industry." Indeed, it was Metro Vancouver's biggest high-tech firm in terms of employees and revenues. Kodak bought Creo in 2005 for US $1.2 billion and according to Michael McCullough Creo basically was hollowed out even as Kodak itself fell into bankruptcy. Thus, its software division was closed, as was the manufacturing plant, R&D was shifted to Israel, and the remaining employees were consolidated at one location (from five). Creo's renowned reputation as a creative, agile organization had become bureaucratized and decimated, without being of any help to Kodak. Although some ex-Creo employees joined other start-ups, its demise was a blow to the local economy, and its acquisition by Kodak served no particular purpose. Apparently, a few employees are still maintained.

Source: M. McCullough, "Creo: The Digitization Printing Company that Could Have Saved Kodak," *Canadian Business,* 2012.

CASE STUDY 3.4 **The Foreign Acquisition**
                and Re-Canadianization of MDA

Policy controversies are rare with respect to FDI in Metro Vancouver's high-tech sector, even with respect to acquisitions where the local benefits are not obvious. One exception to that insouciance was MDA, Metro Vancouver's high-tech flagship and marker of a transforming urban economy. In 2008, the Conservative-led federal government blocked the sale of MDA's space division to Alliant Techsystems, then headquartered in Arlington County, Virginia. Bearing in mind that MDA had received much government support for its space programs, such as RadarSat-2, the government argued, through Investment Canada, that the acquisition would not be of "net benefit" to Canada. The government's concerns pointed to the Canadian Space Agency's funding of MDA's space programs and their role in establishing satellite coverage on Canada's behalf, including with respect to protecting Canada's sovereignty over the Arctic. MDA's satellites provided "free" information to the government in this regard. But this intervention provided a (surprising) exception to the "rule" of openness to FDI. MDA itself had supported the sale, there was no provincial government (or business) opposition, and in its twenty-three-year history Investment Canada had not overturned a single case among the 1,597 foreign takeovers that it had reviewed in detail (CBC News 2008).

Indeed, within ten years, MDA itself had acquired and merged with Digital Globe (of Colorado) in 2017 at a cost of US $2.4 billion, with the two merged companies subsequently becoming part of Maxar Technologies, headquartered in Westminster, Colorado, as the parent company (Pugliese 2017). This shift seems to have been desired by MDA and its new (American) CEO as part of its new "access America" strategy. The transfer of ownership was fully approved by the federal (now Liberal) government, ignoring concerns about the loss of

Second, though both acquisitions can be classified as forms of horizontal integration, the motives of the parent firms differed to some extent. Thus, Glenayre's acquisition was designed in part to reduce competition and to consolidate operations in the United States, whereas Creo potentially was a highly promising related diversification for Kodak. Third, both Glenayre and Creo were locally high-profile companies and pioneers, with the latter still the biggest high-tech company ever to operate in Metro Vancouver. Yet

Canadian sovereignty from opposition parties and others (Pugliese 2017). However, Maxar experienced significant problems following its creation, and to reduce its debt load MDA was sold in 2019 for CDN $1 billion to Northern Private Capital of Toronto, returning MDA to Canadian ownership. According to Northern Private, "separating MDA from Maxar will give the space technology firm more room to pursue partnerships with other companies active in the rapidly growing sector" in which the costs of launching satellites have declined rapidly, involving various other companies, including Apple (McLeod 2019). Apparently, Jim Balsillie, the noted Canadian innovator, champion of Canadian-owned companies, and critic of foreign ownership in the tech sector helped fund Northern Private's acquisition. For the latter's CEO, buying MDA was "an exciting business opportunity but ... the ability to repatriate the company was an added bonus" (McLeod 2019).

As a footnote, how MDA became part of Maxar Technologies remains somewhat cloudy, involving unclear corporate motives and a renaming, and hard to discern benefits to Metro Vancouver from it sale before Northern Private brought it back to Canada at a substantial cost.

Sources: CBC News, "Federal Government Blocks Sale of MDA Space Division," *CBC News,* April 10, 2010, https://www.cbc.ca/news/business/federal-government-blocks-sale-of-mda-space-division-1.703999; D. Pugliese, "Canadarm Creator to Transform into US Company Raising Concerns of Tech Heading South of the Border," *National Post,* November 9, 2017, https://nationalpost.com/news/politics/canadarm -creator-to-transform-into-us-company-raising-concerns-of-tech-heading-south-of-the-border; J. McLeod, "Space-Tech Firm MDA Back in Canadian Hands with $1B Sale to Investors Including Balsillie," *Financial Post,* December 19, 2019, https://financialpost.com/technology/satellite-imagery-company -maxar-to-sell-its-robotics-unit-for-c1-bln; J. Foust, "Maxar to Sell Canadian Unit for $765 Million," *Space News,* December 30, 2019, https://spacenews.com/maxar-to-sell-canadian-unit-for-765-million.

FDI basically eliminated them. Fourth, that the closures of these companies released talent for others to hire and stimulate new entrepreneurial initiatives occurred in spite of rather than because of FDI. Fifth, in neither Glenayre nor Creo was the closure and rationalization helpful to the parent companies continued to experience significant problems. In effect, Kodak failed to restructure to meet the digital age, and Creo got caught up in this failure. Ironically, there is a view that Creo itself could have pointed in the right directions for Kodak's restructuring.[44] These cases also indicate that the rationality, expertise, and know-how of MNCs, even in understanding their own best interests, should not be assumed. They can be prone to mistakes, whether seeking to act in the self-interests of shareholders or in the broader interests of stakeholders. One study has suggested, for example, that high-tech MNCs can restructure by pursuing FDI in clusters around the world as acts of desperation in which they believe that they have "nothing to lose."[45] The Glenayre and Creo case might illustrate such behaviour.

Other companies in Metro Vancouver have been caught up in broader corporate restructurings and acquisitions. Mobile Data International, another once relatively large local firm, became entangled in the restructuring efforts of the Chicago-based Motorola that featured the creation of two companies, one of which (Motorola Solutions) acquired in 2018 another Metro Vancouver firm (Avigilon). Indeed, acquisitions can change ownership (and decision-making control) overnight and unexpectedly. Burnaby's PMC-Sierra, for example, was acquired in 1992 on its start-up by Sierra Conductor of California only to return to Canadian ownership a few years later; Atlanta's Aptean acquired FDM Software of North Vancouver in 2017 only to be acquired by Environmental Solutions Worldwide (ESW) of Texas a year later; and Sweden's Ericsson's acquisition of Redback Networks of California "incidentally" provided it with a small Metro Vancouver office (see Appendix 1). Such changes have uncertain long-term implications for local development.

As a controversial acquisition, MDA is a special case because it was subject to national policy scrutiny as a leading, innovative company not only for British Columbia but also for Canada's space industry (see Case Study 3.4).

MDA remains a high-profile firm locally and a pioneer in the development of Metro Vancouver's high-tech sector. Given its size and expertise, and as a noted supplier to the NASA space program, and the greater United States market, that American corporations were interested in acquiring MDA is not surprising. What is surprising, is that its first proposed acquisition in 2008 was rejected, given long-standing Canadian openness to FDI and acquisitions of domestic companies, and especially given the BC's government and management support for MDA's sale. The rationale for this decision was apparently and legitimately based largely on the grounds of national sovereignty. In this view, MDA was deemed a confidential source of expertise vital to the national interest, especially with respect to satellite communications and maintaining vigilance over Canada's sovereign interests in the Arctic. That MDA had also received much government funding was also noted. Yet, the second (2017) decision to accept foreign ownership of MDA was more in keeping with Canada's openness to FDI, and basically dismissed such a rationale. But what were the expected benefits of foreign ownership? The suggestion that US ownership would provide MDA with better access to the US seems questionable, given the firm's well-established (and continuing) presence there. That the company was locally important within Metro Vancouver with potential as an even bigger anchor company, inherently central to the integrity of Canada's space industry, and that its local and national development roles could be threatened by foreign ownership, seem to have been lesser considerations, if considered at all. In practice, the acquisition was caught up in corporate restructurings and re-namings during which MDA managed to survive. In a confused situation, that MDA subsequently returned to Canadian ownership was entirely due to a Toronto-based financial firm's initiative and motivations, not govern-ment policy. This, story at least hints of some concern within Canadian business for the implications of foreign ownership for sovereignty and local development.

The closures of Creo and Glenayre, and the shenanigans over MDA, illus-trate vulnerabilities exposed by FDI in Metro Vancouver's innovation econ-omy. Admittedly, the hardships of direct and indirect job and business income losses from these and other "downsizings" have been offset and ab-sorbed by the ongoing growth of the high-tech economy. In tandem, the rapidly cumulating contributions of FDI to this evolution are raising new potential problems for the region's innovation economy.

Three issues can be mentioned in this context. First, MNCs generally are able to pay the highest wages within the high-tech sector and, though de-sirable for high-road development in Metro Vancouver, might crowd out local high-tech firms, especially financially challenged start-ups.[46] As one response, Amazon offers help to new (not necessarily high-tech) firms, pre-sumably future suppliers of goods that Amazon will distribute, but the ex-tent of this help and its wider potential is unclear.[47] Second, though MNCs have added expertise and helped the local economy to become a magnet for talent, they are also a pipeline for local talent to leave that economy, most obviously via internal career ladders. In addition, foreign subsidiaries are well placed to attract talent directly from UBC and SFU (and other educational institutions) for immediate employment elsewhere, especially in the United States (where likely they will be better paid). Third, parent companies control intellectual property rights, including those already created by acquired firms as well as those subsequently developed. If this control facilitates the scaling up of innovations for commercial success, then it might also imply a leakage of rights, how they might be pursued, and the benefits of subsequent spinoffs, an issue raised across Canada and relevant in Metro Vancouver.[48]

Regardless of specific costs and benefits, foreign ownership at least imposes nonlocal control over major investment decisions, the nature of local mandating, the scope of local RD&D, and the form and use of patenting. Whether or not local sovereignty matters is a value judgment that for some is an inherent problem itself and for others a nonissue long overridden by the imperatives of globalization. Meanwhile, within Metro Vancouver, foreign ownership is increasingly shaping and institutionalizing the local structure of high tech. Assessing such a trend is not easy, not least because it involves counterfactual questions about what would have happened in the absence of FDI.

Conclusion

In recent decades, the increased momentum of FDI has been a striking feature of Metro Vancouver's high-tech sector and has reinforced its diverse, fragmented structure. MNC acquisitions of existing companies and their building and leasing of offices, along with further investments in modernization, have made important contributions to the sector's vitality, especially evident in and sustained by various forms of the local mandating of RD&D activities. That the sale of local companies to MNCs often has realized considerable wealth for local owners can also be noted. Overall, in terms of governance and identity in Metro Vancouver's high-tech sector, FDI has added new layers of controlled global business organization on top of the previously established, highly dynamic, locally based entrepreneurial culture. Admittedly, FDI has not always worked out for MNCs or locally, ownership changes have occurred, some MNCs have exited the region in short order, and instances of local businesses threatened by giants can be noted.[49] More importantly, the increasing *aggregate* level of FDI in Metro Vancouver high tech raises concerns about the leakage and dampening of locally developed intellectual property by MNCs, further reinforced by the roles of public universities and government funding in supporting these leakages. The scale and development of local intellectual property are important avenues for further research.

Whether or not government policy can be more discerning about the costs and benefits of FDI is questionable. A commitment to free trade and open-door principles to FDI are deeply ingrained in Canada, not least in

British Columbia, and FDI is limited in few sectors (airlines, banking, tele-communications), and these limits are controversial. Otherwise, public and private sector policy makers, along with much economic advice, are largely, if not completely indifferent to criticisms of FDI. This culture is unlikely to change. Openness to FDI, however, has not led to core or anchor compan-ies; MNC subsidiaries remain of modest size, and their frequent entry via acquisition arguably has pre-empted local companies from such a trajec-tory. Nevertheless, FDI is seen – and welcomed – as global recognition of local economic success. But so is local entrepreneurship, after all the basis for a high road of development (see Figure I.1). Indeed, how MNCs interact with local entrepreneurs increasingly will shape Metro Vancouver's future high-tech development, including through their implications for high-tech clustering (see Chapter 4) and the nature of the region's innovation system (see Chapter 5).

4

Local Clustering and Global Connections in Inter-Firm Relations among High-Tech Activities

The impressive growth of high-tech firms in Metro Vancouver, estimated at over 11,000 in 2020, has drawn from and contributed to various agglomeration qua urbanization economies that broadly refer to the benefits available to businesses in all sectors of Metro Vancouver's economy in the form of economic and social infrastructures and recreational, entertainment, and cultural amenities. In addition, Metro Vancouver's high-tech firms gain benefits from being part of distinct localized clusters of related activities.[1] These clustering or localization economies of scale are external to firms but internal to clusters and comprise services of some kind that the former do not wish or are unable to provide themselves. These externalities are diverse, nuanced, and hard if not impossible to measure precisely, but they are vital to business profitability and local development. Indeed, the roles and nature of knowledge-based clustering of innovative high-tech activities have become central to debates on regional and local development and policy around the world.[2] That said, clusters vary considerably in terms of size and scope, business organization, supporting institutional structure, extent and richness of local interactions, and global connections. In this and the next chapter, we probe the nature and implications of high-tech clusterings in Metro Vancouver.

As the world's iconic, most famous, high-tech cluster, Silicon Valley has been the focus of much attention.[3] Comprising several communities in and around San Francisco, Silicon Valley is the pioneering, dominant, and organically developed place-centred force driving (and strongly specialized in) information and communication technologies (ICT). Apple, Google (Alphabet is the parent company), Cisco, Adobe, Intel, Zoom, and Hewlett-Packard (HP Inc. and Hewlett-Packard Enterprises since 2015) are among its high-profile MNCs and supplemented by tens of thousands of other firms of varying sizes. Silicon Valley features not only high levels of competition among its firms but also deep local connections in terms of products and services, spinoffs, information sharing, labour supply, and financing; regarding the latter, for example, Silicon Valley is probably the largest venture capital centre of the world.[4] Its firms have dispersed much manufacturing activity around the United States and the globe, but Silicon Valley remains illustrative of a "complete," highly networked cluster that has global reach through its exports, foreign direct investment (FDI), sources of expertise, and exemplar as a cluster. Indeed, references to "cloning" Silicon Valley are frequent, including across Canada (as various places strive to become Silicon North). The global diffusion of high-tech clusters, however, has been highly differentiated.[5] Indeed, local variations have prompted suggestions for the classification of clusters into different types, ranging from descriptive approaches based on their origins and nature of their specialties, to more conceptual approaches such as Porter's "diamond" model of factor conditions that underlie their operation, to Patchell's exploration of the different ways in which the forces of competition, cooperation, and control are mediated.[6]

For Metro Vancouver, like Silicon Valley, high-tech clustering has been "organically" driven, initiated and largely sustained by local entrepreneurial companies. In contrast to Silicon Valley, notwithstanding its much smaller size, Metro Vancouver's high-tech sector is highly diverse, it lacks large-scale operations and core (giant or very large) high-tech firms, and many of its larger companies are foreign owned (many with Silicon Valley headquarters). As previously noted, its population pyramid is bottom heavy compared with that of Silicon Valley and other high-tech centres (see Figure 2.1). In 2020, for example, the majority of high-tech firms were small, with over 8,000 of the 11,000 estimated high-tech firms in British Columbia having fewer than ten employees. Indeed, Metro Vancouver high tech has evolved around large numbers of small and medium-sized firms (SMEs) supplemented by a few "somewhat" larger locally and foreign-owned firms. With respect to individual clusters, studies of secondary wood manufacturing and new media (film and video) have pointed to "hybrid" behaviours that emphasize the highly varied, independent ("Marshallian") nature of SMEs, with ("flexibly specialized") inter-firm relations evident but relatively weak.[7]

Overall, Metro Vancouver's high-tech clusters are characterized more by active new firm formation, entrepreneurial spinoffs, and spillovers sharing understanding of how to start companies than they are by industry-specific information and ongoing inter-firm linkages. Typically, these clusters comprise specialist firms that pursue strategies of related diversification but with limited functional ties among them. There is considerable reliance on external connections – "mobile" external economies – with other places, often enabled through the "institutional proximity" of shared industry standards and regulations rather than the "geographic proximity" of co-location within Metro Vancouver.[8] Nevertheless, that such clusters generate varying degrees of "local buzz" and "untraded interdependencies" involving informal exchanges of information, not least in meetings and workshops organized by industry associations (see Chapter 5), can be acknowledged.[9] Metro Vancouver's high-tech clusters might not be intensively interactive, but they are not simply congregations of isolated (locally disconnected) operations either.

This chapter begins to probe the nature of high-tech clustering in Metro Vancouver by outlining functional classifications of high-tech activities as a prelude to exploring business behaviour and inter-firm relations in several high-profile clusters, including telecommunications, life sciences, and new media. We also discuss the implications of convergent technologies, which occur when different kinds of technology platforms are combined to create new "hybrid" applications,[10] as extensions of life science and renewable energy clusters. With respect to sources of information, we draw from and update previous studies of telecommunications, life sciences, and new media as seen from cluster perspectives.[11] More recent data on these clusters and information on other clusters, including convergent technology examples, have been drawn from author surveys and various other sources.[12] In the next chapter, we elaborate on the role of high-tech business clusters with respect to their influence on deepening support institutions in the public and private sectors that collectively define Metro Vancouver's high-tech regional innovation system, providing further insights into whether the region's high tech reflects a high- or low-road trajectory of development.

In general, attention to clustering recognizes that local development is driven not simply by the internal abilities of firms but also by how they stimulate external economies, in the first instance with other firms. Local multiplier effects within clusters can generate the most direct and desired impacts in this regard, but global connections are also necessary to support local firms and local development and to avoid "regional lock-in" by providing outside perspectives, especially in an emerging high-tech sector in peripheral places such as Metro Vancouver. Indeed, clustering is important to individual firms (in accessing external economies), industrial sectors (by providing collective benefits and improving resilience), and the region (through related diversification of market opportunities and occupations). Clustering processes also help to appreciate the extent to which the competitive and cooperative interrelations among firms enhance regional competitive advantages.

In terms of the format of the chapter, first we briefly review the classifications of high-tech activities within Metro Vancouver on the basis of related functional types. We then explore in more detail how individual clusters are organized, especially with respect to a long-standing cluster (telecommunications), a growing but still volatile cluster (life sciences), and a growing and thriving cluster (new media). In the last section, we briefly illustrate how innovations that derive from technological convergence have developed in Metro Vancouver, especially as related to clean energy and life sciences. Throughout the discussion, we note the relative importance of local versus global connections, including the impact of FDI.

Classifying High Tech

It is not easy to classify high-tech activities in Metro Vancouver, even in simple descriptive (functional) terms of what they actually supply. Given the difficulties of defining precisely high tech (see the introduction), these activities are highly varied, new, and different, and they do not always fit readily into established categories; they are also dynamic and can be organized by firms diversified across technology boundaries themselves. Moreover, "convergent" technologies create new "hybrid" applications, and individual firms can serve distinct markets. In practice, just about all activities utilize microelectronics, the basis of ICT, and there are other new platform technologies, such as biotechnology and nanotechnology, that intimate convergent tendencies in developing innovative outcomes in Metro Vancouver. Reports on high tech themselves vary in terms of aggregating activities according to clusters or simply to industry groupings.

Given the difficulties of aggregation, an appreciation of the clustered diversity of high tech in Metro Vancouver was given particular profile by publication of the "tech maps" by PricewaterhouseCoopers (PwC), first published in 1997. These maps categorized high-tech activities based on their industry-technology focus, common corporate ancestry, and the splintering of firms through new spinoffs as the basis for summarily organizing their diversity that was gathering momentum in the 1990s. Indeed, PwC's pioneering work preceded the formal promotion of claims for a cluster-based economic development strategy by the provincial government. In general, all BC government–sponsored and related high-tech reports have summarized data on high-tech activities according to subindustries in which constituent firms represent broadly similar functional types (see Table I.3 and below). These surveys usefully communicate key features of local specialties and provide the springboard for more detailed anatomies of individual clusters that reveal the nature of inter-firm relationships, control, and governance.

Functional Types of High-Tech Clusters

PwC's functional classifications qua clusters of high-tech activities in British Columbia provide a comparative static representation of changes for the period 2002–12 (see Table 4.1). Although provincial in scope, the majority (85 percent in 1997 and over 82 percent in 2003 and 2012) are located in Metro Vancouver ("Vancouver and suburbs"), and the sample size is unusually large, with the main exclusions being "tiny" operations.[13] Although not stated precisely, the firms so identified are dependent to an important degree on RD&D in relatively new spheres of activity. PwC's first tech map survey in 1997 identified 410 businesses categorized into nine clusters, with the largest three categories accounting for 78 percent of the sampled population. Subsequent surveys revealed an even more diversified population of high-tech firms and an expansion of the cluster categories. Thus, in the 2012–13 survey, 1,389 firms were recorded and allocated across eleven clusters, with the largest three (software, advanced manufacturing, and electronics) accounting for 63 percent of firms (see Table 4.1).

In these surveys, the top three categories in 1997 (software, electronics and peripherals, and telecommunications) had all expanded by 2003 but had become proportionately less important as firms in other activities grew in number. Individual categories also hide considerable internal variation, with software applications being especially amorphous in this regard. Nevertheless, these maps potentially suggest clusters of activities without

TABLE 4.1 "Snapshot" of British Columbia's high-tech companies as classified in PricewaterhouseCoopers' tech maps, 1997, 2003, 2012

Activity	1997	2003	2012
Software	144 (35%)	309 (34%)	387 (28%)
Digital media	8 (2%)	91 (10%)	125 (9%)
Semiconductors	4 (1%)	9 (1%)	
Mobile and web			138 (10%)
Advanced manufacturing and semiconductors	53 (13%)	118 (13%)	180 (13%)
Cloud integration			14 (1%)
Energy technology	8 (2%)	36 (4%)	42 (3%)
Electronics and peripherals	107 (26%)	137 (15%)	208 (15%)
Clean technology			42 (3%)
Telecommunications and wireless	70 (17%)	127 (14%)	111 (8%)
Services and analytics	12 (3%)	55 (6%)	55 (4%)
Life sciences	4 (1%)	27 (3%)	69 (5%)
Total number	410 (349)	910 (753)	1383 (1139)

Notes: Percentages in parentheses refer to the activity's share of the total for each year shown. The overall number of businesses is listed in an inset figure on the 2013 tech map, with over 80 percent in "Vancouver and suburbs." Not included are public research organizations and another 490 "small firms" known to PwC but not documented. Although companies can operate in several categories, the above distributions assign each company to one dominant type. Because of rounding to single digits, there are small discrepancies between totals listed and activity numbers. Semiconductors were eliminated as a separate category and included in advanced manufacturing in 2012.
Source: PwC, *Tech Map of BC 2013*.

indicating much about the nature of inter-firm linkages and the sharing of information, with one important caveat. In particular, numerous connections are noted in the movement of key people (owners, decision makers) between companies, specifically through the formation of spinoffs. Indeed, such connections are extensive and help to underline the entrepreneurial vitality of Metro Vancouver high tech. Even so, spinoff dynamics themselves do not inform the nature of cluster governance, the extent of subcontracting relations, cooperation regarding innovation, the extent to which rivalrous firms add to local competitiveness and flexibility in responding to market opportunities, or the presence or not of anchor companies.

Unfortunately, the kind of detailed survey data collected on these maps has not been continued since 2012, no doubt in part because of their cost and time-consuming nature. Rather, recent profiles and functional classifications

TABLE 4.2 British Columbia's high-tech employment in manufacturing
and services

Industry	2006	2008	2016	2018
Manufacturing	15,480	15,390	15,350	16,100
Services	70,300	78,990	94,640	107,060
Film, post-film production	5,820	5,690	8,890	11,210
Telecommunications	13,160	13,110	13,430	20,040
Engineering	13,180	15,230	17,290	17,170
Software	7,390	8,500	8,260	9,170
Other computer	18,740	20,220	29,380	32,060
Other services	12,010	16,230	17,390	17,430
High-technology total	85,770	94,380	106,430	123,160
BC employment total	1,828,070	1,944,750	2,132200	2,285,740

Sources: BC Stats, *Profile of the British Columbia High Technology Sector 2017 Edition* (Victoria: Prepared for Ministry of Jobs, Recovery and Innovation, 2017, by Dan Schrier); BC Stats, *Profile of the British Columbia High Technology Sector 2020 Edition* (Victoria: Prepared for Ministry of Jobs, Recovery and Innovation, 2021, by Dan Schrier).

of high tech have been based on census data that do not reveal information on specific firms and are highly aggregated in nature. Recent summaries of high tech in British Columbia by KPMG, for example, provide information on just five broad subsector categories, namely ICT, Interactive and Digital Media, IT/Engineering, Life Sciences, and Clean Technology, without providing much information on any one.[14] Relatedly, BC Stats has published data on high-tech employment in manufacturing and six service categories labelled somewhat differently from KPMG's schema, including a reference to film production (see Table 4.2). In this schema, apart from film and post-production film activities, the identified categories are not especially self-explanatory but highly varied, including the two largest and fastest growing categories of "other computer services" and telecommunications, respectively expanding by 71 percent and 52 percent according to these data. Although these two categories accounted for 44 percent of high-tech service employment in 2016, they likely operate across the economy, including in the resource and transportation sectors. A similar point can be made for engineering and other services that grew by 42 percent and 30 percent, respectively, between 2006 and 2018.

The relatively small high-tech manufacturing segment is also highly diversified, with BC Stats indicating that in 1995 communication equipment, office and business machines, and aircraft parts accounted for 65.6 percent of its total, with the remaining jobs spread over ten other categories. Overall, however, services are clearly dominant in the high-tech sector and increasingly so. Between 2006 and 2018, high-tech employment in manufacturing remained more or less the same, and services expanded by 52.3 percent in this period. As of 2018, BC Stats estimated provincial high-tech employment at 123,160, with 87 percent of jobs in high-tech services and from 70 percent to 75 percent located within Metro Vancouver. In total, in 2019, the high-tech sector accounted for just less than 7 percent of provincial GDP and generated revenues of almost $35 billion. In the next section, we explore in more detail the evolution of three clusters particularly recognized in Metro Vancouver, with an emphasis on their inter-firm (local and global) relations.

Cluster Organization and Dynamics: Case Studies

Summarizing the evolving organization of high tech in Metro Vancouver is not straightforward in the sense that simple stereotypes are not present. For example, there are no "hub and spoke" models dominated by giant companies that organize structured, stable relations with suppliers in some way. Neither are the clusters organized solely by SMEs or branch plants of MNCs. Rather, cluster organization in the region illustrates in-between cases in which many SMEs are supplemented by larger firms, locally and foreign owned. In turn, this organization contributes to both local and global connections, although Marshallian SME independence and the affiliations of branch plants to parent companies imply "weak" local connections. Even so, the "strength of weak ties" among a population of firms – in terms of generating multiplier effects, creating spinoffs, and enabling an agility of response as new opportunities emerge, including boundary-breaking (convergent) practices that cut across recognized clusters – needs to be recognized.[15] Such ties among high-tech clusters around the world are highly varied and can relate to supply sources, marketing, financing, and technological expertise, and they can be traded as part of the price system or untraded.[16]

In Metro Vancouver, the emergent clustering of high-tech firms around the theme of inter-firm (business) ties and collaborations within and beyond the region has been particularly well explored in the telecommunications, medical biotechnology (or life sciences or biomedical), and new media (film and video) industries. These case studies (along with clean energy discussed in the next section) are relatively high profile and comprise important components of high tech within the region. To appreciate further its diversity, other clusters can be noted, including the example of a few small submersible vehicle manufacturers. These firms are locally owned and innovative, and though well known to each other they are not functionally connected and might be summarized best as a (tiny) congregation of otherwise independent (Marshallian) firms (see Case Study 4.1). On a more substantial scale, Ballard Power Systems and Westport Innovations are key firms in a clean-tech cluster focused on energy (see Chapter 2 and Appendix 1) that has expanded by innovations in carbon capture, as led by Svante (Burnaby) and Carbon Engineering (Squamish), and by initiatives in convergent technology (as discussed below).[17] As a service sector example, a cluster of fintech firms has also grown rapidly in recent years, with blockchain a recognized subsector and Metro Vancouver the location of the world's first Bitcoin ATM.

CASE STUDY 4.1 **Submersible Vehicle Producers in Metro Vancouver: A Tiny, Innovative Congregation in the Global Eye**

Since the 1960s, several relatively small entrepreneurial and highly innovative businesses designing and manufacturing small submersible vehicles and related equipment have developed in Metro Vancouver, led by Nuytco Research, International Submarine Engineering (ISE), Hyco Technologies, and Oceanworks International and including others, such as International VentureCraft, Atlantis Submarines, and Aquatica Submarines. Nuytco was formed by Phil Nuytten around the late 1990s in North Vancouver as an extension of an earlier company, Can-Dive, which opened in 1966. Nuytco became the R&D arm and Can-Dive was replaced by Hard Suits. ISE was founded in 1974 in Port Coquitlam by Dr. Jim MacFarlane as a spinoff from International Hydrodynamics, established in North Vancouver in 1962 by two commercial divers and a machinist who designed the famous, pioneering Pisces series of submarines, manufactured until the late 1970s, when the firm folded, with Hyco Technologies of Vancouver subsequently obtaining its technology. Oceanworks International was founded as an offshoot of Can-Dive in 1986 in North Vancouver before moving to Burnaby in expanded facilities in 2010 and taken over by US investment interests in 2014. International VentureCraft started in 1987 in Port Coquitlam.

In the 1960s, diving interests provided the stimulus to Metro Vancouver becoming a global leader of submersible technology design and production. Don Sorte and Al Trice were two commercial divers who recognized the potential of

Telecommunications Cluster

Within Metro Vancouver, telecommunications have relatively long roots through the locally based Electronic Laboratories of Canada (see Case Study 1.1) and the foreign-owned Lenkurt Electric Company (1949), while the predecessors of Telus also existed since the early twentieth century (and IBM had a small office in Vancouver). However, the modern origin of and principal impetus to the growth of the telecommunications cluster in Metro Vancouver were led by Glenayre (1963) and local spinoffs, notably MDI (1979, an MDA spinoff) and MPR Teltech (1979, a Telus spinoff), and by Sierra Systems (1966) that was established to supply IT consulting services. These locally based firms were relatively high profile (see Appendix 1), and their growth in the 1970s and 1980s did much to recruit a large pool of engineering talent.[18]

small submersible vehicles and robots in their work, and they helped to found International Hydrodynamics. That company subsequently designed and built fourteen (three-person) submersibles (by the late 1970s) in the Pisces range that provided exploration and research capabilities. Meanwhile, Phil Nuytten had opened Vancouver's first scuba retail shop before leaving high school prior to graduation and then became a commercial diver and opening his first company in 1965 (Can-Dive), replaced by Nuytco Research in the late 1990s. As Metro Vancouver's submersible technology flourished, ISE and Nuytco Research (and as Can-Dive) became the leading innovators; the former employed over 100 employees, with sales between $20 and $50 millon at its peak, but by 2021 it had declined to 25 employees, with sales between $5 and $10 million (c. 2018). Nuytco Research had about 20–25 employees, with sales in the range of $1–$5 million.

The bigger but still relatively small firm ISE (and ISE Research) developed around telerobotics for submarine work in the oil and gas sector around the world; for the Canadian, American, Australian, and French navies; and for the Japanese military. ISE designs and manufactures remotely operated vehicles, autonomous underwater vehicles, manned vehicles, semi-submersibles, plus various robotic manipulators, with many products representing global firsts and customization. By 2018, ISE had delivered over 200 underwater vehicles and over 400 robotic manipulators. The company developed a supplier network and links with research laboratories established at SFU and UVic (see Chapter 6).

▶

◄

At Nuytco, Phil Nuytten patented numerous products, most famously the Newtsuit in 1986, which uses a rotary arm design and allows "one-atmosphere" (no decompression is needed) deep-sea diving at much lower cost than established practice. Exosuit ADS is another patented ultralight "hard suit" introduced in 2000, and it was rated for 1,000-foot dives by 2010. Since 1985, Nuytco has also developed and patented several types of submersibles, most recently a "flying" model in 2010 and an all-electric remotely operated vehicle in 2016, and in 2018 he was planning experiments for an underwater community. Nuytten was also a co-founder of Oceaneering International, established around 1970 and then sold to a Houston-based company, becoming one of the world's largest underwater contractors, before buying back his original Can-Dive Company in 1979 (50 percent) and 1984 (the other 50 percent). Nuytco's markets have been global, serving the Canadian government's exploration and testing in the Arctic, facilitating oil and gas exploration, supplying Hollywood films such as *Titanic* with submersibles, and undertaking various deep-sea missions, not least for missing space shuttles.

Both ISE and Nuytco Research have been involved with astronaut training for Canada and NASA. Both companies and founding entrepreneurs have received awards for their innovativeness, which included for Nuytten the Order of Canada (2017); as a Métis, he is also an (Indigenous) artist and published author. He died in 2023.

Although ISE and Nuytco are well known to each other, and to other companies with related products, they have operated independently as a congregation rather than a tightly knit cluster. Spinoffs have been important, local machinists have been utilized, and these two leading companies developed high levels of internal manufacturing capability, and products typically are customized. An ISE respondent reported in the late 1990s that, following a seminar on clusters by a Silicon Valley expert, the provincial government, which had organized the seminar, requested a contribution of $75,000. ISE declined the request, apparently with force and some amusement.

Sources: S. McGinty, *The Dive: The Untold Story of the World's Deepest Submarine Rescue* (Toronto: Pegasus, 2021); V. Jensen, *Deep, Dark and Dangerous: The Story of British Columbia's World Class Undersea Tech Industry* (Victoria: Harbour Publishing, 2021); N. Bennett, "B.C. Pioneering Undersea Business Boom," *Technology*, July 12, 2016, https://biv.com/article/2016/07/bc-pioneering-undersea-business-boom. For newspaper stories on Nuytco Research, see R. Richter, "Undersea Tech Pioneer Joins Order of Canada," *North Shore News*, August 25, 2012, www.news.com/local-news/north-vancoiuver-underseas-tech-giant-joins-order-of-canada; and A.A. Davis, "The Prolific Canadian Inventor behind the 'Ironsuit,'" *Maclean's*, June 23, 2021, https://macleans.ca/society/the-prolific-canadian-inventor-behind-the-ironsuit/.

As the largest, Glenayre developed fully integrated and discrete telecom-munications products, although most firms in the cluster supplied modular components that process, coordinate, and transfer information using com-puter, cellular, or radio technologies. About half of the telecommunications sector in Metro Vancouver was foreign owned by the mid-1990s, employing about half of the total workforce of around 3,800.

Two independent studies have examined the extent and nature of collab-orations within the telecommunications cluster: the Rees study sampled eleven firms from a total of about fifty firms in the late 1990s, ranging in size from 21 to 780 employees, with six externally owned (either the United States or Ontario); and the Langford, Wood, and Jacobson sampled forty-six firms out of about seventy a few years later.[19] The former study found that just over half of the sampled firm collaborations (60 of 112) recorded within the telecommunications cluster were with other organizations located out-side Metro Vancouver and that, during the RD&D process itself, most col-laborations emphasized applied research and prototype development to facilitate user-producer integration, particularly with respect to utility pro-viders located elsewhere. Most local collaborations involved prototype developments but were much fewer in number and of relatively low value. Although licensing of research from US-based MNCs occurred, external collaborations were predominantly with the rest of Canada and not espe-cially sophisticated. In practice, as an illustration of institutional proximity, among telecommunications firms, external contacts focused largely on en-suring the compatibility of modular components with hardware from Original Equipment Manufacturers (OEMs), involvement in standard set-ting of new hardware and software protocols, and beta testing of new tele-communications technologies with customers in larger markets than Metro Vancouver. Indeed, external and especially local technological liaisons were shown to be relatively few and weak. Rather, local embeddedness in tele-communications was mainly created by local knowledge among engineers and diffused by their movement among firms, often resulting in new firm formation as the main path of cluster growth. The sense of a weakly con-nected cluster, especially in terms of formal inter-firm relationships, was reinforced by the Langford, Wood, and Jacobson analysis of wireless busi-nesses in Metro Vancouver that further emphasized that the closures of three leading and potential anchor firms (Glenayre, MDI, and MPR Teltech) were a big blow to aspirations for the cluster's viability.

Yet, notwithstanding the closures of three leading pioneering firms, in the past two decades telecommunications employment in British Columbia,

TABLE 4.3 Number of firms in British Columbia's telecommunications industries

2008	2009	2010	2016	2018	2019
293	287 (210)	282	294	731	720 (494)

Note: For 2009 and 2019, the numbers in parentheses refer to microfirms with one to nine employees.
Sources: BC Stats, *Profile of the British Columbia High Technology Sector 2017 Edition* (Victoria: Prepared for Ministry of Jobs, Recovery and Innovation, 2017, by Dan Schrier); BC Stats, *Profile of the British Columbia High Technology Sector 2020 Edition* (Victoria: Prepared for Ministry of Jobs, Recovery and Innovation, 2021, by Dan Schrier).

located mostly in Metro Vancouver, remained stable until experiencing a sharp spurt in growth after 2016 (see Table 4.2). This employment jump was accompanied by rapid growth in telecommunications firms, most of which were small (see Table 4.3).

Indeed, microfirms employing fewer than nine workers in 2019 more than doubled their 2009 numbers, and if their relative share declined it still amounted to 69 percent of industry employment in 2019. Moreover, between 2009 and 2019, firms that employed from ten to forty-nine workers increased almost fourfold, from 55 to 199, with their share of industry jobs rising from 19 percent to 28 percent. That is, in 2019, firms with fewer than fifty jobs accounted for 98 percent of the total number of firms in telecommunications. For sure, the few relatively large firms, led by Telus and Sierra Wireless, account for a significant share of industry employment, with Telus having expanded substantially locally since 2016 (see Table 4.2).[20] At the same time, new firm formation and an entrepreneurial culture remain evident and have helped the industry to diversify to embrace innovative artificial intelligence (AI) activities, led by companies such as D-Wave (see Appendix 1) and Fujitsu (see Appendix 2). Moreover, within Metro Vancouver's telecommunications cluster, Telus is clearly a big firm locally but somewhat of a puzzle whether it is, or could be, an anchor firm (see Case Study 4.2). Although it is a powerful firm in the telecommunications cluster, there is a sense that its R&D and manufacturing uninterest so far have meant that its potential as a local leader has not been fully realized, or even desired.

Life Sciences (Biomedical) Cluster

Kevin Rees's analysis of the telecommunications cluster also involved a comparison with an emergent medical biotechnology cluster, now more commonly labelled the life sciences cluster (see Tables 4.1 and 4.2).[21] Medical biotech (meditech) expanded rapidly in the 1980s and 1990s, with leading companies including QLT, Angiotech, and Stemcell Technologies formed at

CASE STUDY 4.2 **Telus: An Anchor High-Tech Firm?**

Telus was established in 1990 by the Alberta government to control telecommunications in its province. In 1999 Telus merged with BC Tel to form BCT. Telus Communications, with headquarters in Metro Vancouver, becoming Telus in 2000. As with other major telecommunication firms across Canada FDI in Telus is restricted.

It is a puzzle thinking about Telus as a core company in Metro Vancouver. It has basic statistical credentials to be thought of as a large mid-sized company focused on the telecommunications sector, usually considered quintessentially as high tech. In 2018, Telus had revenues of CDN $14.4 billion, 58,000 employees, capital expenditures of almost $3 billion, and R&D expenditures of $303 million. In 2020 and 2021, Research Infosource recorded its R&D expenditures at $799 million and $553 million, respectively, among businesses, easily the largest in British Columbia and the third largest in Canada, and focused primarily on the long-term evolution of its communications networks. From 2007 to 2019, Telus spent about $900 million on R&D. In 2021, revenues reached over $17.3 billion, when its R&D intensity, as measured by R&D budgets to revenues, was 4.6 percent (as in previous years). The web indicates that Telus has submitted eighty-four patents globally, mostly in Canada (twenty-three) and the United States (eleven); twenty-six have been granted. It is an MNC with operations around the world, with about half its workforce located in Canada. About 10,000 or so employees are located in British Columbia, including about 1,000 in its Vancouver head office and R&D centre. (Other R&D units are in Canada, the United States, and India and collectively employ 600.) In the mid-1970s, BC Tel consolidated numerous Vancouver-based offices in a major head office building in Burnaby (just outside the Vancouver-Burnaby border). Although this office still functions, in 2015 Telus built a new head office in downtown Vancouver.

Moreover, Telus is a homegrown company with long roots in British Columbia, with its beginnings in 1891 in the Vernon and Nelson Telephone Company, which subsequently acquired smaller companies, becoming BC Tel in 1904 and receiving a federal charter in 1916 to control telephone services within the province (and beyond). From the 1920s, BC Tel became controlled by a Montreal-based subsidiary of the GTE Corporation of Stamford, Connecticut. Although GTE remains a shareholder, it lost its controlling interest in 1988 when Telus was created by a merger between BC Tel and its Alberta counterpart. Prior to this

▶

merger, in 1979, BC Tel influenced the early development of high tech in Metro Vancouver through its Microtel subsidiary spinoff, which incorporated Microtel Pacific Research, renamed MPR Teltech in 1987, which became an influential incubator of numerous companies developing its innovations (see Chapter 3 and Appendix 1).

Yet caveats to the credentials of Telus as a core high-tech company can be made. Like its predecessor, BC Tel, Telus primarily emphasizes its role as a utility providing services to customers. These services are sophisticated and require sophisticated technological support, and Telus receives revenues from its patents. Even so, it does not highlight itself as an innovator, and it has not wished to be much involved in manufacturing activities – Microtel was spun off as a manufacturing company and to look after innovation potential via MPR/MPR Teltech. Indeed, MPR Teltech was remarkably successful in this regard and the incubator of numerous companies using its innovations. Yet BC Tel chose to close MPR Teltech in 1996 (exiting its SFU Discovery Park location in Burnaby in 1997), sell off its activities in piecemeal manner, and focus on its core business of service provision, possibly in response to the deregulation of the telecommunications market at the time. For Nick Waddell, the selling of MPR assets was "one of the worst examples of foresight in telecommunications history" – illustrated by the selling of the future massively successful ATM technology for "chump change" to an Ontario company that eventually sold the technology to a French MNC for a considerable sum. He makes a similar point about the sale of PMC to Sierra Conductor of California (see Appendix 1). Furthermore, the patenting activity of Telus is not particularly noteworthy for a company of its size and level of R&D expenditures. Neither Telus nor reports on British Columbia's high tech see the company as a local champion of innovation. Rather, it seems to represent a technologically advanced but defensive/dependent company relying on its abilities to implement efficiently the latest developments originating elsewhere. Nevertheless, Telus is big locally, raising the question that, if Metro Vancouver needs a champion of technology, could Telus still evolve into this role?

Notes: As a public corporation, Telus publishes its annual report, readily available on the web. Although much financial data are reported, typically R&D costs are not. However, the R&D expenditures of Telus for 2020 and 2021 are documented in "Canada's Top 100 Corporate R&D Spenders," Research Infosource, 2022, https://researchinfosource.com/top-100-corporate-rd-spenders/2022/list; N. Waddell "Waiting on a Leader: Vancouver's Tech History," Cantech Letter January 27, 2010, https://www.cantechletter.com/2010/01/looking-for-a-leader-vancouvers-tech-history.

that time, with Zymeworks and AbCellera Biologics coming later (see Appendix 1). Out of an estimated total of fifty meditech firms, Rees's study of the situation in the late 1990s sampled sixteen firms, which ranged in size from 8 to 125 employees, including the then two largest in Metro Vancouver. As this study noted, though telecommunications firms often originated through business spinoffs, the meditech cluster featured several firms originating as UBC spinoffs. These firms typically focused on the upstream RD&D stages of drug discovery, especially with respect to applied research, up to and including the point of preclinical trials, and grew out of basic research programs, with their subsequent applied focus often involving contracts with local nonprofit research agencies such as the BC Cancer Agency. Although this cluster of firms has targeted developing biopharmaceutical and biodiagnostic products for global markets, especially the United States, setting up expensive preclinical trials and commitments to commercialization have depended on collaborations with pharmaceutical giants distant from Metro Vancouver, with manufacturing and marketing predominantly taking place outside Canada. In practice, though only two of the sampled firms had created goods commercially produced by 2000, the RD&D focus and organization of this cluster have remained the same during its subsequent growth, reaching ninety companies in 2009, then reputedly the seventh largest in North America and the fastest growing in Canada (but smaller than the Toronto and Montreal clusters).

Despite the local roots of these firms, most of their collaborations were with organizations located outside Metro Vancouver and usually beyond Canada. Thus, of the 113 collaborations identified by Rees, 77 percent were nonlocal. In general, most local collaborations focused on applied and development research with local public institutions, especially UBC and the BC Cancer Research Agency, and most nonlocal collaborations were with large corporations in the private sector. The latter focused on preclinical and clinical trials and subsequent downstream activities such as manufacturing, frequently involving a joint venture or strategic alliance with a major pharmaceutical MNC. Nonlocal links were geographically varied, but in contrast to telecommunications firms they tended to be more sophisticated in nature and were more focused on the United States (many locations), with some links to sources in Asia, Ontario, and Quebec. Although a few clinical trials were held in Vancouver, along with some applied research collaborations with external organizations, the importance of nonlocal trends in these regards is illustrated by reference to the largest respondent firm,

QLT. In its case, basic research was licensed from the United States in 1987, applied research involved collaboration with and financing from another US company, and following an R&D program costing $75 million sales began around the world in 1998. QLT established strategic alliances with nine foreign companies to reduce the financial burdens of clinical trials, production, and marketing, with the latter two organized variously by American, French, Japanese, and British companies. QLT also established technology co-development alliances with two California companies, to develop the hardware component of its new cancer treatment, and two Swiss companies, for the joint development and sale of ophthalmic applications of the drug. In contrast, there were no collaborations with Metro Vancouver firms.

Although local collaborations tended to be "horizontal" between university researchers and not-for-profit research institutions and cluster firms, nonlocal collaborations tended to be corporate and "vertical" in nature, with drug "candidates" being passed on to large pharmaceutical firms based outside the region. The expenses of rigorous clinical trials, the relatively small population of Metro Vancouver in which to conduct clinical trials, and the investment and operating costs of large-scale production facilities have encouraged small Metro Vancouver meditech firms to look globally to access many necessary inputs of materials, processes, know-how, and financial support. This "upstream" focus of British Columbia's medical biotechnology cluster has resulted in a strategic focus on developing expertise in drug discovery, asserting intellectual property, identifying external collaborators, and attracting potential buyers for drug candidates under development or purchase of the entire company. Conversely, expertise in manufacturing, marketing, and distribution of products is rare locally. In the exceptional case in which a Metro Vancouver firm manufactured its pharmaceutical product itself, production was located in China, which in turn limited the product's marketability in North America and Europe because of regulatory constraints. That is, external collaborations have been vital to the commercialization plans of Metro Vancouver's biopharmaceutical or life sciences firms.

The overall nature and scope of the life sciences cluster in Metro Vancouver – broadly including health governance, medical and related faculties, doctors, hospitals, clinics, and biotechnology businesses – as revealed by Rees' early study remains evident. The cluster has been vibrant and grown but also volatile, and faces considerable technological, financing and marketing uncertainties with profitability a challenge. UBC continues as a remarkably fecund incubator of life science firms, but most are small, indeed tiny, and smaller than the Canadian average. Local strengths in life sciences are rooted in pioneering research with development and commercialization dependent on external collaborations, especially with giant MNCs. With respect to UBC's incubator role and firm size, for example, some years ago in a listing of "success stories," reported by its UILO office for the period 2005–16, Kardium, Boreal Genomics and Aquinox Pharmaceutical were among the largest, but then just with 103, 50, and 24 employees, respectively (see Case Study 4.3).[22]

Prior to Kardium's recent growth spurt, a few other life science companies that had become relatively large had emerged. Among companies still operating, Stemcell is the largest, with employment in 2014 of 482, over 1,058 by 2019, and about 2,000 in 2022 in its Metro Vancouver facilities. Zymeworks has reached 250 employees, and AbCellera Biologics had 386 employees by 2019 and has grown since then (see Appendix 1). Before their demise, QLT employed 336, and Angiotech reached 2,000 employees, mostly located elsewhere. All of these firms had important connections to UBC research: Stemcell and AbCellera (and QLT and Angiotech) as professorial spinoffs and Zymeworks by a former PhD student. Both Stemcell and AbCellera, among several other smaller Metro Vancouver–based firms, were strongly active in developing treatments for COVID-19, the former in close collaboration with a Chinese research organization and the latter with the US Department of Defense.[24] Very few companies have scaled up beyond small.

In general, however, life sciences' high-tech activities in Metro Vancouver are dominated by small firms, and the problems of scaling up are formidable. The risks in this field are unusually high and evident globally.[25] R&D is expensive and lengthy, and any resultant specialization is vulnerable to competition, failure, and inability to find replacement initiatives. Further, commercialization depends upon rigorous, trials and upon costly and equally time-consuming regulatory approval that Metro Vancouver firms typically seek in the US and Europe where the largest market potentials exist. It can be well over a decade to move from lab to trials. Even with approval market networks are needed. Many SMEs do not develop successfully, and leading high-profile firms such as QLT and Angiotech have failed (see Appendix 1), the former's experience already noted (see Chapter 2).

In the case of Angiotech, established in 1992 as an R&D-intensive company spun out from the pharmaceutical department at UBC, it focused on cancer-fighting agents as coatings and innovative medical devices. Its Paclitaxel-coated stents help to fight scar formation after cancer surgery

CASE STUDY 4.3 **Leading Examples of UBC's Recent Life Sciences Spinoffs, 2005–16**

The University-Industry Liaison Office (UILO) of UBC identifies numerous life sciences companies as commercially successful spinoffs between 2005 and 2016. The leading three in terms of jobs created are Kardium, Boreal Genomics, and Aquinox Pharmaceuticals, respectively generating 103, 50, and 24 jobs prior to 2016.

Kardium,was co-founded in 2007 by Dan Gelbart and Amos Michelson, respectively the founder and CEO of Creo, where they were working until its acquisition by Kodak in 2005 (see Appendix 1); Dr. Sam Lichtenstein (the head of UBC's cardiac surgery division); and Doug Goertzen. Located in Burnaby, the newly formed company took eleven years and several prototypes to develop the Globe Mapping and Ablation System to treat atrial fibrillation (irregular heartbeats), a widespread condition. Kardium has relied mainly on private investors for funds, and its system was first approved in Europe in 2020 where sales have started. Kardium is also targeting the US market and will likely start sales in Canada in 2020. In early 2021, important funding was obtained to promote commercialization (Silcoff 2021). By 2023 Kardium employed up to 330, sales were over $50 million, and the firm had submitted 257 patents and 168 had been granted, including forty developed by Gelbart. This recent expansion also means Kardium is becoming a large SME, or perhaps larger; it is further distinguished by performing the planning, manufacturing, and distribution of its device in its Burnaby facility, without seeking strategic ties with the giants.[23]

Started in 2007, Boreal Genomics was founded by Andre Marziali, a professor of engineering physics at UBC. It is a campus-based company focused on developing blood-testing instruments for cancer detection (Good 2017). The firm

and have been used on over 5 million patients. Its lead drug, Taxus, was licensed to Boston Scientific and launched in 2004, at the time one of the most successful medical products and second biggest drug launch in history, taking 70 percent of US market share and $1.4 billion in sales in its year of launch. By 2010, Angiotech had a worldwide workforce of 1,030, of which 752 were located in Vancouver. However, sales of Taxus stents declined sharply from 2005 to 2010 because of competition and clinical concerns about a slightly higher risk of late-stent thrombosis, resulting in a fall of opened an office in Silicon Valley in 2011, but this office was closed because of its high costs. Boreal first invented a machine (then developed in a basement) to separate DNA sequences from contaminants. After 2014 and some staff downsizing, the team focused on cancer testing, developing a machine (OnTarget) that separates DNA from tumour cells. Receiving support from UBC and having the spatial proximity enabled by the availability of suitable medical premises for start-ups allowed Marziali to keep his university post while running Boreal, which became profitable in 2016. The company now has less than five employees.

Aquinox Pharmaceutical was co-founded in 2006 by David Main and four scientists at UBC. It was based on the discovery of a new (SHIP1) enzyme (Pharma Boardroom 2018) for the development of small molecule therapeutics for the treatment of cancer and inflammatory diseases. The firm was private until 2014, merged with Neoleukin Therapeutics (Seattle) in 2019, and was acquired in 2020 by Sun Pharma of India for $8.2 million. It had an office in San Bruno, California, that provided information on US regulations. However, in 2018, Rospitor, the lead candidate for treating chronic pulmonary disease and bladder pain, failed in stage three trials. Half of the staff were let go, and the San Bruno office closed.

Sources: University of British Columbia, University-Industry Liaison Office (UILO), uilo.ubc.ca (accessed 2019); S. Silicoff, "B.C. Heart Device Firm Kardium Founded by Creo Executives Raises $115-million from Fidelty, T. Rowe Price Ahead of Going Public," January 25, 2021, https://www.theglobeandmail.com/business/article-bc-medical-device-firm-raises-115-million-from-us-fund-giants-ahead-of/; M. Good, "For Vancouver's Boreal Genomics, Home Proved a Better Bet than Silicon Valley," *BC Business*, March 27 2017, https://www.bcbusiness.ca/industries/tech-science/startups-boreal-genomics/; Pharma Boardroom, "Interview: David Main – CEO and President, Aquinox Phrmaceuticals, Canada" January 26, 2018, https://pharmaboardroom.com/interviews/interview-david-goodman-ceo-pharmascience-canada/.

royalty income from $181 million to $34 million over the period. The Quill knotless tissue closure system, which offered the prospect of diversifying the company's product portfolio, proved to be challenging to put into surgical practice through widespread adoption, not least because of the changes required in training and the surgical practice of using barbed sutures in wound closure, for benefits unclear to some in the medical community.[26] After a costly legal dispute, the firm filed for bankruptcy protection in 2011 to shed $250 million in debt, its share price fell from $25 to $0.79, and it was delisted from NASDAQ. Its story demonstrates the extreme highs and lows of innovation in the life sciences sector: "Once a beacon of hope for B.C.'s biotech industry, Angiotech has also become a lesson about how quickly dreams in this sector can shatter."[27] In 2017, Angiotech was bought by a syndicate led by global investment firm Vivo Capital for an undisclosed amount, primarily for its surgical device products, with a particular focus on expanding market penetration of its medical devices in China.

If the failings of QLT and Angiotech were disappointing and dampened cluster prospects, life sciences in Metro Vancouver have shown resilience and bounced back. According to a recent report the cluster has added 8,000 jobs since 2012 reaching a total of about 20,000 in 2023 and new start-ups are strong, built around "a tight-knit group of universities, agencies, institutes, associations, funders, academics and founders."[28] The two largest companies, Abcellera and Stemcell Technologies both earned considerable revenues recently, the latter reaching $543 million in 2023, and the cluster is presently buoyant. For one executive (of Aspect Biosystems, a still small company) "I want to build a $100 billion dollar company, but it has to be here."[29] Such boosterism can be appreciated. The life science cluster has grown impressively, it has made globally recognized distinctive research-driven substantive contributions, the academic-entrepreneurial culture is thriving, talent is readily attracted, and specialized infrastructure such as lab facilities and educational, financing and subsidy support have all increased (see Chapter 5). Several UBC spinoffs developed important innovations to combat COVID-19, and other serious health problems have been addressed. But as of 2023, there is still only one company that employs more than 2,000. Scaling up remains an issue, some university spinoffs never seem to leave campus, failures occur, and companies can exist for many years through grants, angel investments, and even IPOs without generating revenues or profits. Real estate is expensive and scarce, funding is a challenge and still US dependent, business leadership is an issue, the attractive proximity (and pull) of the US casts a big shadow, and the sense that the cluster is at "a crossroads" between greater or lesser "robustness" has been voiced.[30]

Moreover, this crossroads needs to confront the reality that a few huge pharmaceutical companies, primarily based in the United States and Germany, effectively control a global network of biomedical RD&D, of which Metro Vancouver is one source. Indeed, the dominance of links beyond Metro Vancouver in medical biotech, primarily with MNCs, should also be viewed from a cluster life cycle perspective, in which external collaborations provide access to critical capabilities currently underdeveloped or absent in an emerging cluster yet to develop the full range of functions. Whether the Metro Vancouver cluster can develop or attract these downstream functions is a matter of debate, especially given that the relatively small population of British Columbia is likely to limit its suitability for full-scale clinical trials. Even so, the substantial number of collaborations outside the meditech cluster provides access to outside expertise, extends local knowledge to new applications, and maintains openness to new markets and collaborators. This openness in turn helps to avoid regional lock-ins to outdated practices that can emerge from a dependence on local interactions that become parochial, enabling continued growth and renaissance in the cluster life cycle.[31] In this regard, in comparing the medical biotech and telecommunications clusters, though the quantity of inter-regional collaborations is similar, the quality of such collaborations in the latter suggests fewer opportunities for product development and cluster diversification, with a greater reliance on intracorporate channels of learning and higher risks of a local lock-in.

New Media Cluster

Among the diverse range of high-tech activities, the "new media cluster"[32] within Metro Vancouver, which features the integration of video game producers with film producers,[33] is especially high profile, distinctive, and associated with relatively strong local inter-firm connections. If the film industry can claim longer lineage in Metro Vancouver, the new media cluster has evolved mainly since the 1970s, facilitated by the arrival of several Hollywood films, the existence of a few locally based independent companies, the growth of the local video game industry sparked by Distinctive Software's formation in 1982 (acquired by Electronic Arts in 1991; Appendix 2) and its spinoffs, the setting up of the BC Film Commission in 1978, tax breaks for labour and visual effects, and the development of a productive workforce cooperatively organized by local unions.[34] Growth has been impressive, and in 2008 there were an estimated 569 firms in the new media cluster that, as with high-tech activities in Metro Vancouver in general, were mainly SMEs (and generally small). Among the video game cluster, with over 1,000 employees, Electronic Arts is probably the largest in an otherwise bottom-heavy size distribution of firms. Within Metro Vancouver, small firms tend to be concentrated in the core, especially in Yaletown, East Hastings, and around False Creek. Larger operations, such as the main campus of Electronic Arts and the five major film studios, are located in the adjacent inner suburbs of Burnaby, Richmond, and North Vancouver. A notable exception to the latter is the location of Sony Imagework's animation and visual effects studio, which employs about 800, in the heart of Vancouver, in the same building as Microsoft. The proximity of video game producers and film-based firms allows for ready networking with one another, and easy access to Vancouver's international airport (Richmond) facilitates same time zone–based contacts with Hollywood-based producers.

For the early 2000s, Barnes and Coe mapped the contours of the networking among video game and film producers across Metro Vancouver, drawing from and reinforcing a growing labour pool.[35] In terms of overall size, they estimated that the new media cluster employed around 14,000 in 2005, including about 3,500 in video games. As of 2018, this cluster had grown to include 16,100 in film and post-production (see Table 4.3) plus the video game and related components that probably amounted to about 4,000. As a cluster, new media are distinctive in several ways, most obviously by their focus on entertainment, in which symbolic knowledge and design activities are crucial rather than R&D per se.[36] The provincial government and labour unions have also played unusually proactive roles since the late 1970s, with the latter organizing a stable, cooperative, and productive workforce through collective bargaining. At the same time, the organization of this cluster features important controlling roles by large, foreign-owned firms, especially based in Hollywood, even as SMEs continue to play vital networking roles in the cluster's operations. One illustration is provided by Lux Visual Effects,[37] formed by five partners in 2005 as a spinoff from another computer design company. They started by supplying services to ZOIC BC (a Hollywood-based company focusing on animation) and then won contracts to supply 3D animation to Cinetal, a Hollywood B movie (mainly horror) producer.[38] Lux then gained other contracts with other Hollywood producers, especially in the horror genre. Located in downtown Vancouver among many other similar firms, Lux employed twenty people in 2016, eight permanent and twelve on contract, the latter a reflection of the business's volatility.[39]

The vitality and organization of this cluster remain intact. According to one study, using data from Creative BC, in 2018 there were 450 productions in British Columbia, mainly centred in Metro Vancouver, generating $3.4 billion for the provincial GDP, and at least 15,000 direct jobs, including video games, but possibly more.[40] Foreign and externally controlled companies accounted for 289 of these productions, with local firms organizing 163. In terms of the business population, by 2018 there were over 200 BC-based producers and over 250 local businesses that directly supplied motion picture production, including 65 film studios, 30 post-production companies, and 100 animation and visual effects companies. Metro Vancouver still claims to have the world's largest visual effects cluster. For the most part, the vast majority of visual effects activity within Metro Vancouver is for films made elsewhere. For example, *Maze Runner* was filmed in Louisiana and Capetown, *Independence Day Resurgence* in New Mexico and Utah, and *The Meg* in New Zealand and China, but all were supplied with visual effects by Metro Vancouver firms. As an exception to this tendency, *Deadpool 2* was filmed locally (and in Victoria) and served by local visual effects firms, and it generated over $100 million over eighty days of filming while supporting 3,000 jobs. Indeed, the growth in Metro Vancouver is spilling over into new facilities in the Okanagan (specifically Kelowna) and Vancouver Island.

Metro Vancouver's new media cluster competes with many other locations across North America. In this regard, tax breaks are important in coping with this competition, and builds upon the region's talent pool, specializations, and entrepreneurialism. Meanwhile, natural advantages in terms of the local access to mountains, rivers, and seascapes adjacent to a vibrant urban area provide both a range of locations for filming and important quality-of-life factors for attracting a creative workforce. Yet tax subsidies are often better elsewhere, and filming is extremely mobile geographically, making Metro Vancouver vulnerable to firms that leave the region for better deals elsewhere. The Moving Picture Company's (MPC) closure of its Vancouver office in 2019 to concentrate its Canadian operations in Montreal to obtain better tax breaks illustrates this vulnerability.[41] For Metro Vancouver, competitive advantages in new media[42] will continue to rely on the ability of its firms to compete for visual effects work on a contract basis.

Technology Convergence and Cluster Interdependence
Globally, technologies generated from different platforms are converging to support the emergence of innovative clusters. That evolution is exemplified by the application of genetic engineering that links life sciences research with a chemistry-oriented pharmaceuticals industry to produce "neutraceutical" food products and to connect nanotechnologies with the medical, clothing, and ICT industries to create various "healthware" products.[43] In British Columbia, such converging, "cross-boundary" clusters have been slow to develop. Nevertheless, the potential for technological convergence and cross-fertilization of knowledge between clusters has been recognized. Life Sciences BC, for example, stated that "arguably the most

important driver of the life sciences sector will be the convergence of technologies and medical devices. ICT, biotechnology, and digital and wireless technologies are coming together in an unprecedented manner. As the demand for innovative health technologies grows, BC is ... well-suited to meet the needs of the market."[44] Indeed, there is interest in applying wireless communication technologies to medical applications such as health monitoring or medical provision to all residents of British Columbia wherever located. In addition, within Metro Vancouver, new opportunities for convergence have emerged in response to the climate crisis by applying sustainable energy solutions to transportation and mobile devices, which might also help to revitalize resource towns throughout the province.

Although the extent to which convergent initiatives form new clusters within Metro Vancouver is uncertain, at least they offer the potential to diversify existing clusters, including in clean energy and life sciences. In these activities, noteworthy local firms pursuing technological convergence include Lignol Energy and Angstrom Power (clean energy) and Forbes Meditech and Wireless 2000 (life sciences).

Expanding Clean (Sustainable) Energy Initiatives
Lignol Energy was established in 2000 in Burnaby by Dr. Kendall Pye, a professor at the University of Pennsylvania, and became a public company on the Toronto Stock Exchange in 2007. Lignol illustrates convergence because its RD&D efforts linked technology from the life sciences (specifically biotech) with contributions from the forestry and agricultural sectors to develop a process for clean tech (a different cluster). Pye initially had developed this technology in the United States in collaboration with General Electric, and in a demonstration biorefinery opened in 2009 in Burnaby that converted polysaccharides from plant-based material into fermentable sugars for the production of fuel-grade ethanol. The company had moved to Burnaby for various reasons, including to access expertise within the clean technology cluster, a process led by the hiring of the new head of its RD&D laboratory in 2007 (a former UBC chemistry professor), followed by microbiologists, biotechnologists, biochemists, and organic chemists. The Burnaby location also provided access to the raw materials required by the pilot processing facility and a supply and research agreement with the forestry corporation Weyerhaeuser.

In broad terms, Lignol offered an innovation that differed from the hydrogen-based fuel focus of many local firms, led by Ballard (see Appendix 1) for cleaner energy, giving rise to provincial government aspirations for a biotechnology strategy that raised possibilities for biorefineries to locate in smaller communities throughout British Columbia and provide replacement jobs for declining commodity manufacturing. Indeed, such prospects stimulated its $9 million investment in the Burnaby biorefinery in 2009, including $3.4 million from the provincial government's Innovative Clean Energy Fund, in effect seeking to transform waste wood into liquid fuel. In practice, numerous projects throughout the province received financial support from the fund, and there were hopes of exports of green energy biofuels. However, for Lignol (and the biotechnology strategy), the potential was stunted. In 2015, the firm was acquired by Fibria Cellulose of Brazil to form Fibria Innovations, leaving its Burnaby research facility to continue as Fibrio Innovations but with few employees.

In the case of Angstrom Power, its RD&D efforts relate to Metro Vancouver's established expertise in clean technology centred on Ballard but in a new direction. Angstrom was established in North Vancouver in 2001 by Ged McLean following his departure from the University of Victoria, where he was a professor. His initial idea of small-scale but high-density fuel cells to explore the alternative application of hydrogen fuel cells beyond the automotive sector had been prompted by contacts with Geoffrey Ballard in the mid-1990s. However, his proposal to develop micro hydrogen fuel cells seems not to have been supported at UVic, and he quit his academic job to establish Angstrom, subsequently launching micro fuel cells in 2006. With Ballard's main thrust on relatively large fuel cells to power vehicles, Angstrom's micro fuel cells focused on rapid phone recharging, providing full power within minutes rather than hours of electrical charging, an important feature for users who have limited "downtime" to charge their phones during the day. The company illustrates convergence by its application of hydrogen fuel cells to wireless telecom devices, conventionally seen as two different clusters. For Angstrom, a North Vancouver location was advantageous in its recruitment of product engineers and managers with varied expertise from local fuel cell firms and the local wireless cluster as well as specialists in hydraulics from a locally based pleasure boat firm. In effect, the firm assembled a local multidisciplinary team with expertise in chemistry, electronics, and mechanical engineering to create its competitive advantage, and proximity to other fuel cell firms was vital for accessing the relatively small volumes of material supplies from which to fabricate their components.

Angstrom Power's rapid success led to its acquisition in 2011 by the Canadian subsidiary of French corporation BIC (Société Bic S.A.) for CDN

$18.7 million. For BIC, this acquisition illustrated horizontal integration qua related diversification of its established expertise in replaceable fuel cell cartridges for a variety of consumer products. Meanwhile, Angstrom's operations and its twenty-three employees continued with a globally mandated specialty (see Chapter 3), strengthened by BIC's established product development relationships with major mobile phone developers in North America, northern Europe, and Asia and by an enhanced capacity to access venture capital funds.

Expanding Life Sciences–Related Initiatives

As another illustration of convergence, the nutraceutical products developed by Forbes Meditech are based on linking technologies originating in life sciences, food, and forestry, the latter including Lignol's efforts. Forbes was established in 1992 as a pharmaceutical research company based on technology developed at UBC. In 2000, a company founder was approached to explore the potential medicinal properties of tall oil pitch, a by-product of kraft pulping processes (also identified by Lignol as a by-product from its ethanol production processes). Forbes recognized that the tall oil pitch was a rich source of naturally occurring compounds (including phytosterols) potentially to combat cholesterol in the form of a drug and to contribute health-related benefits as an additive in nutraceutical food products. The company initially focused on the former potential, but after a disappointing second phase of clinical trials for a stand-alone drug (which indicated a 9 percent rather than a 15 percent reduction in "bad cholesterol" after twelve weeks) Forbes out-licensed its pharmaceutical research to an Ontario firm in 2008 and subsequently closed its pharma-focused R&D activities in Vancouver and San Diego, with Vancouver operations specialized on nutraceutical applications. Given that only 10 percent by volume of the tall oil pitch contains the phytosterols required for the anti-cholesterol drug, and with no local market for the waste products (e.g., anti-dust coatings, adhesives, and emulsifiers), a production facility was not viable in British Columbia. Instead, the world's largest tall oil sterol extraction company, Phyto-Source LP, was established in Greater Houston through a joint venture with US speciality chemicals producer Chusei, where a substantial chemicals industry was ready to consume the residual pitch after sterol extraction. Thus, despite access to the expertise of firms in the life sciences cluster, suboptimal results in clinical trials meant a focus on nutraceuticals rather than drug development and, similar to other life sciences firms but for different reasons, a necessity to reach beyond Metro Vancouver for production.

For Forbes Meditech, shifting from drug discovery to nutraceuticals also posed challenges, not least because of a lack of large established food producers with which to partner locally, a lack of aligned industry associations to provide advice, and difficulties in obtaining regulatory approval for nutraceuticals in Canada, where procedures lagged behind those in other countries.[45] Nevertheless, Forbes successfully developed several nutraceuticals, starting with Reducol in milk-based products and later margarine and fruit juice, which have gained approval through the Food and Drug Administration in the United States, European Novel Foods in Europe, and Therapeutic Goods Administration (TGA) in Australia, even as it could not market its products in Canada because of the comparatively slow approval of phytosterols by Health Canada. Forbes also partnered with major sellers internationally, such as Tesco in the United Kingdom, for its products to be incorporated into supermarket "private labels," and Del Monte to serve markets in the Philippines and South Asia. Forbes has also promoted its products through the training of pharmacists, including in the United Kingdom.[46] In this case, innovation has been achieved without much supporting institutional architecture.

Further potential for developing the life sciences (biotechnology) cluster in Metro Vancouver through convergent technologies has been recognized by industry observers for developing new technology platforms in multidisciplinary ways.[47] Within the private sector, AbCellera Biologics is a leading example that integrates AI, genomics, and computation to generate a new biology product (see Appendix 1). Increased support for such convergent technologies in life sciences is also provided by local universities, including UBC's School of Biomedical Engineering and SFU's Faculty of Health Sciences. At the same time, new initiatives can flare up, generate much excitement, but die quickly.[48] In practice, new firms reliant on various technological processes and sources of expertise still confront high levels of uncertainty and cost. Anchor firms remain elusive, and successful development typically involves the close support of MNCs, often involving acquisition.

Conclusion

High-tech clustering processes in Metro Vancouver have occurred around a highly diverse range of activities fuelled by high levels of enterprise formation. Admittedly, new media aside, inter-firm relations tend to be limited in terms of local interactions, and external forms of collaboration are widespread and associated with increasing levels of acquisition and external control. However, there has been a tendency in policy and research to think of clusters in isolation from one another, each with its particular forms of external connections. Yet the sheer diversity of activities at least intimates the role of inter-sectoral dynamics and is reinforced by the emergence of convergent technologies, whether the latter are considered new clusters or add variety to existing ones. Indeed, as the examples of technology convergence reveal, the cluster focus in Metro Vancouver can marginalize activities that do not fall neatly into one or the other of the established clusters. From an economic development perspective, greater investment in boundary-spanning activities by industry associations, to identify and support innovations that "cut across" clusters rather than risk them falling between the cracks, is likely to be important in enabling cluster development and fulfilling the promise of Metro Vancouver as a location well placed to benefit from the convergence opportunities identified by Life Sciences BC.[49]

In the next chapter, we turn to the institutional architecture underlying Metro Vancouver's high-tech clusters to appreciate more fully their implications for local development, including external economies based within and between clusters.

5

Deepening Institutional Support
for Metro Vancouver High Tech

As we elaborated in the previous chapter, literally thousands of businesses (11,000 plus by 2021) comprising Metro Vancouver high tech have created diverse specialties within broadly defined clusters. In so doing they contribute to related variety, new firm formation, supplier networks to some degree, and a growing talent pool. This clustering has further stimulated a deepening of locally supportive institutions in both the private and the public sectors, the former illustrated by industry associations and venture capital businesses and the latter by the targeted initiatives of universities and government policies and programs. Such supportive institutional architecture adds to the ("localized") external economies of scale and scope that benefit high-tech activities in the region.[1] In general, within the literature on business location, the importance of these industry-specific external economies for helping to localize economic activities over time has long been recognized, particularly in relation to information sharing, access to common labour pools, and supplier networks.[2] Indeed, such (evolutionary) trends are evident among high-tech firms in Metro Vancouver to varying degrees (see Chapter 4). Our focus in this chapter on the emergence of support institutions further expresses and elaborates the nature of clustering economies for high-tech activities in Metro Vancouver.[3]

Industry associations, venture capitalists, and targeted university and government policies spearhead the (formal) institutional initiatives and architecture serving Metro Vancouver high tech. Their roles are significant and varied and originate from the collective localized demands of populations of related firms and manifest as various services or inputs to individual firms unable or unwilling to develop them internally.[4] The advantages of clustering in terms of (lower) unit costs for businesses admittedly are hard to measure quantitatively, in part because of their multifaceted, often subjective nature.[5] In this regard, the formation, durability, and performance of industry associations, venture capitalists, and targeted university and government policies in support of Metro Vancouver high tech provide formal institutional indicators of the benefits of clustering. A caveat in this regard is that, for governments in particular, accountability of performance can be marred by self-promotion and delay as well as lack of data. In general, the sustained deepening of institutional architecture expresses the power of clustering for local development.[6]

The various benefits of clustering to firms and the local economy evolve over time, insignificant at the beginnings of new industries but becoming more important. In Metro Vancouver's high-tech sector, as elsewhere, a tempting starting point is to think of the architecture of supporting institutions as an effect rather than a cause of its growth. From this perspective, the establishment of specialized associations, university functions, venture capitalists, and government policies has occurred as a response to the needs of a growing population of high-tech firms in Metro Vancouver. Looking back to its early industrialization, major supporting institutions in the 1920s and 1930s – such as UBC's forestry faculty or the high-profile industry association that became known as the Council of Forest Industries – were established following initial forestry industry expansions. In a high-tech context, Don Hings's pioneering ventures were well ahead of their time – and of the institutional architecture that subsequently developed (see Case Study I.1). Regardless of how momentum is initiated, however, economic activities and their supporting institutional externalities co-evolve, with their interactions reinforcing and strengthening their viability and competitiveness. That is, these institutions are not simply responses to serving the needs of established specialties but also contribute to attracting investments in expanding and new businesses while adding jobs, multiplier effects, and buzz in the local economy. They can also become proactive with respect to export activity and innovation. Furthermore, an exploration of the institutions that underlie Metro Vancouver high tech helps recognize the importance of cooperative behaviour for local competitiveness. Indeed, in Porter's terminology, they illustrate "institutions of collaboration," a role further underlined in recent approaches to the innovation ecosystem.[7]

In this chapter, we review and assess the roles of industry associations, universities, financing, and government policy for promoting high tech in Metro Vancouver. Each of these roles is examined in turn. More generally, this discussion of institutional architecture complements (and extends) the three previous chapters, focused, respectively, on local business, FDI strategies, and clustering, to allow reflections on the nature and deepening of Metro Vancouver's regional innovation system (RIS) for high tech. Clustering qua agglomeration is a powerful driving force of the RIS, and the nature of the former influences the anatomy of the latter. We conclude the chapter with a summary model of the Metro Vancouver high-tech RIS in terms of broad institutional characteristics.

Industry Associations

Industry or business associations are nonprofit organizations (NPOs) normally mandated and funded by private sector members. Their rationale depends on providing collective benefits (services) that members are unwilling or unable to supply themselves and that justify individual membership fees. Whereas the fees are quantifiable costs, the benefits, no matter how real, are often intangible, for example related to market promotion schemes, government lobbying, or information sharing. Participation in these associations is entirely voluntary, and membership does not impose particular obligations beyond payment of fees. Free riding can occur if nonmembers gain access to membership benefits, although such spillovers can be beneficial locally. Beyond their industry contexts, industry associations have little public profile. However, they have evolved in Metro Vancouver's high tech as local expressions of trends occurring in all types of industries around the world and represent a classic form of external, localized economies of scale set up in response to local demands.[8] In a general sense, their key role is to emphasize the importance of collective action and to help businesses share in finding solutions to common problems.

Selected characteristics of ten well-known examples of industry associations serving high tech in Metro Vancouver help to illustrate their roles (see Table 5.1). As expected, these associations are relatively new and have evolved mainly since the 1980s, and several are quite recent, both a response to and a part of the burgeoning rise of high-tech activities in Metro Vancouver. Some earlier initiatives have also been relabelled and given greater profiles and resources. The associations set up to serve the aerospace and fuel cell industries in the early 1980s, for example, were incorporated into national organizations in 2013 and 2009, respectively, both with head

TABLE 5.1 Nonprofit industry associations in Metro Vancouver high tech

Organization	*Development and mandate*
Aerospace Industries Association of BC	Industry association established in 1984, funded by and supporting its members. Became Aerospace Industry Association Pacific in 2013 as part of national organization, head office in Ottawa. In 2014, association and BC government announced a $5 million partnership to support the province's aerospace cluster, comprising about 190 companies.
Vancouver Entrepreneurs Forum	An NPO with one employee established in 1987 to stimulate networking among Vancouver's technology firms. Platform for technology entrepreneurs, hosts eight forums a year, and is financed by members, sponsors, and events. Mandated to support applied R&D in natural sciences in the Canadian Network of Centres of Excellence. After 2007, open to all disciplines. Connections to multiple organizations in British Columbia, main office at UBC.
Canadian Hydrogen Association and Hydrogen and Fuel Cell Association	Established in 1980s or 1990s. Mandated to support development and use of hydrogen and fuel cells. Diverse membership drawn from business, government, and universities. Nine employees in Vancouver, head office at UBC. Merged in 2009 as Canadian Hydrogen and Fuel Cell Association.
BC Technology Industry Association	Established in 1993 and since 2006 called BC Tech Association. Formed by amalgamation of the Electronic Manufacturers Association of BC and the Information Technology Association of Canada. Provides information and lobbying services to over 2,100 members and facilitates partnerships. In 2004, launched an initiative to integrate research for its members; in 2006, partnered with British Columbia Research and Science Technology Network to facilitate collaboration and research. Supports tech companies, dedicates space ("hub") for networking, and develops various programs to support the tech sector involving training, workshops, reports. Supported by private and public sector members.

Organization	Development and mandate
Life Sciences BC	An NPO founded in 1995 to serve life sciences community. Head office in Vancouver, with six employees. Funded by its members and undertakes wide-ranging tasks.
Wavefront Innovation Society	An NPO founded in 2007 by Wireless Innovation Network Society of BC. In 2011, selected and funded as a National Centre of Excellence. Mandated to accelerate growth of wireless companies. Closed in 2018 with debt of $2.1 million with twenty employees in British Columbia (another twelve in Toronto office). Claims of support for new companies unproven.
Wireless Industry Partnership	Established approximately in 2006. Preceded and helped to establish Wavefront. Provides networking for innovation in emerging wireless technology applications, taking an ecosystem perspective to identify emerging opportunities for SMEs. Organizes networking sessions such as Mobile Mondays and JAM brain-storming sessions.
New Media BC	Established in 1998. Enhances professional development in new media (workshops and seminars), provides networking and partnership opportunities, and engages in advocacy work with government (e.g., Vancouver International Partnering Forum).
Wireless Industry BC (WINBC)	Established in 2001. Promotes commercialization of innovation, market access, and talent. Includes mentorship for SMEs (Go WIN) and skill recruitment.
Interactive and Digital Media Industry Association of BC (DigiBC), also known as Digital Media and Wireless Association of BC	A Vancouver NPO established in 2010. Mandated to support digital media and related activities in British Columbia. Formed as a consolidation of Wireless Information Network (established in 2001) and New Media BC (established in 1998). Staff of four and about 400 member companies.

Note: Angel Forum and Vantek are venture capital associations (see Table 5.4).
Sources: Authors' data files.

offices in Vancouver. With earlier roots, BC Tech (formerly BC Technology Industry Association) became more active upon its relabelling in 1993. In the new media and film industries, the formation of DigiBC occurred in 2010 by amalgamating initiatives that had begun in 1998 and 2001. For the most part, members are private businesses, although in some cases there are representatives from government and academia, for example the Canadian Hydrogen and Fuel Cell Association.

In Metro Vancouver high tech, industry associations are tiny, mostly employing between one and nine employees, with one of the largest, Wavefront Innovation Society, closing in 2018 and letting go its twenty employees. DigiBC and Life Sciences BC are exceptions, however, with over 400 and 300 members, respectively, circa 2018. Bearing in mind that membership is voluntary, these associations never include all firms in a particular activity, and the entry and exit of member firms are easily accomplished. Indeed, Metro Vancouver's high-tech associations are vulnerable to maintaining a viable size, with turnover often an issue if individual members believe that their interests are not being served, are concerned about free riders, or simply wish to cut costs. However, notwithstanding some refocusing (or even closure) of activities, industry associations in Metro Vancouver have actively participated in its high-tech growth.

In terms of scope, the majority of the selected associations support particular spheres of activity (aerospace, fuel cells, wireless, digital media, life sciences), with just two associations servicing the high-tech sector as a whole, namely Vancouver Entrepreneurs Forum (since 1987) and BC Tech (since 1993), plus Angel Forum (since 1997) focuses on financial support to the sector (see Table 5.4). Collectively, these associations provide an extraordinarily wide range of services to their members, including shared forums for information generation and exchange, lobbying governments, increasing public awareness, undertaking reports and studies on subjects of collective interest, organizing market promotion, providing space for meetings, helping to train workers, and contributing to liaison activities in seeking funding and research support. Among these many services, the associations' roles in furthering networking and information exchange (and local buzz) can be underlined. The Vancouver Entrepreneurs Forum, for example, stimulates information exchanges across the high-tech sector both online and in-person by scheduling regular forums. Typically well attended, the forums bring together many different perspectives and help to reinforce the identity of Metro Vancouver as an increasingly important high-tech centre. The associations are not particularly involved in RD&D projects, however.

Metro Vancouver's high-tech firms also join associations based elsewhere to access specialized services not available locally, specifically including services related to technology. As discussed in the previous chapter, for example, Angstrom Power's (convergent technology) focus on micro fuel cell technology led not only to collaborations with major American, European, and Asian firms but also to joining international associations and events such as the (annual) Consumer Electronic Show, owned by the Consumer Technology Association in the United States, and conferences such as Wireless World and Japan Fuel Cell Expo. For Angstrom, membership in these associations has been vital since related local associations are more oriented to supporting large-scale fuel cells developed by Ballard Power Systems and other local firms. As another example, D-Wave Systems and other specialist computer companies in Metro Vancouver helped to form Quantum Industry Canada, headquartered in Toronto, to facilitate industry dialogue, attract investments, and develop standards in quantum technologies.

Overall, locally based high-tech industry associations have been important in facilitating networking among otherwise independent firms, mainly SMEs, including by helping with contacts with government bureaucracies. Their activities help to support cluster evolution from embryonic stages (providing services to new entrepreneurs, including access to venture capital) to established stages (enhancing local competence and shared infrastructure) and illustrate localized external economies specific to the high-tech sector. Meanwhile, universities have sought to provide support for high tech within the context of much broader and longer-established mandates.

Higher Education's Growing Proactivity in High-Tech Innovation

Metro Vancouver's high tech is buttressed by an impressive educational system in which tertiary university and college organizations collectively serve to enhance research-driven understandings of the natural and social worlds and to provide educated and sometimes trained human resources for diverse job markets. In general, higher education has become more important with the rise of knowledge-driven, service-oriented societies, inherently contributing to local-global knowledge generation and diffusion. In terms of governance, organizations of higher education are not straightforward to summarize. They are both hierarchical and bureaucratic, perhaps increasingly so, yet decentralized around highly independent faculty "doing their own thing" among an extraordinarily diverse range of research programs. That core academic interests and incentives lie in basic research and understanding for its own sake, rather than being solely motivated by practical relevance, has long been a source of uneasy relationships within universities. Moreover, university attempts to establish new initiatives can compete and overlap with established programs. However, since town-gown relations inevitably are part of broader social dynamics, it is clear that universities and related institutions have become increasingly pushed to be "entrepreneurial" sources of local innovation and diversification, beyond enjoying (complete) freedom in research and educational pursuits or even simply to act as buttresses to established specialties. An abbreviated history of Metro Vancouver's tertiary educational organizations provides a context for their increasingly proactive role in high tech.

Evolutionary Synopsis

The evolution of British Columbia's system of higher education in Metro Vancouver can be seen as part of two main global trends. First, the core institution of that system, UBC, was established in 1908 as part of widespread university expansions that began in the late nineteenth century across advanced countries. These expansions were strongly science oriented and partly a response to the growing technological sophistication of leading countries that included the establishment of in-house R&D or corporate laboratories pioneered in the (research-intensive) chemical and electrical industries. The newly expanding universities provided labour and knowledge for corporate, "professionalized," in-house R&D. In British Columbia, however, corporate R&D was scarcely evident, and its main resource industries, including forestry and farming, were entrepreneurial, with limited capability for research investment. Nevertheless, the need for a scientific basis for the resource industries, and for related technology transfer activities, was evident and led to the establishment of agricultural (1914) and forestry (1922) faculties at UBC, further complemented by a few government laboratories. Within forestry, corporate R&D did eventually expand, if to a limited degree (see Chapter 1).

Second, another major expansion of Metro Vancouver's (and British Columbia's) system of higher education occurred in the 1960s. The key developments featured the establishment of SFU as a research and teaching university in 1965 in Burnaby; the consolidation of a major vocational, industry-oriented institute (BCIT) in Burnaby in 1964; and the establishment of teaching-oriented community colleges, namely Douglas College in New Westminster (1970), Capilano Community College in North Vancouver (1970), Vancouver Community College in Vancouver (1974), Kwantlen Community College in Surrey (1981), and Fraser College in neighbouring

Abbotsford (1974). UBC itself expanded in 1950 with the Faculty of Medicine, which became an important player in Metro Vancouver's biotechnology cluster. Since the early 1970s, the system of higher education as a whole has grown; all of the above-mentioned institutions have established other campuses in the metropolitan area, and several colleges became degree-granting universities around 2008. The relatively small Emily Carr University, with a focus on art and design, including with respect to wood (see Case Study I.1), and with roots dating back to 1925, was also established then and located on the new Great Northern Way Campus in Vancouver.[9] Still, UBC remains the dominant institution of higher education in Metro Vancouver, with recent budgets around $2.2 billion (2020) supporting over 5,500 faculty and 70,000 students, with SFU next at a budget in 2021 of $825 million supporting 1,100 faculty and about 30,000 students.[10]

The considerable expansion of the system of higher education in Metro Vancouver (and British Columbia) in the 1960s and 1970s reflected growing demands for a larger, better-educated, postindustrial workforce, this time with more emphasis on the social sciences and humanities as well as the natural sciences. Assuredly, UBC and SFU have remained committed to pursuing independent, long-run, basic research directed toward enhancing fundamental knowledge about society and nature, including the potential for applied and developmental work. Conventionally, such roles define the distinctive contributions of universities within the R&D core of innovation systems.[11] As a well-known, high-profile illustration of this commitment, in 1968 UBC, SFU, UVic, and the University of Alberta combined to create Triumf, the world-leading laboratory located at UBC to conduct long-term experimentation in particle physics. Still a highly successful operation that lists 600 research-affiliated faculty, Triumf is a reminder of core university mandates for basic research that nevertheless include innovative implications for commercialization that others can pursue. Triumf's collaborations, for example, have occurred with leading high-tech players in Metro Vancouver, including MDA. Indeed, the rise of high tech, policy pressures, and the need to develop knowledge-based specialties to stimulate local development have encouraged universities to become more proactive in commercially motivated innovation.

Local Academic Entrepreneurship

Since the 1980s, universities around the world have become involved in promoting local development through dedicated programs of technological transfer and commercialization.[12] Anticipated by the iconic role of Stanford

University in Silicon Valley, the rise of the "entrepreneurial university" has been stimulated by the rising importance of knowledge inputs and innovations for industrial (and national and local) competitiveness, the remarkable versatility of ICT and biotech, and the increased recognition of the interactive nature of RD&D activities with their commercialization. This trend was given particular momentum in the United States by the Bayh-Dohl Act of 1980, which gave universities ownership of intellectual property rights from federally funded research and the right to reap the associated rewards from commercialization. In turn, interest among universities around the world grew for commercializing knowledge through patents, licensing, spin-offs, incubation activities, technology transfer offices, and industry links. Within Metro Vancouver, led by UBC and SFU, the system of higher education has followed this trend.

In particular, formal administrative support for academic entrepreneurialism was spearheaded by the establishment of University-Industry Liaison Offices (UILOs) at UBC (1984) and SFU (1985). The latter UILO eventually became SFU's Technology Licensing Office, which retained its identity as a key part of the newly formed SFU Innovates in 2016. The creation of these UILOs in the mid-1980s was led by a few academic champions who had been encouraged by the provincial government's new Discovery Park Policy, a "small potatoes" program that established zoned spaces and buildings for innovative developments at both universities (see section 5). That is, the first tentative steps in setting up these UILOs occurred during a deep recession and debate over the future economic directions for British Columbia (and Metro Vancouver). Subsequently, their roles have grown and become more structured. By 2022, for example, UBC's UILO was part of the VP Research and Innovation domain, with thirty-five employees to provide wide-ranging, specialized expertise (legal, financial, technological, start-up, and networking) to faculty and students facing the multifaceted challenges of shifting academic research into business reality.[13] Meanwhile, the broadly similar mandate of SFU Innovates is situated within the VP Research and International office and directed by a seven-person executive team and organized around four main pillars: industry and community research partnerships (including the Technology Licensing Office), incubation and acceleration, entrepreneurship, and social innovation.[14] Start-up help involving mentoring, laboratories and equipment, and (accelerator) financing has been elaborated recently in both universities, for example in the Entrepreneurship@UBC Program since 2013, the UBC Creative Destruction Lab since 2016, and the SFU VentureLabs since 2013.[15] Ideas from all economic sectors are entertained, but innovation and high tech are the focus of these efforts, and increasingly they are associated with environmentally sustainable initiatives.

Indeed, promoting the commercialization of academic research interests, most obviously in high-tech endeavours, was their originating stimulus and continues as a key focus of UBC's UILO and SFU Innovates. Academic entrepreneurs (or, as once called, "boffin-business people") are not a new phenomenon, and for high-tech Metro Vancouver the formation of MDA in 1969 (then MacDonald Dettwiler) and Moli Energy in 1997 as professorial spinoffs from UBC, among a number of others, foreshadowed the role of the new UILOs.[16] As initiatives that reflected individual vision and capability, they nevertheless provided exemplars for the formal UILOs that followed and their focus on providing advice on matters such as funding, technology, collaborators, the patenting process, licensing, and problems associated with start-ups and growth.[17]

Intellectual property (IP) rights are an important theme of discussions between the universities and their clients. In this regard, though both universities require that revenue-generating innovations be disclosed, they have contrasting approaches to the licensing and patenting of academic innovations. Thus, UBC's Policy 88 essentially assigns ownership rights (of commercially motivated patents) to the university, with the IP creators given a share and the university absorbing the costs of technological transfer. Meanwhile, at SFU, IP rights (R30.03) are vested with the creators, reflecting a "commitment to the open exchange of ideas and the publication, dissemination and communication of the results of scholarly activity ... which should be used for the greatest possible public benefit."[18] At SFU, as at UBC, revenue sharing is negotiated within broad limits.

In terms of the scope of their activities, the Canada Foundation for Innovation (CFI) provides some summary data for 2003.[19] By then, UBC's UILO had received 600 disclosures and allocated 150 patents, and 29 licences were granted, adding $13.6 million to university revenues. SFU's UILO had received (since 1985) 409 disclosures and allocated 44 patents, and in 2003 it received $85,874 in royalty fees, licences, and so on, resulting in a total return of $2.7 million between 1991 and 2003. The CFI study also noted that in 2002, in terms of licence income received per $1 million revenue, UBC was ranked second and SFU sixth among twenty-three Canadian universities. This level of activity has continued. At UBC, for example, in 2018–19, there were 144 disclosures, 74 patents issued, and 105 licence agreements completed, and technology licensing revenue reached $8.6 million.

Patenting and licensing are typical prerequisites for the generation of university spinoff companies that in turn provide the readiest indicators of local impacts of UBC's UILO and SFU Innovates activities on high tech. In this regard, the UBC website provides a listing of each case, as well as publishing its patents, and it reported that from the mid-1980s the university had spun off 213 companies by 2019 and 235 by 2022. Although details are not provided, SFU indicates that it had supported more than 400 start-up ventures by about 2018.[20] Comparatively, the CFI ranked SFU first (and UBC seventh) in 2002 among Canadian universities in terms of start-up companies formed per $1 million of revenue.[21] The two universities display somewhat different emphases in this regard, with UBC spinoffs featuring life sciences initiatives and SFU spinoffs featuring information technologies. As UBC data show, an increasing stream of new spinoffs has occurred since a "takeoff" phase in the 1980s (see Table 5.2).

Many of these firms are small, their off-campus locations are hard to find (if they exist), and the failure rate is noteworthy: UBC, for example, indicated that by 2019, out of 213 spinoffs, 130 were still operating, and 83 had closed. SFU has also noted that closures among its spinoffs are frequent.[22] A few UBC spinoffs have grown to become large SMEs or bigger, including QLT, Angiotech, Stemcell Technologies, AbCellera Biologics, D-Wave, and Westport, although QLT and Angiotech are now closed (see Appendix 1). Indeed, the well-known vulnerability of small high-tech companies, especially evident in the life sciences, clearly incorporates university spinoffs.[23] In general, among the largest spinoffs recently highlighted by UBC's UILO, local employment beyond 250 is rare, although sales can be high, based on royalty and licensing fees for web-based applications, without much local employment.[24] Foreign acquisitions of UBC spinoffs have also occurred.[25]

In addition to the services provided by their technology transfer offices, UBC and SFU have connected with Metro Vancouver's high-tech economy through new program developments (not least in engineering and business), the growth of student cooperative work opportunities, and research

TABLE 5.2 Spinoff firms from UBC since the 1980s

1980s	1990s	2000s	2010s
23	60	54	76

Note: The 1980s column includes one firm from the 1970s.
Source: University of British Columbia, University-Industry Liaison Office, uilo.ubc.ca.

programs linked to specific high-tech firms of varying sizes. For example, Metro Vancouver's pioneering developments in submersible technologies (see Case Study 4.1) might be relatively small, but they helped to strengthen a long-term research program at SFU, the establishment of an underwater research laboratory in 1989 under the direction of Professor John Bird. His lab was boosted by a program funded by the Natural Sciences and Engineering Research Council, the Advanced Systems Institute, and International Submarine Engineering (ISE), the Port Coquitlam–based submarine manufacturer, in the late 1990s.[26] In this case, the program designed better instruments and robots for research on underwater acoustics and imaging, not incidentally enhancing technical competence and student experience in the lab, along with the technological capabilities of one of the companies, ISE, its main technology partner. Other SFU examples of industry-research partnerships with bigger local firms (see Appendix 1) include interactions with MPR Teltech when it occupied SFU's Discovery Park and Professor Erik Kjeang's research grant of $6.3 million in 2013 to develop (nano) x-ray technology to analyze the hydrogen fuel cells created by Ballard Power Systems.[27] Such examples can be expanded readily.

In general terms, the various innovative achievements of SFU and UBC have been lauded globally in various third-party ranking schemes of contributions to innovativeness, sustainability, and other criteria.[28] If applied systematically, these rankings admittedly are judgmental. As elsewhere, UBC and SFU claims about spinoff achievements regarding impacts might involve some exaggeration or at least selectivity, and some issues – such as the loss of IP rights to foreign companies – might not be appreciated fully.[29] Nevertheless, as the global rankings underline, UBC and SFU have become aggressive, agile, and important participants in Metro Vancouver's post-industrial economy, adding considerably to the region's desirability for, and performance of, high-tech business.

Beyond these two universities, distinctive specialties introduced at other educational institutions in Metro Vancouver can be noted. BCIT's vocational programs, for example, have adjusted to new needs and provide skills and training for wide-ranging jobs, with dedicated campuses serving aircraft and marine industries and new centres focusing on innovation and health services on the main Burnaby campus. At Capilano University, a highly regarded program for students interested in the video and film industries has been developed, and Kwantlen Polytechnic University introduced a fashion program. Meanwhile, the Emily Carr School of Art and Design has reinvigorated and broadened its programs in various design and art fields.

Emily Carr also symbolizes the importance of "design" in RD&D rather than just R&D. The Great Northern Way Campus included a grant of $1 million from Electronic Arts that supplemented government funding, a collaboration that further underlines this design emphasis and sectoral connection. Several private businesses, all located in downtown Vancouver, have also introduced highly specialized training programs for students interested in careers in the high-tech sector. Five such training and educational organizations have been established since 2008, which include, Launch Academy (2012), Lighthouse Labs (2013), Brain Station (2012), Codecore Bootcamp (2008), and Red Academy (2015) although the latter abruptly closed its doors in 2020 and advised its students to enrol with Brain Station. Largely inspired by Launch Academy, these institutes provide students with digital, coding, and related software training in relatively short, focused courses designed to help them gain work in the high-tech sector.

Emergence of Venture Capital Organizations

In the 1960s and 1970s, Metro Vancouver's pioneering high-tech businesses typically were dependent on financing from local sources such as personal savings, bank loans, and contributions from friends and family members, often while their founders maintained employment in existing jobs and worked in readily available cheap spaces. Often this financing was small, as mentioned in Ballard's history (see Chapter 3), and Glenayre, MDA, and Sierra had similar experiences. Conversely, MPR Teltech's origins were supported by its parent, BC Tel (now Telus). However, the rapid growth of the high-tech sector has increased substantially the demand for high-risk (and high reward) financing beyond personal sources and, in many cases, the interests of conventional stock markets. The closure qua restructuring of the old, albeit ethically questionable, Vancouver Stock Exchange in 1999 underlines the financing challenges facing Metro Vancouver high tech.

In response, in recent decades, the increased size and complexity of the financial needs of this rapidly expanding high-tech population comprising many (financially poor) SMEs, along with the high levels of market and technological uncertainty that many face, have stimulated the rise of specialized sources of high-tech finance such as accelerators, angels, and venture capital organizations. Within the past decade, for example, the previously mentioned accelerator organizations at UBC and SFU, created between 2013 and 2016, have been joined by Innovate BC (since 2016) and many others in the private sector to support start-ups. Such initiatives have complemented the growth of angel investors, who typically simply provide funds, and venture capital firms that provide funds and share the management of high-tech clients. Our discussion principally addresses the bigger, better-documented firms.

Although not a complete list, summary characteristics of several leading venture capital organizations located in Metro Vancouver provide insights into their behaviour (see Table 5.3).

Their evolution is relatively recent, with the first three established in 1994, 1997, and 1999. Of them, the first, Renewal Funds, is a locally based and privately owned family firm, and the Angel Forum and Vantec are nonprofit associations in support of venture capital, and both were created by local entrepreneurs and high-tech promoters. The other nine companies were established in Vancouver between 2000 and 2016. Of them, only Kensington Capital is an "outside" (Toronto-based) firm, establishing a Vancouver office in 2016, stimulated by its choice by the BC government to manage its new tech fund (2018). This surging pattern of locally established venture capital firms reflects growing demands for risk capital among high-tech

TABLE 5.3 Evolution of (selected) venture capital organizations in Metro Vancouver

Organization	Origin and development
Renewal Funds	Started as Renewal Partners in 1994, a family firm founded by Carol Newell and Joel Solomon, joined by Paul Richardson. Became Renewal Funds in 2008.
	Focuses on supporting innovations in food and consumer products to enhance sustainability.
	Invested in forty-one (small) businesses with revenues of from $1 million to $20 million (ten exits).
	Can partner with recipients.
	Employs twelve professionals.
Angel Forum	A nonprofit association founded in 1997 by Bob Chaworth-Musters. New management in 2018.
	Introduces early-stage, private, high-tech companies to private equity angel investors.
	Has fifty members (investors).
	Organizes workshops for members, online meetings between two companies, biannual events, and webinars.
	Links with national angel capital associations in Canada and the United States.

▶

◄

Organization	Origin and development
Vantec	Founded in 1999 by Mike Volker (SFU downtown campus). Connects 120 members (including angel investors) with early-stage (pre-seed, seed one, and seed two companies) high-tech companies in monthly meetings and "start-up" pitches. By 2021, 2,500 companies made presentations, half of which received funding. Average funding is $250,000. Connected to angel associations in the United States and Canada.
Pangaea Ventures	Established in 2000. Also has offices in Arizona and New Jersey. Several MNCs are strategic partners. Focuses on equity growth investments in early- and late-stage companies using advanced materials in energy, electronics, health, and sustainability. Seventy investments by 2020 (with sixteen exits). Employs six–eight professionals.
Yaletown Partners	Founded in 2001 by Hans Kapp. Has offices in Toronto, Montreal, and Calgary. Focuses on emerging growth digital companies (software, data, etc.) that modernize traditional industries, real estate, and so on to provide climate-resilient growth. Seventy-two investments (with sixteen exits) from three funds. Employs ten professionals in British Columbia.
Chrysalix Venture Capital	Founded in 2001 by Wal Van Lierop and Michael J. Brown Focuses on innovations and intelligent systems in resource-intensive industries that enhance productivity. Has 108 investments (with twenty-six exits) across four funds for firms at all stages. Employs eight professionals.
Version One Ventures	Founded in 2007 by Boris Wertz (as W Media Ventures). Version One Ventures established in 2012. Finances high-tech start-ups, with 146 investments, forty-five portfolios, and fifty-four exits. Retains three employees. Focuses on seed and early-stage companies serving consumer internet, software as a service, and mobile sector companies in North America. Average funding is between $250,000 and $500,000.

Organization	Origin and development
Vanedge Capital	Founded in 2010 by Paul Lee. Supports early-stage companies in analytics, hard technology, and computational technology, including video games. Focuses on new companies, series A, and average funding is between $2 million and $5 million. Has fifty-five investments (with twenty-one exits). Manages two funds ($296 million and $380 million). Employs nine professionals.
Quark Venture	Established in 2015 in Vancouver by Jessen Chen and Franklin Jiang. Focuses on supporting innovation in biotechnology and health sciences. Has thirty-three investments (with five exits). Employs four professionals. Partnered with GF Securities, a leading Chinese investment bank, to establish a $500 million investment fund run out of Vancouver. Has other Chinese investors.
7 Gate Ventures	Founded in 2015 by Amir Vohooshi. Has an office in Silicon Valley. Focuses on early-stage start-ups to grow into large-scale companies and on start-ups from seed stage to pre-series A. Highly diverse within high tech. Has thirty-four investments (with ten exits). Retains four professionals.
Vistara Capital	Founded in 2015 by Randy Garg. Seeks equity investments in tech companies in various stages of development, especially growth. Has nineteen investments (with eight exits). Focuses on software as a service, fintech, security, and health care.
Kensington Capital Partners	Vancouver office started in 2016. Head office in Toronto founded in 1996 by Tom Kennedy. Manager of Kensington Venture Fund ($306 million) launched in 2014 under the federal government's Venture Capital Action Plan of Canada. In 2016, BC Tech Fund started with a $100 million commitment from the provincial government, and Kensington became its manager, focusing on series A funding for emerging tech companies.

Note: Firms are headquartered in Vancouver, apart from Toronto-based Kensington Capital Partners.
Source: The Founder Institute 2019: A Comprehensive List of Angel Investors and Capital Venture Firms in Vancouver, https://fi.co/insights-a-comprehensive-list-of-angel-investors-and-venture-capital-firms -in-vancouver.

firms in Metro Vancouver, their relatively small size, and the lack of alternative sources.

In terms of size, these venture capital organizations are small, as meas-
ured by employment, which rarely exceeds ten professionals. However, these
firms play vital networking roles that bring together a myriad of investors
looking for opportunities with a host of clients looking for capital. On the
supply side, the investors can be wealthy individuals, government agencies
with large funds, large and small private equity firms, and other adventurous and deep-pocketed investors. On the demand size, clients range from
many tiny operations wanting seed money to experiment and conduct various forms of RD&D, through those beginning early commercialization, and
growth, to established and relatively large operations looking to undertake
major new and expensive expansions.

Venture Capital Roles
Venture capital organizations provide vital roles in Metro Vancouver's
evolving high-tech ecosystem, first and foremost with regard to risk finance.
In particular, these organizations reduce the transaction costs associated
with bringing together suppliers and demanders of capital in high tech for
projects in various stages of the product life cycle. In this regard, the organizations facilitate search and negotiation processes while reducing opportunity costs in arranging financing. These roles are sophisticated and require
considerable expertise in creating funds, exchanging information, assessing risks, and determining market opportunities associated with new technologies and services. Venture capital firms often take equity positions in
their investments and, especially among smaller firms, can offer managerial
services and participate in strategic decision making. Moreover, if venture
capital markets are highly competitive, in terms of both building up funds
to offer and finding clients, the venture capital operations require trust
and confidence and cooperative exchanges of information. In this latter
regard, the Angel Forum and Vantec are important in connecting interested parties on a regular basis. Both are associated with national associations in Canada and the United States, and by 2021 Vantec, for example,
had arranged for 2,500 company presentations seeking funds, half of which
were successful.

In providing financing, venture capital organizations focus on organizing seed capital, a function in which the main Canadian financial institutions are not especially strong, and in finding different types and sources of
capital. Beyond financing, venture capital firms offer various mentoring ser-

vices, including nurturing entrepreneurs, identifying partners, and providing management support. In seeking to enhance their returns for these services, a primary goal is to enhance the value (payoffs) of their clients, including by preparing for IPOs and for exits by acquisition by wealthy buyers.

Privately owned venture capital firms compete with yet complement one another in serving high-tech firms. Virtually all angels are involved in "seed funding" to move a business idea along, which can be followed quickly by so-called series A, B, and C funds that typically involve equity shares.[30] According to this nomenclature, pre-seed funding is provided by the founders, their friends, and their family members (as illustrated in Ballard's and MDA's origins). With seed funding that anticipates growth, venture capital organizations can become important, providing sums in the range of $10,000 to $2 million or so. Metro Vancouver's venture capital firms provide such seed money; for example, most of the (1,200 or so) companies that received funding (by 2021) after presentations at Vantec are in this range, and most of the venture capital organizations in Table 5.4 have organized funds at this stage. For those companies that want funds beyond seed money, the A, B, and C series come into play and represent progressively larger amounts. Series A fund typically between $2 million and $15 million but with an increasing upper limit have been the particular focus of Vanedge Capital. In 2020, the average series A fund (in Canada) was $15.6 million. In series A funding, companies have already developed a long-term strategy for their innovations; Series B funding is between $20 million and $60 million, and series C funding is larger and oriented toward already successful companies. Series D and series E can also be recognized, whereas larger companies can look to IPOs.

The profitability of venture capital firms themselves depends on their ability to assess the risks of innovative behaviour and to negotiate returns that cover their financial (and managerial) contributions and reward this ability. Local know-how is part of this ability. Compensation for venture capital organizations is provided as fees, equity shares, and in some cases money realized by exits involving acquisitions of recipient firms. In this regard, for Metro Vancouver's venture capital firms, the number of investments that they support and the numbers of exits are important indicators of their activities.

For those organizations serving the high-tech sector, there are variations in focus, bearing in mind that the definition of this sector is elastic. Angel Forum and Vantec are broadly supportive of high tech as a whole. Among the private venture capital organizations, three target innovations directed toward modernizing (different types of) traditional activities, Renewal Funds, Yaletown Partners, and Chrysalix Venture Capital, with the first two also focusing on enhancing sustainability. Pangaea Ventures similarly emphasizes sustainability imperatives along with high tech, and other venture capital firms have specialties within a range of activities, such as Vanedge's interest in video games, Quark's in life sciences, and Version One's in consumer internet software. To an important degree, venture capital organizations in Metro Vancouver serve different market niches.

Geographically, the emergence of venture capital firms in Metro Vancouver illustrates (external) localization economies that have been stimulated by the demands of the rapidly growing high-tech sector. Even so, the building up of funds by venture capital organizations often involves distant (non-local) connections. The BC government, for example, chose Kensington Capital of Toronto to manage its new $100 million high-tech fund in 2018 (from its new Vancouver office), and Quark Venture's main fund has been financed by a Chinese organization (see Table 5.3).

The investment funds procured by Metro Vancouver's venture capital firms have been widely sourced, but predominantly within North America, and have been especially important in providing seed money and early stage (series A, B, and C) financing. With later stage, already established, high-tech firms that seek large-scale financing, the increased role of venture capital organizations based elsewhere, especially in the United States, is evident. In 2019, for example, a record year for high-tech financing deals for Metro Vancouver (and across Canada), with investments amounting to $943 million (and $1.4 billion for British Columbia as a whole), US-based venture capital firms dominated the biggest deals. Indeed, in the six largest deals in the region (accounting for over $700 million in investments), all but one (General Fusion) relied on US-based firms, and none involved local firms. In the case of General Fusion, the lead venture capital organization was based in Singapore, with much funding from the federal government's Innovation Fund. Other big financing initiatives in Metro Vancouver in 2019 included the initial public offerings of two life sciences companies, Zymeworks and Sierra Oncology, on the New York Stock Exchange (see Table 5.4 notes).

As these deals indicate, venture capital firms often cooperate in creating funds. For example, in 2019, funding of $65 million for Chinook Therapeutics involved three such firms, and in 2020 the company arranged further funding that involved more than eight such firms.[31] In the case of Angstrom Power, a convergent technology firm discussed in Chapter 4, financing was

TABLE 5.4 Big venture capital deals in Metro Vancouver high tech, 2019

Recipient firm and activity focus	Funding and main providers
Clio, Burnaby, cloud-based legal technology	$330 million in series D funding from TCV (Menlo Park, CA) and JMI Equity (La Jolla, CA).
PDFTron Systems, Vancouver, document-processing tools for software developers	$95 million in funding led by Silversmith Capital Partners (equity firm), Boston.
General Fusion, Burnaby, fusion power devices	$86 million in series E funding led by Temasek, an investment company based in Singapore. Also $50 million from Canada's Strategic Innovation Fund.
Trulioo Information Services, Vancouver	$70 million in funding led by Goldman Sachs (New York) and other banks (Citigroup, American Express, and Spain's Banco Santander SA).
Terramera, Vancouver, new (clean tech) technologies for food production	$60 million in series B equity funding led by new investor Ospraie Ag (New York) and Seed2Growth Ventures (Chicago).
Chinook Therapeutics, Vancouver, medicines for kidney diseases	$65 million in series A funding led by Versant Ventures (San Francisco) along with Apple Tree Partners (New York) and Samsara BioCapital (Palo Alto, CA). In 2020, Chinook received another $106 million in funding supplied by more than eight venture capital firms.

Notes: This source noted four other "big deals," including two initial public offerings by life sciences companies located in Vancouver, namely Zymeworks ($200 million) and Sierra Oncology ($103 million). The other two were Aurinia Pharmaceuticals of Victoria, which raised $250 million in an initial public offering (Nasdaq), and Carbon Engineering, located in Squamish, which received $90 million in equity funding from multiple, largely US, sources. All figures are in Canadian dollars.

Source: T-Net, "BC Tech Companies Raise Record Financing in 2019 (Well over $2b), 10 Largest Deals Bring in over $1.4b," *T-Net*, December 27, 2019, https://www.bctechnology.com/news/2019/12/27/BC-Tech-Companies-Raise-Record-Financing-in-2019-(Well-Over-2-Billion)-10-Largest-Deals-Bring-in-Over-1.4-Billion.cfm.

obtained from a variety of local venture capital organizations (Ventures West, VantagePoint Ventures Partners, OPG Ventures, as well as Crysalix Energy (managed by Chrysalix Venture Capital) and from different sources within the federal government, especially through the National Research Council of Canada's (NRC) Industrial Research Assistance Program (IRAP),

NRCAN-PERD (Program of Energy Research and Development, Sustainable Development Technology Canada (see Table 5.5), plus some military funding and tax credits. In general, the sizes of financing deals have increased over time, and in 2021, for example, an increase in high-tech "unicorns" – firms receiving at least $1 billion in valuation on the stock exchange – was recorded for high-tech firms in Metro Vancouver.[32]

More surprisingly, Metro Vancouver's venture capital firms have funded clients in other parts of North America, in effect becoming a mobile external economy, reinforcing an important global trend in financing. Nevertheless, the local venture capital–based cluster remains modest, lagging behind Toronto and Montreal in Canada, which itself lags behind other leading countries. As a cluster, local venture capital organizations have enriched local connections, but global (especially US) sources of funding are dominant. The BC government's Tech Fund of $100 million (for a five-year period) is noteworthy but still modest, less than one-third of the financing needs of one company (Clio) in one year (2019). The shallowness of Metro Vancouver's capital pool for high tech remains a concern.

High-Tech Policy Evolution, BC Style

Provincial government support and enthusiasm for innovation and especially high tech have gathered considerable momentum in recent decades. "Innovation" is routinely touted in speeches, reports, programs, and policies on economic development. Yet, in 2022, as Castle's lucid analysis begins, "British Columbia has no overt, consolidated innovation policy."[33] Admittedly, regarding high tech, the first tentative steps of the 1970s have been supplanted by much more substantive programs and funding, often in partnership with federal initiatives. For the most part, however, policy interventions have been reactive, responding to (diverse) established trends and needs rather than being proactive. BC governments have also maintained enthusiastic boosterism for both local entrepreneurship and FDI while rarely, if ever, opposing the latter's acquisition of the former. BC governments, for example, offered no opposition to the foreign acquisitions of local high profile firms such as Glenayre, Creo, and MDA, and have "given away" other promising firms, such as Moli Energy (see Case Study 2.1) and Westech Information Systems, over which it had control (see Appendix 2). With both conservative (Social Credit and Liberal) and NDP governments sharing power in recent decades, if policy differences can be detected, then the lack of an "overt, consolidated innovation policy" is a combined legacy.[34] With the exception of the ill-fated fast-ferry project, British Columbia's innovation and high-tech policies have not followed the proactive path associated with dirigisme but sought to support emerging trends, albeit with increasing commitments.

Gathering Policy Momentum ... Definitely not Dirigiste

The failure of the fast-ferry project helps to explain BC government reticence to entertain "picking winners" as an overt strategy while indicating the experimental nature of high-tech policy-making. This project was the brainchild of the new NDP government elected in 1991, replacing the soon-to-be-defunct Social Credit party. Given Metro Vancouver's shipbuilding and marine engineering traditions and expertise, and British Columbia's extensive ferry service providing local demand, a proposal to design and build advanced ferries locally made sense. Its execution, however, was flawed. Rather than rely on local innovation and expertise, the ferry design was imported from Australia, possibly a cheap but low-road approach. Furthermore, manufacturing was dispersed among different communities on equity and local development rather than efficiency grounds, and overall management was provided by a former union boss in forestry with no shipbuilding experience. It was also not clear why "fast" ferries were needed. They had lower capacities than regular ferries, they were less passenger friendly with more limited seating and less strolling space to view "Beautiful BC," and in operation they had to slow down on approach to ports to reduce tidal wash. Several ferries were manufactured but soon taken out of service and sold for a substantial loss.[35]

Subsequently, high-tech policy gradually if sporadically regained momentum, not least by building on "experiments" from the 1970s, notably the Discovery Park Policy introduced in 1979. This policy, along with the related establishment of the Science Council of BC in 1978, stemmed largely from the prescience of Pat McGeer, a Social Credit government minister and UBC faculty member, and developed from his suggestion in the early 1970s of a "Science City." The Discovery Park Policy was nevertheless rather modest in scale and scope, involving the designation of relatively small parcels of zoned land and buildings with three (of four) located on or near the campuses of UBC, SFU, and BCIT in Metro Vancouver, each "vaguely" anticipating (business R&D) interactions with campus expertise, without assigning any priority focus. Indeed, beyond McGeer, the extent of provincial government enthusiasm for this policy wasn't apparent, and its relevance was questioned.[36] Afterall, in 1980, high-tech activities in Metro Vancouver or across British Columbia were of minor importance to the provincial economy, and in the midst of a prolonged, deep recession economic policies seemed to be confused, even chaotic, offset only by the impacts and optimism of Expo 86.[37] Tenants were attracted, most famously Electronic Arts in BCIT's Discovery Park in Burnaby, where it has become a mainstay of the local video game industry. However, the Discovery Parks largely failed to generate much "incremental activity" in the form of new firms and investments in the region, and by 1990 the policy was privatized as an autonomous "real estate" organization. By 2004, only about fifty companies had been established in the Discovery Parks, mostly relocations of existing, locally based facilities, some of which remain on the BCIT and UBC sites. Subsequently, several were either closed, including MPR Teltech at SFU, or relocated elsewhere, as was the case with Xantrex, which left SFU's Discovery Park after being acquired by French firm Schneider Electric (see Appendix 1).

Notwithstanding its limited impacts in stimulating new innovative businesses, the Discovery Park Policy undoubtedly helped to encourage the universities to establish UILOs and think about how they might engage technological transfer and commercialization. The Science Council of BC has also continued to be a vibrant voice supporting local innovation, rejuvenated in 2005 as the BC Innovation Council and in 2018 as Innovate BC as a crown agency. The latter continues to showcase and support the high-tech sector by providing information services, public presentations, and special programs, the latter including accelerator support for Indigenous businesses, life sciences, and new media. Beyond the Discovery Parks, two other early if less high-profile provincial initiatives have become increasingly influential in Metro Vancouver's innovation economy.

First, the BC Cancer Centre as a research organization was established in 1979 in Vancouver. It had originated as a small treatment centre in 1938 (employing two part-time doctors), funded by an anonymous donation, and had expanded to become provincial in scope by 1971, with the provincial government acquiring control in 1974. As a growing, important source of R&D and patented innovations in cancer treatment, the BC Cancer Treatment Centre is now part of Metro Vancouver's life sciences cluster. It expanded in 2005 in a new building that employed 93 faculty, 400 research staff, and 340 trainees, plus 3,000 staff employed across the province. It has maintained this size and scope, continues to patent, publish, license, engage in clinical trials, and create spinoff companies, with funding in 2021 provided by nonprofits (34 percent) and industry (20 percent) as well as the government (46 percent).[38]

Second, in 1978, the provincial government established the Film Commission, becoming Creative BC in 2013, as an independent, nonprofit organization, headquartered in Vancouver, initially to support the emerging film industry and then a wider range of artistic endeavours.[39] Although a relatively small organization, Creative BC documents innovative developments in new media and related artistic endeavours; provides information and helps to facilitate projects, large and small, by indicating various forms of tax credits in filmmaking and other sources of financial help or competitions; and provides creative assistance for films, music, and publishing. It employs between 25 and 100, with a budget that sometimes reaches $5 million while the film industry continues to enjoy tax breaks and subsidies.

These expanded initiatives have been reinforced by newer commitments to innovation. In 1998, the BC Knowledge Development Fund responded to the federal government's Canadian Innovation Fund established the previous year to provide matching funds for research infrastructure projects in universities and hospitals. The 2009 Innovative Clean Energy Fund (which has since morphed into a broader climate mitigation plan) has helped to support the energy transition, in 2016 the new BC Technology Fund was more broadly based, and in 2023 the province joined with the federal government and industry to announce a new $700 million life sciences cluster for Vancouver.[40] Since 2018, successive provincial governments have also welcomed the federal government's Super Cluster plan for British Columbia for digital technology. Indeed, whether as a funding partner and/or facilitator, the province has been part of a proliferation of federal government programs available to stimulate innovation in Metro Vancouver. Locally, these initiatives have been endorsed by creation of the Vancouver Economic Commission in 1996 that provided information, advice, and support for high-tech developments, until a surprising decision in 2023 by the newly elected Mayor Ken Sim to wind it down.

Connecting with the Federal Government

Federal government programs supporting innovation have been truly labyrinthian in recent decades, including many that have sought to rejuvenate or modernize the traditional industrial mainstays of the economy, such as steel, autos, and forestry, as well as high-tech industries, such as aerospace, electronics, and renewable energy. In a recent opinion piece, for example, Andrew Coyne noted that the then (2014) government "found more than 60 [federal innovation programs], worth billions of dollars annually, spread across 17 different federal agencies," many well-established.[41] While some government policies focus on particular sectors others apply across the economy. In Metro Vancouver, numerous firms such as Ballard and MDA have long received federal support for innovation and for MDA the federal government is an important customer. Selected initiatives are illustrated in Table 5.5.

As the oldest of the selected initiatives, the National Research Council was established in 1916 mainly to support university research with industry potential and evolved as a "generic" part of wider federal government support programs for innovation that included control of R&D laboratories, especially in the resource sector. NRC's IRAP was introduced in the 1950s and since then has been accessed widely by university researchers in collaboration with industry interests. It remains active and is now part of the Ministry of Innovation, Science and Development (ISED) formed in 2015. Support for R&D, principally in the form of tax credits controlled by the Canada Revenue Agency, is another long-standing policy that continues to

TABLE 5.5 Federal agencies supporting high tech

Organization	Mandate and development
The National Research Council of Canada's (NRC) Industrial Research Assistance Program (IRAP).	The NRC is within the Ministry of Innovation, Science and Economic Development, with the head office in Ottawa and a contact office at UBC. Formed in 1916; IRAP introduced in the 1950s. IRAP seeks to help businesses and in recent years especially has supported research collaborations with university faculty. IRAP is national in scope, and in British Columbia in 2020 IRAP and Innovate BC signed a memorandum of understanding to invest $2 million in R&D funding in twenty-two companies, organized within the BC Fast Pilot Program.
The scientific research and experimental development tax credit, administered by the Canada Revenue Agency	Can be traced to 1944 when introduced as part of the Income Tax Act. Designed to encourage Canadian firms in all sectors to conduct R&D through income tax credits, investment tax credits, and sometimes refunds. Replaced by a cash grant system between 1965 and 1977, when tax credits were reintroduced. "Scientific research and experimental development" first referenced in 1986.

Organization	Mandate and development
Innovation, Science and Economic Development Canada (ISED)	Established in 2015, head office in Ottawa. Department renamed from Industry Canada, which in 1993 renamed the Department of Industry, Trade and Commerce established in 1969. With an annual budget of about $5 billion and over 4,000 employees, controls four ministries, including Innovation, Science and Industry (others relate to trade, rural development, and tourism). Mandated to support economic development across Canada. Controls regional development agencies, the Canadian Foundation for Innovation, the Strategic Innovation Fund, the Innovation Super Cluster Initiative, and Western Economic Diversification Canada.
Canadian Foundation for Innovation	An NPO established in 1997, head office in Ottawa, part of ISED. Funds research facilities and equipment mainly for university research hospitals to attract and retain researchers and train personnel with a broad focus. Budgeted expenditures in 2019 were $400 million.
MITACs (Mathematics of Information Technology and Complex Systems)	An NPO formed in 1999 by mathematicians as a centre in the Canadian Network of Centres of Excellence at UBC (its head office). Jointly funded by federal and provincial governments and academic and research partners. By 2020, received almost $200 million from the federal government. Mandated to support student education and research that encourages innovation in partnership with industry, government, and academia. Strong research collaboration and graduate training focus. Originally supported R&D in the natural sciences and after 2007 open to all disciplines. Supported over 3,300 projects in BC alone by 2022.
Genome Canada	Founded by the federal government in 2000 as an independent NPO with twenty to forty-five employees. Head office in Ottawa and an office in Vancouver. A catalyst and bridging organization in stimulating genomic research and commercialization in life sciences linking the public and private sectors.

▶

◄

Organization	Mandate and development
	By 2020, Genome BC generated more than $1.1 billion in investment in over 425 research projects in several different sectors (especially resource based).
Sustainable Development Technology Canada	An NPO established in 2001 by the federal government as an independent foundation, with the head office in Ottawa. Supports small and medium-sized companies for clean technology developments from seed to scale up. Invested $1.3 billion in 450 companies across Canada by 2019.
Institute of Fuel Cell Innovation	Established in 2002 at UBC by the National Research Council of Canada (part of ISED). Mandated to research, test, and evaluate fuel cell innovations. Collaborates with Ballard Power Systems among others.
Centre for Drug Research and Development	Established in 2007 with the head office in Vancouver. A nationally mandated organization with 101 employees. Liaises with ISED. Multiple funding sources within governments and industry. Conducts R&D in several laboratories to help commercialize innovations by creating spinoffs, assisting companies to scale up, and providing training. Has registered seventy-two patents.
Canada's Innovation Super Cluster Initiative	An NPO established in 2017 and renamed Global Innovation Clusters in 2021 with renewed funding. Part of ISED, with the head office in Ottawa. Five super clusters located across Canada, initially supported by $950 million in funding over five years. In British Columbia by 2019, its Digital Technology Super Cluster had 34 members and more than 450 associates. Seeks to accelerate the development of digital technologies to improve productivity and reduce climate impacts.
Strategic Innovation Fund	An NPO established in 2018 as part of ISED, with the head office in Ottawa. Supports investments and collaborations in all sectors. Commitments of about $5 billion by 2021.

Notes: The Natural Sciences and Engineering Research Council and the Social Sciences and Humanities Research Council are not included. Other established programs omitted include: the Innovation Program, the Technology Demonstration Program, the Strategic Aerospace and Defence Initiative, the Strategic Networks Grants, and the Networks of Centres of Excellence. Also, in early 2023, the government announced a blueprint for the establishment of the Canada Innovation Corporation, planned to start in 2026.

be accessed widely by all industries. In addition to the continuation of these programs, the clamour for greater support for innovation across Canada has led to new national initiatives and organizations to support developmental research and technology transfer, several of which apply across all sectors, including high-tech activities. The recency of these initiatives reflects the need to support emerging trends in an innovation economy.

As an umbrella framework for many programs, the formation of ISED in 2015, though it relabelled long-established bureaucracies, nevertheless reflected a shift in thinking toward highlighting innovation. In practice, the mandate of this large department is far-ranging, embracing four ministries, including the Ministry of Innovation, Science and Industry, and it has governance over the NRC and IRAP, along with the Canadian Foundation for Innovation established in 1997 with its health sector orientation. Recently, the commitment of the Department of Innovation, Science and Economic Development to support innovation has been highlighted by establishment of the Innovation Super Cluster Initiative (2017), since 2021 called Global Innovation Clusters, and the Strategic Innovation Fund (SIF) in 2018. There are five super clusters located across the country, and Metro Vancouver is the home of the Digital Technologies Initiative, with the broad (vaguely stated) goal to support such technologies potentially relevant to firms in different sectors, from forestry to health care. Meanwhile, the Ottawa-based SIF, whose goals are also broadly stated in support of economic development, is potentially accessible to firms in all sectors seeking to invest in Canada. In Metro Vancouver, the SIF listed nine projects involving eight firms that had received over $400 million in funding between 2018 and 2021, with AbCellera Biologics accounting for over 40 percent of the funds (see Table 5.6).

Although relatively diverse, four of the nine projects were in the life sciences and two in renewable energy, both important industry thrusts in the region. ISED also controls regional agencies (established at various times since 2008) that fund development projects. Services for Metro Vancouver firms were provided from Edmonton until 2021, when an office was established in Vancouver. In addition to the tentacles of ISED, the federal government was involved in the formation of MITACs (1999), Genome Canada (2000), Sustainable Development Technology Canada (2001), the Institute of Fuel Cell Innovation (2002), and the Centre for Drug Research and Development (2007). The last two agencies are located in Metro Vancouver and a response to local expertise in the renewable energy and drug development

TABLE 5.6 Strategic innovation funds for Metro Vancouver high-tech firms, 2018–21

Firm	Project	SIF funds ($ million)	Total investment	New jobs (new and maintained jobs)
AbCellera Biologics, Vancouver	Improve discovery platform and biomanufacture antibodies for clinical trials to combat COVID-19	175.5 (n/a)	287.4	113 (230)
D-Wave Systems, Burnaby	Software development funding for quantum computers	40.0 (n/a)	119.9	84 (200)
General Fusion, Burnaby	Build prototype plant powered by nuclear fusion	49.3	153.3	100 (170)
Mastercard Technologies, Vancouver	New cybersecurity R&D centre	49	420 (by 2029)	268 (380)
Precision Nano Systems, Vancouver	Develop vaccines to combat COVID-19	18.2	24.3	35 (125)
Precision Nano Systems, Vancouver	New plant to biomanufacture vaccines	25.1	50.2	90 (125)
Stemcell Technologies, Burnaby	Plant to manufacture products for clinical trials in cell therapy	22.5 (22.5)	138.1	675 (1,484)
Switch Materials, Burnaby	Develop advanced glazing technology for vehicles	8.3	16.5	63 (94)
Svante, Vancouver	Centre to develop low-cost carbon recapture and scale up manufacturing	25	97.2	53 (125)

Notes: In nearby Squamish, Carbon Engineering received $25 million from SIF in a total investment of $114.6 million to support 400 jobs. In 2023, the federal and BC governments announced $300 million in support for AbCellera Biologics to build a new biotech campus and enlarge others as part of a $701 million project focused on clinical testing and production.

Source: Government of Canada, "Announced Projects from Innovation, Science and Economic Development Canada," 2021.

fields. MITACs originated and is headquartered in Vancouver (at UBC), and Genome BC, also an NPO, has a Vancouver office; the head offices of most federal agencies mentioned are in Ottawa. With a few exceptions (energy transition projects and life sciences research), federal programs are broadly mandated, typically involve (partial) funding, and are voluntary.

Policy Evolution: A Learning as Well as Political Process?

Government policies on innovation are driven inevitably by "political" self-interest, possibly to an increasing degree in recent times, and rarely if ever without self-applause, albeit usually enhanced by a public rationale. Indeed, the commitments that different levels of government have made to promoting innovation in Metro Vancouver's economy, not least in high tech, are to be appreciated. Their programs have grown substantially in providing financial help (tax breaks, capital cost subsidies, infrastructure provisions) and in supporting various services, ranging from helping the incubation of new business to hiring foreign talent. From a related perspective, public commitment to promoting Pacific Rim connections, including with respect to the Cascadia Corridor that anticipates stronger connections with the US Pacific Coast, can be recognized as helping to further Metro Vancouver's high-tech potential. Government programs are generally widely available, even as the choices of support involve specific companies and projects. Compared with the "simple" Discovery Park, a zoning exercise hoping to attract high-tech investments whatever their nature, policy on innovation has been a learning experience in Metro Vancouver, including policies on promising developments.[42]

Nevertheless, questions can be raised about whether government support for high-tech in Metro Vancouver is sufficient, appropriate and/or too diffuse. Moreover, such questions are evident in the mainstream business community. As David Main, then the CEO of Vancouver-based Aquinox, and now the CEO of Notch Therapeutics, states,

> when you add up all the investments of federal and provincial governments in Canada, you come to the conclusion that the government is doing more than its fair share. Nonetheless, the coordination is poor and the investment landscape highly fragmented. It is composed of a multitude of individual initiatives rather than pursuing a concerted focus which would encourage efficiency ... Canada spends a lot on basic research, all universities are subsidized by government, but nothing translates truly into action. For instance, having a life sciences dimension in the recent super cluster

initiative that identified industries of focus ... would have been very beneficial and an important sign for the right direction. What is lacking in Canada
is the focus on moving research from the early stages all the way through to
commercialization, to capture the value of the full ecosystem.[43]

These comments are especially apropos regarding Metro Vancouver's high-
tech policy environment. As an example, though the Global Clusters announcement came with much fanfare, its not inconsequential promise of
$960 million in funding to occur over five years for Metro Vancouver, at the
time of the program's renewal in 2021, has meant about $173 million in
commitments. That amount translates to a relatively modest $35 million or
so per year – Ballard's R&D losses alone have been greater in some years.
Moreover, what was the particular rationale in the rather generic Digital
Technologies label in terms of specific local assets upon which it hopes to
build and direct? Coordination in any specific sense between this super cluster and the SIF program (and other programs, for that matter) is not obvious. Furthermore, participation is voluntary; there are no particular
targets regarding industry priorities, global leadership, or overall levels of
employment. Canadian control is also (apparently) not an issue, and how
intellectual property is to be promoted is not clear. Given that the super
cluster and SIF programs are recent, and so far few firms have participated
in them, how are these programs to be assessed? And is this super cluster
more important than life sciences or renewable energy clusters? Or new
media (or value-added wood)? Other questions about high-tech policies for
Metro Vancouver can be raised. For example, governments seem to want
core firms, without saying why or what they are (or how to help create them).
   In broad terms, the mounting plethora of policies in support of innovation introduced by the federal and BC governments that are accessible to
Metro Vancouver firms suggests a growing understanding of the importance of innovation for national and local economic development, particularly for enhancing productivity, increasing wealth per capita and, it might
be added, for meeting green goals. Within high-tech, governments have
learned of the multi-faceted needs required to help start-ups and in scaling
up processes, and are doing a lot, for example in terms of funding, providing facilities and helping to access talent. Yet, a consolidated, more coherent
policy on innovation remains a challenge, both nationally and provincially
in BC[44]. Although the issues are complex, that Canadian productivity trends
are globally poor, and have been so for decades, is scarcely an endorsement
of the effectiveness of innovation policies, and unclear that enough has been

learned. Recent commentaries by well-informed experts, for example, provide lucid understandings of the weaknesses of Canadian innovation policies, but suggestions to establish an advisory body (presumably like the old Science Council of Canada), or to modify the tax credit system seem rather minor.[45] Despite (or because of?) their proliferation, truly critical assessments of the effectiveness on innovation policies in terms of promoting development and productivity are lacking. For other experts such as Jim Balsillie and Dan Breznitz a stronger focus needs to be placed on supporting *and* elaborating intellectual property rights among high-tech firms within Canada.[46] If such thinking has hitherto been policy terra incognita it needs to be reversed.

Conclusion

Institutional architecture support for high tech in Metro Vancouver has deepened in tandem with the sector's growth, vibrancy, and breadth. Within high-tech, this deepening has occurred around the continued proliferation of SMEs (see Chapter 2) and increasing flows of FDI (see Chapter 3) that together feature a clustering of wide-ranging activities involving various forms of inter-firm relations (see Chapter 4). Further, as this chapter has shown, localized external economies, diverse forms of industry associations, university involvements, venture capital suppliers, and government policies have complemented the diverse specializations among high-tech firms. In so doing, this supporting institutional architecture has contributed much to "local buzz" and "global pipelines."[47] Locally, this developing architecture can be summarized as the core of Metro Vancouver's regional innovation system (RIS).

In broad terms, RISs comprise networks of public and private (formal and informal) institutions and policies that support the local creation and diffusion of economically useful knowledge (see Figure 5.1). RISs are locally distinct in particular sectors, closely integrated within national systems, yet also connected globally.[48] RISs take on different forms and trajectories, but as in Silicon Valley–style exemplars and in the case of Metro Vancouver, they are driven fundamentally by business. High-road trajectories imply an evolution to RISs that are sophisticated, coherent, well networked (locally and globally), and driven to support innovation-based competitive advantages. In contrast, low-road-derived RISs are simple, fragmented, and cost based. From this perspective, the evolution of high-tech in Metro Vancouver is at least consistent with the high-road trajectory, with clusters of business firms that provide innovative products and processes are at its heart. Tied

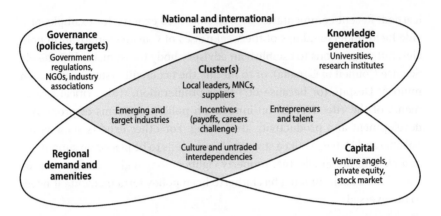

FIGURE 5.1 This model shows the main institutional drivers of locally concentrated innovation systems and clusters. Businesses, both local and MNCs, in various activities, and how they are connected, including with respect to incentives, are the core of the system. Institutions involved in governance, knowledge creation, and financing provide crucial roles in shaping the innovation system, as do regional demand and the supply of amenities.

together by traded and untraded interdependencies, these clusters are fed directly by pools of entrepreneurship and talent, and, within emerging or possibly targeted industries, leading firms can be local or MNCs and supply final or intermediate goods. For these firms, innovativeness and creativity draw from in-house R&D programs and/or from experience, design activity, imagination, and intuition, strongly shaping rewards and incentives in terms of careers, financial returns, prestige, size, market share, et cetera. Over time, the deepening of cluster or agglomeration economies implies increasing local connections among institutions in support of a stronger global presence.

In this interpretation of a high-tech RIS for Metro Vancouver, the clustering qua agglomeration of individual firms draws from an array of services from other institutions to help promote their innovativeness. These institutions complement businesses in different ways that generally relate to governance, knowledge generation, and finance. In terms of governance, national and BC governments exercise particularly important influences on Metro Vancouver's economy and society, including policies targeting high tech, in terms of providing infrastructure, subsidies, planning regulations, and immigration. In more focused, limited ways, industry associations and related organizations further assist the governance of Metro Vancouver's high-tech activities in terms of the collective challenges that they face. With respect to knowledge generation, Metro Vancouver's universities and colleges, led by UBC, play particularly powerful and diverse roles in the region's RIS as suppliers of sophisticated research, creators of talent, sources of business spinoffs, and (wide-ranging) cultural amenities. Regarding finance, high-tech firms in Metro Vancouver, as elsewhere, can access personal sources and public stock exchanges, but their demands for substantial amounts of high-risk capital have stimulated the development of venture capitalists and angels. Ultimately, the overall goal of RISs is to create products in demand, even as individual actors have their own distinct motivations, and this reality needs to be kept in mind. Suffice it to say that many innovative firms and clusters in Metro Vancouver anticipate roles within global production systems, and local demands are important in stimulating new opportunities, allowing new firms to reach the minimum efficient size, and attracting MNCs that seek to extend their market horizons.

More critically, the value of thinking about Metro Vancouver's high-tech RIS is to raise questions regarding the distinctive roles, nature, and sizes of different public and private sector institutions, how these roles are articulated, and the balance between local and global connections as they evolve. For Metro Vancouver, such questions at least raise conundrums (see Chapter 7). Questions can be raised, for example, regarding the adequacy or not of the overall size and scope of the contributions of business (large and small, local, and foreign), universities and governments, and of their interdependencies. More specifically, for example, is the level of business R&D sufficient? Is the diversity of business clusters appropriate for local development Is local risk financing sufficient? Are university spinoffs appropriately organized and should they better supported or not? Are there too many government policies that are too driven by short-term considerations? And how might increased FDI, as a two-way global pipeline bringing benefits in and taking them out, change the region's underlying institutional architecture? Metro Vancouver's high-tech RIS both helps reveal the actual anatomy of its institutional architecture and raises issues that deserve research and policy attention.

6
Lifestyle Innovators, West Coast Style

What is a better-known symbol of Metro Vancouver's new economy, MDA, Electronic Arts, Amazon's new subsidiary, or Lululemon? The corporate innovators that have raised Vancouver's global profile are not necessarily high tech. Rather, the region's lifestyles have propagated fashion, outdoor equipment, restaurant and beer products, and businesses that contribute much to the region's identity and, unlike the city's high-tech contributions, sit at the apex of the value chain. Lululemon, in 2023, only second to Nike in valuation among athletic fashion companies, leads this cohort, but there are several others that have created national or global brands. Principally, the innovations of these companies occur not in research laboratories but in the conceptualization and design inspired by the city's way of living. That this type of innovation and scaling up can occur in Metro Vancouver is both interesting in its own right and helps to illuminate the difficulties facing high tech. Whereas lifestyle innovators draw inspiration for their products from local demand and then diffuse these fashions globally, the majority of tech innovators attempt to discover some element of universal significance that will contribute inputs to larger technological value chains. This chapter thus serves the dual purpose of illustrating how a peripheral city can use its innate advantages to integrate into and grow within the global economy while further revealing the challenges of growing an economy out of a lab. Moreover, there is an interdependence between the sectors. The high-tech and West Coast lifestyle activities reinforce each other because the former have evolved within Metro Vancouver around talent pools attracted to and made sticky by desirable lifestyles and amenities. In a virtuous cycle, these activities have stimulated local entrepreneurs to establish innovative businesses that serve, reflect, and shape those lifestyles and a local identity. To understand Metro Vancouver's high-tech economy, lifestyle innovation must also be understood.

The lifestyle products that Metro Vancouver generates provide direct, if somewhat ironic, benefits of the postindustrial economy that forestry and resource incomes afforded the region's citizens from earlier times. Yoga, mountain biking, skiing, hip fashions, rounded out with casual dining and craft beer, have been generated in a city that enjoys a substantive leisure capacity. Globally, such a trend illustrates the emergence of postindustrial cities from their industrial origins, evocatively characterized as a transformation from "landscapes of production to landscapes of consumption."[1] This perspective complements the hitherto emphasized themes of urban transformation from industrial economies to service and especially knowledge-based or creative economies highlighted by high-tech activities.[2] In this view, increased creativity and consumption are related trends, both associated with rising per capita incomes and service-centred employment. Thus, talent provides the knowledge inputs to the competitive advantages of creative businesses, most obviously expressed in high-tech activities, and seeks places that offer (various) preferred urban amenities and lifestyles while rejecting places characterized by low levels of amenities and unwanted lifestyles. But amenities and lifestyles are not simply "given" locational factors that attract or repel talent.[3] Rather, rising pools of higher-income talent help to fuel changing habits of consumption, preferences, and lifestyles, including goods and services that serve recreational, amenity, health, and quality-oriented markets. Indeed, this servicing of lifestyle desires reinforces the trend (of deindustrialization) away from manufacturing as an engine of growth and toward the connections between the "cognitive" and "cultural" assets of creative, postindustrial cities.[4] Such servicing is profoundly shaped by place.

Changing consumer habits that value creativity, distinctive design, and service, and enable an association with a specific place and its lifestyles, can be seen as reactions to the homogeneity and mass production of previous decades. This evolution allows consumers to diversify and distinguish their demands by emphasizing aesthetics and symbolism, thereby increasing their "cultural capital."[5] In effect, in creative, craft, and lifestyle industries, products are consumed on the basis of where they are produced, with such place identification providing added symbolic value through reputation, exclusivity, cachet, and a sense of product authenticity to the consumer, a trend summarized as "neo-localism."[6] That consumers are prepared to pay a premium for products with particular place-specific origins and associations provides producers with a form of "monopoly rent" relative to competitors' locations, where it is not easy for the place-specific characteristics to be replicated. For Allen Scott, how the identity of places imbues products with additional value through association contributes to virtuous processes of "recursive intensification" in which place identity and product innovation reinforce each other.[7] In summary, products enjoy monopoly rents because of the association of innovativeness and creativity with a "unique place," possibly by making a connection to its history, famous landscape, lifestyles, or reputations of notable firms, in which "favorable geographical stories, certified or not, create entry barriers for products from other places."[8] This identification of products with specific places, enhancing their reputation and attraction as sites of and for consumption, both local and nonlocal, in turn contributes to distinctive local-global dynamics.

An emphasis on lifestyle and the generation of innovation should not obscure, however, the importance of industrial structuring within and outside Metro Vancouver. How do these companies – all entrepreneurial in origin – scale up to become globally significant companies? Which further attributes does the region have beyond lifestyles that enable the companies to grow efficiently? If attributes, such as textile raw materials or inexpensive textile labour, are lacking, then how are these challenges overcome? Are these innovators capable of generating a cluster? Metro Vancouver demonstrates a deep and broad capacity in what Porter[9] termed "demand conditions" (too often an overlooked aspect of his cluster diamond model), but does it generate external economies through a network of suppliers or interact with related industries? Does the region generate externalities through labour pooling, competitive rivalry, or governmental and associational support? How are its national and global connections structured to take advantage of the efficiencies offered elsewhere and to overcome the weakness within the region? Despite the apparent lifestyle innovators' products and scales of performance, answering these questions helps to determine whether these innovators are delivering a more deeply rooted local economy, one capable of providing a broader base of high-road jobs. The evidence is that, although apparel and food and beverages are often regarded as mature, low-tech sectors, Metro Vancouver's lifestyle businesses prosper through innovation, design, and experiential activities that support substantial high-level local employment, organized by head offices that control continental and global organizations.

The following discussion is selective because lifestyle businesses are not an established industry category used for reporting purposes, and some overall contribution to provincial or local GDP or employment is not possible. However, estimates of the size of the industries examined in this chapter are available, and the discussion references the leaders in Metro Vancouver in these activities. Information is drawn principally from published studies, including business reports and websites, articles in business journals and newspapers that feature interviews with key actors, and in one case (Lululemon) an autobiography.[10] A loose categorization of lifestyle business is proposed. Among apparel and fashion activities, the discussion particularly highlights Lululemon, Arc'teryx, Aritzia, and Mountain Equipment Co-op (MEC) as the largest, best-known businesses that have significantly expanded beyond British Columbia through exports and investments. In broad terms, these firms serve the urban and outdoor recreational lifestyles of consumers, as do a number of innovative SMEs, some of them also well known. In addition to apparel, the Metro Vancouver lifestyle is lived through its food and beverages. Led by The Keg and Earls, the growth of several restaurant chains captures a West Coast dining style and, along with the emergence of microbreweries across Metro Vancouver, further illustrates the influence of local lifestyle-driven consumption on distinctive, creative business development. A discussion of microbreweries further illustrates how localized consumption reflects local distinctiveness.

Acknowledging (Canadian) Lifestyles as Consumption-Based Business Generators

If the idea of "lifestyle" is broadly associated with "ways of life" among groups of people, then in contemporary rich economies the term is often expressed as the "quality of life," in relation to people's tastes, preferences, and consumption patterns of goods and services in their leisure time or often for related amenity, recreational, health, prestige, and spiritual purposes. It has been long recognized that, as dynamic city-regions become bigger and wealthier, local demands for goods and services become inherently more important as wealth generators, with consumers able and willing to spend increasing shares of their (increasing) disposable incomes on discretionary purchases. Within the context of the "old" staples thesis of urban and regional development in Canada, including in British Columbia, the growing importance of local consumption is expressed through the creation of "final demand linkages" that complement the growth provided by re-source exports and their generation of backward (supply) and forward (further processing) linkages.[11] Potentially, such final demands strictly in-volve not only the local consumption of relatively standardized goods and services but also the evolution of innovative lifestyle businesses that can con-tribute new, consumer-driven, autonomous forms of urban growth, divers-ification, and export income.

Indeed, as the geodemographic marketing industry informs us, consumer tastes and demands vary among and within countries, regions, and cities. These variations can be highly nuanced. Environics Analytics of Toronto, for example, is a leader in this field and uses extensive data sources on house-holds to map and label detailed variations in consumer types within cities and regions, including Metro Vancouver.[12] Environics Analytics basically provides a marketing guide for businesses, in effect allowing them geograph-ically to target existing distinct consumer profiles strongly associated with distinct lifestyles. In a more generalized, subjective fashion, the online pub-lication *Strategy* debated the views of professional advertising firms on the extent to which Metro Vancouver constitutes distinctive or shared "main-stream" marketing opportunities.[13] They concluded that, though sharing con-sumption patterns in North America, Metro Vancouver "harbors a unique consumer market that is ever-changing and growing," such that the forms of advertising that work in Toronto might not apply on the West Coast. For example, as Terry O'Reilly's popular marketing series on CBC Radio rec-ords, one interesting expression of Metro Vancouver's distinctive consump-tion is its unusual preference for luxury autos.[14] Indeed, this program (and series) illustrate that "where you live dictates what you buy," and, "what you chose is greatly influenced by what you see others doing" – helping to reinforce a long-standing theme in the literature that much consumption is socialized, interdependent rather than independent.[15]

Metro Vancouver well illustrates these co-evolving trends between crea-tivity and consumption, including by businesses that implement innovative opportunities that extend, promote, or identify consumer lifestyle prefer-ences. As a newspaper profile recently observed, Metro Vancouver has been remarkably prolific in creating high-profile, locally rooted, distinctive life-style businesses and forms of consumerism that in turn have exerted influ-ence across Canada, North America, and beyond.[16] This article especially cited apparel businesses such as Lululemon, Aritzia, Arc'teryx, MEC, Herschel, Sugoi, Kit and Wilson, and Fluevog Shoes and restaurant chains such as Earls, The Keg, Milestones, and Browns Socialhouse that originated in Metro Vancouver. Such lists can be expanded readily to include restaurant chains such as the Cactus Club and Moxie's Grill and Bar and a related proliferation of microbreweries such as Horseshoe Bay Brewery and Granville Island Brewing, both of which claim to be Canada's first microbreweries. Other lifestyle-driven initiatives can be noted, such as the formation of mountain bike and kayak producers. These initiatives express the particular amenity-related conditions and lifestyle aspirations of Metro Vancouver. As a senior manager at Arc'teryx stated, "for brands rooted in outdoor activity ... there's not a better place in the world ... We can take an idea from one of our designers, whip up a prototype, and two hours later take it up into the mountains."[17] As another example, restaurant innovations such as Earls reflect a casual premium style, and "their menus are more adventurous, with influences from many different cuisines, in keeping with the ethnic makeup and collective palate of Vancouverites, who have been shifting away from the North American diet for half a century."[18] In more general terms, such business initiatives elaborate the emergence of Metro Vancouver as a postindustrial city, made iconic with the False Creek–Granville Island Market developments starting in the 1970s and Expo 86 and recently popularized, albeit boosterishly, as Vancouverism, a distinct planning framework for embracing local living and lifestyles.[19]

If MacDonald Dettwiler and Associates (MDA) in 1969 was a marker for high-tech expansion, then the creation of Fluevog Shoes and MEC in 1970 and 1971, respectively, provides similar early indications of the growth of locally owned, consumer-driven, innovative lifestyle businesses rooted in West Coast cultures. MEC, of course, had environmental credentials and started at a time when the environmental movement was developing rapidly, not least through the formation of GreenPeace in Vancouver in 1971. In practice, in British Columbia, environmental NGOs focused their opposition on resource production, allowing Metro Vancouver to celebrate high tech, consumerism, and the environment as part of its brand, seemingly without much appreciation of any contradictions in these relationships. Indeed, the labelling or branding of Metro Vancouver in distinctive lifestyle terms is not straightforward, in part because of the global nature of consumerism that links and standardizes as well as differentiates cities and regions.

The Evolutionary Dynamics of Signature Apparel Companies

According to a recent report, Metro Vancouver's apparel and fashion cluster, circa 2015, comprised an estimated 375 firms, supporting almost 8,000 jobs, including design, manufacturing, and retail activities, with Lululemon, MEC, Aritzia, and Arc'teryx cited as international leaders and several others, including Fluevog Shoes, contributing to globally recognized brands.[20] The recent growth of the apparel and fashion cluster has been impressive, driven by wide-ranging entrepreneurial firms, albeit without policy anticipation.

The distinctiveness of Metro Vancouver's lifestyle apparel and fashion cluster is well illustrated by its signature "leading" companies (see Table 6.1).[21]

TABLE 6.1 Seven signature "lifestyle" apparel companies originating in Metro Vancouver since 1970

Firm founders and focus	*Size and scope*
Fluevog Shoes	
Founded in 1970 in Vancouver (Gastown) by John Fluevog and Peter Fox as Fox and Fluevog. Both had worked in a local shoe store. Name changed in 1980s as Fluevog took control. High-end designer ("unique") shoes; mainly sells its own brands.	Estimated revenue in 2019 of over $100 million with 100 employees. Relocated the Vancouver store in 1973. Opened stores in Seattle (1985), Boston (1987), Toronto (1989), San Francisco (1997), and Chicago (1999). Reopened a store in Vancouver's Gastown. Ten stores by 2010 and twenty-five by 2018 located across North America and recently in Amsterdam (2018), Australia, and Germany. Adopted a green philosophy based on recycled, sustainable materials.
Mountain Equipment Co-op	
Sporting goods store founded in 1971 in Vancouver by four members of the UBC outdoor club. Similar to a Seattle store, REI (Recreational Equipment, Inc.) but organized as a cooperative with memberships. Started as a climbing and outdoor gear retail company, becoming a diversified supplier of outdoor apparel and equipment. Membership fee of five dollars (as in 1971) until 2020.	Sales in 2018–19 of $462 million with 2,583 employees across Canada. Run by volunteers in the first three years; membership grew from 6 (1971) to 700 (1974), 57,000 (1981), 250,000 (1990), 1 million (1997), 3 million (2009), and 5 million (2017). Expansions in Vancouver and new stores opened in Toronto (1983), Calgary (1987), Ottawa (1992), Edmonton (1998), and Halifax (2001). By 2018, twenty-two stores across Canada. Follows green and fair labour philosophies.

Firm founders and focus	Size and scope
	Contract supplies increasingly come from China. Income losses during COVID-19 led to acquisition by Kingswood Capital Management of Los Angeles in 2020; now a private company, not a cooperative.
Aritzia	
Founded in Vancouver in 1984 by Brian Hill. Began as a stand-alone boutique within a family-owned department store. Focuses on high-quality women's "fashion" clothing.	Sales in 2018 of $743.3 million with 4,000–4,500 employees. Listed on the Toronto Stock Exchange in 2016. Quickly built five stores in Vancouver, the basis for national expansion in the 1990s. In 2005, Boston-based Berkshire Partners bought a majority share, helping to finance US growth. By 2018, eighty-four stores or boutiques in North America, sixty-three in Canada and twenty-one in the United States.
Sugoi Performance Apparel	
Founded in 1987 in Burnaby by Carol Prantner and David Hollands, a wife-husband team, to design and manufacture performance apparel for mountain biking. Carol had obtained a degree in fashion from Kwantlen university and had worked for a couple of independent design stores before starting her own (with David).	Started as a two-person team in a home basement and reached $1 million in sales by 1990. Acquired in 2005 by Cannondale, a US company just out of receivership (founders leaving the company), which in 2008 was acquired by Dorel Industries of Montreal ($2.6 billion in revenue in 2018). Acquired Sombrio of North Vancouver (founded by Dave Watson in 1998) in 2014, supplementing mountain bike apparel. Moved into new Burnaby facilities in 2010, with manufacturing outsourced in 2011. Peak employment of about 250 with sales of about $50 million. The Sugoi and Sombrio clothing brands sold to Louis Garneau Sports in 2018; sales and design (100 jobs) to be kept in Vancouver as Sugoi Global, with other activities transferred to Quebec.

▶

◄

Firm founders and focus	*Size and scope*
Arc'teryx	
Founded in 1989 in North Vancouver as Rock Solid by David Lane and Jeremy Guard; name changed in 1992. Maker of high-end outdoor clothing. Moved head office to Burnaby in 1999 and back to North Vancouver in 2005.	Estimated revenue in 2018 of over $500 million with over 800 employees in Metro Vancouver. Opened in Montreal in 2006; by 2018, sixteen brand stores in North America (five in Canada), with others in Switzerland, France, the United Kingdom, Japan, and China. Products distributed through 3,000 retail locations in forty countries. Manufactures in New Westminster and outsources to China and elsewhere. Acquired by the Salomon Group in 2001 and by Amer Sports of Finland in 2005; China's Ante bought 56 percent of Amer Sports in 2019.
Lululemon Athletica	
Founded in 1998 in Vancouver by Chip Wilson. Makes athletic clothing especially for women. Began as a design studio by day and a yoga studio at night; first stand-alone store opened in Kitsilano in 1999. New head office planned (Great Northern Way, Vancouver.	Revenue in 2019 of $3.3 billion with 5,200 employees in Canada (2,600 in 2012), 2,000 jobs in the Vancouver head office, and globally 15,700 employees. Went public in 2007. By 2019, 506 stores worldwide, 305 in the United States and 63 in Canada, also in greater China (38), Australia (31), the United Kingdom (14), New Zealand (7), Japan (7), Germany (6), South Korea (5), Singapore (49), France (3), Sweden (2), and Ireland (1).
Herschel Supply Company	
Founded in 2009 in Vancouver by Lyndon and Jamie Cormack. Designs backpacks, other bags, and accessories	In 2016, revenues of $156 million with 200 employees globally. A new flagship store opened in Vancouver in 2018. There are forty-four retail locations worldwide, including in Hong Kong, Dubai, and Paris.

Sources: Authors' research files.

In particular, Lululemon, Aritzia, Arc'teryx, MEC, Fluevog Shoes, Sugoi, and to some extent Herschel developed as locally high-profile consumer companies that, as representatives of West Coast lifestyles, have developed significant brand name presence across Canada, in the United States, and in some cases beyond. These apparel and fashion signature companies might be regarded as surprising or unexpected in that they stemmed not from established textile or clothing specialties within the region but as entrepreneurial initiatives reflecting the diversity of Metro Vancouver's distinct lifestyles. Indeed, though the seven identified apparel firms collectively operate in the same industry, their market roles differ and largely complement one another. Their evolutionary trajectories illustrate the interrelationships between place and lifestyle businesses led by design-oriented innovation and creativity.

Entrepreneurial Origins and Overall Growth

The highlighted firms are part of Metro Vancouver's contemporary post-industrial development, with the first two founded in 1970 (Fluevog Shoes) and 1971 (MEC) and the remainder beginning after the recessionary crash of the early 1980s, starting with Aritzia (1984). Their founders were locally born and raised or had become residents within Metro Vancouver, once again underlining the importance of the seedbed hypothesis and the benefits to new firm formation of local know-how and connections.[22] In this regard, Chip Wilson, the founder of Lululemon, has a more complicated biography that nevertheless emphasizes the importance of local understanding in company start-ups.[23] Although born in California, he was raised in Alberta from the age of five (becoming a swimmer at the University of Calgary), and he developed a successful company before arriving in Vancouver in his thirties, joining a couple of entrepreneurial friends. He then founded Lululemon, stimulated by observations made at a local yoga class. These firms were soon challenged by the need to "scale up" from ideas and individual examples of new products to a minimum size of profitable operations, requiring minimum levels of materials to be purchased to be cost effective, along with investments in production and labour, prior (hopefully) to serving a sufficient number of customers. Wilson describes such struggles in the early months of Lululemon when his new fabric had to be produced in sufficient quantities to be economic and the resulting output sold. The initial start-up problems facing Fluevog Shoes and Arc'teryx would have been similarly acute though softened in the case of Aritzia by its creation within an established (family-owned), large department store. MEC, conversely, did not face the same challenges because at start-up it sought to sell an already established line of goods and only later developed its own line of products.

Since start-up, the growth of these signature apparel companies has been impressive, at least until 2018 (see Table 6.1). Lululemon, for example, started from one location in Vancouver in 1998–99 and soon faced cash-flow problems. However, by 2019, it had generated revenues of $3.29 billion from over 500 stores globally in support of 15,700 employees, with 2,000 based in Metro Vancouver. As such, Lululemon illustrates a "big firm locally," bigger than most leading, locally based, high-tech firms (see Chapter 2). Similarly, the growth in revenues generated by MEC, Aritzia, and Arc'teryx have been rapid, with Aritzia's revenues in 2018 of $743.3 million the next largest after Lululemon. Meanwhile, as the smallest of the identified companies, Sugoi reported almost $50 million in sales in the early 2000s. Also, from single-location beginnings, by 2018 MEC had twenty-two stores and 2,583 employees, Aritzia had eighty-four stores and over 4,000 employees, and Arc'teryx had sixteen stores and over 800 employees. Fluevog Shoes is smaller but has grown rapidly in the past two decades to generate $100 million in revenue by 2018–19 for twenty-five stores across Canada and beyond supporting 100 employees. Herschel Supply Company also illustrates noteworthy increases in revenues, store locations, and employees in recent years from a Metro Vancouver base. Meanwhile, Sugoi, just when it might have begun inter-regional expansion to meet its growing sales, was unexpectedly acquired first by a US firm struggling for viability and then more successfully by Dorel Industries of Montreal.

Growth on such a scale inevitably has required changes in decision-making structures and in some cases shifts in ownership and control. Yet, as of 2020, John Fluevog continued to help his sons control his company, as did Brian Hill of Aritzia, while the more recently established Herschel Supply Company is still run by its founders. In contrast, Arc'teryx's principal founder, David Lane, left the company in 1995, and it was later acquired by the Salomon Group in 2001 and then by Amer Sports (Finland) in 2005, the latter in turn acquired by China's Ante. Arc'teryx, however, in effect retains a global product mandate in its established area of operations, and its (subsidiary) head office and R&D remained (as of 2020) located in North Vancouver. Sugoi similarly retained design, marketing, and for a while some manufacturing in Burnaby following its acquisition by the conglomerate Dorel Industries and subsequent move into new facilities. Its subsequent acquisition by the smaller Louis Garneau Sports of Quebec in 2018 has seen a downsizing of operations, but its design, marketing, and brand name products, including Sombrio, remain. Lululemon's and MEC's evolution have been higher profile. Indeed, Lululemon become a public company in 2007, but not without controversy, and Wilson's decision-making role ended, especially since Wilson resigned as chairman in late 2013 (and he is no longer a board member). MEC's future is perhaps in particular doubt, the company having lost money in the financial crisis of 2009 and reportedly experiencing losses of about $80 million between 2017 and 2020 before COVID-19 made matters even worse.[24] MEC seems to have overexpanded across Canada, established a too-expensive new head office, and experienced various managerial inefficiencies and worsening relations with its membership. Indeed, MEC recorded losses in 2019 and during COVID-19, on sales of $462 million, and was acquired in 2020 by the Los Angeles–based Kingswood Capital Management under a credit arrangement scheme.[25] MEC (now Mountain Equipment Company) is no longer a cooperative, and as a private company it has restructured, retaining seventeen of its twenty-two stores and still maintaining a Vancouver head office with about 1,332 jobs.

Notwithstanding the distress created by COVID-19 across the retail sector, since their formation Metro Vancouver's signature apparel companies have pursued strategies of horizontal integration that exploit economies of scale and scope in expanding outlets to other jurisdictions. These strategies have been driven by the branding of design-based product innovations and services.

Importance of Design-Led Innovation

Metro Vancouver's signature apparel businesses were founded and subsequently grew based on innovation-driven, design-centred principles (see Table 6.2). In particular, these firms were built on the insights and principles of (local) founders formulated by their experiences and interests. For example, John Fluevog had worked in a shoe store, MEC's founders were hikers who bought their gear from a Seattle store that became one of their suppliers, Brian Hill's family had established a large department store in the early twentieth century, David Lane was a mountaineer disappointed with available backpacks and clothing, and Chip Wilson had founded a successful athletic wear business and had just enrolled in a yoga class. For Fluevog Shoes, Aritzia, Sugoi, Lululemon, and Arc'teryx, the keen observations of market opportunities by their founders stimulated design-led innovations to promote those markets. In MEC's case, recognition of market opportunities

TABLE 6.2 Focus of design-led innovations by Metro Vancouver apparel/fashion companies

Start-up focus	Subsequent related initiatives
Fluevog Shoes	
John Fluevog and Peter Fox, without formal training, made their first designer shoes in 1970 based on fifty-year-old Mexican footwear that John had discovered. A focus on unconventional designs that "embrace peculiarity" (Ebner 2018) has been the firm's guiding principle, including the design, the Pilgrim, a Victorian inspired buckle tea-strap loafer, one if its first designs for women.	By the 1980s, John Fluevog, in full control, founded the landmark Angel Soles design at a shoe fair in England in 1985. Harvested from the Hevea tree, Angel shoes were tough, resoleable, and engraved with the logo "Resists alkali, acid, fatigue and Satan." The opening of the Seattle store popularized Angel shoes. Angel boots were created in the 1990s. Began to sell and modify Doc Martens. After faltering around 2000, a new mini design became popular, eco-friendly tanned leathers and water-based glues were innovated, and in 2002 Open Source was launched to allow shoe wearers to be designers for Fluevog to make a (3D) shoe. Store expansions followed. In 2018, cut ties with Amazon to control brand distribution. Designs about seventy-five shoes a year and employs seven designers, with sons increasingly running the business. Aritzia, Lululemon, and MEC are customers.
Mountain Equipment Co-op	
Stimulated by a Seattle outdoor retail store MEC set up as a cooperative to serve local demands in Metro Vancouver, mainly supplied by imported goods, including from Seattle.	In 1979, MEC and Hine-Snowbridge set up a factory to make their own brand of backpacks and panniers, becoming Serratus Mountain Products (until 2005, when closed). In-house products began again in 1988 with the Nevé Gore-Tex Parka (based on Gore-Tex technology introduced in 1978). In 1994, made a fleece jacket and pants from recycled polyester (from soda bottles). In 1998, made garments from organically grown cotton. In 2010, produced a line of MEC bikes.
Sugoi Performance Apparel	
Founder Carol Prantner, was a keen cyclist, with associated fashion interests.	From 1987, inspired by Vancouver and its environs, Sugoi focused on designing high-quality cycling shorts (and then related apparel) with the North Shore mountains as a logo.

Start-up focus	Subsequent related initiatives
These interests became business focus.	In 2018, Sugoi became part of Quebec's Louis Garneau Sports. The Japanese word *sugoi* translates into English as "incredible."

Aritzia

Brian Hill's boutique focused on high-quality "fashion" clothing targeting women in their late teens to thirties.	Developed by designing and selling in-house brands, including Babaton (1994), Talula (1996), TNA (1997), Wilfred (2006), and Denim Forum and Wilfred Free (2009). Each brand treated as an independent label and sometimes sold in their own boutiques. Exercises tight control over suppliers from around the world. Each boutique is designed to be sensitive to local influences and natural materials and to incorporate custom furniture and art. Carrier bags have artistic designs and in-store music organized by a music director. In 2014, introduced two handbag lines: SIXELEVEN and Auxiliary. Personal shopping appointments can be booked at many of their boutiques. Exclusive brands provide 90 percent of revenues, and the principal design studio is in Vancouver.

Arc'teryx

Focused on high-quality rock-climbing harnesses and backpacks by applying the then new lamination technology. Vapor climbing harness became a top seller. Uses an "evolutionary design process," and its name refers to the earliest known bird that evolved wings to adapt to its hazardous environment (Finkle 2017).	Developed an outdoor apparel line based on licensed Gore-Tex and invented a WaterTight zipper. Innovative focus is on details (zippers, stitching, seams), and manufacturing in British Columbia allows close collaboration between design and production workers, the former based in North Vancouver. Focus is on high-quality, reliable products. With Polartec, created big-selling softshell jackets that provide thermal insulation with breathability. Arc'teryx LEAF is a separate division that began in 2003 to make military and police equipment, including Bora backpacks for US Navy Seals.

▶

◄

Start-up focus	Subsequent related initiatives
Emphasizes serving niche markets of outdoor enthusiasts.	Entered retailing in 2006, expanded ski and snowboard garments line in 2010, and started a footwear line in 2015. Main design centre is in North Vancouver, with emphasis on field testing and collaboration.

Lululemon Athletica

Founder Chip used funds from the sale of his previous company (Westbeach). Initial stimulus came when Wilson joined a yoga class in 1998 to address his aches and pains (Wilson 1998, 126). Wilson recognized that, "in 1998, gym fashion was simply your worst throw away clothes" (1998, 127). With advice from his yoga teacher, he designed fashionable yoga wear that felt good, did not stink or shrink, and looked wicked for "Super Girls" (145).	After noticing that women were wearing his new yoga outfits outside the gym as "streetwear," Chip set up design meetings, gained funds through a house mortgage, and perfected Luon, a proprietary fabric blending nylon and Lycra, trademarked in 2005. Developed distinctive employee relations and consumer relations models. In 2008, diversified into eye glasses and sun glasses. Launched stand-alone men's stores in 2016 (men's apparel comprising 12 percent of sales), including running shorts and underwear that started in 2013. Partnered with Athletic Propulsion labs and introduced men's and women's shoes in 2017. Lululemon has an R&D group (fifty employees) in its Vancouver head office.

Herschel Supply Company

Named after a hamlet in Saskatchewan where the founders' grandparents settled.	Flagship Vancouver store opened in 2018. Focus on exclusive backpacks and other goods that evoke Canadian history. Sells over 130 products and accessories.

Note: Kit and Ace was founded by Shannon Wilson and her stepson in 2014 as a Lululemon spinoff focusing on luxury cashmere brands. It became profitable in 2018 and was sold to its manager. Since then, international operations have been closed with a shift to technical apparel for commuters and more online sales.

Sources: D. Ebner, "Canadian Footwear Company Fluevog Prepares for Life without Founder," *Globe and Mail,* March 18, 2018, https://www.globeandmail.com/report-on-business/small-business/canadian -footwear-company-fluevog-prepares-for-life-without-founder/article38298110/ ; C. Finkle, "Lifestyle Brand Case Study Arc'teryx," *Brand Marketing Blog,* September 5, 2017, https://brandmarketingblog. com/articles/good-branding/lifestyle-brand-case-study-arcteryx/; Wilson, *Little Black Stretchy Pants.*

helped to stimulate a new (actually rejuvenated) cooperative approach to retailing.

From their origins, these firms have sought to establish high-quality products that target customers willing to pay relatively high prices. That is, competitiveness for these firms is based on design-created functional and aesthetic characteristics, not on low prices. The original designs that sparked the growth of Fluevog Shoes, Aritzia, Arc'teryx, and Lululemon included highly unusual, funky shoes; high-fashion dresses; resilient backpack frames; and washable, durable, and nonsweat yoga outfits (which also proved to be attractive casual wear). MEC has pursued a similar market focus. Indeed, design activities have been ongoing for these firms. In 2018, for example, as the smallest of the apparel firms, Fluevog Shoes had a design team of seven people, and Lululemon has invested in an R&D (and design) laboratory of fifty people. Meanwhile, Arc'teryx's North Vancouver location specializes in design, Aritzia has design studios in Vancouver, organized around each of its major brands, and MEC's in-house design activity was sparked in the late 1980s in relation to Gore-Tex-based clothing.

For these firms, competitiveness based on design-led innovation poses ongoing challenges for the creation of new products and their marketing and distribution. In this emphasis on design, several features can be noted (see Table 6.2). First, design activities are labour intensive and lengthy and require highly skilled, experienced, and often formally educated workers ("designers"). The resulting products are subsequently protected by trade-marks that reinforce the sense of "exclusive brands" that the firms provide. Fluevog shoes, Aritzia dresses, Sugoi biking outfits, Arc'teryx anoraks, and Lululemon yoga pants are all relatively expensive, a reflection of the high ongoing costs of design; the sometimes limited runs (especially obvious re-garding Fluevog shoes); the complex value chains that need to be built in support of design activities, including manufacturing and marketing func-tions; and the close attention paid to detailed, "high-quality" performance and aesthetic characteristics. That some designs fail also adds to costs. Overall, the sales of these firms are largely their own brands. As a more di-versified retailer, MEC sells some of its own trademarked goods (its logo is a registered trademark seen on its Gore-Tex rain jackets) while emphasizing quality branded products of other companies.

Second, as the sketch maps of company histories reveal, strikingly evi-dent is the importance attached by the founders of Lululemon, Arc'teryx, Aritzia, Sugoi, Herschel, and Fluevog Shoes to the smallest details (a stitch, a zipper, a seam) in meeting specifically desired performance and aesthetic requirements for their products. This attention to detail is part of these companies' "DNA" that reinforces control over marketing and desires for quality, in terms of the image and the reality, of their products.

Third, the design activities of these firms are typically collaborative and since their origins have been connected closely to marketing opportunities. Thus, given that design activities are typically team based, Arc'teryx routinely develops its fabrics in relation to field testing in the nearby North Shore mountains, and Aritzia and Lululemon constantly have sought outside advice and expertise throughout their value chain activities. For Fluevog Shoes, whose philosophy has been to "embrace peculiarity" and to provide "unique soles for unique souls," collaboration within its largely family-based team was extended in 2002 by the introduction of an Open Source program, an online site on which anyone was invited to submit designs, an initiative that led to fifteen manufactured products (with the designer's signature).[26]

Fourth, for these growth-oriented companies, there is ongoing pressure to innovate. The decline in Fluevog Shoes sales around 2000 was reversed by the successful innovations of mini designs and by renewed commitment to design activities; in recent years, the firm has introduced about seventy-five new designs per year. In the case of Aritzia, design activities are organized independently of one another around its major brands – Babaton, Talula, TNA, Wilfred, Denim Forum, and Wilfred Free. Arc'teryx and Lululemon have also diversified around their original specialties, the former from recreational backpacks to clothing, then to military-style backpacks, and most recently to snowboard garments and footwear, based on design work in North Vancouver. Meanwhile, Lululemon has diversified into a men's line of athletic clothing and more recently into footwear, the latter in partnership with Athletic Propulsion, an innovative shoe company founded in 2009 in Los Angeles.

Fifth, Metro Vancouver's design-driven apparel firms have emphasized the importance of marketing their products and services in their own outlets. Indeed, the selected companies have expanded their locations in the form of specialized retail outlets and boutiques throughout Canada and the United States. Fluevog Shoes also recently (2018) cut ties with Amazon to emphasize its unique products better and to control distribution through its stores, typically found in premium downtown locations, and by direct online arrangements.[27] Aritzia exercises similar corporate control over its products, with its brand name boutiques typically occupying prestigious sites within cities and often selling their specific brands. Both of these firms have benefited from celebrity influences. In the case of Fluevog Shoes, the influences began in 1971 when director Robert Altman bought a pair of knee-high boots while filming *McCabe and Mrs. Miller*, and in the 1990s publicized purchases by Madonna and Lady Miss Kier, among other celebrities, further promoted the firm's global reputation as a high-quality, distinctive, funky supplier. In 2020, Fluevog designed shoes for Dr. Bonnie Henry, British Columbia's chief and highly respected medical adviser during the COVID-19 pandemic, a line that had sold out by June. Aritzia has also used celebrities – such as Meghan Markle, Gigi and Bella Hadid, and Kendall Jenner – to promote its reputation. Lululemon is similarly based on developing close relations directly with its customers, which it terms "clients," and in unpressured ways encourages independent choices. Meanwhile, Arc'teryx sells its products through specialized outdoor stores along with related products and through its own stores.

Clustering as Congregation?

Metro Vancouver's signature apparel companies have stimulated local clustering benefits in the form of training, spinoffs, sewing activity, a degree of rivalry, and supportive education programs, notably at Kwantlen Polytechnic University, that amount to almost 400 companies and over 8,000 employees. That these companies themselves have added much to local vibrancy is underscored by Lululemon's announcement in 2023 of 2,600 managerial, computing, and software engineering jobs at its downtown head office over the next five years.[28] Even so, although a subjective judgment, largely informed by the selected signature companies, the local interdependencies among apparel and design firms within Metro Vancouver as a whole seem to be modest, reflecting tendencies toward loosely connected congregations rather than strongly connected clusters. The signature companies emphasize vertically integrated operations in design and testing, prototype creation, and sales and distribution. Such integration facilitates the realization of internal economies of scale and, just as importantly, control over issues of quality. In practice, the overall apparel and fashion business is still relatively small, and the signature companies, a caveat to the connections between MEC and Arc'teryx aside, operate in separate subsegments with distinct supply and market systems. Lululemon's head office expansion is apparently also predicated in part on an agreement with the federal government to allow the company to import talent without the need to obtain labour market assessments. That Metro Vancouver's signature apparel companies have attracted FDI (see Table 6.1), mostly if not always supportive of their activities, further reinforces the strength of global integration.

Furthermore, though local sewing has been stimulated, for the most part, manufacturing is contracted out to overseas suppliers, many in less-developed countries, in order both to lower costs and to access expertise not readily available by the designer firms themselves. At the same time, the need to maintain high-quality standards requires careful selection of suppliers and attention to training and close interactions with suppliers that in turn emphasize the importance of stable relations. Lululemon, for example, has long-standing arrangements with a Taiwanese supplier. Fluevog shoes are manufactured by established suppliers in Portugal, Peru, China, and Vietnam. Aritzia has developed suppliers in Hong Kong, China, Cambodia, and Vietnam, and Arc'teryx has perhaps the most geographically diversified range of suppliers of manufactured and material inputs among these firms. Thus, its recently published data, as illustrated selectively below (see Table 6.3), indicate that Arc'teryx obtains supplies from sixty-seven different operations variously located in northeastern United States, Central America, Europe, and Asia (apparel, backpack frames, footwear, fabric, and trim). Its head office and design centre in North Vancouver are closely integrated with its nearby New Westminster factory, with manufacturing capability to test new designs and produce items for consumer demands that range from Veilance (technically sophisticated urban clothing) to its Law Enforcement and Armed Forces (LEAF) line. Otherwise, it reaches out around the world for materials, products, and manufacturing.

Several features of Arc'teryx's supply chain are worth noting. Geographically, its supply sources are global and diverse, with inputs obtained from several rich as well as developing countries, with the main concentrations in Asia. However, there are no African supply sources and only one in Latin America. In terms of timing, the sources have been developed recently, with the oldest involving two Chinese suppliers that began in 2003–05. Arc'teryx chooses its suppliers carefully, emphasizing firms with established reputations for quality products, innovativeness, and an ability and willingness to learn new techniques to lower costs and enhance quality. Indeed, training periods can be lengthy – over several years – and often this training is interactive as Arc'teryx looks for solutions from suppliers. Thus, since 2005, Arc'teryx has worked with Huizhou Charming Enterprises in Guangdong, China, a key (apparel) supplier of its most technically difficult products: "A willingness to train employees and adapt facilities made Charming an ideal candidate for formal training in our GORE-TEX construction methods.

After five years of mastering the technicalities in our Gamma and Covert products, the staff moved on to intricate GORE-TEX designs."[29] In addition, all of its suppliers subscribe to the HIGG Facility Environmental Module (FEM), which provides a methodology and indicator of ethical and environmental business practices. Indeed, to reduce transaction costs in making new arrangements, both Arc'teryx and its suppliers look for long-term relationships, which in some cases have become exclusive.

Finally, the suppliers themselves typically are "large firms" with employment usually over 900 and often much higher. For Arc'teryx, its suppliers offer lower costs and higher productivity rooted in distinct specialties. In broad terms, Arc'teryx uses suppliers that specialize in apparel goods, hard goods, trim, and fabric. Within these categories, suppliers are specialized, with the major concentrations occurring across Asia. With respect to apparel and hard goods, for example, Arc'teryx has developed wide-ranging inputs from seventeen different locations, principally in Asia but including sources from El Salvador and Latvia (see Table 6.3). These goods include different components for backpacks; brand name jackets, knitted and Gore-Tex; hoods; conventional caps and "technical" caps; gloves; and footwear. Indeed, these firms basically produce the Arc'teryx range of brand name goods (along with its New Westminster facility).

Metro Vancouver as Design Incubator

Locally founded, design-driven apparel companies reflect and contribute to the sense of Metro Vancouver's identity as a creative place that embraces healthy, green or environmentally friendly, cool, desirable, West Coast lifestyles. Could these founders have succeeded elsewhere? Such a counterfactual question is not easy to answer. After all, Fluevog shoes, Aritzia dresses,

TABLE 6.3 Arc'teryx's apparel and "hard good" (external) suppliers, 2020

Company, country	Supply focus
Dong In Entech, Philippines	Backpack components (stays, parts), including RotoGlide hip belt (since 2007)
Huizhou Charming Enterprises, China	Technically difficult jackets (e.g., Macai) and Gore-Tex-designed products (since 2005)
Karian (Taicang) Sports Apparel, China	Since 2003, selected Gore-Tex jackets (e.g., Zeta SL), help with technical ball caps, taped duffle bags (exclusive to Arc'teryx)

▶

◀

Company, country	Supply focus
Madison 88 (with U-Jump Arts and Craft Company), China	US owned, makes most of Arc'teryx's knit hats and toques (since 2014)
Mensa Industries, Vietnam	Down specialist, has Gore-Tex test facilities, makes various down and knit products for Arcteryx (since 2020)
Nanyang, Vietnam	Cotton specialist has supplied DryTech fabric (since 2008); main graphics T-shirt maker for Arc'teryx (since 2018)
PRO DEPT, El Salvador	Knit specialist since 2013 supplying knit and woven apparel
PT. PANCAPRIMA EKABROTHERS, Indonesia	Since 2014, developing sewing skills, and in 2019 began training on Arc'teryx Gore-Tex methods
QVT (Quang Viet Enterprise), Vietnam	Since 2015, major supplier of insulated hooded jackets
Santa Clara, Vietnam (Huizhou Charming)	Opened in 2016, supplying Arc'teryx (since 2018) with jackets, and Gore-Tex products planned
Spectre Garment Technologies, Vietnam, Latvia	Danish-owned, supplies knit fabrics using innovative gluing and cutting technology (since 2020)
Sungjin Inc., Vietnam	Supplies duffle bags, day packs, and trekking packs (since 2014)
SUPERCAP, China	Taiwanese owned, supplies technical ballcaps (since 2013)
Takashima Sports, Myanmar (moved from China in 2017)	Specializes in high-quality gloves (since 2009)
Vast Apparel, Cambodia	Since 2017, has supplied woven shirts and dresses
Youngone (Cepz), Bangladesh and Vietnam	Two facilities supplying knitwear and synthetic insulation jackets, moving into sportswear lines (since 2011)
Pou Chen Footwear, Taiwan	Supplies high-tech footwear for Arc'teryx (since 2015)
ZKG Asia, Myanmar (no clarification needed.	Hong Kong-owned down specialist supplying Arc'teryx (since 2015), now knit and down Gore-Tex, pieces in Veilance
Zplus, China	Hong Kong owned, as above (since 2013)

Source: Arc'teryx, "Supply Chain Partners," 2020, https://arcteryx.com/ca/en/explore/supply-chain -partners.

Arc'teryx jackets, and MEC kayaks are widely bought across North America and beyond. Yet new businesses typically locate where their founders live, and Metro Vancouver has been a stimulating place for designer-led businesses in activities beyond its resource specialties, complementing its role as a high-tech incubator (see Chapter 2). Moreover, the founders of these businesses recognize the stimulus provided by local experiences and observations. The founders of Arc'teryx, Sugoi, and MEC, for example, were active outdoor enthusiasts, hikers, bikers, and mountaineers who saw market opportunities in these enthusiasms. Chip Wilson's identification of his version of Super Girl was made at a Vancouver yoga class that allowed Wilson to connect the dots between "her" and what would become Lululemon wear. Expensive shoes and women's fashion clothing are not so automatically connected locally, but Fluevog's funky shoes fit with a local cool, laid-back, lifestyle image, often associated with Metro Vancouver, not to mention the founder's personality, while providing a suitable match for the elegance of Aritzia wear.

These companies are also part of Metro Vancouver's promotion of a green identity, and its celebration of links with nature, not least through their logos and names. MEC's name starts with the word *mountain*, Arc'teryx is named after a bird that lived 140 million years ago (one of the first feathered dinosaurs), and its logo is a fossil of that creature, and the word *sugoi* means "awesome" in Japanese, its logo is of the North Shore mountains, and its main co-founder, Carol Prantner, is a mountain bike enthusiast who wanted to design specialized clothing for the sport. Indeed, biking has been the stimulus for several well-known, innovative SMEs in Metro Vancouver, including with a special focus on mountain biking (see Case Study 6.1). Water sports have generated still other SMEs.[30] Indeed, all lifestyle companies have been sensitive to encouraging environmentally friendly processes of production, including Fluevog and Herschel, now use more sustainable materials.

Moreover, in Metro Vancouver, creativity to enhance lifestyle consumption has also occurred to meet and differentiate local tastes by the establishment of pioneering restaurant chains and microbreweries, adding further to the region's economic base and identity.

West Coast–Inspired Restaurant Chains, with Craft ("Designer") Beers

As part of its postindustrial economy, new types of restaurant chains and microbreweries have co-evolved, if from independent beginnings, to enliven and redefine Metro Vancouver's food and beverage industry, long

CASE STUDY 6.1   **SME Bike Innovators from Metro Vancouver**

Innovative design-driven SMEs that have arisen in response to these opportunities include mountain bike manufacturers led by Norco (1964), Brodie Bikes
(1986), and Rocky Mountain Bikes (1981). Founded by local residents and biking
enthusiasts in Port Coquitlam, Vancouver, and North Vancouver, these firms
have remained small, though Norco and Brodie in particular have established
reputations for quality, innovative products.

Norco, for example, introduced the first full-suspension BMX bike to the
Canadian market in 1973; manufactured ten-speed, drop-bar road bikes by
1975; diversified into mountain bikes in 1984, introducing the world's first
front-suspension (mountain bike) model in 1991; introduced variable-point
suspension for mountain bikes in 1997; designed the world's first street/dirt
jump-specific mountain bikes in 2001; and won design awards for further innovations in 2015 and 2016. Exports started in 1995 and by 2014 embraced 125
models. Design and engineering remain in Port Coquitlam, with suppliers
around the world.

Brodie Bikes, employing just five people, has a similar reputation for innovation, including with respect to the sloping top tube. Paul Brodie, the founder,
left the firm while continuing to make customized bikes from the past, including
the Excelsior, originally built in the 1920s, for $139,000. Rocky Mountain Bikes
was acquired by Procycle (Quebec) in 1990 but operates independently, with
design and marketing based in North Vancouver, and in 2018 became the parent company's name. There are several other mountain bike suppliers in the
region, including Spawn Cycles, which started in 2012 in nearby Squamish, designing trail bikes specifically for kids and youth.

characterized as low tech. Both trends occurred as pioneering, entrepreneurial, creative, differentiated, neo-local responses to established mass production practices. Both trends illustrate neo-localism, recursively wrapped
up with Metro Vancouver's cool lifestyle characterization as an intimate expression of its emerging postindustrial economy.

Beginning with The Keg in 1971 and then with Earls and others in the
1980s, the new West Coast–inspired restaurant chains developed around
"casual premium," "casual fine dining," or "upscale casual" experiences, in

contrast to widely prevalent, cheap, fast-food, self-service chains and their highly standardized options and with expensive, top-end restaurants. Casual premium offered distinctive menus, often emphasizing health, taste, and local sourcing, for reasonable prices and within elegant, casual, convivial surroundings that bespoke attractive social experiences with widespread appeal to many types of customers, including families and young adults. If self-identifying as restaurant chains, and not as pubs offering food, they are also drinking establishments in which microbrewed beers are featured offerings, reinforcing their sense of localness.

As for micro- and craft breweries, their emergence in the early 1980s was unabashedly expressed as a response to prevailing beer standardization and to becoming part of postindustrial Metro Vancouver. John Mitchell, the acknowledged grandfather of microbrewing in Metro Vancouver (and Canada), following the announcement of Vancouver Expo 86 in late 1980, was recorded as saying that "people are going to be coming from all over the world, and all we have to serve them is this rubbish? You can't have a good country without good beer."[31] The "rubbish," of course, referred to the remarkably similar-tasting beers offered by the dominant breweries, several of which were then located in Metro Vancouver. In a related pioneering venture, Mitch Taylor and Bill Harvey, the founders of Granville Island Brewing, had been leading participants in the Granville Island Market revitalization, the iconic symbol of Vancouver's postindustrialism. Innovative microbrewing sought to revive older methods of beer making with an emphasis on creating distinct tastes on a small scale and offering them in convivial pubs. That local microbreweries (and their pubs) and casual premium dining evolved together was not coincidental. Both were entrepreneurially driven trends that took off in the 1980s, especially after Expo 86, as part of a related lifestyle drive but reflecting entrepreneurial responses to increasingly differentiated consumer lifestyle–driven tastes.[32]

Entrepreneurial Foundations

Founded in 1971 by George Tidball, The Keg (The Keg and Cleaver then) was well ahead of the curve in establishing casual premium as a distinct West Coast style that awaited the 1980s for it to become a discernible "movement" with the formation of Earls by the Fuller family (see Table 6.4). Both the Tidball and the Fuller families were long-time residents of Metro Vancouver, with earlier connections to Alberta, and both founding entrepreneurs learned the restaurant trade in fast-food outlets. Tidball, who was born in

TABLE 6.4 Five signature "lifestyle" restaurant chains originating in Metro Vancouver since 1971

Firm founders and head offices	*Size and scope*
The Keg	
Founded in North Vancouver in 1971 in an old industrial building by George Tidball (as The Keg and Cleaver). Acquired by David Aisenstat and in 2018 by (Toronto-based) Cara Operations (now Recipe Unlimited Corporation), a Canadian food giant, for $200 million. Head office in Richmond.	By 2018, controlled 160 locations across Canada (except in Prince Edward Island) and the western United States. Estimated to have over 10,000 employees. A core group of 106 restaurants in the "Royalty Pool," created in 2002 and requiring 4 percent of gross sales from members, had reported revenues of $161 million in 2018.
Earl Restaurant Chain	
Founded in 1982, initially in Edmonton, by Bus and Stan Fuller, a father-and-son team living in Vancouver by the 1970s. First restaurant in British Columbia opened in 1984 in North Vancouver with the head office nearby.	Expanded to control sixty-eight locations across western Canada, Ontario, and the United States. Reported revenue of $250 million and 5,000 employees by 2014. Fullers are part owners of Joey's and Cactus Club Café. Committed to sustainable supply chains.
Cactus Club	
Founded in 1988 by Richard Jaffray and Scott Morison, two former waiters at Earls, in North Vancouver, the head office location. Morison left in 2004 to form Browns Socialhouse.	By 2018, had nineteen locations in British Columbia and Alberta; by 2013, had twenty-seven locations across Canada. Estimated revenues in 2018 of $93 million and 4,500 employees.
Milestones Grill and Bar	
Founded in 1989 in Vancouver, becoming part of the (Vancouver-based) Spectra Group of restaurants founded by Peter Bonner and Wayne Holm. Acquired by Cara in 2002 for $34.4 million; head office moved to Vaughan, Ontario. Acquired in 2021 by Foodtastic (Quebec).	By 2002, expanded to twenty restaurants, with estimated sales of $70 million. Further expansion to more than forty-five locations, especially in Ontario, and one in Washington State. Had 4,100 employees by 2018.
Browns Socialhouse	
Founded in North Vancouver in 2004 by Scott Morrison. Head office in Vancouver.	Expanded to sixty-nine locations across Canada and Washington State. Estimated annual revenues of $43 million.

Note: Moxie's Bar and Grill (Calgary) and Joey's are related restaurant chains.[33]

Alberta and attended UBC, had introduced McDonald's in Metro Vancouver in 1967, selling the franchise to help fund The Keg. Meanwhile, Leroy "Bus" Fuller had acquired fast-food retail experience in Montana before managing such outlets, including A&W operations, in Edmonton by the late 1950s and Metro Vancouver by the 1970s. In fact, Fuller established his first Earls in Edmonton in 1982 before opening one in North Vancouver, close to the family head office and where he lived. Earls has also spawned competitive casual premium chains, notably the Cactus Club and Browns Socialhouse, founded by former Earls waiters, respectively, in 1988 and 2004. Joey's is another related chain, founded by the Fullers, first opened in Calgary in 1992, and with the same Vancouver head office address as Earls. That is, as casual premium's leaders, The Keg and Earls have provided important incubator functions, spinning off entrepreneurs who have established related chains while being important sources of financing for new franchisees. In addition, Milestones was independently founded in 1989 by the Spectra Group of local businesspeople.

Popularly regarded as the grandfather of microbrewing in Metro Vancouver (and Canada), John Mitchell left England for Canada in 1953 and worked in a variety of jobs before becoming an entrepreneur and brewer. As a supporter of the Campaign for Real Ale formed in the 1970s in England (with a Vancouver chapter), his dislike of the bland options offered by Big Beer was reinforced in British Columbia when he became an owner of the Troller Pub in Horseshoe Bay. His efforts to create more tasty beer first came to fruition, albeit briefly, in 1982 with the opening of the Horseshoe Bay Microbrewery (close to his pub), using second-hand (dairy) equipment, and with advice from a noted BC brewing authority, Frank Appleton.[34] Mitchell became the first brewmaster (and pulled the first pint in 1984) at Spinnakers, which he co-founded with Paul Hadfield and Ray Ginever as a specifically designed brew pub that used new equipment imported from England. In tandem, the Granville Island Brewing Company was opened in 1984 by Mitch Taylor and Bill Harvey, along with help from Vern Labourne, a brewmaster from Germany. Microbreweries have also been important sources of spinoffs. John Mitchell, for example, was involved in a couple of ventures, and Dix BBQ and Brewery, which started in Yaletown in 1998, developed a reputation as an incubator for young brewing talent, beginning with Tony Dewald as its first brewmaster, who notably stated that "there's way more acceptance out there for esoteric, alternative beers nowadays. It was like alternative music in the 1980s. We shared knowledge with each other and tried to change tastes one person at a time."[35]

In contrast to the ease of entry for new restaurants, microbrewing in Metro Vancouver had to overcome formidable opposition from the dominant breweries, whose powers were entrenched in provincial regulations.[36] In 1980, for example, it was illegal for breweries to sell beer on their own premises, and the British Columbia Liquor Distribution Board controlled all sales of beer, whether to pubs or to individual customers. The board, which employed thousands of unionized workers, controlled distribution outlets throughout the province and the beers (and wines) offered for sale. Linking food with beer sales was also limited, and neighbourhood pubs (not breweries) had been allowed in Metro Vancouver only since the 1970s. In practice, the relaxation of these regulations, still rooted in prohibition-era thinking, depended on the lobbying efforts of John Mitchell and others. Regulatory changes were nevertheless slow to implement, and Mitchell, for example, only received his brewing licence at Horseshoe Bay just before the opening date in 1982, and he was required to have a "commercial road" between his brewery and pub. Granville Island and Spinnakers, however, were able to sell to consumers on site. Since then, regulations governing craft breweries and brew pubs have continued to be loosened, with several key changes occurring as recently as 2011.[37]

The casual premium restaurant chains were pioneering initiatives nationally as well as locally, and the Horseshoe Bay and Granville Island microbreweries claim, justifiably, to be Canada's first such ventures (and Victoria's Spinnakers Canada's oldest continuously running brew pub). However, though the formation and expansion of casual premium restaurants and microbreweries reflect their local origins and innovative thinking about differentiated consumer demands, their organization and geographical structures have evolved differently. While the restaurant chains have expanded "internally" by controlling multiple establishments locally, across Canada and sometimes the United States, the microbreweries have expanded around new, small, independently run companies throughout Metro Vancouver.

Locational Dynamics: Casual Premiums

The casual premiums have developed as horizontally integrated retail chains as their competitive advantages have allowed them to expand geographically into new markets and to become large, multiple-plant organizations ("chains") with widely recognized brands. These restaurants have grown by exploiting internal economies of scale and scope that have allowed them to take advantage of existing know-how, experience, and branding in different locations within Metro Vancouver and across Canada. As the two largest, The Keg and Earls had estimated revenues of about $250 million in 2018, respectively employing 10,000 and 5,000 workers. The Keg has expanded across Canada (except for Prince Edward Island), often showing a preference for renovating industrial heritage buildings, such as its location in New Westminster in an old CPR building. Earls has focused more on western Canada and Ontario, and both chains have made limited inroads to the United States. The other chains are smaller but still bigger than conventionally defined SMEs. In all cases, successful locations need access to consumers willing to reach them and/or benefit from flow-throughs of traffic. These restaurants are typically found in downtown locations and in suburban retail centres, where several began, and they are pulled to places readily accessible by consumers. Often rival establishments occupy adjacent or nearby locations. Collectively, the casual premiums have emphasized ambience, layout, service, and, above all, distinctive menus to meet more varied consumer tastes. These chains have also evolved around particular distinctions. The Keg, the first and highest priced of the group, has focused on steak and fish dishes while introducing the salad bar to Metro Vancouver; Earls has diversified from its initial focus on hamburgers by adding items from around the world; Milestones has emphasized giving a "twist" to favourite foods; and the Cactus Club's distinctive menus have been enhanced by the hiring of a renowned chef.[38] Conviviality and social interaction are important to the casual premium experience, a goal captured in the very name Socialhouse.

These firms have become well-known brand names, exporting their lifestyle-related offerings across Canada and often including BC-based craft beers. For the casual premium restaurants, geographical expansion has involved some shift in control and ownership to central Canadian–based firms. In particular, The Keg is now owned by the Toronto-based giant Recipe Unlimited Corporation (formerly Cara), although it is still run from its Richmond head office, and Milestones is now controlled from Quebec. Earls, Cactus Club, and Browns Socialhouse, however, fully retain their Metro Vancouver controlling bases.

The Inherent Localness of Microbrewing

Within Metro Vancouver, the proliferation of craft breweries, defined as microbreweries and regional breweries, has occurred by the establishment of independently run, small, site-specific, entrepreneurial operations that have offered a variety of beer choices for consumers. This proliferation has occurred especially since 2000, with at least forty or so established by 2018 and more by 2021. By 2020, some estimates placed the number of craft breweries in the region at seventy-seven.[39] Indeed, craft breweries have accounted for an increasing share of beer consumption in British Columbia, estimated to have reached 10 percent by 2005 and over 24 percent by 2016.[40] Although individual operations are small, by 2016 there were 2,500 people directly employed in craft brewing and another 1,500 in brew pubs, totals that substantially exceed the closure of two conventional breweries and a number of the Liquor Board's distribution outlets. Invariably higher priced than mass-produced beers, the craft beers have won consumers by providing a range of different tastes based on combining old-fashioned methods of brewing and extensive experiments with hops, malts, and other ingredients, including to produce "seasonal" beers.[41] The extraordinary range of craft beer types and tastes is captured by imaginative naming and wide variations in their alcohol by volume and level of bittering.

Although not precisely defined legally, the smallness of craft breweries, especially microbreweries, is inherently associated with their entrepreneurialism, differentiated offerings, and consumer appeal.[42] They still need to be big enough to reach the minimum efficient scale (MES) while – importantly – creating a range of options produced in relatively small batches. Both Horseshoe Bay Brewery and Granville Island Brewing began with just one featured beer, respectively Bay and Island Lager (the latter in distinctive tall-necked bottles). But serving just one option limits consumer appeal, and following the lead of Spinnakers in Victoria craft breweries since then have opened with three or more different beers on tap.[43] Indeed, the noted brewmaster Tony Dewald, who introduced cask brewing to Vancouver, was recorded as noting that at Dix's new Yaletown pub (opened in 1998) he tried to produce a new variety every week.[44] If such a goal is hard to sustain, it nevertheless captures the need to exploit economies of scope while achieving the MES.

In general, the locations of microbreweries, like restaurants, are "market oriented," dependent on ready consumer access. For the original breweries at Horseshoe Bay and Granville Island, their locations attracted both nearby residents and tourists. However, though the locational imperative has encouraged the dispersal of microbreweries throughout Metro Vancouver, clustering tendencies are also evident, typically supported by local municipalities that hope to reinvigorate declining industrial areas by using craft breweries as catalysts for gentrification and "trendy consumption" in return for available, cheap spaces.[45] For example, both south and east Vancouver are home to designated brewery clusters, each home to approximately a dozen craft breweries; Brewery Row emerged in Port Moody in 2014 after the municipality became one of the first outside the City of Vancouver to pass a bylaw allowing microbreweries to establish in the old industrial warehouse district; most recently, a brewery quarter was designated in North Vancouver in 2019, converting light-industrial premises east of Lonsdale Quay into brewpubs.

More generally, as illustrations of neo-localism and recursive intensification, craft breweries in Metro Vancouver, and the imaginative naming of their beers, are "often proudly and self-consciously local ... In fact, microbreweries are marketing 'place' as much as they are marketing beer, and they actively seek out distinctly local imagery, local landscapes, and local stories to position themselves as intrinsically rooted in place."[46] For the pioneering firms that had little if any place-based reputation and monopoly rent to exploit, the construction of a local brand identity has been based on a particular feature of the city's heritage, for example Granville Island, or on the natural landscapes and landmarks for which Vancouver is famous, in the case of Horseshoe Bay Brewery, or more frequently in the naming of beers, such as Stanley Park Lager, Lions Gate Lager, and English Bay Ale. Steamworks Brewery, established in 1995, is another noteworthy example, with its association with the Gastown Steam Clock, itself constructed as a symbol of successful local community opposition to the proposed demolition of the historic Gastown neighbourhood in Vancouver's Downtown Eastside to make way for a highway, as well as other city landmarks (see Figure 6.1). With its central location on Vancouver's waterfront, Steamworks has become a significant meeting place for locals and visitors alike that traces its "origins to the happy accident of finding the original piping from a steam distribution system in our historic Vancouver building ... [W]e are inspired by history and tradition on the one hand and a constant re-imagining of our future on the other."[47] Interestingly, in contrast to an emphasis on place-based imagery of the pioneers, later entrants into the Vancouver craft brewing industry have become less reliant on local branding.[48]

If Metro Vancouver's craft breweries themselves have not sought geographical expansion, their success has occasionally attracted FDI seeking to regain market share and "cash in" on the monopoly rent of place identity by co-opting the local.[49] Indeed, Granville Island Brewing itself was acquired by Molson Coors Canada in 2009 under its subsidiary Creemore Springs,

FIGURE 6.1 The two logos use images of well-known local landmarks, a gas-fired clock and the Lions Gate Bridge. | Permission provided by Steamworks Brewing.

which has maintained the original Granville Island brands.[50] But for giant breweries the advantages of acquiring tiny operations such as craft breweries are not obvious, given their small size and not infrequent failure.[51]

Local Supplier Networks and Headquarter Functions

Casual premiums and craft breweries have further shaped local development by generating local supplier networks regarding ingredients and stimulating supporting institutions qua localization economies. Regarding the former, though both industries emphasize high-quality, sustainable, and local ingredients, supply chains are organized differently. With their national operations generating large-scale demands for food, the casual premiums rely considerably on contracts with major national, and often giant, food suppliers based in Vancouver, Calgary, and Toronto. The involvement of Cara in The Keg and Milestones reflects this type of connection.[52] The scale of the demands of the restaurants has led to controversy, as when Earls sought to use cheaper meat from the United States but then backed down and resumed its preference for local, sustainable supplies.[53] Meanwhile, the growth of craft breweries within Metro Vancouver has helped to stimulate the revitalization of local hops production.[54] Hops had once been a significant specialty within British Columbia, peaking in the 1940s, but as breweries increasingly consolidated into large-scale operations hop production became similarly concentrated, with the last of British Columbia's original hop farms closing in 1997. The continued growth of craft breweries in the province, however, has stimulated investments in new farms down the Fraser Valley and on Vancouver Island in particular. In part, this stimulus reflects that the fully flavoured India Pale Ales that are a large part of craft brewery production require more hops per litre than lighter, more standardized lagers. Furthermore, the use of local hops has added to the creativity of craft beer. As Fumano records, "the rise of local hop production has also made it easier for craft brewers to create wet-hop beer, limited edition small batch beers brewed with fresh hops, rather than the more commonly used dried or pellitized hops."[55] These locally produced fresh hops add aroma and flavour and are readily combined with other ingredients. Indeed, variety, design, and innovation are related activities.

Casual premiums and craft breweries have also helped to stimulate local education initiatives. The Pacific Institute of Culinary Arts, for example, was founded in 1997, and culinary training has become an important program at the La Salle College of Arts in Vancouver, beginning in 1982 in Burnaby as the Dubrulle International Culinary and Hotel Institute of Canada. A new campus is planned for 2024. Meanwhile, training in brewing has been developed at Kwantlen Polytechnic University, where British Columbia's only brewing diploma (one of only three across Canada) has been established as a two-year program, providing an important source of locally trained specialists in all aspects of brewing, stimulated by the collective demands of craft brewing. Indeed, Kwantlen Polytechnic University has its own award-winning brewery. The buzz surrounding craft brewing is also underlined by the Vancouver Craft Beer Week – first occurring in Victoria in 1993 – an annual festival celebrating craft beers from around North America, especially British Columbia and the West Coast. The evident success of this microbrewing cluster is also indicated by the commemoration of the fortieth anniversary of John Mitchell's first craft beer in July 1982 by a new "dark ale" brewed at Russell Brewing, developed from Mitchell's original brew sheets and supplied by malts, hops, yeast, labels, and coasters from other local companies. Sales proceeds will help to fund the John Mitchell Legacy Scholarship in Kwantlen's brewing program.[56]

The casual premiums, although generated locally and serving a local clientele, are also an export industry because of the expansion of their Canadian and American chains. These investments not only bring returns to Vancouver but also, more importantly, require headquarter functions that provide high-level jobs. These headquarters promote occupations such as restaurant and menu design, training, accounting, upper management, and so on, although after buyouts some functions have shifted to Toronto. The export function of both the casual premiums and the craft breweries are further extended by adding to the attractiveness of Metro Vancouver as a tourist destination, thereby deriving income from external demand just as more obvious exports of goods and services provide.

Conclusion

Metro Vancouver's transformation toward an innovation economy has involved co-evolutionary trends toward consumption and the knowledge economy. Lifestyle businesses have complemented high tech's growth, both gathering much momentum since 1980. Moreover, inspiration for these trends in both cases has been local and entrepreneurial, even as the forces of globalization, including the influence of MNCs, have become more powerful. Indeed, desirable lifestyles and high-tech employment seemingly go hand in hand in enabling such a transformation in Metro Vancouver. Furthermore, the importance of locality and the influence of Metro Vancouver as a place of creativity should be understood as a facet of globalization rather than in spite of it. Consumers are looking to reconnect with places in a meaningful way through the products that they purchase, with local pride, a desire for authenticity, a sense of community, and attempts to reduce carbon footprints all influential. At the same time, globalization is enabling firms to reach larger and more distant markets and customers from afar to consume products from Greater Vancouver, such as clothing, food, and drink. Amenities and lifestyles are consumption-oriented activities that have stimulated innovative initiatives in the region as well as provided important attractants to talent for Metro Vancouver's burgeoning high-tech roles. The region has a work-to-live reputation rather than the other way around, but this mantra has generated many business opportunities and contributions to an innovative economy. For postindustrial Metro Vancouver, local market demands have become increasingly important as a stimulus for business and a reminder of the region's own credentials as a centre of consumerism.

7
Metro Vancouver on the Thin Edge of Innovation and Associated Conundrums

Metro Vancouver's transformation toward a new innovation economy has arisen within the context of its past as a resource-based industrial city on the edge of Canada, North America, and the Pacific Rim. This emergence, though not necessarily spectacular or singular, is distinctive, significant, and promising. Whether it is substantial in regard to fostering a form of development that supports a strong middle class, however, is questionable. The foundation for Metro Vancouver's innovation economy was laid by the resource industries that generated sufficient service industries to support a postindustrial society attractive to high-tech entrepreneurs and, importantly, encouraged high-level university and research aspirations. From that postindustrial hearth, generations of small, innovative firms have sprung up within the region, most obviously in high tech but in other sectors too. This development has been real and heralded as a high-road approach. But this approach has not dominated local development thinking and itself has been arrested by its internal dynamics rooted in highly diverse innovation initiatives limited in size and spread thin without sinking many local roots and cultivating increasingly rich local clusters and industrial foundations. Indeed, Metro Vancouver's postindustrial innovation economy confronts a conundrum. Should the region be satisfied with this constant generation of highly varied sources of innovation, which individually do not expand much locally and often are volatile, or should it try to scale up its firms to generate local clustering with core companies and jobs? If pursuing the former, then Metro

Vancouver might be in a high-tech version of a "run of the red queen," a form of development in China's Pearl River Delta in which, for several decades, companies were compelled constantly to compete at the margins and to work furiously just to stay in the race.[1] But rather than firms being unable to improve their situations through RD&D, which happened in the Pearl River Delta, Metro Vancouver's running on the spot has resulted from an inability to extend into related activities to reap more of the rewards of its innovation. Can Metro Vancouver constantly churn out innovation across a diversity of fields and reap sufficient benefits from its investments in universities and innovation subsidies? On the other side of the conundrum, if Metro Vancouver wishes to move deeper into production stages, then the question is how can this happen? Such deepening has not occurred organically or been a policy focus. The task might be more difficult than hiring professors who can pump out innovations and innovators.

Even so, Metro Vancouver's post-industrial transformation has involved the emergence of a vibrant innovation economy pioneered by local entrepreneurs. This emergence was neither anticipated nor straightforward. After all, resource-based – especially forestry – activities had provided considerable wealth and high expectations for its citizens, a major source of political power within BC, and did not see or welcome diversification away from their dominance as meaningful. That the rise of the innovation economy did not become particularly evident until the 1980s when the forest sector in Metro Vancouver was in the throes of secular decline is not coincidental. If the innovation economy's rise since then is impressive, its continuation remains problematical.

In this chapter, we address both sides of the conundrum as to whether to maintain or deepen the present trajectory, not with answers per se but with elaborations of key problematic themes arising from the evolutionary trajectories toward an innovation economy that have been pursued in relation to the possibilities of deepening the local impacts of innovation along a high road of local development. These themes relate to the core company question, the extent of local diversification, and the issue of self-generating momentum, the jack-of-all-trades policy approach, and the casual association typically made between high tech and greening. In addition, albeit tentatively, we note the conundrum raised by Metro Vancouver's real estate dynamics for its innovation economy. Although these reflections might expose the limitations of this book, they point to the need for further research on innovation behaviour in the region.

A Cautionary High Road and the Core Company Ghost

A high-road trajectory to an innovation-driven local economy that provides distinct competitive advantages and global roles typically envisages entrepreneurial initiatives in endogenous knowledge creation and application at its foundation that over time become consolidated and enriched by the emergence of core companies. Although not easy to define with empirical precision, the sense of core (high-tech) firms is that they are dominant private sector employers that have achieved significant firm-level economies of scale, size, and growth, usually supplemented by operational-level economies of scale that generate considerable benefits for their home locales. Core firms provide locally major head-office and R&D operations that offer high-income, challenging occupations that powerfully shape local identity by globally leading innovations, exports, and international expansions while promoting strong clustering benefits for local suppliers, universities, and related external economies.[2] In Metro Vancouver high tech, the entrepreneurial animus is clearly evident, the emergence of core companies less so.

In Metro Vancouver, a high road toward a contemporary innovation economy originated and largely evolved through local entrepreneurship, especially in relation to high tech. As pioneering "Hall of Famers," Donald Hings and John MacDonald (with Vern Dettwiler), Ian Reed, and Klaus Deering began this entrepreneurially inspired shift toward high tech in the 1960s. Other icons – such as Rudi Haering, Geoffrey Ballard, Dan Gelbart, and Norman Dowd – reinforced these initiatives in the 1970s. Typically, these pioneers were born in British Columbia or were established residents and, except for the self-taught Hings, typically had obtained PhDs. Hings and MacDonald were also raised in remote, small, resource communities in the province, a reminder that the genus of innovation is not just a "city thing." Moreover, these entrepreneurs were dedicated to Metro Vancouver and Canada and as socially motivated as individually inspired. Greedy entrepreneurialism has always existed in Metro Vancouver (and British Columbia), from the early days of forest exploitation to present-day housing bubbles and Bitcoin manipulations. The high-tech pioneers of Metro Vancouver, however, better reflect the Schumpeterian ideal of the innovative entrepreneur's role in the creative side of capitalist development.

As part of Metro Vancouver's march toward postindustrialism, the pioneering entrepreneurial firms in a new globally competitive innovation economy did not exert much of a collective impact locally until the late 1980s, when high tech's growth became measurable, and rapidly gathered momentum. Like the pioneering exemplars, this growth has been fuelled substantially by the formation of new locally based companies, the majority of which are small, and led by entrepreneurs who have received high levels of formal education, although exceptions can be noted. Don Mattrick (with Jeff Sember) and Phil Nuytten, for example, began their careers before leaving high school, the former to establish the gaming industry (see Case Study 2.1) and the latter to become a leading innovator in submersible technology (see Case Study 4.1). The growth of entrepreneurial companies in high tech (and lifestyle activities) has attracted attention from foreign-based MNCs, giant and mid-sized. In this regard, Mattrick's (voluntary, proactive) sale of his company, Distinctive Software, to Electronics Arts signalled growing inflows of FDI and its enduring success. Indeed, although there have been exceptions in which local interests have been undermined, hitherto MNCs have been largely supportive of locally innovative operations. Nevertheless, FDI has become an important presence in Metro Vancouver's innovation economy, especially in high tech, and a dominant entrepreneurial culture is becoming more of a hybrid that includes subsidiaries whose behaviour is ultimately controlled from elsewhere.

Yet, despite impressive entrepreneurial dynamics and (or because of) the growing presence of FDI, Metro Vancouver high tech lacks so-called core companies, an absence that raises questions about the scope and depth of the sector's development. As a potential candidate within Metro Vancouver, Telus is large locally but perhaps seen mainly as a utility company rather than a technological driving force orchestrating local supplier networks. As for the high-tech companies that pioneered in Metro Vancouver, MDA (1969) and Creo (1982) reached peak local employment of close to 2,000 and just over 4,000, respectively. Although locally impressive, neither firm reached mid-sized giant or core status. Indeed, both were acquired, and Creo closed. The provincial government had controlling influences on Moli Energy (the lithium battery pioneer) in the 1970s and Westech Information Systems (BC Hydro's innovative offshoot) in the 2000s but chose to sell them cheaply to foreign interests, to little effect (see Chapter 2). But could not the very considerable intellectual strengths of BC Hydro, rooted in massive dam-building and related infrastructure projects, have been promoted more fully on a global stage? In recent decades, life sciences companies such as Stemcell and AbCellera have grown rapidly, though still around the level of 2,000 jobs, and they operate in highly uncertain businesses strongly dependent upon MNC giants located elsewhere. Overall, given over a fifty-year period of evidence, it seems unlikely that locally based companies will ever reach core status – their acquisition is much more possible. In British Columbia, entrepreneurs are for sale, just like land, mines, forests, water, and housing. Meanwhile, subsidiaries within Metro Vancouver might have specialized roles but nevertheless are organized by MNCs as components in integrated global systems of operation. MNCs evolving to invest in locally based subsidiaries qua core firms also seems to be unlikely, even as the collective implications of their presence and power become more evident. As of 2021, Electronic Arts (1,500 jobs) and Sony (800 jobs) were probably the largest employers among branch plants, although Amazon's plans for a Vancouver head office employment of 4,000 would make it the biggest.

That the lack of core high-tech firms implies a concern for local development is often intimated, if not elaborated, in government and industry reports. If so, then should it not be addressed? If not, then core companies will continue to be present only as ghosts. In practice, the need for firms to scale up to become profitable is recognized, and support for their incubation and growth, including financing, is increasingly available. But the government's characterization of high-tech firms as large when they employ only fifty people is delusional, undermining any true effort to promote core firms.[3] Would the sophistication of Metro Vancouver's high-tech regional innovation system benefit if a few were to become such dominant players? Alternatively, does the number of relatively big high-tech firms, with ten or so having more than 1,000 employees, collectively capture, to some extent, the implications of core firm status? Have the ghosts collectively become more virtual in this regard, imposing pragmatic limits on local development expectations? Suffice it to say that, with a problematic nod to Telus (see Case Study 4.2) there are limited signs of "true" core firms emerging in Metro Vancouver.

Looking beyond high tech, core firms do not have presence in wood value-added activities in Metro Vancouver, and this is unlikely to change. Most such firms are small and face increasing difficulties in remaining profitable in the region, R&D support in the sector is declining, and forestry policy is highly politicized, with no clear commitment to innovation. Among innovative lifestyle activities, several fashion apparel companies have grown impressively based on their design capabilities and global reach, with Lululemon exceptional in terms of its size. Yet, within Metro Vancouver, fashion apparel is diverse and limited in overall scale, and foreign ownership has become more important. There is little sense of this industry or these companies developing core-like status in the region.

With or without core companies, an important question to consider is whether or not high tech in Metro Vancouver has become self-generating. In core firm–dominated local economies, such as Silicon Valley and the nearby Metropolitan Seattle area, this question requires a focus on the behaviour of core firms themselves and the key sectors in which they operate. In Metro Vancouver, however, SMEs have been an important driving force in high-tech growth in many different activities that have generated many different kinds of externalities. Indeed, the resilience of Metro Vancouver's innovation economy requires consideration of the nature and extent of its specialties.

The Unexpected Range of ("Thin") Diversified Specialties

The emergence of Metro Vancouver's globally competitive innovation economy, especially if not exclusively in relation to high tech, has been driven by new specialties, the range of which is unusually large and can be regarded as "thin." In employment terms, for example, recent estimates place about 122,000 jobs in the high-tech sector, with film and video game firms forming the most coherent with the strongest inter-firm relations. Yet this cluster, often categorized as new media, provides just one-sixth of local high-tech employment (and there are game developers not linked to film producers). Moreover, new media, telecommunications, life sciences, clean or renewable energy, social media, and artificial intelligence, among other high-tech activities that can be mentioned (submersibles, biochains), have been touted as locally important clusters, and plans for the digital technology super innovation cluster add another dimension of applauded local priorities to this list. These categories themselves are highly diverse. Renewable energy initiatives, for example, have been led by essentially independent (and relatively small) companies focused on large and small lithium batteries, hydrogen as an energy source, improved fuel consumption, biofuels, and carbon capture.[4] Many high-tech firms also do not fall into the above categories in employment terms, including the two most prominent, locally owned, high-tech companies to have existed in Metro Vancouver, MDA and Creo, situated primarily in aerospace and printing categories, respectively. Value-added forestry and consumer-driven lifestyle initiatives reinforce the emergence of the highly diversified nature of Metro Vancouver's innovation economy.

In a functional rather than industry categorization, many innovative high-tech businesses in Metro Vancouver comprise producer services. These businesses, similarly, are highly varied, often independent of one another, and involve novel ways of improving accounting, marketing, bookkeeping, legal work, game design, schedule organizing, and so on, and suppliers to the film industry take on many different functions. Meanwhile, high-tech manufacturing might be relatively small and declining but nevertheless comprises wide-ranging, independent activities. In transportation-related activities, for example, there are businesses that supply airplane wings, custom-made hydrogen buses, and mini subs for deep-sea exploration. Beyond high tech, the business diversification of Metro Vancouver's innovation economy in services and manufacturing is further extended by developments in value-added forestry and consumer-driven, lifestyle initiatives, both comprising an impressive range of different, often segmented activities. Although diversification is hard to measure, the remarkable scope of activities is surely a signature feature and driving force of Metro Vancouver's innovation economy.

The (Paradoxical?) Diversification of a Metropolitan Periphery

For Metro Vancouver, its highly diversified, newly emerging innovation economy is surprising, especially given its inheritance as a peripheral core at the edge of Canada, North America, and the Pacific Rim. Peripheries, after all, are characterized by their specialized nature. Other cities and regions of similar or even larger size are typically associated with particular high-tech foci, not least the iconic Silicon Valley, with its emphasis on ICT. But in Metro Vancouver, the innovative specialties are highly varied. Its emerging innovation economy has turned the idea of (narrowly) specialized peripheries on its head. Furthermore, its highly diversified nature, originating mainly through local entrepreneurial companies, has been reinforced by FDI and the development of supportive institutions. MNCs from around the world have participated in this FDI, although tendencies toward the United States, especially the Pacific Coast, can be noted. With respect to supporting institutions, UBC and SFU have long recruited globally and them-selves are highly diversified sources of advanced knowledge, readily able to support a wide range of commercial activities through education, training, and research. As for the provincial and federal governments, their natural inclinations have been to support diverse market trends rather than to dictate particular ones. Metro Vancouver's innovative specialties have been re-inforced further by specialized forms of financing and industry associations.

   A less surprising feature of Metro Vancouver's peripherality is the reliance of its innovative companies on global connections for their viability, not just for markets but also for expertise, talent, and finance. In newly emerging peripheral spaces, such as Metro Vancouver, innovation based on local initiatives often requires such connections, even in the early stages of growth. Necessary inputs simply are not available locally, even if some can be developed over time. Hitherto, however, the emergence of clusters with strong inter-firm connections and supplier networks has been relatively weak in Metro Vancouver. Indeed, in conventional terminology, its diversified specialties can be regarded as driven in general by Jacobs-style externalities and implemented in many cases by rather independent Marshallian firms. Rejuvenated forestry aside, Metro Vancouver's emerging innovation economy is a marked departure from its industrial past, stimulated by new ideas and thinking based on the region's inherent dynamism and its difficult-to-predict implications for entrepreneurship. At the same time, this dynamism has been implemented largely through the (thinly) related diversification strategies of independent entrepreneurial firms, a few caveats aside.

Toward a Self-Generating "Smart" High Road?

Metro Vancouver's innovation economy clearly has evolved via a diversified range of specialties. Is this smart? According to recent literature, a "smart specialization" approach to local development is not simply a question of how narrow or diversified specialties are.[5] Rather, smart specialization asks broadly whether Metro Vancouver's new innovation economy of diversified specializations is directing the region along a high road of sustainable, self-generating (long-run) development (see Figure I.1). A related question is whether or not local (regional) innovation systems are becoming more coherent and sophisticated. Answers are not straightforward. After all, smart specialization is not preordained but problematic and contingent. Even defining self-generating growth or size for a population of firms is judgmental, and scarcely pinned down precisely, and in Metro Vancouver will vary among different clusters. As a starting point, however, self-generating growth implies that business failures and employment losses are more than offset by expansions by new or existing companies, with a high-road trajectory requiring continuing enrichment of innovative capabilities and systems. Metro Vancouver's experiences suggest that there are pros and cons in its evolutionary pathway.

That Metro Vancouver's economy is rooted in, and has continued to be enriched by, bottom-up, endogenous (organic) sources of knowledge and knowledge transfer among multiple small entrepreneurial companies strongly indicates an effort to build a high road – by entrepreneurs, policy makers, and universities. Overall, that high tech, including new media, achieved about 120,000 jobs by 2021 is impressive in absolute terms, and its entrepreneurially fuelled growth is an encouraging sign of self-generating momentum in an aggregate sense. Such growth (to which innovative forestry and lifestyle businesses add to some extent) inevitably has generated many direct and indirect multiplier effects, and its highly diversified nature has stimulated various external economies particularly highlighted by spin-off businesses and support for a wide-ranging institutional architecture embracing universities, associations, venture capitalists, and government policies. Furthermore, the highly diversified specialties of Metro Vancouver offer wide-ranging opportunities for further growth and, significantly, more resilience to recession, problems of parochialism, and other forms of upheaval that threaten the dependency on single or just a few industries. That is, this structure provides insurance against the "eggs-in-one-basket" syndrome. In tandem, the new innovation economy, with its cornucopia of new products and services, has meant new global roles for Metro Vancouver, with far-reaching implications for supply lines, exports, and attracting FDI.

Nevertheless, there are concerns that the region's diversified specializations are a skin-deep form of development, each part never quite fulfilling its potential while remaining vulnerable to market dynamics, whether in relation to funding, competition from elsewhere, or acquisition by MNCs. If 120,000 high-tech jobs are impressive, apart from new media, then various specialties forming Metro Vancouver's new economy are relatively small and segmented around distinct labour markets, each comprising highly specialized talent pools with limited interconnections among them. Reference to value-added forestry and lifestyle clusters reinforces this point. That many relatively small clusters of talent within the region have not necessarily achieved self-generating momentum, and remain vulnerable to downsizing and even collapse, needs to be recognized. As a pioneering cluster, for example, telecommunications have witnessed considerable restructuring. In addition, regarding two of the larger, still growing clusters, developments in the life sciences typically face significant technological, financial, and marketing risks, and the new media cluster, especially in relation to film-making, has depended in part on subsidies. That death rates (globally as well as locally) are the highest among new and small firms, including those spun off from universities, also needs to be kept in mind, especially in view of Metro Vancouver high tech's unusually bottom-heavy population structure.

The Local Entrepreneurship-FDI Dynamic

As a foundational force in Metro Vancouver's innovation economy, especially in regard to high tech, local entrepreneurship has helped to attract growing levels of foreign direct investment that now include the world's largest MNCs. Arguably, FDI not only has reinforced thin diversification across Metro Vancouver high tech but also has been stimulated by it, with local firms in each cluster seeking support to upscale and globalize.[6] Hitherto, this evolving organizational mix realized an impressive high-road trajectory of overall growth. But will this continue? MNCs bring mixed blessings to local development that can change over time. They are pipelines to global markets, finance, talent, and expertise in support of local development and pipelines that extract know-how, talent, and profits from local circulation. They can invigorate local operations, stimulate local suppliers, replace local ownership, and favour exogenous, often affiliated suppliers. Further, whatever assets and services MNCs provide, subsidiaries will be charged for them. They can become big employers but cannot aspire to be true local champions given that strategic decision-making control and local discretion to expand and diversify lie elsewhere. That is, subsidiaries forfeit their autonomy for strategizing (making long-run commitments), not least with respect to new R&D programs, patenting and the local realizing of their intellectual properties beyond what is specifically mandated from afar. MNCs both stimulate and compete with entrepreneurs, not least for labour, and rely on them and buy them out. Indeed, MNCs benefit from British Columbia's nurturing of a high-tech workforce but pay substantially less than in the United States while drawing talent from there as convenient (and often within the same time zone).

Moving forward, whether or not the balance between FDI and local ownership across high tech and within particular clusters can be maintained depends on a continuing supply of entrepreneurship and talent and the region's continuing attractiveness to FDI. But neither is guaranteed. How will Metro Vancouver's innovation economy be affected if the former dries up or slows down and the latter becomes dominant? Such a scenario is not impossible: locally based innovation is uncertain, and there are (virtually) no restrictions on FDI. Suffice it to say that changes in the balance between local and global corporate ownership can be anticipated. In practice, "thin diversification" is defining a new competitive reality for innovation in Metro Vancouver, a periphery where talent flourishes and likes to live but where vulnerabilities to maintaining growth trajectories and adapting to change are not far below the surface. Indeed, it would be interesting to know whether similar (high-amenity, peripheral) places are following suit or not, not least as a way of assessing the potential of alternative approaches. Suffice it to say that, notwithstanding a growing layer of FDI, the effectiveness of thin diversification is a model dependent on a local supply of entrepreneurship, in effect on Metro Vancouver's reliance on its own wits. At least these wits have access to supportive institutional architecture and government policies.

Jack-of-all-Trades Innovation Policies (and Support)

The diverse flourishing of innovative behaviour in Metro Vancouver has been supported by a corresponding range of policies introduced by the BC and federal governments, most obviously in relation to high tech. Developed primarily in reaction to market trends, these high-tech policy initiatives reflect a jack-of-all-trades approach that in effect reinforces thin diversification. In practice, government policies that support high tech have provided various types of support that, within broad guidelines, are often generic and invariably voluntary. Picking winners is not the style. Such an approach is no doubt politically sensible, offering support to diverse interests – across many business and university activities – that allows for frequent announcements of government actions that can involve renewal and/or modification as experience is gained and that can be responsive to new demands. Indeed, government programs – whether as subsidies, tax breaks, loans, grants, or immigration help – are vital for high-road development and a sophisticated regional innovation system (RIS) for Metro Vancouver. Undoubtedly, government support directly helps businesses to sustain costly, lengthy, and highly uncertain RD&D programs and innovation, provides crucial contributions for incubation and scaling-up processes beyond the reach of private sector interests, and helps to combat similar policies in rival jurisdictions. Similarly, the extensive public support channelled through the education system, including the hundreds if not thousands of projects supported by Mitacs and Genome BC (plus the Industrial Research Assistance Program), among others, in Metro Vancouver can be readily appreciated. Such programs provide vital sources of education, training, experience, and talent; foundational, basic knowledge that is valuable in itself and raises new possibilities for innovation; and all kinds of contributions to applied, development, and technology transfer activities delivered to businesses, all the while enlarging the local talent pool and the region's capacity to understand global scientific and technological developments. Indeed, the cornucopia of government support for innovation in British Columbia can be endorsed readily.[7]

Yet an underlying concern is that government policies in support of thin diversification in Metro Vancouver are thinly spread themselves, representing a jack-of-all-trades policy approach but a master of none. Even if picking a winning model is an impractical alternative, the scattershot approach to supporting innovation raises questions of effectiveness since it is driven by politics more than coherent long-term thinking. Typically, government-funded innovation policies have broad guidelines and serve proposals that can have highly varying foci. Innovation goals are typically stated only in vague ("apple pie") terms without a precise indication of how they might be evaluated. British Columbia's digital technology super cluster, one of five super clusters located across Canada, with its base primarily in Metro Vancouver, and arguably innovation policy's central recent thrust, nationally and locally, is a case in point. Indeed, its label is scarcely informative (what isn't digital?), and how is this cluster to evolve in terms of size, scope, export, and governance? Are some players, whether leaders or not, already in place, and what will be their roles? Is this super cluster expected to increase efficiencies across the economy, especially those companies that seek to reduce climate impacts or be more product and export oriented? In fact, how are constituent players to be defined? Will client firms, after receiving support, be allowed to move elsewhere? Is foreign ownership an issue? Will Metro Vancouver's super cluster rival, complement, or be independent of other super clusters? How is this cluster to be evaluated, if at all, for example in terms of patents, publications, employment, market share, or global leadership? How will we know that this cluster is actually super or when it has become super?

Meanwhile, where does the forestry sector fit into government thinking (federal or provincial) about innovation? In practice, innovation scarcely has been central to forestry policy or corporate ambition in British Columbia, and – if a relatively sophisticated R&D system evolved in Metro Vancouver – then it had a limited mandate, and opportunities were missed. Even now forestry management R&D regarding silviculture, and coping with diseases, pests, and fires, and in manufacturing (value-added activities, machinery), offers considerable potential. Technological responses have been made to natural threats to forests, but they tend to be short term rather than sustained and proactive, and the value-added imperative remains ambiguous in government policy. Instead, forestry sector R&D is in decline, and enthusiasm and selected policy initiatives for engineered wood scarcely constitute an overall policy approach to innovation in the sector. High levels of conflict over forest ownership and use have also seemed to militate against, rather than stimulate, increasing commitments to research and innovation.

In practice, high-tech innovation policies appear to be destined to support thin diversification, always raising the concern that the full innovative potential of a particular specialization are not fully realized or that collective efforts are effectively coordinated. Policy makers usually make general references to the key issues of incrementality, indicating how policy will change business behaviour in desired ways and generate significant benefits to overall development. However, rigorous analyses along these lines are lacking.[8] The significant benefits generated by government innovation policies are often summarized by association with the direct impacts of recipient projects or firms, for example in the number of jobs generated or the investments made. Occasionally, particularly for federal programs across Canada, ex post summaries of the cumulative impacts of programs in these terms are offered. Follow-ups on the longevity of significant benefits nevertheless are rare, with little or no attention given to foreign or Canadian ownership in implementing or evaluating domestic innovation programs. Indeed, beyond a few sectors (banking, airlines, telecommunications utilities), Canada rarely objects to foreign ownership of high tech or innovative activities in general, including acquisitions of firms that have received substantial government support.

Moreover, as the formal, legal expression of knowledge-based competitive strengths, IP seems to be terra incognita in Canadian innovation policy thinking, both with respect to its protection and support. Its neglect may be a puzzle, although it can be understood in part. If core firms are welcomed rhetorically by policy makers, not least in British Columbia, the idea of national champions is widely derided, even as MNCs (global champions), and their commitment to control IP, are welcomed. A significant policy challenge is how IP developed within Metro Vancouver (and Canada) can be elaborated locally. Part of this challenge also needs to recognize the role of US-owned subsidiaries in particular in luring Canadian engineering, science, and computing graduates with lucrative co-op experiences, that in turn offer potential careers to their bigger R&D groups in the United States.[9]

Yet, though there are many programs that support innovation in Metro Vancouver (as across Canada), with many deemed successful, at least by the sponsoring departments, overall conventional measures of innovativeness, such as per capita RD&D investments or employees and patent counts, continually show Canada as a whole and British Columbia in particular lagging behind other developed countries. Such a verdict applies not only to high-tech activities but also to forestry (see Chapter 1), British Columbia's dominant comparative advantage for over 100 years, and represents an indictment of deficiencies in long-term commitment to and thinking about innovation in Metro Vancouver as well as across the country. In practice, a jack-of-all-trades policy approach, more diverse than deep, supports short-term initiatives for the most part, in policy terms representing a follower rather than a shaper of market trends. From this perspective, or the evolving RIS within Metro Vancouver, the network of public and private institutions supporting high-tech innovation (see Figure 5.1) is broadly consistent. Even so, the balance of the contributions can be questioned and requires further investigation. For example, both governments and universities might be doing both too much and too little – too much across the board and too little in particular activities. Regarding the private sector, are businesses relying too much on university expertise and not enough on their own? Can the latter effectively substitute for the former? As noted, there is also the thorny issue of technology leakage and the problem of local innovations and their potential to add jobs and increase productivity to become increasingly controlled by MNCs and diverted elsewhere.

Regardless of its particular makeup, there is increasing policy and public pressure for Metro Vancouver's high-tech innovation system to help resolve environmental problems. Indeed, within British Columbia, governmental ambitions to green the economy have become a priority that in turn is associated positively with the high-tech sector along with hopes for a more equitable economy. These claims are both legitimate and problematic.

Innovation for a Greener Future: Potentials and Ambiguities
We have not systematically explored the extent to which Metro Vancouver's emerging innovation economy is addressing green hopes, although such a trend is apparent, and positive links between innovation and environmental imperatives are often touted. Yet there are ambiguities as well as strengths and potentials in this association. The deep interdependencies among all economic activities, locally and globally, are often ignored, and though strong support for greening the economy is good an anti-resource prejudice can be counterproductive.

Politically, within British Columbia and Metro Vancouver, commitments to greening the economy were given forceful expression by Andrew Weaver, as leader of the provincial Green Party (2015–20), and Gregor Robertson, as mayor of Vancouver (2008–18). Both were vociferous opponents of re-source industries, and both emphasized high tech, especially the role of clean technology as part of a future green economy for Metro Vancouver (and British Columbia). Shortly after his election as mayor in 2008, for ex-ample, Robertson established a "Greenest City Action Team" to meet just such a goal by 2020. A recent report has reflected on the achievements of this action plan while prescribing continued action.[10] The "economy" part of this plan, it is interesting to recall, promised that Metro Vancouver would become a "mecca of green enterprise" and create 20,000 new green jobs.[11] Indeed, environmental sustainability has become a major priority of urban planning in the region.[12] Whether or not Metro Vancouver is such a mecca, the report recognizes that the region is home to a thriving high-tech sector that includes innovative clean tech companies such as Ballard, Westport, and Xantrex (see Appendix 1). Indeed, such initiatives in high tech, along with other innovative behaviours in forestry and lifestyle activities, reveal the potential of Metro Vancouver to become a postindustrial economy of-fering greenness with innovative behaviours and high incomes.

This potential is appealing and makes sense. After all, innovative and es-pecially high-tech activities in Metro Vancouver largely provide service jobs as part of widespread postindustrial trends away from old-style manufac-turing and its association with dirty, dangerous jobs and various negative externalities related to pollution, aesthetics, and hazards. Furthermore, high tech is a key driving force in the knowledge-based component of the post-industrial economy capable of providing relatively high incomes as part of resilient forms of locally distinct competitive advantages. An impressive lit-erature on local development enthusiastically endorses such a perspective, associated with a high-road approach (see Figure I.1).[13] Service and know-ledge sector office jobs are the economic complements of wider trends toward healthier, safer, and higher-amenity lifestyles within attractive and convenient urban environments, much in evidence in postindustrial Metro Vancouver, not least through much virtuous signalling among residents, if less so through SUV purchases and square footages of their homes.

However, notwithstanding their evident contributions, the associations between the innovation economy, especially high tech, and Metro Vancou-ver's environmental and developmental hopes too often are made facilely. In particular, the "simple" conflation of a green economy with high tech, along with the simultaneous berating of resource industries, fails to appreciate sectoral and geographic interdependencies among *all* economic activities.

Many of Metro Vancouver's high-tech activities provide inputs to resource and manufacturing operations, including and perhaps especially so to other parts of the world. In turn, the region's high tech is supplied with energy, various resources, and manufactured components from both local and distant sources. Similar comments can be made about tourism. Indeed, these interdependencies are deep and deepening and a *sine qua non* for Metro Vancouver's participation in the global economy. Yet the separation of "good" high tech from "bad" industry, especially resource industries, in terms of their environmental impacts ignores economic interdependencies even as it is often reinforced by British Columbia's divisive politics. If the need for sustainable resource use is a policy given, then the continued resource basis of modern economies and their multiscalar connections need to be recognized. The literature on energy transition rightly points to a shift toward renewables, and perhaps nuclear power, but this transition will take a long time: fossil fuels remain the globe's dominant energy sources, they are even necessary to provide base loads in regions with plentiful renewable power (if not so in British Columbia), and they provide inputs for an incredible range of goods consumed by modern societies, not least by Metro Vancouverites. Furthermore, high-tech activities themselves not only require energy but also are dependent on mining a wide range of "rare earth" minerals, the search for which is of interest to Vancouver's mining exploration cluster.

The antagonism toward the resource sector seems to preclude any promotion of it as an innovative activity. Yet, for a senior Microsoft executive, Metro Vancouver's recent proposal for a super cluster is "an opportunity to build a technology ecosystem and economy that will span British Columbia by energizing investment in multiple areas, especially around natural resources, around health and around new industries."[14] Indeed, an innovation priority for the resource sector, including but not limited to forestry, makes sense, and it speaks volumes that a giant cloud company representative should see Metro Vancouver's emerging innovation economy in this way. After all, the region has established expertise and access to a vast, rich, and renewable forest resource (see Chapter 1) and hosts a mining community, with considerable expertise in exploration, that could focus on discovering rare minerals vital to many modern innovations, not least in batteries and other forms of energy sources being pioneered in Metro Vancouver and used in electric vehicles and many other products.[15] The region's recent innovative developments in carbon capture are another obvious link with the resource sector that could be part of a local cluster of activities rooted in an array of competitive advantages for ongoing growth while re-engaging metropolitan hinterland ties. New facilities could also feature engineered wood. Whether such cooperative connections between the high-tech and resource sectors can be made is debatable, not least because of strident opposition to resource exploitation. But this opposition is too blinkered, a case of "cutting off your nose to spite your face."

In summary, Metro Vancouver's innovation economy is not to be conflated solely with high tech or its greening, even if innovation is vital to its (green) realization. An innovation-led, hopefully green economy will require decades to unfold – and involve deepening global as well as local interdependencies. Indeed, although beyond the scope of this study, the interdependencies among economic activities need to be appreciated better, including their environmental implications throughout global as well as local value cycles. Even so, the region's commitment fully to promote an innovation economy, however green, cannot be taken for granted. Questions about this commitment remain, not least regarding the ongoing real estate conundrum and its relationship with a high-road innovation economy.

The High-Road/Low-Road Conundrum

In recent decades, Metro Vancouver has case-studied a high road toward local development in which innovation and local entrepreneurship have been reinforced through clustering tendencies and the formation of a more sophisticated local innovation system. However, in tandem with this trajectory, and in addition to its internal conundrums, the region has embraced a low-road, or at least a lower-road, development through more facile place-selling strategies centred on tourism and housing that have led to a decoupling of house prices and incomes. Admittedly, local development dynamics in Metro Vancouver inevitably are multidimensional, and in practice the high-road and low-road distinction is blurred. After all, property investments and tourism have added wealth and jobs, made contributions to the region's amenity value, and been reinforced by the growth of the innovation economy. Yet the decoupling of house prices and incomes is also a threat to that economy and its ability to attract talent. The vaunted idea of Metro Vancouver's innovation economy as a developing ecosystem is at least threatened if not ruptured by this decoupling. Arguably, the innovation economy is less the culprit than a part of the solution in this regard.

Conventional wisdom argues that, for Metro Vancouver, innovation-driven growth is important for the region to develop and sustain competitive advantages, potentially able to offer diverse jobs and increasing incomes commensurate with high costs of living, including for housing. Indeed, within Metro Vancouver, business and political leaders have urged such a commitment, along with a desire to lessen dependence on property development and rapidly rising real estate prices and revenues. Even within the business community this dependence has been portrayed as an unsustainable source of economic growth, unlikely to realize cumulative productivity gains or meet wider employment and income objectives. Moreover, in conventional locational terms, the shift toward an innovation economy makes sense for Metro Vancouver as a high-amenity, highly desirable place to live with a sophisticated infrastructure, excellent accessibility and attractive to entrepreneurs and highly skilled workers. That the region is part of the globally leading Pacific Coast centres of technological innovation, admittedly mainly in the United States, also buttresses aspirations for innovation.

Yet whether or not the region is moving toward an innovation economy hangs in the balance. As the core of the innovation economy, high tech (including new media), although growing, remains a small part of the economy in terms of gross national product or jobs. Furthermore, though average wage levels in high tech are higher than wages as a whole, they have not increased at anything like the rising real estate values over the past couple of decades. The mismatch between household incomes and house prices is evident in the high-tech sector as well as throughout the local economy. In contrast, high-tech incomes and house prices in nearby Seattle and Silicon Valley are more in lock-step with each other, providing for a more coherent (innovative) ecosystem. High-tech growth might have contributed to real estate dynamics to some extent, but other factors are also at play and likely have been more important.

In the meantime, the mismatch between property prices and high-tech incomes poses a conundrum, one that might worsen. As of late 2022, the indications are that the property development industry retains a powerful influence in Metro Vancouver. The newly elected mayor, like his predecessor, and council expect Vancouver to grow by several hundred thousand over the next decade or so and propose massive increases in densification to accommodate such expansion. Yet discussions about these proposals make little or no reference to the innovation economy. For example, how will increasing densification (and congestion and house prices) affect Metro Vancouver as a desirable place to live for innovative workers? How will interactions throughout the metropolitan area be affected? Will continued rapid population growth better fuel real estate and construction rather than innovation? Will banks continue to prioritize real estate lending over innovation? Where are innovative workers expected to live and work? And to what extent will this growth and densification help to stimulate the innovation economy to ensure its sustainability? If Metro Vancouver has successfully developed a pool of mobile innovative talent, how is the balance between in- and outflows evolving? Or to what extent do the green ambitions associated with growth plans depend on innovative local responses? Answering such questions is beyond the scope of this study and will require a more aggregate methodology and comprehensive focus on population growth, income level and inequality, environmental impacts, and employment patterns and structures. For such macro analyses, this study at least provides some behavioural insights. Suffice it to add here that, in the old days of industrial Metro Vancouver, employment forecasts, especially for the dominant global industries, used to be the basis of population projections and local planning. Where do employment considerations, including in the innovation economy, now contribute to planning projections?

In broad terms, a fascinating comparative perspective on Metro Vancouver's postindustrial trajectory is provided by the global power city index (GPCI) that assesses the performance of forty-eight leading cities in terms of their "magnetism" or "ability to attract people, capital, and enterprises from around the world."[16] The GPCI is derived from an integrated analysis on six dimensions, namely economy, R&D, cultural interaction, livability, environment, and accessibility.[17] For our purposes, the GPCI offers a useful proxy for comparing urban performances in the postindustrial search for a knowledge-based economy and society. From this perspective, the GPCI offers support for thinking of Metro Vancouver in terms of arrested development. Indeed, that Vancouver is included within the set of forty-eight cities reflects recognition of its global postindustrial status, and Toronto is the only other Canadian city included. In 2018, Vancouver was also ranked an impressive twenty-first overall. Yet in 2022 the city's rank had fallen to thirty-four, and only the environment dimension scored highly among the forty-eight cities.[18] With respect to economy and R&D, Vancouver was just above and below median scores and performed relatively poorly on the livability and especially accessibility and cultural interaction dimensions. For one well-known, locally astute observer, these scores provide caution about local boosterism and "narcissism," suggesting that civic leaders "could do less preening and more innovating."[19] Metro Vancouver's future trajectory in these terms remains problematic. The GPCI recognizes both its core status, by virtue of its inclusion, and the vulnerability of its peripherality as expressed in the rapid decline of its overall ranking (from twenty-one to thirty-four) in four years (2018–22).

In recent decades, Metro Vancouver has deepened its metropolitan postindustrial credentials, including through the emergence of innovation-driven activities, most obviously, if not limited to, high tech. At the same time, the region's peripherality has powerfully influenced this emergence, albeit in an unexpected and highly diversified range of activities. Metro Vancouver has effectively enjoined globalization in multiple innovative ways or specializations without becoming a dominant global player in any one or two. Its innovation economy is evolving as a peripheral form of arrested development that can be summarized as a highly diversified cluster with relatively weak, local, inter-firm tendencies supported by diversified global connections. An interesting question in this regard is whether or not this model is Metro Vancouver's best bet for moving toward an innovation economy (and whether it might be a model for other peripheral cities). Alternatively, would fewer, and more tightly knit, clusters be a better option? After all, local multipliers are increased by local connections. In either scenario, global connections are vital, particularly so for peripheral regions, and there are interesting questions about the balance of local-global dynamics as they evolve over time. For Metro Vancouver, if fewer tightly knit clusters are not possible, implying a degree of social engineering simply not feasible, then is its present model at least heading in appropriate directions? Answers to this question, along with concerns about greenness and inequality, pose fascinating research challenges for evolutionary economic geography.

Reflections on Evolutionary Economic Geography

In this book, an economic geography of Metro Vancouver's search for a new innovation-based economy, we have pursued an institutional qua evolutionary approach in the Schumpeterian tradition. In this view, innovation is the backbone of "creatively destructive" economic development and comprises social processes and choices driving socio-economic changes that are "permanent and irreversible," as "time repeats, never repeating."[20] The role of economic geography in this tradition is to insist that history shapes and is shaped by geography, that places, like time periods, are connected but different, unique but not singular. More prosaically, innovations have geographical as well as historical origins and diffuse over time across space in particular trajectories, often with adaptations and modifications.

In contemporary times, industrial cities looking to rejuvenate themselves offer different starting points for innovative and creative activities, and such an evolution is inherently uncertain, crisis ridden, and varied, the aspirations for development part of a kaleidoscope of opportunities.[21] Metro Vancouver's illustration of an "adaptive city" incorporates a postindustrial innovative future shaped by the particular nature of its peripherality, resource-based history, and diverse entrepreneurialism, creating its version of a unique but not singular economy, both different and connected.[22] There has been development along high-road prescriptions, but this development has been arrested.

Overall, in this study, we have emphasized an integrative perspective centred on business, an approach designed to communicate a broader, and more representative, picture of Metro Vancouver's innovation economy (and to a broader audience) than offered by anatomies of individual clusters, not least by revealing the extent of their collective diversification and entrepreneurial origins. Related future research could readily enrich this perspective with systematic analyses of supplier networks, inter-firm collaborations, the characteristics of innovations and innovative processes, and more emphasis on employment and work-related processes. In general, there is a need for research and policy to regain an appreciation of the interdependent nature of economies, locally as well as globally. Economic interdependence used to be a basic foundation for understanding local economies but now often seems to be forgotten, not least in public debates. Moreover, in governing these interdependencies, the question of cooperative behaviour might regain consideration. That cooperative behaviour and trust are vital for successful local development is often lost. As a social process, however, innovation can be directed toward agreed-upon social goals.

Appendix 1

Locally Founded "Larger" Firms in Metro
Vancouver High Tech to circa 2019

Firm, start-up features	Evolutionary synopsis
Glenayre Electronics	
Established in 1963 in Vancouver. Restructured from the closure of Chisholm Industries, a Vancouver-based family firm controlled by Jim, Edward, and James Chisholm (Pitman Business School, Vancouver Technical School), starting in the late 1940s. Began as a small equipment manufacturer. In 1969, hired Klaus Deering (high school in West Vancouver) to focus on radio telephone systems, becoming an early core firm of the wireless cluster.	Became a public company in 1983. With over 600 employees, became British Columbia's largest electronics manufacturer, producing its first mobile phone in 1974, pioneering pager development in 1983, and installing its first pager systems in the United States (1985), China (1990), and Europe (1994), with production in a new facility opened in 1984. Acquired by Simmonds and Sons of Toronto in 1987 and then by locally based Celtel (of TransCanada Glass, owned by the Skidmore family) in 1989. In 1992, became Glenayre Technologies and sold its manufacturing plant to a US company and closed in 2001. Evolved as Glentel, a Burnaby-based retail firm selling mobile phones, linked with Rogers (Toronto). Glenayre filed thirty-eight (Canadian) patents.

Firm, start-up features	Evolutionary synopsis
Sierra Systems Group	
Co-founded in 1966 in Vancouver (as Computech Consulting) by Ian Reid (UVic), Grant Gisel (University of Manitoba), and Dave Bowman. Involved in IT services and management consulting.	A private company with sales in 2001 of $128.8 million and 909 employees in 2002. Became part of the Sierra-Cedar group (US) in 1994–95. In 2018, with 700 employees across Canada, 340 in Vancouver, acquired by NTT Data Services of Japan via its Texas-based head office. Registered no (Canadian) patents.
MacDonald Dettwiler and Associates (MDA)	
Founded in 1969 in Richmond by John MacDonald (UBC, MIT) and Vern Dettwiler UBC), both UBC professors. Developed satellite and remotely driven information technologies with applications in space exploration, robotics, and property and resource evaluations.	Became a public company in 1993. In 2016, global sales of $2,063.8 million and 5,800 employees, with up to 2,000 in British Columbia. In 2023 global employment around 3,000 with main centre in Richmond. Once called the "epicentre of Canadian space industry," MDA built the Canadarm for NASA. Has offices in Europe and the United States and manufacturing plants in Ontario. Acquired by Orbital Sciences Corporation (US) in 1995 for US $67 million, which sold 70 percent of MDA to the Ontario Teacher's Pension Fund in 2001. Acquired by US-based Maxar Technologies (head office in Colorado) in 2016, then by Northern Private Capital of Toronto in 2020 for CDN $1 billion, still as MDA, a private, independent company, with the head office in Brampton, Ontario. Filed thirty-seven patents.
Alpha Technologies	
Founded in 1975 in Burnaby by Fred Kaiser and Grace Borsari, the former educated at Ohm Technical School, Germany, and BCIT. Focused on power solutions, initially for cable TV, then for broadband cable, telecommunications, et cetera.	A private company that relocated much activity to Bellingham, Washington, in 1976–77. Corporate sales of $79 million in 2001, $600 million in 2015, with 1,300 jobs (employment in Burnaby about 350). Acquired adjacent Argus Technologies of Burnaby (founded in 1986) in 2010 and by US-based EnerSys (Reading, Pennsylvania) for $750 million in 2019. Filed thirty-six patents.

▶

◄

Firm, start-up features	*Evolutionary synopsis*
Mobile Data Inc. (MDI)	
Began in 1978 in Vancouver as a spinoff from MDA, led by Dan Gelbart (Israel Institute of Technology). Pioneered the world's first mobile data system. Involved in the design and manufacturing of radio data communications products.	A private company that grew from twenty employees in 1981 (sales of less than $2 million) to 440 employees (sales of around $44 million) in 1987 to over 500 employees in six locations and over $50 million in sales in 1988. Acquired by Motorola (US) in 1988 for $105 million and expanded to over 1,000 employees and $100 million in sales. Operations terminated in 1989; some activities shifted to China. Filed three patents (see MDSI below).
Ballard Power Systems	
Founded in 1979 in Burnaby (as Ballard Research) by Geoffrey Ballard (Queen's University, Washington University in St. Louis), Keith Prater (University of Texas), and Paul Howard (University of Kansas) to R&D high-energy lithium batteries.	Became a public company in 1993, with 630 employees and revenues of over S100 million in 2019. Revenues fluctuate greatly, and viability has depended on support and contracts with MNCs, governments, and other organizations from around the world. As Ballard Power Systems, the company focused on hydrogen-based fuel cells (discussion in the text). Filed 252 patents in Canada (over 1,400 in total).
MPR Teltech	
Founded in part by Norman Dowds (education unknown) in1979 in Burnaby. Originated as Microtel Pacific Research, part of Microtel, a telecom equipment manufacturing company owned by BC Tel (now Telus). Relabelled MPR Teltech in 1987 when BC Tel sold Microtel. Focus on telecommunications.	Independent in 1987 but still owned by Telus. Employed 450 at its peak, located in SFU's Discovery Park. Fertile innovator of numerous important telecom products sold, usually cheaply, to other companies, including Newbridge Networks (Ontario), which commercialized its core (ATM) technology, and the California-based Sierra Conductor, which acquired Microtel Pacific Research's PMC group and its ATM and networking, semiconductor chip technology. Incubated other companies in British Columbia and elsewhere. Closed by BC Tel in 1996 and finally disbanded in 1997 (see Case Study 4.2). Dr. Alan Winter (Belfast, Queen's University) was CEO from 1985 to 1996. Filed seventeen patents.

Firm, start-up features	Evolutionary synopsis
Delta Controls	
Founded in Surrey in 1980 by Brian Goodchild (University of Saskatchewan) and Raymond Rae (University of Saskatchewan). Created an intelligent building automation system and controls.	A private company that established 300 distributors in eighty countries to sell its open protocol building automation systems. Had over 300 jobs and sales up to $25 million. Acquired by Delta Electronics BV (Denmark) in 2016, an MNC with sales of more than $7 billion, with offices in China (2003) and Europe (2005). The Surrey operation continues, with 262 employees in 2018 and 287 in 2022. Filed one patent.
Quadra Logic Technologies (QLT)	
Co-founded in Vancouver in 1981 by Dr. Julia Levy (UBC, University of London) and Dr. James Miller (University of Western Ontario), plus Ronald Mackenzie (Queen's University and University of Western Ontario), Ronald Chase, and John Brown. A UBC spinoff – Levy and Miller were professors there (microbiology and medicine. respectively). Focused on anti-cancer drugs and treating blindness.	Julia Levy became the sole leader by 1985, and QLT became a public company in 1986. Helped to develop photofrin as an anti-cancer drug with limited success. Achieved commercial success around 2000 through sales of Visudyne, a drug combatting macular degeneration. In 2002, sales were $110 million (and over $186 million in 2004), with 336 employees. Merged in 2004 with Atrix Laboratories of Quebec in an attempt to diversify, but sales plummeted "by 2008. Merged with Aegerion, becoming Novelion in 2016, liquidated in 2020. Filed fourteen patents.
Creo	
Founded in 1983 in Burnaby by Ken Spencer (UBC, SFU) and Dan Gelbart (Israel Institute of Technology), former MDA employees. Focused on digitized printing technologies.	Became a public company in 1999. Had 100 employees in 1992, 270–350 in 1995 (sales of $45 million), and 1,023 by 1998. Acquired the rival Israel-based Scitex in 2000 and reached over $1 billion in revenue, with 4,200 jobs globally and over 700 at its Burnaby manufacturing plant and head office. Acquired by Kodak for $1.05 billion in 2005, and its operations were gutted in 2009, leaving only a skeletal office. Filed twenty patents.

▶

◄

Firm, start-up features	Evolutionary synopsis
Xantrex Technology	
Established in 1983 in North Vancouver, moved to Burnaby in 1990.	Became a public company in 2004.
	In 2001, had $170 million in sales and 600 employees; by 2008, it had sales of $234 million
Founded by Jim Dotson, Hazar Muji (education unknown), and others by acquisition of the power supply division of Anatek Electronics.	and 800 employees (300 in SFU's Discovery Park, subsequently relocated nearby).
	In 2008, acquired by Schneider Electric of France for $415 million (its San Diego–based programmable power business was acquired by Ametek [Pennsylvania] for $120 million), an MNC with sales of $17 billion (2007).
Focused on alternative power technologies (wind, solar).	
Developed rapidly after 1998 when Mossadiq Umedaly (from Ballard) became CEO.	Opened a new lab in Burnaby in 2013, purchased by Mission Critical Electronics (California) in 2018. Filed eighteen patents.
Aim Global Technologies	
Founded in 1983 in Delta by Steven de Jaray (UBC).	A private company with sales in 2001 of $123 million and 987 employees.
Involved in contract manufacturing services of original equipment manufacturers OEMs in various sectors.	In 2004, admitted (to British Columbia's Security Commission) to insider trading violations.
	Failed in 2010 following federal government charges of exporting equipment that threatened Canada's security (could be used in weapons); charges were withdrawn in 2011, and in 2015 Aim won a lawsuit against the federal government and was awarded compensation estimated at about $10 million.
	No (Canadian) patents filed.
Quartech Systems	
Founded in 1984 in Vancouver by Paul Huffington and Bill O'Brien (education unknown) to provide ICTs and consulting, initially for a BC government ministry.	A private company that has employed 250, with reports of sales ranging from $38 million to over $61 million.
	Has a diversified clientele in public and private sectors.
	Acquired and run by David Marshall (SFU), originally hired in 1988.
	No (Canadian) patents.
Fincentric Corporation	
Established in 1986 in Richmond.	A private company with over $61 million in sales in 2001 and 273 employees.

Firm, start-up features	Evolutionary synopsis
Until 2001, known as Prologic and co-founded by Greg Hope, Paul Oeuvray (UBC), and Wes Warner. Develops software for banks.	Has strategic alliances with several major companies and provides financial services (software) in twenty-five countries for banks and credit unions. Acquired in 2007 by Open Solutions, Glastonbury, Connecticut, and has 100 jobs. Has filed several patents.
Avcorp Industries	
Founded in 1986 in Delta by Kenneth R. Patrick (a wing commander in the Second World War, honorary degrees, Order of the British Empire). Original location was in Richmond, predecessor companies can be traced back to 1959. Subcontractor of aircraft parts, especially wings, and advanced manufacturing.	A public company since 1993. In 2005, revenue was $79.5 million, with about 350 jobs; in 2020, revenue was $150.9 million, with 650 employees. Acquired Comtec Advanced Structures in Ontario (aircraft parts and ninety jobs) in 2007. Sales dominated by parts for Cessna, Bombardier, and Boeing. Between 2009 and 2016, Panta Holdings BV (Netherlands) – an investment company – obtained majority control, providing financing to Avcorp. In 2022, Latecoere (France) acquired Avcorp for CDN $41 million. No patents filed.
Seanix Technology	
Established in 1986 in Richmond by Paul Girard (Hudson Technology University, Ottawa). Designs and manufactures personal computers.	In 2001, sales of $152 million; following a merger with a Quebec company, had 300 employees and estimated sales then of $300 million. Went bankrupt in 2009 Had acquired A&B Sounds (Vancouver) when it was bankrupt (2008). Once the largest Canadian personal computer manufacturer. Filed three patents.
Microserve	
Founded in 1987 in Burnaby by Jay Ayer (Harvard University). Provides IT support and solutions for businesses.	A private company. Reports of size vary, with two indicating sales of over $100 million in 2021, with 373 employees. Has offices across Canada but sales mainly in British Columbia and Alberta. No patents filed.

◄

Firm, start-up features	*Evolutionary synopsis*
ACL Services	
Established in Vancouver in 1987 by Hart and Harold Will, a UBC (commerce) professor and his son. Rebranded in 2019 as Galvanize. Provides audit, security, risk assessment, and related software.	A private company with over 500 employees by 2020. Offices in London, Singapore, Tokyo, and New Jersey. Hart Will ran the company until 2011. Acquired several companies, including Workpapers.com in 2012, to provide a cloud-based business model. Acquired by Diligent Corporation of New York in 2021. Filed one patent.
Westech Information Systems	
Founded in 1989 in Vancouver by David Mclean (University of Alberta) as a spinoff of a BC Hydro division but still owned by it until a partial employee buyout in 1991 (with much business between the two). Provides IT management, power, and computing services for utilities.	A private company that employed 240 people in 1991 and 365 in 2001. In 2003, Westech's operations were contracted out controversially to Accenture Business, started in 2001 as a giant spinoff from a New York–based consulting company and since 2007 headquartered in Dublin. Part of a ten-year contract in which the BC government agreed to pay Accenture Business $1.45 billion to run several BC Hydro assets, including Westech. The contract was renewed for five years, but the benefits to Westech were unclear; the contract ended in 2018, and Westech closed. No patents were filed.
Creation Studios	
Began in 1989 in North Vancouver as Anatek, a small manufacturing firm acquired by Barry and Jane Henderson (both University of Waterloo). Renamed Creation Technologies in 1991 and relocated to Burnaby in 1996. Started by supplying inputs to the music industry, then provided design, manufacturing, and services.	A private company with important employee ownership. Revenues in 2018–19 were $94.2 million, with 450 jobs in British Columbia and 2,500 in total. Operates eleven manufacturing facilities in Canada, the United States, Mexico, and China. In 2019, acquired by Lindsay Goldberg (Boston), a private investment firm. In 2022, over 500 jobs in the Burnaby operation, still the headquarters. Sales are global, and no patents filed.

Firm, start-up features	Evolutionary synopsis
PMC-Sierra	
Began in 1992 in Burnaby. Originated as Pacific Microelectronics Centre (PMC), stimulated by Greg Aasen, who worked at MPR Teltech, but funded by Sierra Conductor (California), founded by Colin Harris (University of Rhode Island) and James Diller (UBC). MPR retained 15 percent ownership, and Sierra obtained 80 percent ownership for a $5 million investment, and the head office shifted to California. Returned to Canadian control (and head office) in 1997 as PMC-Sierra. Fabless company focused on developing ATM and networking semiconductor chips.	If PMC had Canadian origins, it quickly became part of Sierra Conductor (a public company). Retained its Burnaby operation, and when Sierra Conductor moved out of the model chip business PMC acquired that business and in 1996 established its Burnaby head office. Had $531 million in revenue, with 500 employees in British Columbia (1,500 in total). In 2015–16, acquired by Microsemi (California) for $2.5 billion. In 2018, Microsemi was acquired by Microchip Technology (Arizona) for US $10.2 billion.
Angiotech	
Founded in 1992 in Vancouver as a UBC spinoff by Drs. William L. Hunter (UBC), Lindsay Machen, and Larry Arsenault (UBC). Arsenault was a UBC professor and Machen a radiologist. A life sciences company focused on developing technologies to combat diseases and complications arising from implants.	Became a public company in 2003. From 1992, first developed the Taxus drug-eluting coronary stent, co-developed and sold by Boston Scientific Group, whose Irish factory manufactured the stent. Taxus was sold in Europe in 2003 and approved for sale in the United States in 2004. In 2005, sales reached US $200 million. Acquired American Medical Instruments (US) in 2006 for CDN $900 million, with its 1,450 employees, while expanding its R&D activities to include manufacturing and marketing. Had ninety-six employees in Vancouver. Acquired Surgical Specialities in 2006. Rapid decline led to filing for bankruptcy in 2011; partial recovery with sales back to $128.8 million in 2013.

▶

◄

Firm, start-up features	*Evolutionary synopsis*
	Manufacturing relocated from the United States to Mexico; also located in Puerto Rico, Germany, and England.
	In 2017, Angiotech employed 2,000 globally and was acquired by a consortium led by Vivo Capital (US) and ZQ Capital (China), both investment firms, the former focusing on health care.
Absolute Software	
Founded in 1992 in Vancouver by Christian Cotichini (Singularity University) and Fraser Cain (UBC), joined by John Livingstone (University of Guelph). Specializes in computer security systems, anti-theft software, and risk management.	A publicly traded company since 2000. Employment of 350 in 2013 and revenue close to $100 million. Revenues of US $99 million in 2019, with 440 total employees (269 in Canada), and US $197.3 million in 2022. Offices are located in the United States, United Kingdom, and Vietnam. Partners with leading OEMs (e.g., Dell, Samsung, Hewlett-Packard, and Lenovo) that use its patented technology in their factories. By 2015, its persistence technology was reportedly embedded in half a billion devices. Thirty-one patents filed.
Mobile Data Solutions Inc. (MDSI)	
Founded in1993 in Richmond as a spinoff by Erik Dysthe (Concordia University) and other former employees of Mobile Data International (itself an MDA spinoff).	A private company with revenues in 2001 of about $90 million, with 500 employees, declining in 2002 to 325 employees and US $38.7 million. Acquired in 2005 by Vista for $70 million and consolidated in 2007 as part of Ventyx of Atlanta, Georgia Ventyx acquired in 2010 by ABB, a Swiss engineering group, for over US $1 billion, and in 2018 Hitachi Energy (Japan) acquired ABB's power grid division for US $11 billion, deals that retained key talent from MDSI, which dissolved.
Stemcell Technologies	
Founded in Vancouver in 1993 by Dr. Allen Eaves (Acadia University, Dalhousie University, University of Toronto), a UBC professor who, with his (doctor) wife, had started the Terry Fox	A private company, the largest biotech firm in Canada. In 1993, employed 8 people, over 1,000 employees by 2017, 850 located in Metro Vancouver, 1,500 by 2019, 2,000 in 2022, and 2500 in 2023. 2023 revenues of $523 million.

Firm, start-up features	Evolutionary synopsis
Laboratories in 1981, focusing on blood cancer research and cell cultures. Focused on life sciences and biotechnology.	Focused on developing, manufacturing, and selling scientific instruments, reagents, and a variety of cell cultures. MethoCult globally recognized in a study of hemotopoietic cells. Estimated revenue per year of around $447.9 million. Offices in the United States, Europe, Asia, and Australia and sales in 120 countries. In 2018, received $45 million in government grants to build an advanced manufacturing facility in Burnaby. Filed thirty-one patents.
Sierra Wireless	
Established in 1993 in Richmond by Norman Toms (Trinity College, Dublin) and Andrew Harris (SFU grad) after they left MDI. Designer and manufacturer of wireless communication equipment.	A public company since 1999. In 2016, sales of US $615 million, with 1,400 employees in 2018; in 2021, sales of $473.3 million, with 1,007 employees. Filed 550 patents by 2018. Funded an SFU chair position since 2003, and Andrew Harris appointed an SFU professor in 2016. Launched the world's first cellular-embedded module in 1997. An internet of things solutions provider, had global sales and acquired several foreign companies. Acquired by California-based Semtech in 2022 for $1.2 billion.
Pivotal CRM	
Founded in 1994 in Vancouver by Norm Francis (UBC) and Keith Wales (UBC?), the former a UBC computer science grad. Grew out of earlier start-up of Basic Software Group that provided accounting software and acquired by Computer and Associates in 1985. Then developed a pen computing software company before establishing Pivotal CRM (meaning customer relationship	A public company since 1999, with revenue in 2001 of $128.8 million and about 400 employees. In 2000, Microsoft was a partner and customer in stimulating its growth but then became a rival. Acquired by CDC of Hong Kong in 2004, with Pivotal continuing its Vancouver operations as part of CDC Software until the parent CDC went bankrupt in 2011. CDC Software as a stand-alone company merged with Consona Corporation to form Aptean, headquartered in Atlanta. Provides CRM and other business services, with eighty employees in Metro Vancouver.

▶

◀

Firm, start-up features	*Evolutionary synopsis*
management) and employing people from Basic Software Group. Became Pivotal Corporation in 1999.	In 2018, Aptean acquired by ESW (Engineers for Sustainable World) Capital, Austin, a private equity firm that specializes in controlling business companies.

Westport Innovations

Co-founded in 1995 in Vancouver as a UBC spinoff by Professor Philip Hill (Queen's University, MIT) and David Demers (University of Saskatchewan), based on the former's research (in mechanical engineering). Focused on replacing diesel fuel with a cleaner energy source such as liquid natural gas and compressed natural gas, hydrogen, and biofuels. Became Westport Fuel Systems in 2016 following a merger with (Calgary-based) Fuel Systems Solutions.	Became a public company on the Alberta Stock Exchange and in 1999 on the Toronto Stock Exchange. Negotiated various joint ventures with MNCs in the United States, Sweden, and China and a long-term partnership with Cummins (Detroit). Employment of 725 in 2015, reached 1,751 in 2016, and in 2018 over 1,200 employees, with $360 million in sales; in 2021, employed 1,761 globally and had sales of $312 million. Sales in seventy countries and supplies over twenty OEMs. Made over 1,400 patent applications but filed only one.

PNIDigital Media

Established in 1995 in Vancouver; began as InMedia Presentations, renamed PhotoChannel Networks in 1999 and PNI Digital Media in 2009 (founders unknown). Provides software services for printing, fraud checks, and so on by retail giants and others in the United States and Canada.	A private company, PhotoChannels Network was small, with 10 employees in 2001, but increased to 50 in 2008 and 250 in 2017. Revenues also increased from $25 million in 2010 to $40.5 million in 2017 and have been as high as $68.5 million. Offices have been established in the United Kingdom (from 2007), and there are exports around the world. Operates PNI Digital Media Platform, which provides transaction processes and order routing services for major retailers such as Walmart, Tesco, and Fujifilm. No patents filed.

Point Grey Research

Founded in 1997 in Richmond by Donald Murray (University of Alberta), Malcolm Steenburgh	A private company that employed 300 people in 2015 with offices in Germany, Japan, China, and Italy as well as Richmond.

Firm, start-up features	Evolutionary synopsis
(Queen's University), Stewart Kingdon, Vladimir Tucakov (Brock University), and Rod Burnham (UBC). Developed as a spinoff from UBC's Computer Science Department. Designs and manufactures high-performance digital cameras for industrial, medical, traffic, bio-metric, geographic information system, and people-counting applications.	Has a global network of distributors and patented products. Produces over 200,000 cameras per year, with revenue around $20 million. Acquired by Flir Integrated Imaging Solutions (Wilsonville, Oregon) in 2016 for $253 million. Had 272 employees in British Columbia in 2018 and over 300 in 2021.

iQmetrix

Established in 2010 in Vancouver but originally founded in 1999 by Christopher Krywulak (high school, Regina). Head office relocated to Vancouver shortly after Krywulak moved there in 2009. Provides retail management solutions for the wireless industry. A key part of Chrysalis Software as an original flagship company.	A private company with employment of 400 (85 in British Columbia) and estimated sales of $80 million in six offices across North America, but Regina is still the biggest Canadian location. First flagship development was a retail management system known as RQ. Has become the continent's leading provider of telecom retail management software. Acquired Viva Tracker (Detroit) in 2021 and two companies in 2022 for $14 million, adding 100 employees in India, the United States, and Europe. Filed five patents.

D-Wave Systems

A UBC spinoff founded in 1999 in Burnaby by Dr. Geordie Rose (UBC), Haig Farris (UBC, University of Pennsylvania), Bob Wiens (University of Calgary, Columbia Business School), and Dr. Alexandre Zagoskin (A.M. Gorky Kharkiv State University, Ukraine). Creates an extremely fast, large-scale computer using subatomic particles.	A private company until 2022. Reports of 180–214 employees (2019) and contracts worth $75 million over twenty-one years. The first company to sell a computer including quantum effects; following earlier models, it became commercially available in 2015. Offices established in California and Maryland, and early customers included the University of Southern California, Lockheed Martin, and NASA/Google. Extensive collaborations with Canadian universities and American organizations.

▶

◄

Firm, start-up features	*Evolutionary synopsis*
	Struggles to maintain profitability despite substantial funding; 2022 revenue and employment were low. Filed 40 patents in Canada plus 200 in the United States.
Global Relay	
Founded in 2000 in Vancouver by Warren Roy, Duff Reid, and Eric Parusel (all Okanagan College). Involved in cloud archiving and information governance, becoming focused on finance (rather than architecture and construction).	A private, employee-controlled company with 393 employees in 2018, over 500 in 2020, and globally over 1,000 in 2022. Offices established in the United States (New York, Chicago, Raleigh), London, Singapore, Halifax, and Vancouver. Global sales and revenue over $100 million in 2019. About 20,000 clients, typically banks, private equity firms, hedge funds, et cetera. Owns its own data centre in North Vancouver to enable control of all its services. One patent filed.
Vision Critical	
Founded in 2000 in Vancouver by Andrew Reid (University of Manitoba) and Angus Reid. Builds software to link businesses continuously with customers (especially) and stakeholders to enhance decision making.	A private company with 257 employees in Vancouver in 2018 and estimated sales of $80 million in 2012 and over $100 million in 2022. In 2020, acquired by (and renamed) Alida (Toronto), partially owned by Andrew Reid's father since 2005 and in similar business. One patent filed.
Zymeworks	
Co-founded in 2003 in Vancouver by Dr. Ali Tehrani (University of Waterloo, UBC) and Dr. Anthony Fejes (UBC, University of Massachusetts). Focused on therapeutic approaches to cancer treatment drug development. A clinical-stage life sciences company.	A public company since 2017 that employed 250 (45 of whom have PhDs); in 2018, it had 183 employees. A new Vancouver lab opened in 2017. Had venture capital funding of US $61.5 million in 2017, one of the largest in Canadian biotech history. Its lead product is ZW25, a novel antibody. Has many licensing agreements with leading pharmaceutical firms but by 2022 was still awaiting drug approval. Revenues are from funding sources rather than drug sales, and income losses have been reported publicly. Filed fifty-four patents.

Firm, start-up features	Evolutionary synopsis
Avigilon	
Founded in 2004 by Alexander Fernandes (high school, Montreal), who, after military service, moved to Vancouver in the early 1990s, worked for Creo, and set up Qimaging in 1999. Sold Qimaging for $20 million in 2002 and used the profit for Avigilon. A leading supplier of surveillance software and products, integrated solutions, and recently AI.	A public company since 2011. First sales were in 2007, with 500 employees in British Columbia in 2021 (1,200 employees in total), with revenue in 2017 of $408.6 million. Manufactures in Richmond (also R&D) and Texas. In 2018, sold its downtown head office for $107.5 million and then leased it back. In 2018, acquired by Motorola Solutions of Chicago (along with a UK company) for $1.2 billion, and Fernandez left the company. Filed 750 American patents and 45 Canadian patents.
Broadband TV	
Founded in 2005 in Vancouver by Shahrzad Rafati (UBC). Provides secure platforms to create and distribute video content for online consumption.	A private company that became public in 2020. Control of 51 percent acquired by European business interests in 2013; in 2020, control reacquired by Rafati. Revenues reached $33 million in 2014 and grew to $388 million by 2020, with 350 employees (260 full time).
Traction on Demand	
Established in 2006 in Burnaby by Greg Malpass (SFU). Provides software services for salesforce platform consulting.	A private company that grew rapidly to over 700 employees by 2019 and 1,200 by 2022. Self-funded until 2019 when it obtained external funding for the first time. Traction Guest, an early product spun off as an independent company, acquired by Boston-based equity firm PSG (Providence Strategic Growth) in 2021. Traction on Demand acquired by Salesforce (San Francisco) in 2023 (it had obtained a minority position in 2019). No patents filed.
Clio	
Founded in 2008 in Vancouver by Jack Newton (SFU) and Rian Gauvreau (University of Alberta) and moved to Burnaby in 2012.	A private company with 425 employees in 2019 and over 500 in 2021. Estimated revenue of about $176 million with global markets and offices in Toronto, Calgary, Los Angeles, and Dublin.

▶

◀

Firm, start-up features	*Evolutionary synopsis*
Provides cloud-based legal software.	Received much external funding and in 2020 achieved unicorn status after receiving $136 million in funding from American venture capital sources. Filed two patents.

Hootsuite Media

Established in 2009 in Vancouver by Ryan Holmes (high school, Vernon), David Tedman (Vancouver Film School), and Dario Meli (Vancouver Film School) as a spinoff from Invoke Media, which they founded in 2005. Holmes moved to Vancouver in the early 1990s. Focuses on social media integration.	A private company with 1,500 employees in 2019 and estimated sales of over $200 million in 2018 with 16 million users. Developed software to allow users to keep track of all log-ins across all accounts. First Hootsuite app launched in 2008 and by 2010 had 1 million customers. Established fourteen offices around the world by 2018. In 2019, laid off 10 percent of its staff and in 2022 a third; probably employs about 1,000 people worldwide. Filed one patent in Canada (others in the United States).

Visier

Founded in 2010 in Vancouver by John Schwarz (University of Manitoba), Ryan Wong (UBC), Jan Schwartz (Western University), and Brett Schwartz (University of Toronto). Provides cloud-based analytics and workforce planning.	A private company with eleven employees in 2011, 340 employees in 2018, and over 600 employees globally by 2022 in seven offices in Europe, the United States, and Asia as well as Vancouver and Toronto. Secured external funding, reaching unicorn status ($1 billion in evaluation) in 2021 (with $100 million investment injection). Revenue $50–$100 million in 2022. Filed one patent.

Bench Accounting

Founded in 2012 in Vancouver by Ian Crosby (UBC) and Jordan Menashy (York University) as 10Sheet Services in 2010. In 2012, joined by Adam Saint (Vancouver Film School) and Pavel Rodionov (Tomsk State University) to form Bench. Provides online bookkeeping software services.	A private company with more than 300 employees by 2018 and over 600 jobs by 2022. Revenue estimates vary a lot, but some reach $90 million or so. Primarily services small businesses across most industries and has integrated its services with banks and digital firms. Delivers constant reports and year-end tax packages. No known patents.

Firm, start-up features	Evolutionary synopsis
AbCellera Biologics	
A UBC spinoff founded in 2012 in Vancouver by Dr. Carl Hansen (UBC, California Institute of Technology), Dr. Véronique Lecault (UBC), Dr. Kevin Heyries (UBC), Daniel Da Costa (UBC), and Dr. Oleh Petriv (UBC). Researches and develops human antibodies.	Started with six employees in 2012 and still affiliated with UBC. Became a public company in 2020 (Nasdaq) when revenue was $233 million, up from just $11.6 million (research fees) in 2019. In 2021, revenue was $375.2 million with 386 employees. Hansen became the full-time CEO in 2019. From UBC-based research, developed a patented cell-screening platform to help with medical antibody countermeasures. Multiple partnerships with pharmaceutical companies and funding agencies. Developed COVID-19 antibody and partnered with Eli Lilly, generating $5 billion in royalties. New office opened in 2022 (480 employees). Multiple patents, fifty including Hansen (and fighting lawsuits as both defendant and accuser).
Slack	
Established in 2013 in Vancouver, soon became Slack Technologies. Lead founder was Stewart Butterfield (UVic, University of Cambridge); co-founders included Eric Costello (Cabrillo College, California), Cal Henderson (Birmingham City University), and Serguei Mourachov (National University of Science and Technology, Moscow). Grew out of internal use in an earlier gaming company, Tiny Speck (2010), and initial funding came from the sale of part of Butterfield's first start-up, Flickr, for $20–$25 million to Yahoo.	Extremely rapid growth, achieving a $1 billion valuation within a year of start-up. By 2016, had 430 employees and went public in 2019, with revenue that year of US $401 million and 1,664 employees. First office established in 2015, and new head office in San Francisco in 2018, becoming a US company. Offices in New York, Toronto, Denver, London, Tokyo, Pune (India), Paris, Istanbul, and Melbourne. In 2020, acquired by Salesforce of California for US $27.7 billion. Over 100 patents filed.

Notes: Firms identified are those achieving employment of 250 people or more and/or $50 million in sales or more and are/were locally owned and controlled within Metro Vancouver for some time. Patent filings are with the Canadian Intellectual Property Office (until 2019–20); filings made elsewhere are not recorded.
Sources: Authors' research files and multiple newspaper and business journal articles.

Appendix 2

Foreign Firms in Metro Vancouver's High-Tech Sector, 1980–2019

MNC	Entry timing and mode
Nintendo	
Founded in 1889 in Kyoto, Japan. A public company with revenue in 2018 of ¥1.2 trillion or about US $9.960 million. Creator of video games.	In 1983, Nintendo Entertainment Centre, a small office mainly for marketing. Firm's North American operations are in the United States, headquartered in Redwood, Washington.
Motorola	
Founded in Chicago in 1928. After big losses in 2009, split into two public companies: Motorola Mobility and Motorola Solutions. The former company acquired by Google in 2012, which sold it to Levano in 2014.	In 1988, for US $105 million, acquired Mobile Data International in Vancouver with its 500 employees, reaching 1,000 jobs and $100 million in revenue with global sales (see Appendix 1). Closed in 1999, some operations transferred to China by Motorola.
Raytheon	
Founded in 1922. Relocated from Lexington to Waltham, Massachusetts, in 2003. A public company with sales in 2018 of US $27.1 billion and 67,000 employees. Involved in the aerospace and defence industries.	In 1989 in Richmond, had 150 employees in two buildings, with sales in the $10–$25 million range. Focus is on the design and development of large-scale software systems for air traffic management.

MNC	Entry timing and mode
Japanese Consortium	
Includes NEC, a giant Tokyo-based electronics company formed in 1898. Plant became Moli Energy, then Nippon Moli Energy, in 1994 and NEC Moli Energy in 1997. In 1989, acquired by E-One Moli Energy, formed in 1977 as a research group and part of Taiwan Cement Corporation, a public company (since 1962) and conglomerate with revenue in 2018 of US $4.1 billion.	Moli Energy acquired in 1977 by Japanese interests that were customers in a fire sale by the BC government for $5 million (see Case Study 2.1). Manufacturing stopped, but the operation was stabilized in 1998 on its acquisition by E-One Moli Energy, which then developed the lithium-ion battery and became the first to sell it for use in large-scale power tools; also supplies ventilator companies and NASA. In 2020, the Maple Ridge operation had an estimated eighty-five employees and planned to add jobs by re-establishing manufacturing to complement its Taiwanese factory.
Electronic Arts	
Formed in Redwood City, California, in 1982 as an Apple spinoff. A public company since 1989, with revenue in 2018 of US $5.2 billion and 9,300 employees. Focus is on video games.	In 1991, acquired Distinctive Software of Burnaby, which started in 1982 (see Case Study 3.1). The Burnaby facility has remained a key part of Electronic Arts, with employment reaching 1,500.
Sierra Semiconductor	
Established in 1984 in San Jose and became a public company in 1991. Focus is on semiconductors.	In 1993, acquired PMC-Sierra in Burnaby. PMC became independent again (BC based) in 1994. Supported 1,703 jobs (see Appendix 1).
Seagate Technology	
Founded in 1979 in Fremont, California. Sought to enter the software business to diversify its hardware focus on data storage products. A private corporation with 40,000 employees in 2022. Sold Crystal Decisions qua Seagate Software to Business Objects (France) in 2003, which sold it to SAP in 2008.	In 1994, acquired Crystal Decisions (initially Crystal Services) started by Terry and Mark Cunningham in Vancouver for $18.6 million. Produced business intelligence reports, notably Crystal Reports, for SMEs. Still small when acquired, Crystal Decisions grew rapidly with the same owner, who made further acquisitions for Seagate Technology between 1947 and 1997. Crystal Reports continued as a major product.

▶

◄

MNC	Entry timing and mode
IBM	
A public company in Armonk, New York. In 2018, revenue of US $13.2 billion and 350,600 employees. Sells information technology.	Opened a Vancouver office in 1921. In 1997–98, IBM extended the Toronto-based centre for e-business innovation to Burnaby as the Pacific Development Centre. Employs 280 people in a cross-functional team for diverse projects mainly outside British Columbia, in cooperation with IBM's Global Services. Has filed twenty-nine patents.
Broadcom Corporation	
Founded in Irving, California, in 1991 and a public company since 1998. In 2012, revenue of US $8 billion and 11,000 employees. Merged with Avago Technologies (United States and Singapore) in 2015, operating as Broadcom Incorporated (San Jose). In 2016, acquired by Cypress Semiconductors.	In 1999, acquired (for US $280 million) Hothaus Technologies in Richmond, a spinoff from Spectrum Signals (Burnaby) in 1995 led by Ross Mitchell. Hothaus specialized in voice-over IP software (and can use chips provided by Broadcom), employing 60 and expanding to 197 in 2016. Sales office established in 2018.
Redback Networks	
Founded in 1996 in Sunneyvale, California. Listed on Nasdaq in 1998. Had 800 employees worldwide, acquired by Ericsson (Sweden) in 2006–07 for US $2.1 billion. Provides hardware and software used by ISPs to manage broadband services.	In 1999, acquired Siara Systems of California in a US $4.3 billion deal, including its Vancouver software development office with forty employees. In 2000, acquired Abatis Systems of Burnaby (founded in 1998 by Adam Lorent and Paul Terry) for $US 676.7 million, with 126 employees providing IP services (no revenue to date). The two facilities are located next to each other. In 2018, there were 226 employees.
Sulzer Medica	
Located in Switzerland; provides mechanical and tissue-based heart valves. Acquired by Italy's Sorin in 2003 for $27 million.	In 1999, acquired Mitroflow International of Richmond for $50 million. Mitroflow was established in 1991 by Paul Geyer (UBC grad) with 9 employees, growing to 125 in 1999 with global sales.

MNC	Entry timing and mode
Fortinet	
Founded in Sunneyvale, California in 2000 by Ken and Michael Xie. A public company since 2009 with revenue in 2022 of US $4.42 billion and 12,091 employees. Focuses on cybersecurity software, appliances, and services.	In 2000, established its global R&D centre in Burnaby, where it employed 100 by 2009. By 2022, almost 600 employees in Burnaby R&D (and 1,059 across Canada).
Boeing	
Founded in 1916 in Seattle. A public company with revenue in 2018 of US $101.1 billion and 153,027 employees. Established a Canadian head office in Vancouver in 1929 and in 1939 built a huge factory in Richmond, making PBY flying (patrol) boats and B-29 parts during the Second World War. Factory closed in 1945 with 7,000 layoffs.	In 2000, acquired Aeroinfo Systems in Richmond. By 2018, had 200 employees (software engineers and data scientists). In 2016, opened a facility in Vancouver (Yaletown) to add fifty data analyst jobs focusing on flight routing.
Business Objects	
Founded in 1990 in Paris and San Jose. A public company with revenue in 2007 of over US $820 million and 4,977 employees (2,153 employees in 2003). Acquired by Germany's SAP in 2008.	In 2003, acquired Crystal Decisions (qua Seagate Software since 1994), a rival company, and rights to its flagship product, Crystal Reports, used by many MNCs (IBM, Microsoft, etc.). Major Crystal facilities retained in Vancouver but R&D in Ipswich, England, closed. Had revenue of $270 million when acquired.
Sorin	
A spinoff in Italy in 1956 from the Fiat Group, transforming itself from nuclear research to the biomedical field and specializing in cardiac devices. Acquired by the Snia Group (Milan) in 1986, but soon spun-off as independent company. A public company with offices in France, the United States, and Japan. Revenue in 2014 of €176.3 million.	In 2003, acquired Sulzer Carbonedics that included Sulzer Medica that controlled Mitroflow in Burnaby, founded in Richmond in 1991 to develop heart valve technology. Expanded especially after 2007 when the US Food and Drug Administration approved its valve (previously accepted in Europe). By 2011, 240 employees and produced its 100,000th heart valve.

▶

◄

MNC	Entry timing and mode
In 2015, Sorin merged with Cyberonics to form the UK-based LivaNova, with sales in 2018 of $1.1 billion.	

Sophos

Founded in 1985 in Abingdon, United Kingdom. A public company with sales in 2019 of US $710.6 million and 3,319 employees in 2018. Creates security hardware and software.	Acquired in 2003 ActiveState (Vancouver), a developer of programming tools for dynamic languages, for $23 million. Became independent in 2006 when sold to Pender Financial, a venture capital firm, and employees.

CDC Software

Founded in 2002 in Hong Kong to focus on company software applications in relation to customer experience. Merged in 2012 with Consona Corporation to form Aptean (head office in Atlanta).	In 2004, acquired Pivotal CRM, founded in 1994 in Vancouver, for US $56.6 million (see Appendix 1). Aptean in control from 2012 to 2018 when acquired by ESW (Engineers for a Sustainable World) (Georgia), a private equity firm.

Vista

A private equity company in San Francisco that acquired MDSI, rebranded as Ventyx in 2007 by combining it with the newly acquired Indus. Ventyx (head office in Atlanta) acquired in 2010 by ABB, a Swiss engineering group, for over US $1 billion. In 2018, Hitachi Energy (Japan) acquired ABB's power grid division for US $11 billion.	In 2005, acquired MDSI for $70 million (see Appendix 1). Ventyx is relatively small, but ABB and Hitachi are huge MNCs. An agreement in 2004 for MDSI to be acquired by AT Road (California) was cancelled.

Kodak

Founded in 1888 in New York. Dominant in camera products but failed to transition to the digital era. Bankrupt in 2012 but survived, had sales in 2018 of $1.3 billion and 5,400 employees.	In 2005, acquired Creo for $1.05 billion and gutted its operations in 2009, leaving only a skeletal office (see Appendix 1).

MNC	Entry timing and mode
Nexon Publishing	
Founded in 1994 in Seoul, head office moved to Tokyo in 2005. Focuses on video games. Revenue in 2018 of ¥53.7 billion. Became a public company in 2011.	Established in Vancouver in 2006 as Human Nature Studios division of Nexon. Closed in 2009 with 100 jobs lost. In 2016, joined with Vancouver's Game Studio, founded in 2015, to provide global marketing.
Microsoft	
Founded in 1975 in Redmond, Washington. Became a public company in 1986. In 2019, had sales of US $125.8 billion and 144,106 employees. Focuses on software et cetera.	In 2007, created the Vancouver Development Centre with 300 employees to develop code and test software systems. In 2016, consolidated three offices in new building to house 750 employees on Granville Street, its largest Canadian development centre.
Activision (becoming Activision Blizzard)	
Founded in 1979 in Santa Monica, California. A public company with revenue in 2018 of US $5.7 billion and 400 employees. Creator of video games.	In 2007, acquired DemonWare of Ireland and Vancouver, the latter office employing eighty people providing online software and services.
Open Solutions	
Founded in 1992 in Glastonbury, Connecticut, to provide financial services to banks and credit unions. Acquired in 2013 by Fiserv of Brookfield, Wisconsin, for US $55 million (and much debt), expected revenue of US $75 million.	In 2007, acquired Fincentric in Richmond, which continued its operations (see Appendix 1). After the Fiserv acquisition, a small office was retained in Vancouver.
Schneider Electric	
Founded in 1836, head office (since 2000) in Rueil-Malmason, France. Shifted from steel and shipbuilding to electronics in the 1980s. Sales in 2007 of $17 billion and in 2018 of about $30 billion and 155,286 jobs globally.	In 2008, acquired Xantrex (see Appendix 1) for $415 million (and its programmable power business acquired by Ametec for $120 million). Focus on solar energy (inverter technology) with new labs in Burnaby in 2013 and 2014. Employed 750 in Metro Vancouver in 2014. Purchased by Mission Critical Electronics (California) in 2018.

▶

◄

MNC	*Entry timing and mode*
SAP (System Applications and Products in Data Processing)	
Founded in 1972 in Germany as a spinoff from IBM. A public company with revenue in 2018 of €24.7 billion and 96,498 employees. Develops enterprise software.	Several acquisitions since 2008, including Business Objects, consolidated in SAP Labs in Yaletown (Vancouver) with about 1,400 employees, its largest Canadian development centre. Continued with Crystal Reports. Major renovation in 2016.
Sony	
Founded in 1946 in Tokyo. A public company with sales in 2019 of ¥8.665 billion and 114,4000 employees. Focuses on consumer electronics but highly diverse, including films and video games.	In 2010, production office opened by Sony Pictures Imageworks, initially with eighty employees. Head office moved from Culver City, California, to downtown Vancouver in 2014, with 800 employees.
Salesforce	
Founded in San Francisco in 1999 as a software as a service (SAAS) company. Revenue in 2022 of US $26.5 billion and 73,542 employees. Creates cloud-based customer relationship managmeent technologies.	In 2010, acquired Sitemasher, Vancouver, for $20 million, and operations closed. In 2018, acquired (for US $15.3 billion) by Tableau Software, which had opened a Vancouver office in 2015. Had 175 employees by 2019 in a new, central location. In 2022, acquired Traction on Demand and its 1,500 employees (500 in British Columbia); given the long-time relations, the operations of Traction likely to continue. In 2020, Salesforce had also acquired Mobify Research and Development of Vancouver (which developed an e-commerce platform) and Slack Technologies (which had been founded in Vancouver and still has offices there).
Disney	
Founded in 1923 with the head office in Burbank, California. A public company with revenue of US $67.57 billion and 201,000 employees.	In 2012, through its subsidiary Lucasfilm, opened a workshop in Vancouver (Gastown); opened a second studio in 2017. An estimated 400 people are employed.

MNC	Entry timing and mode
Amazon	
Now in Seattle, founded in 1994 in Arlington, Virginia. A public company with sales in 2018 of US $232,9 billion and 647,500 employees. Focused on e-commerce, cloud computing, AI, et cetera.	In 2013, expanded an existing small office in a new space with the potential to employ 1,000. In 2020, a new "first purpose built" office building planned for downtown Vancouver in two towers (seventeen and eighteen storeys) opened late 2023 with potential for 3,000 employees. Anticipates supporting 5,000 jobs in Vancouver.
Facebook (now Meta)	
Founded in 2004 by Mark Zuckerberg in Menlo Park, California. A public social media company with revenue in 2018 of US $55.8 billion and 39,651 employees.	In 2013, opened an office in Coal Harbour (Pender Street). Employed 150 at its peak as a training centre. Another office was planned, not started by 2020.
Oracle Corporation	
Founded in 1977 in Redwood City, California. A public software company with revenue in 2018 of $39.8 billion and 137,000 employees.	In 2013, established a Burrard Street office with 220 employees as Oracle Labs working on the RAPID project in software design.
Samsung	
Founded in 1938 in Seoul. Samsung Electronics alone has sales of $280 billion.	In 2013, Samsung R&D Canada opened a facility on Great Northern Way as one of forty-two global R&D centres; employs about 100. Focuses on cloud technologies related to mobile security et cetera.
Double Negative	
Founded in 1998, a private company headquartered in London, United Kingdom. Focuses on motion pictures and TV.	In 2014, took over vacated office space (the former head office of Mountain Equipment Co-op) in the Mount Pleasant area of Vancouver as its first North American office. Also located in numerous other cities worldwide.

▶

◄

MNC	Entry timing and mode
Tableau Software	
Founded in Seattle in 2003. An interactive data visualization company with sales in 2018 of US $1.2 billion and 4,181 employees. Acquired by Salesforce in 2019.	Established an office in 2015 in Vancouver. One of the founders is from Vancouver and an SFU grad.
Microsemi	
Headquartered in California.	Acquired PMC-Sierra in 2015–16.
Delta Electronics	
Founded in 1971 in Hoofddorp, the Netherlands. A global leader in switching power solutions for electronic software and acoustics. In 2018, revenue of $7.9 billion.	In 2016, acquired Delta Controls, founded by Brian Goodchild and Raymond Rae in 1971 (see Appendix.1), a global leader in building automation systems.
Flir Systems	
Founded in 1978 in Winslow Oregon. In 2018, revenue was US $1.8 billion; in 2018, had 2,800 employees. Creates sensor systems (thermal imaging cameras and components).	In 2016, acquired Point Grey Research (Richmond) for $253 million (see Appendix 1) to develop advanced visible images and solutions (digital cameras) for multiple purposes. Employed 300 globally with global sales.
Maxar Technologies	
An IT company founded in 1969 in Westminster, Colorado. In 2018, $2.1 billion in sales and 5,900 employees.	Acquired MacDonald Dettwiler and Associates in 2016 for $6.4 billion. Acquired by Northern Private Capital of Toronto in 2019 for CDN $1 billion (see Case Study 4.4, Appendix 1).
Mastercard	
Founded in the early 1960s in Purchase, New York. A public company with sales in 2017 of about US $12.5 billion and 13,400 employees. Provides financial services.	In 2017, acquired NuData Security to focus on biometrics and behavioural analytics. Had eighty employees plus thirty employees in another downtown office leased in 2018.

MNC	Entry timing and mode
Aptean	
Created in 2012 in Atlanta by consolidation of CDC Software (which had acquired Vancouver's Pivotal in 2004) and Consona Corporation.	In 2017, acquired FDM Software in North Vancouver, founded in 1990 as a software company for records management. About $5 million in sales and forty employees. In 2018, Aptean was acquired by ESW Capital.
Vivo Capital and ZQ Capital–led Consortium	
Along with others, based in Hong Kong and China. Both are investment companies, with Vivo (formed in 1999) focused on health care and ZQ (founded in 2016) focused on MNCs interested in China.	In 2017, acquired Angiotech (Vancouver), a leading medical device manufacturer (see Appendix 1). Surgical Capital (Angiotech's US subsidiary) sold in 2021 for $800 million. Current operations in Vancouver unclear but likely small.
Motorola Solutions	
Based in Chicago and created in 2009 as a restructuring spinoff from Motorola. In 2018, US $7.3 billion in sales and 17,000 employees. Provides advanced video surveillance technologies for police and others.	In 2018, acquired Avigilon (Richmond) for $1.2 billion (see Appendix 1). Revenue of $354 million in 2016 with 1,200 employees in Richmond and Vancouver and Plano, Texas. In 2020, Plano's manufacturing relocated to Richardson, Texas.
Enterprise Software Capital	
Based in Austin, Texas, and founded in 1988. A private company that specializes in acquiring business software firms. In 2018, acquired Aptean (Atlanta) and Pivotal's former operations. Controls seventy-five companies located in forty-five countries.	In 2018, acquired ResponseTek (Vancouver), founded in 1999. With seventy employees in offices on four continents, ResponseTek developed patented software in customer experience management.
Enersys	
Founded in 1999 in Reading, Pennsylvania. In 2018, sales of $2.6 billion and 9,000 employees.	In 2018, acquired Alpha Technologies of Burnaby for $750 million. In 2018 Alpha had 500 local employees (1,300 in total) and revenues of CDN $591 million.

▶

◄

MNC	*Entry timing and mode*
A global leader in AC and DC power for industry, manufactures and distributes reserve power and batteries, battery accessories, et cetera.	In 2004, worked with Ballard Power Systems to supply broadband uninterruptible power to the Canadian cable TV market.
Fujitsu	
Based in Tokyo and founded in 1935 (second oldest IT company after IBM). A public company with sales in 2018 of ¥4.098 billion or US $36.8 billion and 140,365 employees globally.	In 2019, chose Vancouver for its global R&D centre in AI and quantum computing and to be close to its investment in IQBit.
Tile	
Founded in 2012 in San Mateo, California. Reached US $100 million in revenue in 2016 with an estimated 125 employees. Creates key finder devices that use Bluetooth.	Established a new office in Vancouver in 2019, the first outside San Mateo, to add to engineering software capability. Also in partnership with Herschel Supply Company, which supplies wallets for Tile devices.
Grammerly	
Founded in 2009, originating in the Ukraine, headquartered in San Francisco, with offices in Kiev and New York. An estimated 240 employees in 2018. Creates digital writing tools using AI.	In 2019, established a small Vancouver office employing about ten in 2020. Vancouver was chosen to access talent and collaborates closely with other offices.
Asana	
Founded in San Francisco in 2008. By 2019, had 900 employees and US $142.2 million in revenue. Provides work management tools.	In 2019, established a Vancouver Development Centre. Started with about ten employees, including three transferred from the San Francisco head office. The local office serves local markets and has development responsibility for Asana's product line.
Streak	
Based in San Francisco and founded by Canadians in 2011. A software company with a management platform for Gmail. Has a special relationship with Google.	In 2019, established a Vancouver office with three engineers, and hiring ten more. Plans to be closely coordinated with the parent company with its own projects.

MNC	Entry timing and mode
Zenefits	
Founded in San Francisco in 2013 by Parker Conrad. Develops management software for human resources. Revenue in 2016 of US $43.5 million. About 500 employees in 2020.	Established a small office in Vancouver in 2019.
Apple	
Based in Cupertino, California, and founded in 1976. A public company with sales in 2018 of $265.6 billion and 132,000 employees.	Issued an announcement in 2019 to complete a new twenty-four-storey office on Georgia Street across from the Vancouver Public Library, opened in 2022. Apple planned to use 60,000 square feet of the 370,000 square feet of total floor area; Amazon's new offices are across the street.
Lindsay Goldberg	
A private investment firm in Boston founded in 2001. Funds family-based businesses.	In 2019, acquired Creation Technologies and its nine manufacturing locations, two design centres, and a prototyping centre with 3,000 employees in Canada, the United States, Mexico, and China (see Appendix 1). Remains operating as Creation Technologies.
Rivian Automotive	
Founded in 2009 in California. A public company that manufactures electric vehicles. Revenue in 2021 of US $55 million and 11,500 employees.	In 2022, established an office in Vancouver employing about 150 software and marketing people.
Latecoere	
Based in Toulouse, France; founded in 1917 as an aircraft manufacturer. In 2021, employed 4,764 with sales of around $500 million.	In 2021, acquired Avcorp (Delta) for $41 million (see Appendix 1). Likely to continue to serve the North American market.
Diligent Company	
Founded in New York in 1994. In 2020, employed 1,805 and had revenue of $45 million. Provides software for corporate governance, risk, and compliance.	In 2021, acquired Galvanize (originally ACL Services) for $1 billion. Galvanize provides related services.

▶

◄

MNC	*Entry timing and mode*
PSG (Providence Strategic Growth) Equity	
Founded in 2014 in Boston.	In 2021, acquired Traction Guest, spun off
An equity firm that acquired Traction through its affiliate Shield Company.	(incubated) from Traction on Demand as an independent company in 2015 (see Appendix 1).
Semtech	
A public company in California founded in 1960.	In 2023, acquired Sierra Wireless for $1.2 billion (see Appendix 1).
Revenue in 2022 of US $741 million and 1,439 employees.	A complementary acquisition in serving the internet of things.
Supplies analog and mixed-signal semi-conductors and advanced algorithms.	

Notes: Foreign-owned high-tech companies continue to invest in Metro Vancouver, including Rivian in 2020. This appendix likely does not fully document FDI in Metro Vancouver high tech.

Notes

Introduction: Metro Vancouver's Post-Industrial Transformation toward an Innovation Economy

1 D. Breznitz, *Innovation in Real Places: Strategies for Prosperity in an Unforgiving World* (New York: Oxford University Press, 2021), 3.

2 OECD, *Innovation in Firms: A Microeconomic Perspective* (Paris: OECD, 2009), https://doi.org/10.1787/9789264056213-en.

3 C. Freeman and C. Perez, "Structural Crises of Adjustment, Business Cycles and Investment Behaviour," in *Technical Change and Economic Theory*, ed. G. Dosi, C. Freeman, R. Nelson, R. Silverberg, and L. Soete (London: Pinter, 1988), 36–66.

4 Bob MacDonald and Vern Dettwiler were the two professors at UBC who founded MDA. MacDonald, born in British Columbia, was appointed to UBC's electrical engineering department in 1965, leaving in 1973 to focus on leading MDA. Dettwiler, who had immigrated from Switzerland in 1947, also taught at UBC (electrical engineering and computing science), where he was recruited by MacDonald to co-found MDA.

5 BC Stats has been documenting high tech in the province since the mid-1990s. The accounting firms KPMG and PricewaterhouseCoopers are also important sources of information on high tech.

6 See T. Barnes and N.M. Coe, "Vancouver as Media Cluster: The Cases of Video Games and Film/TV," in *Media Clusters across the Globe: Developing, Expanding, and Reinvigorating Content Capabilities*, ed. C. Karlsson and R.G. Picard (Cheltenham, UK: Edward Elgar, 2011), 251–77; N.M. Coe, "The View from Out West: Embeddedness, Inter-Personal Relations and the Development of an Indigenous Film Industry in Vancouver," *Geoforum* 31 (2000): 391–407; C.H. Langford, J.R. Wood, and A. Jacobson, *The Evolution and Structure of the Vancouver Wireless*

Cluster: Growth and Loss of Core Firms, https://www/researchgate.net/publication/ 265533886, 2005; K. Rees, "Collaboration, Innovation and Regional Networks: Evidence from the Medical Biotechnology of Greater Vancouver," in *Proximity, Distance and Diversity: Issues on Economic Interaction and Local Development,* ed. A. Lagendijk and P. Oinas (London: Ashgate, 2005), 191–215; and K. Rees, "Inter-regional Collaboration and Innovation in Vancouver's Emerging High-Tech Cluster," *Tidjschrift voor Economische en Social Geografie* 96 (2005): 298–312.

7 Breznitz, *Innovation in Real Places.*

8 The classic reference to creative destruction is J. Schumpeter, *Capitalism, Socialism and Democracy* (New York: Harper, 1943). For pioneering (economics) literature that elaborates the Schumpeterian approach to economic development, see G. Dosi et al., eds., *Technical Change and Economic Theory* (London: Pinter, 1988); C. Freeman, "Continental, National and Sub-National Innovation Systems – Complementarity and Economic Growth," in *Systems of Innovation: Essays in Evolutionary Economics,* ed. C. Freeman (Cheltenham, UK: Edward Elgar, 2008), 106–41; C. Freeman and F. Louçã, *As Time Goes By: From the Industrial Revolution to the Information Revolution* (Oxford: Oxford University Press, 2001); and R.R. Nelson, ed., *National Innovation Systems: A Comparative Analysis* (Oxford: Oxford University Press, 1993).

9 D.R. Audretsch, *Innovation and Industry Evolution* (Cambridge, MA: MIT Press, 1995); D.R. Audretsch, M. Keilbach, and E.E. Lehmann, *Entrepreneurship and Economic Growth* (Oxford: Oxford University Press, 2006); D.R. Audretsch and M.P. Feldman, "Knowledge Spillovers and the Geography of Innovation," in *Handbook of Urban and Regional Economics,* vol. 4, *Cities and Geography,* ed. J.V. Henderson and J.-F. Thisse (Amsterdam: Elsevier, 2004), 2713–39.

10 B. Asheim and M.S. Gertler, "The Geography of Innovation: Regional Innovation Systems," in *The Oxford Handbook of Innovation,* ed. J. Fagerberg, D. Mowery, and R. Nelson (Oxford: Oxford University Press, 2005), 291–317; P. Oinas and E.J. Malecki, "The Evolution of Technologies in Time and Space: From National and Regional to Spatial Innovation Systems," *International Regional Science Review* 25 (2002): 102–31.

11 Richard Florida's creative class thesis and Allen Scott's cognitive-cultural theory of contemporary capitalist development are especially well known in this regard. See R. Florida, *The Rise of the Creative Class* (New York: Basic Books, 2002); and A.J. Scott, *A World in Emergence – Cities and Regions in the 21st Century* (Cheltenham, UK: Edward Elgar, 2012).

12 R. Martin, P. Sunley, and P. Tyler, "Local Growth Evolution: Recession, Resilience and Recovery," *Cambridge Journal of Regions, Economy and Society* 8 (2015): 141–48; R. Boschma and R. Martin, eds., *The Handbook of Evolutionary Economic Geography* (Cheltenham, UK: Edward Elgar, 2010). The adaptive city theme is referenced in P. Sunley, R. Martin, and P. Tyler, "Cities in Transition: Problems, Processes and Policies," *Cambridge Journal of Regions, Economy and Society* 10 (2017): 383–90.

13 For a review of the literature on regional competitiveness organized around the low- and high-road distinction, see E.J. Malecki, "Economic Competitiveness and Regional Development Dynamics," in *Handbook of Regions and Competitiveness,* ed.

R. Huggins and P. Thompson (Cheltenham, UK: Edward Elgar, 2017), 136–52. As Malecki notes, high-road approaches are associated with terms such as "knowledge economies," "innovative milieus," "regional systems of innovation," "learning regions," "entrepreneurial ecosystems," and "associational economies."

14 As a low-road approach, Malecki, "Economic Competitiveness," 138–39, Table 6.1, emphasizes the low-wage branch plant option. Place selling is noted as part of such approaches and typically is associated with low-taxation regimes. In the case of Metro Vancouver, place selling in recent decades generally has involved boosterish attitudes and an openness to property investment whatever its source or motive, including sweetheart deals to foreign developers.

15 A.F. Cullen, *Commission of Inquiry into Money Laundering in British Columbia* (Victoria: Province of British Columbia, 2022). As this "Cullen Report" records, concern about money laundering was evident by 2008–09 with little effective government response. If hard to quantify, estimates of money laundering in British Columbia between 2015 and 2019 are between $1 billion and $5 billion per year.

16 M.P. Feldman, "The Character of Innovative Places: Entrepreneurial Strategy, Economic Development, and Prosperity," *Small Business Economics* 43 (2014): 9.

17 On the idea of local models, see T.J. Barnes, "Homo Economicus, Physical Metaphors and Universal Models in Economic Geography," *Canadian Geographer* 31 (1987): 299–308; and T.J. Barnes and R. Hayter, "No 'Greek-Letter Writing': Local Models of Resource Economies," *Growth and Change* 36 (2005): 453–70.

18 A. Rodríguez-Pose and J. Griffiths, "Developing Intermediate Cities," *Regional Science Policy and Practice* 13 (2021): 441–56; M. Fritsch and M. Wyrwich, "Is Innovation (Increasingly) Concentrated in Large Cities? An International Comparison," *Research Policy* 50 (2021): 4–32.

19 The main communities of Metro Vancouver are Vancouver itself, the adjacent "inner suburbs" of North and West Vancouver, Burnaby, and Richmond, and the "outer suburbs" of New Westminster, Surrey, Maple Ridge, Coquitlam, Port Coquitlam, Port Moody, and Delta. These and other smaller communities have a shared history, and their functional integration extends eastward to include Abbotsford and northward to include Squamish. Initially called the Greater Vancouver Regional District (GVRD) in 1967, the area was relabelled Metro Vancouver in 2017. Administratively, Vancouver and surrounding communities have been formally recognized as a metropolitan area since 1967, formally named Metro Vancouver in 2017.

20 D. Ley, "Liberal Ideology and the Post-Industrial City," *Annals of the Association of American Geographers* 83 (1980): 238–58. Vancouver's postindustrialism was anticipated in W.G. Hardwick, *Vancouver* (Don Mills, ON: Collier-Macmillan Canada, 1974). Both studies drew from D. Bell, *The Coming of Post-Industrial Society: A Venture in Social Forecasting* (New York: Heinemann, 1974). In Bell's view, postindustrialism and the overall rise of services are particularly spearheaded by knowledge-intensive activities (then forecast mainly by growing jobs in R&D, education, and health care, with the internet economy, and related initiatives, only in early stages of development).

21 G. Wynn, "The Rise of Vancouver," in *Vancouver and Its Region,* ed. G. Wynn and T. Oke (Vancouver: UBC Press, 1992), 69–148; P.D. McGovern, "Industrial Development in the Vancouver Area," *Economic Geography* 37 (1961): 189–206; W.

Hardwick, *Geography of the Forest Industry in British Columbia,* Occasional Papers in Geography No. 5 (Vancouver: Canadian Association of Geographers, British Columbia Division, 1963).

22 K. Edenhoffer and R. Hayter, "Restructuring on a Vertiginous Plateau: The Evolutionary Trajectories of British Columbia's Forest Industries 1980–2010," *Geoforum* 44 (2013): 139–51.

23 G.P.F. Steed, "Intrametropolitan Manufacturing: Spatial Distribution and Location Dynamics in Greater Vancouver," *Canadian Geographer* 17 (1973): 235–58.

24 Sawmills were big structures occupying large river-front lots, major traffic generators, and readily observable, not least by the smoke columns that they generated.

25 R.C. Allen and G. Rosenbluth, eds., *Restraining the Economy* (Vancouver: New Star Books, 1986), documents the social protests and implications of the recession in the 1980s for Metro Vancouver.

26 MB's head office was sold in 1983 but remained a widely used name until 2021, when it was renamed for the architect who had designed it.

27 Suggestions for services to be classified as the tertiary, quaternary, and quinquenary sectors, partly based on the nature and extent of knowledge inputs, have been made. However, these distinctions are rarely cited now, and the service and tertiary labels are often used as synonyms.

28 In the 1950s and 1960s, the urban planning literature, including in Vancouver, often distinguished between basic and nonbasic activities, respectively serving export and local markets. It was typically assumed in making growth predictions that the latter depended on the former. Other autonomous (nonexport) sources of growth are now recognized.

29 K. Peacock, "A Brief Primer on BC's Export Base," Business Council of British Columbia May 12, 2022, https://bcbc.com/insights-and-opinions/a-brief-primer-on-b-c-s-export-base. See also J. Finlayson and K. Peacock, "Opinion: Export of Services Plays a Strong Growing Role in B.C. Economy," *Business in Vancouver,* June 15, 2020, https://bcbc.com/insights-and-opinions/opinion-export-of-services-plays-a-strong-and-growing-role-in-b-c-economy.

30 For example, forest revenues provided $1.85 billion to the BC government in 2021–22, mainly because of a spike in the price of lumber, although they are expected to decline substantially in the coming years. Gas revenues indicate a similar story. See C. Smith, "The B.C. Economy and the Broadway Plan: An Explainer," *Georgia Straight,* May 9, 2022.

31 See J. Munro and W. Gill, "The Alaska Cruise Industry," in *Cruise Ship Tourism,* ed. R.K. Dowling (CAB eBooks, 2006), 135–60; and A.M. Gill and P.W. Williams, "Rethinking Resort Growth: Understanding Evolving Governance Strategies in Whistler, British Columbia," *Journal of Sustainable Tourism* 19 (2011): 629–48. By 2017, the City of Vancouver estimated that tourism provided about 70,000 full-time jobs and about $4.8 billion to the metropolitan area's GDP. In addition to its own multiple attractions and amenities as a tourist destination, since 1986 Vancouver "anchored" the development of the coastal cruise ship industry and became an important global link with the Whistler resort. From the first cruise ship in 1986 to 2019, Vancouver welcomed 298 cruise ships that injected an estimated $864 million into the local economy.

32 This deal has been regarded as transformational by its replacement around False Creek of former industrial uses with attractive housing and related commercial and leisure uses centred on the Granville Island Market and for its stimulus to further Asian investment. See K. Olds, *Globalization and Urban Change: Capital, Culture and Pacific Rim Mega-Projects* (Oxford: Oxford University Press, 2001); and J. Proctor, "Deal of the Century: Expo 86 Land Purchase Changed Vancouver," *CBC News*, May 4, 2016, https://www.cbc.ca/news/canada/british-columbia/expo-86 -china-business-vancouver-1.3560255.

33 D. Ley, "Global China and the Making of Vancouver's Residential Property Market," *International Journal of Housing Policy* 1 (2017): 17–34; D. Ley, "A Regional Growth Ecology, a Great Wall of Capital and a Metropolitan Housing Market," *Urban Studies* 58 (2021): 297–315; C. Cheung, "Inside the 'Growth Machine' that Made Vancouver-World Class Unaffordable," *TheTyee.ca*, February 13, 2020, https://thetyee.ca/ Analysis/2020/02/13/Gov-Real-Estate-Vancouver-Housing-Unaffordable/.

34 In this context, decoupling refers to big increases in the ratio between average annual incomes and average house prices in Vancouver from 1:3 in the early 1970s to about 1:15 or more in recent years. According to J. Gordon, foreign investment is a key factor decoupling income from house prices and creating tax avoidance. See J. Gordon, "Solving Puzzles in the Canadian Housing Market: Foreign Ownership and Decoupling in Toronto and Vancouver," *Housing Studies*, 2020, https://doi.org/ 10.1080/02673037.2020.1842340. Also D. Todd, "Hidden Foreign Ownership Helps Explain Metro Vancouver's 'Decoupling' of House Prices, Incomes," *Vancouver Sun*, December 4, 2020, https://vancouversun.com/opinion/columnists/douglas-todd -hidden-foreign-ownership-helps-explain-metro-vancouvers-decoupling-of -house-prices-incomes; and T. Davidoff, P.B. Akaabre, and C. Jones, "Policy Forum: The Prevalence of Low Income Tax Payments among Owners of Expensive Homes in Vancouver and Toronto," *Canadian Tax Journal* 70 (2022): 843–59.

35 Ley, "A Regional Growth Ecology."

36 J. Young, "Vancouver Became a Byword for Money Laundering, Fuelled by Chinese Cash. Can It Flip the Script?," *South China Morning Post*, December 21, 2021, https:// www.scmp.com/news/china/diplomacy/article/3160485/vancouver-became -byword-money-laundering-fuelled-chinese-cash; Cullen, *Commission.*

37 The minister of finance in the provincial government observed that by 2017 residential real estate constituted about 15–17 percent of market activity in Metro Vancouver. H. Woodin, "B.C. Budget 2017: Government Plans for a Lower Housing Market," *Business in Vancouver*, February 21, 2017, https://www.biv.com/news/real-estate/ bc-budget-2017-government-plans-slower-housing-mar-8248845. Especially after 2019, housing revenues (drawn from property transfer taxes and from 2016 foreign house buyers' taxes) helped BC governments to balance their budgets, amounting to $2.1 billion in the 2017–18 fiscal year (just over 4 percent of overall revenue). R. Shaw, "Housing Revenues Help Balance B.C. Budget Again, but Downtown Looms," *Vancouver Sun*, August 28, 2018, https://vancouversun.com/news/local-news/b-c -maintained-budget-surplus-for-2017-18-despite-increased-spending.

38 D. Todd, "How Global Liveability Rankings Cursed Vancouver," *Vancouver Sun*, March 2, 2023, https://vancouversun.com/opinion/columnists/douglas-todd-how -global-livability-rankings-cursed-vancouver.

39 Lenkurt Electronics, originating in California in the 1940s, established a substantial manufacturing operation in Burnaby by the 1950s. Lenkurt eventually closed, some of its assets becoming part of Telus (formerly BC Tel), the telecommunications giant now headquartered in Burnaby that has its (entrepreneurial) roots in the first decades of the twentieth century (see Case Study 4.2).

40 The first reports seem to be BC Stats, *The British Columbia High Technology Sector 1988–1995* (Victoria: Government of British Columbia, 1996); J. Lawrance and S. Miller, *Defining the High Technology/Knowledge Sector in British Columbia* (Victoria: BC Stats, 1995); and J. Lawrance and S. Miller, *The British Columbia High Technology Sector, 1988–1994* (Victoria: BC Stats, 1996). These reports use an input-output table to identify industry-based groupings of high tech.

41 For recent, ongoing sources of comprehensive data on BC high tech, see the notes to Tables 1.3, 1.4, and I.5.

42 BC Stats, *The British Columbia High Technology Sector 1988–1995*.

43 KPMG, *The British Columbia Technology Report Card: Tackling the Scale Up Challenge* (Vancouver: KPMG, 2020). The data on overall R&D expenditures are provided on pages 36–39 and include trends from 2007 to 2017. In 2019, Telus is recorded as spending $307 million on R&D, probably mainly but not solely in British Columbia, and as the second largest (ranked twenty-sixth in Canada) Sierra Wireless spent $122 million. The three life sciences companies noted are Arbutus Biopharma ($75 million), Zymeworks ($73 million), and Aurinia Pharmaceuticals ($54 million).

44 BC Stats, *The British Columbia High Technology Sector 1988–1995*.

45 PricewaterhouseCoopers (PwC), *British Columbia TechMap 1997, 2003*, and *2013*; the main author is Michael Calyniuk, with each edition of the maps based on an increasing size of the survey, the last edition being based on over 4,000 respondents. The data presented seem to be for the year preceding publication. PwC kindly provided Hayter with these maps for classroom and educational purposes. Note: only aggregated data derived from these maps is provided here.

46 In PwC's 2013 map (2012 data), the twelve high-tech categories are software; digital media; mobile and web; advanced manufacturing and semiconductors; cloud integration; energy technology, electronics, and peripherals; clean technology; telecommunications; service and analytics; and life sciences. KPMG, *The British Columbia Technology Report Card*, cites five categories of high-tech activity, namely information and communication technology; interactive and digital media; IT/engineering services; clean technology; and life sciences. Both sets of categories are discussed in Chapter 4.

47 P. Wei, "Silicon Valley 150 Rankings of the Top 150 Public Tech Companies in the Bay Area," *Mercury News*, May 1, 2017, https://www.mercurynews.com/2017/05/01/sv150-top-10-the-best-and-worst-performances/.

48 KPMG, *The British Columbia Technology Report Card*.

49 On the decline of the wireless industry, see Langford, Wood, and Jacobson, *The Evolution and Structure of the Vancouver Wireless Cluster*, and Chapter 4. Although data are not available, new small firms typically have high death rates, but hitherto in Metro Vancouver high-tech birth rates have been higher than death rates.

50 KPMG, *The British Columbia Technology Report Card*, documents per capita R&D spending compared with other jurisdictions, along with information on patents (and

wage levels), both of which are lower than national or (appropriate) international averages. Relatively low levels of per capita spending by Canadian business have been a well-documented characteristic for decades and apply to high tech as well as more mature segments of the economy.

51 BC Stats, *Profile of the British Columbia High Technology Sector* (Victoria: BC Stats, 2013).

52 As part of its resource inheritance, Vancouver arguably has the world's largest cluster of sophisticated mining engineering and exploration and related service activities, around 2000 comprising about 700 mostly small companies that serve global markets.

53 R. Hayter and A. Clapp, "Towards a Collaborative (Public-Private) Partnership Approach to Research and Development in Canada's Forest Sector: An Innovation Systems Perspective," *Forest Policy and Economics* 113 (2020), https://doi.org/10.1016/j.forpol.2020.102119.

54 C.S. Binkley, "Creating a Knowledge-Based Forest Sector," *Forestry Chronicle* 69 (1993): 294–99.

55 J. Sutherland, "Everything Cool Comes from Vancouver," *Globe and Mail,* November 24, 2016, https://www.theglobeandmail.com/report-on-business/rob-magazine/sorry-toronto-everything-cool-comes-from-vancouver/article32955661/.

56 Lululemon fits into a segment of large firms much bigger than SMEs and global in scope but not as big or diversified as the biggest MNCs. See Chapter 6.

57 With reference to broader literatures on postindustrial cities, see Florida, *The Rise of the Creative Class;* and Scott, *A World in Emergence.*

58 For a discussion of "deindustrialization" as the term was developed in the late 1970s and 1980s, see R. Hayter, *The Dynamics of Industrial Location* (Chichester, UK: Wiley, 1997), 401–23 (available on the author's website, hayter@geog.sfu.ca).

59 One important trend associated with globalization has been the shift of secondary manufacturing activities toward poorer countries, especially in Asia.

60 See Schumpeter, *Capitalism, Socialism and Democracy;* Freeman and Louçã, *As Time Goes By;* and Dosi et al., *Technical Change and Economic Theory.*

61 For discussion of Fordist transformation toward ICT or post-Fordism in a Metro Vancouver and BC context, see T. Barnes, D.W. Edgington, K.G. Denike, and T.G. McGee, "Vancouver, the Province and the Pacific Rim," in *Vancouver and Its Region,* ed. G. Wynn and T. Oke (Vancouver: UBC Press, 1992), 171–99; and R. Hayter and T. Barnes, "Labour Market Segmentation, Flexibility and Recession: A British Columbian Case Study," *Environment and Planning C* 10 (1992): 333–53.

62 For recent reviews within the scholarly literature emphasizing the importance of innovation-based growth for local development, see R. Huggins and P. Thompson, "Introducing Regional Competitiveness and Development: Contemporary Theories and Perspectives," in *Handbook of Regions and Competitiveness,* ed. R. Huggins and P. Thompson (Cheltenham, UK: Edward Elgar, 2017), 1–31; and Malecki, "Economic Competitiveness."

63 A. Saxanian, "The Genesis of Silicon Valley," *Built Environment* 9 (1981): 7–17; A. Saxanian, *Regional Advantage: Culture and Competition in Silicon Valley and Route 128* (Cambridge, MA: Harvard University Press, 1994); J.S. Engel, "Global Clusters of Innovation: Lessons from Silicon Valley," *California Management Review* 57

(2015): 36–66; J.S. Engel and I. del-Palacio, "Global Clusters of Innovation: The Case of Israel and Silicon Valley," *California Management Review* 53 (2011): 27–49.

64 B. Asheim, H. Lawton Smith, and C. Oughton, "Regional Innovation Systems: Theory, Empirics and Policy," *Regional Studies* 45 (2011): 875–91; P. Cooke, "Regional Innovation Systems, Clusters, and the Knowledge Economy," *Industrial and Corporate Change* 10 (2001): 945–74. This focus evolved from studies of national innovation systems. See Freeman, "Continental, National and Sub-National Innovation Systems"; B.-Å. Lundvall, ed., *National Systems of Innovation: Towards a Theory of Innovation and Interactive Learning* (London: Pinter, 1992); and Nelson, *National Innovation Systems*.

65 H. Etzkowitz, *The Triple Helix: University-Industry-Government Innovation in Action* (London: Routledge, 2008); Freeman, "Continental, National and Sub-National Innovation Systems"; P. Benneth, L. Coenen, J. Moodyson, and B. Asheim, "Exploring the Multiple Roles of Lund University in Strengthening the Scania Regional Innovation System: Towards Institutional Learning?," *European Planning Studies* 17 (2009): 1645–64.

66 R. Brown, "Mission Impossible? Entrepreneurial Universities and Peripheral Regional Innovation Systems," *Industry and Innovation* 23 (2016): 189–205; also see A. Bonaccorsi, "Addressing the Disenchantment: Universities and Regional Development in Peripheral Regions," *Journal of Economic Policy* 20 (2017): 293–320.

67 See A. Malmberg and A. Maskell, "The Elusive Concept of Localization Economies: Towards a Knowledge-Based Theory of Spatial Clustering," *Environment and Planning A* 34 (2006): 429–49; and A. Potter and H.D. Watts, "Evolutionary Agglomeration Theory: Increasing Returns, Diminishing Returns, and the Industry Life Cycle," *Journal of Economic Geography* 11 (2010): 417–55.

68 For example, the Economist Intelligence Unit in its Global Liveability Index ranked Vancouver first for many years, the third "most livable" city in 2016 in the world, and the fifth best in 2022. Note that livability or urban quality of life is informed by subjective assessments of stability, health care, culture, environment, education, and infrastructure. In Metro Vancouver, critics have argued that its livability is threatened by high housing prices, traffic and other use congestion, and increased residential densities. See Todd, "How Global Liveability Rankings Cursed Vancouver"; and S. Fralic, "Vancouver, Once Heaven, Now Merely a Mess Choking Itself to Death," *Vancouver Sun*, May 16, 2021, https://vancouversun.com/opinion/columnists/shelley-fralic-vancouver-once-heaven-now-merely-a-mess-choking-itself-to-death.

69 For reference to mobile/immobile external economies, see R. Hayter and D.W. Edgington, "'Getting Tough' and 'Getting Smart': Politics of the North American–Japan Wood Products Trade," *Environment and Planning C: Government and Policy* 17 (1999): 319–44.

70 A. Saxanian, *The New Argonauts: Regional Advantage in a Global Economy* (Cambridge, MA: Harvard University Press, 2007); Engel, "Global Clusters of Innovation"; Oinas and Malecki, "The Evolution of Technologies in Time and Space."

71 G. Bridge, S. Bouzarovski, M. Bradshaw, and N. Eyre, "Geographies of Energy Transition: Space, Place and the Low-Carbon Economy," *Energy Policy* 53 (2013): 331–40.

72 Within Metro Vancouver, Ballard Power Systems and Westport Fuels have been long-time leaders seeking replacements for fossil fuel production (see Chapter 2). In recent years, increasing references to a "clean tech" sector involve several companies engaged in carbon capture and its use. For a general reference to economy and environment as an innovation-driven positive sum game, see R. Hayter, "Environmental Economic Geography in Institutional Perspective," *Geography Compass* 3 (2008): 831–50, compass.com/subject/geography/article.

73 Feldman, "The Character of Innovative Places."

74 C. Beaudry and A. Schiffauerova, "Who's Right, Marshall or Jacobs? The Localization versus Urbanization Debate," *Research Policy* 38 (2009): 318–37.

75 D. Rigby, "The Geography of Knowledge Relatedness and Technological Diversification in US Cities," *Papers in Evolutionary Economic Geography* 12.18 (Utrecht University, Department of Human Geography and Spatial Planning, 2012); R. Boschma, "Designing Smart Specialization Policy: Relatedness, Unrelatedness or What?," *Papers in Evolutionary Economic Geography* 21.28 (Utrecht University, Department of Human Geography and Spatial Planning, 2021).

76 On the edge metaphor for Vancouver's earthquake hazard frames, see J. Clague and B. Turner, *Vancouver: City on the Edge* (Vancouver: Tricouni Press, 2003). More recently, the edge metaphor has been used to understand the region's planning processes; see P. Gurstein and T. Hutton, *Planning on the Edge: Vancouver and the Challenges of Reconciliation, Social Justice, and Sustainable Development* (Vancouver: UBC Press, 2019).

77 L. Evenden, ed., *Vancouver: Western Metropolis*, Western Geographical Series, vol. 16 (Victoria: University of Victoria, 1974). See also Wynn, "The Rise of Vancouver."

78 T. Hutton and T. Barnes, "Vancouver and the Economy of Culture and Innovation," in *Growing Urban Economies: Innovation, Creativity and Governance in Canadian City-Regions*, ed. D. Wolfe and M. Gertler (Toronto: University of Toronto Press, 2016), 109–38; T. Hutton, "Post-Industrialism, Post-Modernism and the Reproduction of Vancouver's Central Area: Re-Theorising the 21st Century," *Urban Studies* 41 (2004): 1953–82.

79 Economist Intelligence Unit, "The Global Liveability Index," *Economist,* June 2022, https://www.eiu.com/public/topical_report.aspx?campaignid=liveabilityindex22.

80 For example, see "The Global Power City Index 2022," Institute for Urban Strategies, The Mori Memorial Foundation, 1, https://mori-m-foundation.or.jp/english/ius2/gpci2/index.shtml. In this ranking, which focuses more on economic development performance, Vancouver is ranked thirty-four of forty-eight "influential" cities around the globe, led by giant metropoles such as New York, London, Tokyo, and Paris.

81 L. Beasley, *Vancouverism* (Vancouver: UBC Press, 2019). See also J. Punter, *The Vancouver Achievement: Urban Planning and Design* (Vancouver: UBC Press, 2003).

82 Peripheries refer to various types of regions, rich and poor. The core sense of a periphery, however, is a remote and relatively underpopulated region that specializes in resource exploitation and is dependent on demand from (and control by) core regions. See J. Eder, "Innovation in the Periphery: A Critical Survey and Research Agenda," *International Regional Science Review* 42 (2019): 119–46.

83 A. Rodríguez-Pose and R.D. Fitjar, "Buzz, Archipelago Economies and the Future of Intermediate and Peripheral Areas in a Spiky World," *European Planning Studies* 21 (2013): 355–72; H. Bathelt, A. Malmberg, and P. Maskell, "Clusters and Knowledge: Local Buzz, Global Pipelines and the Process of Knowledge Creation," *Progress in Human Geography* 28 (2004): 31–56.

Chapter 1: Rethinking Forestry's Roles in Value and Innovation
1 This chapter draws particularly from the so-called Innisian staple thesis of Canadian economic development. See D. Drache, ed., *Staples, Markets and Cultural Change: Selected Essays, Harold A. Innis* (Montreal and Kingston: McGill-Queen's University Press, 1995).
2 R. Schwindt and T. Heaps, *Chopping Up the Money Tree: The Distribution of Wealth from British Columbia's Forests* (Vancouver: David Suzuki Foundation, 1996).
3 E. Grass and R. Hayter, "Employment Change during Recession: The Experience of Forest Product Manufacturing Plants in British Columbia, 1981–1985," *Canadian Geographer* 33 (1989): 240–52.
4 For a discussion of staple diversification via the development of forward, backward, final demand, and fiscal linkages, see M. Watkins, "A Staple Theory of Economic Growth," *Canadian Journal of Economic and Political Science* 29 (1963): 141–48; for BC-based elaborations, see R. Hayter and T. Barnes, "Innis' Staple Theory, Exports and Recession: British Columbia 1981–86," *Economic Geography* 66 (1990): 156–73; and D. Ley and T. Hutton, "Vancouver's Corporate Complex and Producer Services Sector: Linkage and Divergence within a Provincial Staple Economy," *Regional Studies* 21 (1987): 413–24.
5 R. Hayter, "'The War in the Woods': Post-Fordist Restructuring, Globalization and the Contested Remapping of British Columbia's Forest Economy," *Annals of the Association of American Geographers* 93 (2003): 706–29; K. Edenhoffer and R. Hayter, "Restructuring on a Vertiginous Plateau: The Evolutionary Trajectories of British Columbia's Forest Industries 1980–2010," *Geoforum* 44 (2013): 139–51.
6 R.C. Allen and G. Rosenbluth, eds., *Restructuring the Economy: Social Credit Policies for BC* (Vancouver: New Star Books, 1986).
7 C. Binkley, "Creating a Knowledge-Based Forest Sector," *Forest Chronicle* 69 (1993): 294–99.
8 J. McWilliams, *Profile of the B.C. Wood Products Value-Added Sector*, FRDA Report (Vancouver: Forintek Canada, 1991); R. Kozak and T. Mannes, "Towards a Value Focused Forest Sector in British Columbia," *BC Forum on Forest Economics and Policy Issues Brief: IB 05-01*, 2005, http://conservation economics.com/pdf_pubs/issue_brief/IB050_ValueFocusedForestry.pdf. Government publications that offer estimates of the sizes of wood-based, value-added operations include Canadian Forest Service, *Secondary Wood Manufacturing in BC* (Victoria: Ministry of Forests, 2003); and British Columbia Government, *Generating More Value from Our Forests: A Vision and Action Plan for Further Manufacturing* (Victoria: Ministry of Forests, 2009). See also R. Hayter and K. Edenhoffer, "Shakeouts, Shakeins and Industry Population Dynamics: British Columbia's Forest Industries 1980–2008," *Growth and Change* 47 (2016): 497–519.

9 Support for entrepreneurial forestry was boosted by P.H. Pearse, *Timber Rights and Forest Policy in British Columbia: Report of the Royal Commission on Forest Resources* (Victoria: Queen's Printer, 1976). Simply stated, Pearse argued that corporate concentration in BC forestry, especially its underpinning by guaranteed, large-scale timber rights, was too high and that higher prices for wood products, along with higher government revenues, could be realized by more competitive timber markets involving small firms. Subsequently, the role of SMEs in adding value was emphasized in M. M'Gonigle and B. Parfitt, *Forestopia* (Madeira Park, BC: Harbour Publishing, 1994); and O.R. Travers, "Forest Policy: Rhetoric and Reality," in *Touch Wood: BC Forests at the Crossroads*, ed. K. Drushka, B. Nixon, and R. Travers (Madeira Park, BC: Harbour Publishing, 1993), 171–224.

10 R. Hayter and A. Clapp, "Towards a Collaborative (Public-Private) Partnership Approach to Research and Development in Canada's Forest Sector: An Innovation Systems Perspective," *Forest Policy and Economics* 113 (2020): https://doi.org/10.1016/j.forpol.2020.102119.

11 B. Parfitt, "Raw Logs and Lost Jobs: How the BC Government Has Sacrificed Forest Communities," *Tyee*, February 27, 2017, https://thetyee.ca/opinion/2017/02/27/raw-logs-lost-jobs/; B. Parfitt, "BC's Chief Forester Jumps to Multinational Wood Pellet Corporation," *Tyee*, April 7, 2022, https://thetyee.ca/Analysis/2022/04/07/BC-Chief-Forester-Jumps-Multinational-Wood-Pellet-Corporation/; B. Parfitt, "How Monster Mills Ate BC's Timber Jobs," *Tyee*, March 6, 2023, https://thetyee.ca/Analysis/2023/03/06/Monster-Mills-Ate-BC-Timber-Jobs/.

12 Essentially, environmental interests have been driven by conservation and preservation values, Indigenous interests by sovereignty and control values, and the US sawmilling industry by protectionist motives. See Hayter, "'The War in the Woods.'" It is argued that forest policy in British Columbia has shifted from a hierarchical model to a more diffuse stakeholder governance model, with the Great Bear Rainforest Agreement an oft-cited exemplar. M. Howlett, J. Rayner, and C. Tollefson, "From Government to Governance in Forest Planning? Lessons from the Case of the British Columbia Great Bear Rainforest Initiative," *Forest Policy Economics* 11 (2009): 383–91; J. Affolderbach, R. Hayter, and A. Clapp, "Environmental Bargaining and Boundary Organizations: Remapping British Columbia's Great Bear Rainforest," *Annals of the Association of American Geographers* 102 (2012): 1391–1408; A. Clapp, R. Hayter, J. Affolderbach, and L. Guzman Flores, "Institutional Thickening and Innovation: Reflections on the Remapping of the Great Bear Rainforest," *Transactions of the Institute of British Geographers* 41 (2016): 244–57.

13 A. Clapp, "The Resource Cycle in Forestry and Fishing," *Canadian Geographer* 42 (1998): 129–44; Hayter and Edenhoffer, "Shakeouts, Shakeins and Industry Population Dynamics." An extensive literature on long-run industry life cycles, especially in relation to secondary manufacturing, is reviewed, respectively, from business and regional development perspectives by M. Peltoniemi, "Reviewing Industry Life Cycle Theory: Avenues for Further Research," *International Journal of Management Reviews* 13 (2011): 349–75; and A. Pike, A. Rodríguez, and J. Tomaney, *Local and Regional Development* (London: Routledge, 2017), 94–96. See also A. Markusen, *Profit Cycles, Oligopoly and Regional Development* (Cambridge, MA: MIT Press, 1985).

14 W.G. Hardwick, *Geography of the Forest Industry in British Columbia,* Occasional Papers in Geography No. 5 (Vancouver: Canadian Association of Geographers, British Columbia Division, 1963). This study identifies an initial "pioneering period" (1860–84) followed by a period of "Development and Speculation 1885–1908." G. Wynn, "The Rise of Vancouver," in *Vancouver and Its Region,* ed. G. Wynn and T. Oke (Vancouver: UBC Press, 1992), 69–148.

15 P. Marchak, *Green Gold: The Forest Industry in British Columbia* (Vancouver: UBC Press, 1983); J. Wilson, *Talk and Log: Wilderness Politics in British Columbia 1965–96* (Vancouver: UBC Press, 1998); R. Hayter, *Flexible Crossroads: The Restructuring of British Columbia's Forest Economy* (Vancouver: UBC Press, 2000).

16 M. Clark-Jones, *A Staple State: Canadian Industrial Resources in Cold War* (Toronto: University of Toronto Press, 1987); R. Hayter, "International Trade Relations and Regional Industrial Adjustment: Implications of the 1980s' North American Softwood Lumber Dispute for British Columbia," *Environment and Planning A* 24 (1992): 153–70.

17 R. Hayter, "Corporate Strategies and Industrial Change in the Canadian Forest Product Industries," *Geographical Review* 66 (1976): 209–28; Edenhoffer and Hayter, "Restructuring on a Vertiginous Plateau."

18 Sawmilling was Metro Vancouver's dominant, most export-oriented forest commodity, with softwood plywood and veneer, particleboard, and shingle and shake mills also important wood-processing activities. For production profiles of other forest commodities from 1946 to 2010 in British Columbia, see Edenhoffer and Hayter, "Restructuring on a Vertiginous Plateau."

19 On British Columbia's failure to pursue sustainable forestry, and possible solutions, see C.S. Binkley, "A Crossroad in the Forest: The Path to a Sustainable Forest Sector in BC," *BC Studies* 113 (1997): 39–61; and Clapp, "The Resource Cycle in Forestry and Fishing."

20 F.L.C. Reed and Associates, *Canada's Reserve Timber Supply,* 1974, report prepared for the Department of Industry, Trade and Commerce, Ottawa. On declining forestry harvests in British Columbia after 1980, see P. Marchak, S. Aycock, and D. Herbert, *Falldown: Forest Policy in British Columbia* (Vancouver: Ecotrust Canada, 1999). From 1980, forest harvest levels in British Columbia have fluctuated greatly, not least because of a pine beetle epidemic that encouraged the government to increase harvest rates before the loss of timber values. However, timber harvests have declined relentlessly, from about 65–70 million cubic metres in 1980 to 45 million cubic metres in 2020 (with less than 40 million cubic metres expected in 2022).

21 After early exploitation (and urbanization) reduced local supplies, the log supply to Metro Vancouver wood-processing mills dispersed throughout coastal and interior British Columbia, much of it via water-based transportation. The area's wood-processing mills in turn shipped their waste products and chips as energy and fibre inputs to coastal pulp and paper mills. Particleboard operations in Metro Vancouver also relied on "waste" supplies from local sawmills.

22 Parfitt, "How Monster Mills Ate BC's Timber Jobs."

23 Kruger Products' New Westminster Paper Company is the largest old forestry operation surviving in Metro Vancouver. It opened in 1922 as New Westminster Paper, manufacturing paper napkins and then tissue paper mainly for regional markets. It

was acquired by Scott Paper (of Philadelphia) in 1952 (and its R&D facility closed) and by Kruger (of Montreal) in 1997. It employed 370 in 2022.

24 The decline of the pulp and paper industry was especially strong on the coast with mill closures in Prince Rupert, Kitimat, Gold River, and Campbell River and significant downsizing at Powell River, Port Alberni, and Crofton. More recently, pulp mills have also closed in the interior (e.g., at Prince George and Mackenzie), with remaining mills also downsizing employment.

25 Jack Munroe was president of the International Wood Workers of America in British Columbia from 1973 to 1992, when it had over 50,000 members, and he was a well-known, influential public figure. The Canadian branch broke away from its American parent in the midst of the beginning of American protectionism against BC lumber exports. Union head offices are in Metro Vancouver, connected to a series of locals throughout the interior.

26 R. Kronbauer, "The Site of the Last Sawmill in Vancouver Might Be Your New Residential Neighbourhood," *Vancouver Is Awesome,* June 11, 2013, https://www.vancouverisawesome.com/real-estate-news/the-site-of-the-last-sawmill-in-vancouver-might-be-your-new-neighbourhood-1930825; J. Lee, "Memories of Marpole Mill Offer Up Name for New Park," *Vancouver Sun,* February 5, 2014, https://vancouversun.com/news/staff-blogs/memories-of-marpole-mill-offer-up-name-for-new-park; J. Cleugh, "Developer Eyes Granville Island–Type Project on Coquitlam Water Front," *TriCity News,* April 26, 2022, https://www.tricitynews.com/local-business/developer-eyes-granville-island-type-project-on-coquitlam-waterfront-5303342.

27 The financial background to this decline is indicated by a turnaround in profits among publicly held companies, mainly headquartered in Vancouver, from a $500 million profit in 1979 to a $500 million loss in 1981. Such losses lay behind the onset of unusually high debt-equity levels and major layoffs. See Grass and Hayter, "Employment Change during Recession."

28 MB's pursuit of value-added flexible mass production strategies is discussed in R. Hayter and T. Barnes, "The Restructuring of British Columbia's Coastal Forest Sector: Flexibility Perspectives," in *Troubles in the Rainforest: British Columbia's Forest Economy in Transition,* ed. T. Barnes and R. Hayter (Victoria: Western Geographical Series, 1987), 181–202; and Hayter, *Flexible Crossroads.* In 1999, MB was acquired by the US-based Weyerhaeuser, which, following continuing difficulties, closed or sold former MB operations while almost completely divesting itself from British Columbia. Over the past two decades, the remaining large BC-based forestry corporations increasingly have invested elsewhere. B. Parfitt, *After the Windfall: Plotting a New Course for BC beyond the SLA* (Vancouver: Canadian Centre for Policy Alternatives, 2010); V. Palmer, "B.C. Forest Companies Expanding at a Rapid Pace, but not at Home," *Vancouver Sun,* December 17, 2021, https://vancouversun.com/opinion/columnists/vaughn-palmer-b-c-forest-companies-expanding-at-a-rapid-pace-but-not-at-home. Foreign MNCs have been leaving the province since the 1980s. See Edenhoffer and Hayter, "Restructuring on a Vertiginous Plateau."

29 D. Haley and J. Leitch, *The Structure and Product Mix of the Solid Wood Products Sector,* report prepared for the British Columbia Forest Resources Commission,

1992, 31–32. See McWilliams, *Profile of the B.C. Wood Products Value-Added Sector*; Kozak and Mannes, "Towards a Value Focused Forest Sector in British Columbia"; Canadian Forest Service, *Secondary Wood Manufacturing in BC*; and British Columbia Government, *Generating More Value from Our Forests.*

30 S. Klepper and J. Miller, "Entry, Exit, and Shakeouts in the United States in New Manufactured Products," *International Journal of Industrial Organization* 13 (1995): 567–91. They define shakeouts as a "persistent fall in the number of firms" with a sustained net exit of at least 30 percent of peak numbers over a "lengthy period" (567). Shake-ins can be similarly defined. See S. Klepper and S. Simmons, "Industry Shakeouts and Technological Change," *International Journal of Industrial Organization* 23 (2005): 23–43; and Hayter and Edenhoffer, "Shakeouts, Shakeins and Industry Population Dynamics."

31 Note that all of the operations in Table 2.2 add value. However, in the BC forest sector, secondary manufacturing firms often are classified as its "value-added sector," and secondary manufacturing firms mainly comprise the value-added wood and paper converting categories in Table 2.2.

32 Woodbridge Associates, *Opportunity BC 2020. BC's Forest Industry: Moving from a Volume Focus to a Value Perspective,* 2009, report prepared for the Business Council of British Columbia; Hayter and Edenhoffer, "Shakeouts, Shakeins and Industry Population Dynamics."

33 K. Mclhenney and R. Hayter, "Sustaining Jobs and Environment? The Wood Industry in Vancouver-Metro, British Columbia," *Local Environments* 19 (2014): 605–25.

34 The export sales ratios of these firms were high, with the smallest (case D) being 50 percent, and higher than for secondary wood manufacturers as a whole, including numerous tiny firms (fewer than ten employees) strongly connected to local markets.

35 Mclhenney and Hayter, "Sustaining Jobs and Environment?"

36 H.R. Gilani, R.A. Kozack, and J.L. Innes, "The State of Innovation in the British Columbia Value-Added Wood Products Sector: The Example of Chain of Custody Certification," *Canadian Journal of Forest Research* 46 (2016): 1067–75.

37 R. Hanna, R. Hayter, and A. Clapp, "Threshold Firms: Innovation, Design and Collaboration in British Columbia's Forest Economy," *Growth and Change* 48 (2017): 700–18; T. Reiffenstein, R. Hayter, and D.W. Edgington, "Crossing Cultures, Learning to Export: Making Houses in British Columbia for Export in Japan," *Economic Geography* 78 (2002): 195–220.

38 In recent years, British Columbia's previous premier, John Horgan, often lauded the value-added potential of engineered wood, and his enthusiasm culminated in a new action plan. See Government of British Columbia, *B.C.'s Mass Timber Action Plan* (Victoria: Government of British Columbia, 2022). This plan hopefully will have positive impacts, even if it was introduced thirty-five years after "mass timber" qua Parallam was innovated at Expo 86, when it could have been proactive in establishing global leadership.

39 H. Manninen, *Long-Term Outlook for Engineered Wood Products in Europe,* European Forestry Institute Technical Report 91, 2014.

40 A. Silverwood, "Weyerhaeuser Uses Strong Scraps," *Canadian Forest Industries,* October 17, 2017, https://www.woodbusiness.ca/weyerhaeuser-strong-scraps-1859.

41 In CLT technology, softwood layers are bonded under pressure at right angles to each other to form load-bearing walls et cetera. Although the technology originated in Europe in the early 2000s (Austria and Germany), substantial adaptations were required to serve the specifics of North American markets, and Structurlam added a second factory in British Columbia in 2013 and one in the United States in 2020. See W. Downing [president of Structurlam Products], "Statement to the Natural Resources Committee," 2017, http://www/search/q+witness%3A+%22235919%22; and M. Church, "Leading the Masses: Structurlam Expands Okanagan Mass Timber Operation," *Canadian Forest Industries,* February 8, 2019, http://www.wood business.ca/leading-the-masses-structurlam-expands-okanagan-mass-timber -operation/.

42 Church, "Leading the Masses."

43 Church, "Leading the Masses."

44 Examples include Kalesnikoff Lumber's $35 million investment in a new CLT plant in the southern interior, StructureCraft Inc. opening a plant in Abbotsford to manu-facture dowel laminated timber, and in nearby Squamish Fraser expanding its re-manufacturing capabilities in glulams.

45 Information in this section is taken from "Brock Commons Tall Wood House," *Think Wood,* n.d.; T. Fletcher, "BC's Engineered Wood Leadership Many Years in the Making," *Campbell River Mirror,* May 14, 2019, https://www.campbellrivermirror. com/business/b-c-s-engineered-wood-construction-leadership-years-in-the -making-1483543; L. Givetash, "Wood Tower at the University of British Columbia a Game-Changer for Construction," *Winnipeg Free Press,* June 14, 2016, https:// www.winnipegfreepress.com/arts-and-life/life/greenpage/2016/06/14/wood -tower-at-the-university-of-british-columbia-a-game-changer-for-construction; and P.A. Fast and R. Jackson, *Brock Commons: A Case Study in Tall Timber,* 2017.

46 "Brock Commons Tall Wood House," 3.

47 Downing, "Statement to the Natural Resources Committee."

48 Tall wood buildings have proliferated around the world. See E. Hunt, "Plyscraper City: Tokyo to Build 350m Tower Made of Wood," *Guardian,* February 16, 2018, https://www.theguardian.com/cities/2018/feb/16/plyscraper-city-tokyo-tower -wood-w350; and A.K. Hurley, "The Weird, Wooden Future of Skyscrapers," *Atlantic,* December 2017, https://www.theatlantic.com/magazine/archive/2017/12/timber -land/544146/. In 2020, Microsoft's new Silicon Valley head office was reportedly the tallest new wood building in the world, replacing the Mjosa Tower near Oslo in Norway as the tallest new wood building at 85.4 metres in 2019. With respect to British Columbia and Canada, see D. Penner, "Prince George Centre Opens as Towering Experience in All-Wood Construction Sector," *Vancouver Sun,* Novem-ber 18, 2014, https://vancouversun.com/business/commercial%20real%20estate/ prince-george-centre-opens-as-towering-presence-in-all-wood-construction -sector; D. Penner, "New Bentall Tower to Be Focal Point of Timber in Vancouver's Concrete Jungle," *Vancouver Sun,* September 23, 2021, https://vancouversun.com/ news/local-news/new-bentall-tower-to-be-focal-point-of-timber-in-vancouvers -concrete-jungle; P. Kuitenbrouwer, "Mass Timber Movement Breaking Ground on Ontario's Tallest Wood Building," *Globe and Mail,* December 14, 2021, https:// www.theglobeandmail.com/canada/article-mass-timber-movement-breaking

-ground-on-ontarios-tallest-wood-building/; E. Andreasen, "B.C. Mass Timber Is Ready for Global Prime Time," *Vancouver Sun,* September 18, 2020, https://vancouver sun.com/opinion/op-ed/eric-andreasen-b-c-mass-timber-is-ready-for-global -prime-time; and W. Hamilton, "It's Glory Days for Heavy Wood Timber in British Columbia," *Resource Works,* 2014, https://www.resourceworks.com/-it-s-glory -days-for-heavy-wood-timber-in-british-columbia. In 2018, Sumitomo announced plans for a new wood-based, seventy-floor "plyscraper" tower, 250 metres in height, in Tokyo, a few metres higher than an eighty-floor proposal in Chicago.

49 H. Kitching, "Is Timber the Future for Highrise Buildings? Lakehead Researchers Develop Patent to Help Make It Happen," *CBC News,* May 3, 2022; H. Dhokia, A. Khan, J. McNally, and C. Meier, "Framing British Columbia's Low-carbon Future." PLACE Centre. Smart Prosperity Institute (Ottawa, 2024), https://institute.smart-prosperity.ca/sites/default/files/MT1-PLACE-Cluster-Report-EN.pdf.

50 This rethinking was stimulated by the early 1980s recession. See Woodbridge Reid and Associates, *British Columbia's Forest Industry: Constraints to Growth. Report Prepared for the Ministry of State for Economic and Regional Development* (Vancouver 1984).

51 Historically, in British Columbia, as across Canada, public sector institutions were important in establishing forestry R&D, with efforts for privatization always a struggle. See Hayter and Clapp, "Towards a Collaborative (Public-Private) Partnership Approach." In British Columbia, the need for scientific support for the forest sector was formally recognized in the Royal Commission of 1908–12, the provincial and federal governments established research units, and UBC's forest faculty opened in the 1920s. Subsequently, a couple of small-scale laboratories were established by firms adjacent to their pulp and paper operations by the 1930s, including one at Powell River, relocated to Burnaby in the 1960s, as MB's major R&D facility.

52 R. Hayter, *Technology Policy Perspectives and the Canadian Forest Product Industries,* Background Study No. 56 (Ottawa: Science Council of Canada, 1988).

53 For example, for the new Gold River Pulp Mill in 1967 (now closed), a pipeline was constructed to release effluent into deep water as a classic example of an end-of-the -pipe solution, in this case wrongly assuming that the effluent would naturally disappear without damage. Similarly, at Kamloops, the large chimney to disperse air pollution beyond the surrounding valley from a pulp mill opened in 1965 is still evident as another example of an end-of-the-pipe "solution."

54 Canfor operates the surviving in-house R&D unit in New Westminster, employs fewer than ten professionals, and is primarily concerned with pulp mill efficiencies.

55 As an example of private sector R&D as a weak link in Metro Vancouver's (and Canada's) forest sector, in 1980 Weyerhaeuser employed over 500 professionals in its main R&D lab in Washington State, roughly five times more than corporate R&D as a whole in British Columbia (and bigger than totals across Canada). See R. Hayter, "Research and Development in the Canadian Forest Product Sector – Another Weak Link?," *Canadian Geographer* 26 (1982): 256–62. As an unusual example of the "reverse" flow of technology from the United States to Canada, Cancar's growth in the 1950s and 1960s was predicated on the purchase of patents from an American inventor for "chip-n-saw" processing and the sale of over 500 units, many to the

United States. See A. Froome, "A Sawmill Icon," *Logging and Sawmill Journal*, February 2005, 12.

56 For example, Westmill and FPInnovations (initially as Forintek) co-developed Light-SORT™, first introduced in 2006, to improve the accuracy of measuring green veneer moisture content. Westmill has exclusive global distribution and development rights for LightSORT™ and continues to collaborate with FPInnovations.

57 Hayter and Clapp, "Towards a Collaborative (Public-Private) Partnership Approach."

58 Hayter and Clapp, "Towards a Collaborative (Public-Private) Partnership Approach."

59 Related members are also technological suppliers to the forest sector, such as Canfor, Noram Engineering, and Fitnir Analyzers, and related nonmembers include UBC's Centre for Advanced Wood Training and other programs in institutes of higher learning. In addition, there are non–forest industry members, especially transportation companies as well as others such as BC Hydro, similarly concentrated in Metro Vancouver.

60 For example, Fitnir Analyzers is an interesting example of a spinoff company from FPInnovations that sells its patented technology developed out of collaboration with others, including Sweden's Modo-Chemetics (soon acquired by Kvaerner Chemetics) and Paprican in Vancouver. The technology measures pulp and paper properties during processing. In 2007, ABB assumed 50 percent of the patent rights from Kvaerner and supplies the hardware, while Fitnir Analyzers Inc. was established in 2008 as a local UBC-based company, led by a scientist who had helped to develop the technology, as the exclusive distributor, first introduced in 2000 in Prince George.

61 Hayter and Clapp, "Towards a Collaborative (Public-Private) Partnership Approach."

62 See D. Levy, "ORNL Researchers Invent Tougher Plastic with 50% Renewable Content," 2016, https://www/news/orni-researchers-invent-tougher-plastic-50 -percent-renewable-content; D. Nighbor, "FPInnovations Needs Renewed Government Funding to Help Turn Trees into Airplane Parts," *Vancouver Sun*, November 4, 2016, https://vancouversun.com/opinion-turning-trees-into-airplane-parts; S. Perkins, "How to Make Window 'Glass' from Wood," *Science News for Students*, 2016, https://www.snexplores.org.org/article/how-to-make-window-glass-wood; N. Tajusu and T. Shiraki, "Tougher than Steel: Japan Looks to Wood Pulp to Make Lighter Auto Parts," 2017, Reuters, https://www.reuters.com/article/us-autos-japan -wood/tougher-than-steel; L. Williams, "The Wood Fibre Solution to the World's Plastic Problem," *Eureka*, June 13, 2018, https://eureka.eu.com/innovation/wood -bre-plastic; and J. McCrank, "Nanotechnology Applications in the Forest Sector," in *Natural Resources Canada* (Ottawa: Canadian Forest Service, 2009), https:// publications.gc.ca/collections/collection_2009/nrcan/Fo4-27-2009E.pdf.

63 V. Palmer, "Unions Report on NDP failings in Response to Forestry Crisis," *Vancouver Sun*, March 13, 2024, https://vancouversun.com/opinion/vaughn-palmer-unions -report-on-ndp-failings-in-response-to-forestry.

Chapter 2: Metro Vancouver High-Tech Firms in Arrested Transition?

1 D.R. Audretsch, *Innovation and Industry Evolution* (Cambridge, MA: MIT Press, 1995); D.R. Audretsch, M. Keilbach, and E.E. Lehmann, *Entrepreneurship and Economic Growth* (Oxford: Oxford University Press, 2006).

2 E.J. Malecki, "Economic Competitiveness and Regional Development Dynamics," in *Handbook of Regions and Competitiveness,* ed. R. Huggins and P. Thompson (Cheltenham, UK: Edward Elgar, 2017), 136–52.

3 M.P. Feldman, "The Character of Innovative Places: Entrepreneurial Strategy, Economic Development, and Prosperity," *Small Business Economics* 43 (2014): 9–20.

4 KPMG, *British Columbia Technology Report Card* (Vancouver: BC Tech Association, 2020). KPMG reports that the situation in 2020 was similar to that in 2018, with almost 11,000 companies in the high-tech sector, the great majority of them small. Only twenty-two companies employed 500 or more people in 2020, and with a total employment estimated at about 120,000 the average employment size of British Columbia's high-tech companies is just 11. This report notes the lack of "anchor" firms in the province, implying a problem without saying why.

5 Telus is large and a potential anchor company in high-tech Metro Vancouver. See Case Study 4.2. However, KPMG and other reports do not cite Telus as a high-tech anchor company.

6 OECD, *OECD SME and Entrepreneurship Outlook 2005* (Paris: OECD, 2005).

7 We identified locally originating "transitional" firms from personal knowledge, lists of high-tech firms provided in sources such as BC Business, and mentions in various publications (academic studies, newspapers, news releases, etc.). Individual firms were then googled for background information on history, size, et cetera.

8 KPMG, *British Columbia Technology Report Card,* 1.

9 The idea of business segmentation in a local development context is discussed in R. Hayter, J. Patchell, and K.G. Rees, "Business Segmentation and Location Revisited: Innovation and the Terra Incognita of Large Firms," *Regional Studies* 33 (1999): 425–42. For pioneering studies, see J.K. Galbraith, *The New Industrial Estate* (Boston: Houghton Mifflin, 1967); and A.D. Chandler, *Strategy and Structure: Chapters in the History of American Industrial Enterprise* (New York: Doubleday, 1962). The former distinguished the giant MNCs of the so-called planning system from the smaller firms of the market system, and the latter argued that decision-making structures responded to the implementation of new growth strategies.

10 Mid-sized companies are portrayed as dynamic, highly innovative, job-creating firms that might employ from 2,000 to over 100,000. See H. Simon, "Lessons from Germany's Midsized Giants," *Harvard Business Review* 70 (1992): 115–23; H. Nakamura, *New Mid-Sized Firm Theory* (in Japanese) (Tokyo: Tokyo Keizai Shinpansha, 1990); and R.L. Kuhn, *To Flourish among Giants* (London: John Wiley, 1985).

11 G.A. Knight and S.T. Cavusgil, "Innovation, Organizational Capabilities, and the Born-Global Firm," *Journal of International Business Studies* 35 (2004): 124–41; G. Knight and P. Liesch, "Internationalization: From Incremental to Born Global," *Journal of World Business* 51 (2016): 93–102; H. Bathelt, A. Malmberg, and P. Maskell, "Clusters and Knowledge: Local Buzz, Global Pipelines and the Process of Knowledge Creation," *Progress in Human Geography* 28 (2004): 31–56.

12 G.P.F. Steed, *Threshold Firms: Backing Canada's Winners. Science Council of Canada* (Ottawa: Ministry of Supply and Services, 1982). For Steed, threshold firms are Canadian-owned and -controlled innovative firms operating in high-tech sectors that have grown successfully to at least medium size and have the potential to become much larger. His argument that Canada lacks such firms still resonates.

13 The level of capitalization is another indicator of size cited in studies of high-tech companies. This indicator, however, can be speculative and does not have the same comparative sense as revenue or employment.

14 The formidable problems facing firms in overcoming the valley of death have provided the rationale for various kinds of policy support for new firms.

15 For an introduction to the seedbed hypothesis, see R. Hayter, *The Dynamics of Industrial Location* (Chichester, UK: Wiley, 1997), 224–26.

16 Both Deering and Patrick were decorated Second World War veterans and subsequently gained considerable business experience, the former in the family's (West Vancouver–based) logging business and the latter in a major manufacturing enterprise in eastern Canada before moving to Victoria.

17 Among other achievements, UBC's award citation of Gelbart noted the 100 patents that he had filed and that sales from these products had reached over $1 billion.

18 PricewaterhouseCoopers, *British Columbia TechMap 2012,* 2013. This survey draws from data on over 2,000 companies (plus other organizations) and is not so much a map (since the locations in British Columbia are not identified) but an inventory of firms that shows their genealogy (by decadal cohort) and their "connections" as spin-offs or in some related way. Visually, the data are presented on a large canvas (five feet by three and a half feet) and classified in multiple ways hard to "read" and sort out. Yet the very "messiness" of the lines connecting the survey firms in PwC's maps underlines the importance of spinoffs.

19 This privatization was unusual in that it involved a management contract to Accenture, a US-based consulting company that for a substantial fee oversaw the running down of Westech. Accenture became controversial in Canada again in 2023 when it was revealed as the company (secretly) contracted by the federal government to implement its $146 million CEBA (Canada Emergency Business Account) program to fund businesses through the COVID-19 pandemic.

20 See K.G. Rees, "Innovation in the Periphery: Networks or Fragments in the High Technology Industries of Greater Vancouver" (PhD dissertation, Department of Geography, Simon Fraser University, 1999).

21 Gelbart, for example, left Creo and soon helped to co-start Kardium, a life sciences spinoff from UBC (see Chapter 4).

22 Apart from PMC-Sierra, MPR spun off small firms such as Abatis Systems, OctigaBay Systems, Convedia Corporation, Motion Technologies, and Open Text. See Rees, "Innovation in the Periphery"; and D. Jordan, "Innovation Calling: Norman Dowds," *BC Business,* August 5, 2009, https://www.bcbusiness.ca/people/general/innovation-calling-norman-dowds/.

23 Rees, "Innovation in the Periphery"; Jordan, "Innovation Calling."

24 The categories are noted in Chapter 1 and cited in Table 4.1.

25 Information for the synopsis of Ballard Power Systems is derived from various sources, including its annual reports since 1993, when it became a public company, and from several studies. See T. Taylor, "Ballard Power and the Quest for Profitability," *BC Business,* May 2, 2011, https://www.bcbusiness.ca/industries/general/ballard-power-and-the-quest-for-profitability/; Innovation Canada, *Case 2: Ballard Power Systems,* 2005, https://web.archive.org/20051217125101/http://www.innovation.gc.ca/gol/innovation/site.nsf/en/in04204.html; Ballard Power Systems, "Our History," 2019,

https://www.ballard.com/about-ballard/our-history; British Columbia Innovation Council (BCIC), *Ballard's Fuel Cell Project: Next Stop – Changing the World*, BCIC Case Study Library No. 0009 (Burnaby: SFU Business Studies, 2008), prepared by L. Papanalia and J. Hall (online for classroom use only); T. Koppel, *Powering the Future* (Chichester, UK: Wiley, 2001). Along with many other newspaper and magazine articles, Wikipedia provides information on Geoffrey Ballard and Ballard Power Systems.

26 The three principals had strong, complementary scientific backgrounds: Geoffrey Ballard had a BSc from Ontario and a PhD from the United States, Keith Prater was a chemistry professor at the University of Texas, and Paul Howard was a mechanical engineer.

27 Ballard famously said, "What is a fuel cell?"

28 Ballard sold this company in 2007, a year before he died, to Plug Power of New York for US $10 million, quickly integrated with Cellex Power of Richmond, also acquired by Plug Power. General Hydrogen's work included using fuel cell stacks contracted from Ballard for forklift trucks, and Cellex similarly used Ballard fuel stacks.

29 M. Jaganmohan, "Gross Revenue of Select Fuel Cell Companies Globally from 2013 to 2016," January 29, 2021, https://www.statista.com/statistics/478631/gross-revenue-of-key-fuel-cell-companies-globally/.

30 Other privately owned firms have not released information on R&D expenditures or stopped doing so following their acquisition.

31 B. Jang, "Chasing the Hydrogen Dream: Ballard in Quest to Transform Long-Haul Transportation," *Globe and Mail*, December 4, 2020, https://www.theglobeandmail.com/business/article-chasing-the-hydrogen-dream-ballard-on-quest-to-transform--long-haul-transportation.

32 David Baines, a highly respected former financial journalist writing in the *Vancouver Sun*, expressed concern about Ballard's future and warned investors. See Taylor, "Ballard Power and the Quest for Profitability."

33 More big company customers are becoming interested in sustainable energy, and the overall policy environment is more supportive, as reflected by the seventy-five countries that have established targets for zero carbon emissions, with many also investing in supportive infrastructure.

34 Taylor, "Ballard Power and the Quest for Profitability."

35 The hiring of Rasul reflected Ballard's recognition that new organizational capabilities were required.

36 J. Kay, "RIP PLC: The Rise of the Ghost Corporation," *Prospect*, March 3, 2021, https://www.prospectmagazine.co.uk/ideas/economics/37397/rip-plc-the-rise-of-the-ghost-corporation.

37 Initially (2007), Automotive Fuel Cell Corporation was owned by Daimler (50.1 percent), Ford (30.0 percent), and Ballard (19.9 percent). In 2008, it became a private company, and in 2018 Ballard sold its share of the company to Weichai Power of China, with which it had entered a partnership.

38 Ballard has also been awarded various government grants in support of its R&D.

39 Jang, "Chasing the Hydrogen Dream."

40 In March 2021, Ballard announced fuel cell sales for Canadian Pacific's Hydrogen Locomotive Program; six were delivered that year, and more have been ordered

since. Ballard also announced fifty fuel cell modules (thirty-four already delivered) for Wrightbus of the United Kingdom and manufactured in Ireland. The Joint Initiative for Hydrogen Vehicles across Europe Program helped to fund 295 buses, 85 percent of which have Ballard fuel cells.

41 With production based in Ontario as well as Metro Vancouver (Delta), Avcorp is another strongly export-oriented company, in its case mainly to the United States: American customers, led by Boeing and Lockheed Martin, accounted for about half of the firm's $173 million in sales in 2016 and $183 million in sales in 2018, the latter including sales to the Japanese-based Subaru.

42 Avcorp, for example, has long-term subcontracting relations with its main customers, such as Boeing, MDA was a stable supplier to NASA, the biotechs seek licensing arrangements with big pharmaceutical companies, and Ballard and Westport are strongly linked in selling to their partners.

43 Several firms, including Ballard and MDA, developed important early contracts with central Canadian consumers, including the Canadian government. In general, however, transitioning firms are as likely to look south as to look east to develop nonlocal markets.

44 For example, KPMG, *British Columbia Technology Report Card.*

45 Simon, "Lessons from Germany's Midsized Giants"; Hayter, Patchell, and Rees, "Business Segmentation and Location Revisited."

Chapter 3: The Influence of FDI in Metro Vancouver High Tech

1 In this chapter, we focus on corporate equity investments in foreign branch plants and subsidiaries that they control. Portfolio-type investments, when lenders provide funds to borrowers for a monetary return but without implications for control or management, are not considered. In high tech, angel investors provide such portfolio funds (see Chapter 5).

2 In 2019, Apple and Amazon were ranked eleventh and thirteenth on *Fortune's* Global 500 list, when both had revenues of over US $230 billion, and in 2020 Apple was ranked as the world's most valuable company.

3 That throughout the twentieth century foreign control of the Canadian economy was unusually high globally is well documented; see H. Marshall, F.A. Southward, and K.W. Taylor, *Canadian-American Industry: A Study in International Investment* (Toronto: Ryerson, 1936); J.N.H. Britton and J.M. Gilmour, *The Weakest Link: A Technological Perspective on Canadian Underdevelopment,* Background Study 22 (Ottawa: Science Council of Canada, 1978); and M. Wilkins, "Comparative Hosts," in *The Making of Global Enterprise,* ed. G. Jones (London: Frank Cass, 1994), 18–50. The reasons for Canada's (and British Columbia's) historical openness to FDI are beyond the scope of this study.

4 The idea that FDI can "truncate" – remove and pre-empt – local R&D activity and innovation potential was developed in a Canadian context in the manufacturing and resource sectors. See Marshall, Southward, and Taylor, *Canadian-American Industry*; Britton and Gilmour, *The Weakest Link;* and R. Hayter, "Truncation, the International Firm and Regional Policy," *Area* 14 (1982): 277–82.

5 Various work-related characteristics and where-to-live preferences have long been recognized as significant locational considerations for high-tech activities. See E.J.

Malecki and S. Bradbury, "R&D Facilities and Professional Labour: Labour Force Dynamics in High Technology," *Regional Studies* 26 (1992): 123–36; and R. Florida, "The Economic Geography of Talent," *Annals of the Association of American Geographers* 92 (2002): 743–55.

6 Jim Balsillie, the former head of BlackBerry and the chair of the Council of Canadian Innovators, has long been critical of the leakage of Canadian technological expertise (and patents) to foreign MNCs. See, for example, J. Synder, "Unclear Intellectual Property Rules Put Canada at Risk amid Higher Threat of Foreign Takeovers," *National Post,* June 15, 2020, https://nationalpost.com/news/unclear-rules-around -intellectual-property-put-canada-at-risk-amid-increased-threat-of-foreign -takeovers-experts-say; and D. Breznitz, *Innovation in Real Places: Strategies for Prosperity in an Unforgiving World* (New York: Oxford University Press, 2021).

7 H.W. Yeung, "Regional Worlds: From Related Variety in Regional Diversification to Strategic Coupling in Global Production Networks," *Regional Studies* 55 (2020): 989–1010; N.M. Coe and H.W. Yeung, *Global Production Networks: Theorizing Economic Development in an Interconnected World* (Oxford: Oxford University Press, 2015); N.M. Coe and H.W. Yeung, "Global Production Networks: Mapping Recent Conceptual Developments," *Journal of Economic Geography* 19 (2019): 775–801.

8 Information sources are derived from author research and numerous, overlapping stories in business magazines and newspapers that record and discuss the arrival of MNCs and major events affecting their performance in Metro Vancouver, typically based on interviews with key decision makers. PwC's techmaps also identified foreign ownership of the high-tech companies surveyed in British Columbia in 2002 and 2012.

9 Key early theories of MNCs include P.J. Buckley and M.C. Casson, *The Future of the Multinational Enterprise* (London: Macmillan, 1976); R.E. Caves, "International Corporations: The Industrial Economics of Foreign Investment," *Economica* 38 (1971): 1–27; J.H. Dunning, *Explaining International Production* (London: Unwin Hyman, 1988); S.H. Hymer, *The International Operations of National Firms: A Study of Direct Foreign Investment* (Cambridge, MA: MIT Press, 1960); and J. Johansson and J.E. Valhne, "The Internationalization Process of the Firm – A Model of Knowledge Development and Increasing Foreign Market Commitments," *Journal of International Business Studies* 88 (1977): 23–32.

10 Conglomerate growth implies that firms expand in product market areas functionally unrelated, except in overall control and financial terms. FDI, however, mainly features horizontal and/or vertical integration.

11 For a recent review of branch plant truncation, see J.W. Sonn and D. Lee, "Revisiting the Branch Plant Syndrome: Review of Literature on Foreign Direct Investment and Regional Development in Western Advanced Economies," *International Journal of Urban Sciences* 16 (2012): 243–59.

12 Knowledge exchanges between parent companies and subsidiaries are an important theme in contemporary business literature on MNCs. See J. Cantwell, J.N. Dunning, and S.M. Lundan, "An Evolutionary Approach to Understanding International Business Activity: The Co-Evolution of MNEs and the Institutional Environment," *Journal of International Business Studies* 41 (2010): 567–86; A.M. Rugman and A. Verbeke, "Subsidiary Specific Advantages in Multinational Enterprises," *Strategic*

Management Journal 22 (2001): 237–50; S. Michailova and Z. Mustaffa, "Subsidiary Knowledge Flows in Multinational Corporations: Research Accomplishments, Gaps and Opportunities," *Journal of World Business* 47 (2012): 383–96; L. Rabbiosi and G.D. Santangelo, "Parent Company Benefits from Reverse Knowledge Transfer: The Role of the Liability of Newness in MNEs," *Journal of World Business* 48 (2013): 160–70; and Y. Wang and S. Chung-Sok, "Towards a Re-Conceptualization of Firm Internationalization: Heterogeneous Process, Subsidiary Roles and Knowledge Flow," *Journal of International Management* 15 (2009): 447–59.

13 E. Jarrett, "New Lessons from the Epic Story of Moli Energy, the Canadian Pioneer of Rechargeable Lithium Battery Technology," *Electric Autonomy Weekly*, September 18, 2020, https://electricautonomy.ca/2020/09/18/moli-energy-lithium-battery -technology. As Jarrett notes, a cellphone battery produced by the company in its new Maple Ridge factory caught fire (in Japan), and Moli went into receivership in 1989, which led to significant financial problems. The BC government removed its funding, and after the firm went into receivership it sold its assets for around $5 million to a Japanese consortium, a small fraction of its real value. A local newspaper rightly labelled it a "give away." Following its further sale in 1998 to E-One of Taiwan, Moli became more active. Meanwhile, as the company's founder one of Rudi Haering's (see Case Study 2.1) graduate students, Jeff Dahn, has become a leading authority on lithium batteries as a professor at Dalhousie University.

14 R. Littlemore, "Vancouver's High Tech Makeover," *Globe and Mail*, March 26, 2015, https://www.theglobeandmail.com/report-on-business/rob-magazine/vancouvers -high-tech-makeover/article23614007/; A. Gibbon, "Greenbacks Flow to BC Tech Sector," *Globe and Mail*, January 10, 2000, updated March 23, 2018, https://www. theglobeandmail.com/report-on-business/rob-magazine/greenbacks-flow-to-bc -tech-sector/article4158645/.

15 The sticky metaphor comes from A. Markusen, "Sticky Places in Slippery Space: A Typology of Industrial Districts," *Economic Geography* 72 (1996): 293–313.

16 E.J. Malecki, *Technology and Economic Development: The Dynamics of Local, Regional and National Change* (Harlow, UK: Longmans, 1991); Malecki and Bradbury, "R&D Facilities and Professional Labour"; Florida, "The Economic Geography of Talent."

17 E. Duggan, "International Visual Effects Firm Makes Vancouver Its First Anchor in North America," *Vancouver Sun*, November 11, 2014, https://vancouversun.com/ business/international-visual-effects-firm-makes-Vancouver-its-first-anchor -in-north.america.

18 E. Duggan, "International Visual Effects Firm."

19 Locational surveys of high tech typically focus on subjective "rankings" of various locational factors in which labour cost is just one of many such factors. See Malecki and Bradbury, "R&D Facilities and Professional Labour." Similarly, see Florida, "The Economic Geography of Talent." His aggregate analysis of the spatial distribution of talent across the United States is rooted in multiple attributes and subjective assessments with emphasis on the value created by talent rather than its cost.

20 BC Stats, *Profile of the British Columbia Technology Sector 2020 Edition* (Victoria: Ministry of Jobs, Economic Recovery and Innovation, 2021), 18. See also Vancity Credit Union, *Help Wanted: Salaries, Affordability and the Exodus of Labour from Metro Vancouver, 2015* (Vancouver, British Columbia, Vancity, 2016).

21 BC Stats, *Profile of the British Columbia Technology Sector 2016 Edition* (Victoria: Ministry of Technology, Innovation and Citizens' Services, 2017), Tables 16 and 18.

22 P. Evans, "Big Tech Hiring Cements Canada's Status as Silicon Valley North – But There Is a Catch," *CBC News*, April 24, 2022, https://www.cbc.ca/news/business/canada-tech-sector-boom-1.6425879.

23 E. Duggan, "Amazon to Take over Entire Former Canada Post Office Building in Downtown Vancouver," *Vancouver Sun*, December 10, 2019, 4, https://vancouversun.com/business/commercial-real-estate-amazon-to-take-over-entire-former-canada-post-building.

24 See Canadian Human Computer Communications Society, "Canadian Digital Media Pioneer Award: Don Mattrick," 2016, https://graphicsinterface.org/awards/cdmp/don-mattrick/.

25 Duggan, "International Visual Effects Firm."

26 Duggan, "International Visual Effects Firm."

27 E. Kirkwood, "Tile Expands to Canada, Opens Engineering Hub in Vancouver," *Betakit*, May 29, 2019, https://betakit.com/tile-expands-to-canada-opens-engineering-hub-in-vancouver/; T. Orton, "Consumer Electronics Firm Tile Taps Vancouver as New Engineering Hub," *Business in Vancouver*, May 29, 2019, https://biv.com/article/2019/05/consumer-electronics-firm-Tile-taps-vancouver-new-engineering-hub; T. Orton, "Big Tech Expansion in Vancouver a 'Magnet for U.S. Firms," *Business in Vancouver*, June 20, 2019, https://big-tech-expansion-vancouver-magnet-us-firms.

28 Orton, "Big Tech Expansion in Vancouver."

29 W. Johnson, "Meet Rivian, the $80b EV Maker with Offices in Yaletown," *Vancouver Tech Journal*, October 18, 2021, https://www.vantechjournal.com/p/rivian-vancouver?s=r.

30 Orton, "Big tech expansion in Vancouver a 'Magnet' for U.S. Firms."

31 Littlemore, "Vancouver's High Tech Makeover."

32 Littlemore, "Vancouver's High Tech Makeover."

33 Slack Technologies relocated its headquarters from Vancouver to San Francisco and in 2019 went public on the New York Stock Exchange. With revenue in 2019 of over $400 million and a workforce of over 1,600, this Vancouver-born company has global sales focusing on business, with IBM as its leading customer. In 2020, it was acquired by Salesforce (San Francisco; see Appendix 1).

34 Avcorp is another long-time, unionized, high-tech firm in Metro Vancouver.

35 T. Barnes and N.M. Coe, "Vancouver as Media Cluster: The Cases of Video Games and Film/TV," in *Media Clusters across the Globe: Developing, Expanding, and Reinvigorating Content Capabilities*, ed. C. Karlsson and R.G. Picard (Cheltenham: Edward Elgar, 2011), 251–77.

36 Britton and Gilmour, *The Weakest Link*.

37 J. Lee, "SAP Unveils $11-Million Vancouver Office Reno," *Vancouver Sun*, April 12, 2016, https://vancouversun.com/business/local-business/sap-unveils-11-million-vancouver-office-reno.

38 Meta's Metro Vancouver office, at least prior to 2018, was mainly involved in training and recruitment and is not included in Case Study 3.2. See K. Chan, "Facebook to

Open New Major Downtown Vancouver Office on Burrard Street," *Vancouver Urbanized*, November 17, 2017, https://dailyhive.com/vancouver/facebook-vancouver-office-200-burrard-street.

39 T-Net, "Fortinet to Add 1,000 New Tech Jobs in Vancouver in New State-of-the-Art Data Centre," BC Technology.com, September 12, 2017, https://brainstation.io/magazine/fortinet-announces-operations-expansion-in-burnaby.

40 Molicel, "Strengthening Battery Manufacturing in British Columbia to Secure Good Jobs and Keep our Air Clean," November 15 2023, https://www.molicel.com/corporate/strengthening-battery-manufacturing-in-british-columbia-to-secure-good-jobs-and-keep-our-air-clean/; Jarrett, "New Lessons from the Epic Story of Moli Energy."

41 D. Penner, "Japanese Giant Fujitsu Picks Vancouver for Global Artificial Intelligence HQ," *Vancouver Sun*, July 9, 2019, https://vancouversun.com/business/local-business/japanese-tech-giant-fujitsu-picks-vancouver-for-global-artificial-intelligence-hq. This facility started with nine employees from Japan in 2018, and by 2019 it employed twenty. Penner also notes that the Royal Bank of Canada opened a research institute for artificial intelligence (Borealis AI) that includes a Vancouver office employing thirty.

42 DH Vancouver Staff, "Samsung Research & Development Centre," *Daily Hive*, December 19, 2017, https://dailyhive.com/vancouver/samsung-research-development-centre-vancouver.

43 Amazon Staff, "Amazon's Economic Impact in Canada: How We're Investing in Local Communities," https://www.aboutamazon.com/news/policy-news-views/amazons-economic-impact-in-canada-2023, 2023. See also C. Wilson, "Virtue of Being a Single Corporate Tenant: A Peek Inside Amazon's New Vancouver Office," *Times Colonist*, May 21, 2023, https://www.timescolonist.com/real-estate/virtue-of-being-a-single-corporate-tenant-a-peek-inside-amazons-new-vancouver-office-7023892.

44 M. McCullough, "Creo: The Digitization Printing Company that Could Have Saved Kodak," *Canadian Business*, February 16, 2012, http://www.canadianbusiness.com/business-news/industries/technology/creo-the-digitization-printing-company-that-could-have-saved-kodak/.

45 R. Mudambi and T. Swift, "Leveraging Knowledges and Competencies across Space: The Next Frontier in International Business," *Journal of International Management* 17 (2011): 186–89.

46 M. Ma, "Amazon Is not a 'Big Win' for the Vancouver Technology Sector," *Vancouver Sun*, May 4, 2018, https://vancouversun.com/opinion/op-ed/melody-ma-amazon-not-a-big-win-for-the-vancouver-technology-sector; P. Evans, "Big Tech Hiring Cements Canada's Status as Silicon Valley North – But There's a Catch," *CBC News*, April 24, 2022, https://www.cbc.ca/news/business/canada-tech-sector-boom-1.6425879.

47 Amazon Staff, "Amazon's Economic Impact in Canada."

48 Synder, "Unclear Intellectual Property Rules"; Breznitz, *Innovation in Real Places*.

49 For example, note Microsoft's ruthless behaviour toward Pivotal. P. Brethour, "The Decline of Vancouver's Pivotal Corp Shows the Perils of Partnering with Microsoft," *Globe and Mail*, April 17, 2002, https://www.theglobeandmail.com/report-on

-business/rob-magazine/the-decline-of-vancouvers-pivotal-corp-shows-the-perils
-of-partnering-with-microsoft/article1022868.

Chapter 4: Local Clustering and Global Connections in Inter-Firm Relations among High-Tech Activities

1 Economic geography and regional economics textbooks provide extensive discussions of external qua agglomeration economies (and diseconomies) and their various subcategories. See A. Potts and H.D. Watts, "Evolutionary Agglomeration Theory: Increasing Returns, Diminishing Returns, and the Industry Life Cycle," *Journal of Economic Geography* 11 (2011): 1–39.

2 For recent reviews of this literature, see R. Huggins and P. Thompson, "Introducing Regional Competitiveness and Development: Contemporary Theories and Perspectives," in *Handbook of Regions and Competitiveness*, ed. R. Huggins and P. Thompson (Cheltenham, UK: Edward Elgar, 2017), 1–31; E.J. Malecki, "Economic Competitiveness and Regional Development Dynamics," in *Handbook of Regions and Competitiveness*, ed. R. Huggins and P. Thompson (Cheltenham, UK: Edward Elgar, 2017), 136–52; and M. Storper, "Explaining Regional Growth and Change," in *Handbook of Regions and Competitiveness*, ed. R. Huggins and P. Thompson (Cheltenham, UK: Edward Elgar, 2017), 35–48.

3 A. Saxanien, "The Genesis of Silicon Valley," *Built Environment* 9 (1981): 7–17.

4 R. Florida and D.F. Smith, "Venture Capital Formation, Investment and Regional Industrialization," *Annals of the Association of American Geographers* 83 (1993): 434–51.

5 M. Kenney and D. Patton, "The Coevolution of Technologies and Institutions: Silicon Valley as the Iconic High-Technology Cluster," in *Cluster Genesis: Technology-Based Industrial Development*, ed. P. Braunerhjelm and M.P. Feldman (Oxford: Oxford University Press, 2006), 38–60; S.B. Adams, "Growing Where You Are Planted: Exogenous Firms and the Seeding of Silicon Valley," *Research Policy* 40 (2011): 368–79; J.S. Engel and I. del-Palacio, "Global Clusters of Innovation: The Case of Israel and Silicon Valley," *California Management Review* 53 (2011): 27–50; S. Manning, "New Silicon Valleys or a New Species? Commoditization of Knowledge Work and the Rise of Knowledge Service Clusters," *Research Policy* 42 (2013): 379–90.

6 See G.P.F. Steed and D. Genova, "Ottawa's Technology-Oriented Complex," *Canadian Geographer* 27 (1983): 262–78; M. Porter, *The Competitive Advantage of Nations* (New York: Free Press, 1990); and J. Patchell, "Kaleidoscope Economies: The Processes of Cooperation, Competition, and Control in Regional Economic Development," *Annals of the Association of American Geographers* 86 (1996): 481–506.

7 N.M. Coe, "A Hybrid Agglomeration? The Development of a Satellite-Marshallian Industrial District in Vancouver's Film Industry," *Urban Studies* 38 (2001): 1753–75; K.G. Rees and R. Hayter, "Flexible Specialization, Uncertainty and the Firm: Enterprise Strategies and Structures in the Wood Remanufacturing Industry of the Vancouver Metropolitan Area, British Columbia," *Canadian Geographer* 40 (1996): 203–19.

8 In theory, localized or immobile external economies can be accessed only by being close to particular places, whereas mobile external economies can be accessed from

around the globe. See R. Hayter and D.W. Edgington, "'Getting Tough' and 'Getting Smart': Politics of the North American–Japan Wood Products Trade," *Environment and Planning C: Government and Policy* 17 (1999): 319–44; and R. Boschma, "Proximity and Innovation: A Critical Assessment," *Regional Studies* 39 (2005): 61–74.

9 See M. Storper, "The Resurgence of Regional Economies, Ten Years Later: The Region as a Nexus of Untraded Interdependencies," *European and Urban Regional Studies* 2 (1995): 191–221; and H. Bathelt, A. Malmberg, and P. Maskell, "Clusters and Knowledge: Local Buzz, Global Pipelines and the Process of Knowledge Creation," *Progress in Human Geography* 28 (2004): 31–56.

10 D.K.R. Robinson, A. Rip, and V. Mangematin, "Technological Agglomeration and the Emergence of Clusters and Networks in Nanotechnology," *Research Policy* 6 (2007): 871–79.

11 T. Barnes and N.M. Coe, "Vancouver as Media Cluster: The Cases of Video Games and Film/TV," in *Media Clusters: Spatial Agglomeration and Content Capabilities,* ed. C. Karlsson and R.G. Picard (Northampton, MA: Edward Elgar, 2011), 251–77; T. Barnes and T. Hutton, "Situating the New Economy: Contingencies of Regeneration and Dislocation in Vancouver's Inner City," *Urban Studies* 46 (2009): 1247–69; N.M. Coe, "The View from Out West: Embeddedness, Inter-Personal Relations and the Development of an Indigenous Film Industry in Vancouver," *Geoforum* 31 (2000): 391–407; N.M. Coe, "On Location: American Capital and the Local Labour Market in Vancouver's Film Industry," *International Journal of Urban and Regional Research* 24 (2000): 79–94; C.H. Langford, J.R. Wood, and A. Jacobson, *The Evolution and Structure of the Vancouver Wireless Cluster: Growth and Loss of Core Firms,* 2005, https://www.researchgate.net/publication/265533886_The_evolution_and_structure _of_the_Vancouver_wireless_cluster_Growth_and_loss_of_core_firms; K.G. Rees, "Collaboration, Innovation and Regional Networks: Evidence from the Medical Biotechnology Industry of Greater Vancouver," in *Proximity, Distance and Diversity: Issues on Economic Interaction and Local Development,* ed. A. Lagendijk and P. Oinas (Aldershot, UK: Ashgate, 2004), 191–215; K.G. Rees, "Interregional Collaboration and Innovation in Vancouver's Emerging High Tech Cluster," *Tijdschrift voor Economische en Sociale Geografie* 96 (2005): 298–312.

12 Rees has regularly contacted high-tech firms in Metro Vancouver, and unpublished insights from these contacts are included in this and the next chapter.

13 These excluded micro firms likely have no employees or maybe one or two; many would not have reached profitability.

14 KPMG, *British Columbia Technology Report Card: Tackling the Scale-Up Challenge* (Vancouver: KPMG, 2020), https://wearebctech.com/2020-bc-technology-report -card/. KPMG has published several such report cards.

15 M.S. Granovetter, "The Strength of Weak Ties," *American Journal of Sociology* 78 (1973): 1360–80.

16 J.N.H. Britton, "High Technology Localization and Extra-Regional Networks," *Entrepreneurship and Regional Development* 16 (2004): 369–90; Rees, "Collaboration, Innovation and Regional Networks."

17 The Burnaby-based Svante was founded in 2007 in a garage and by 2022 had almost 200 professionals. The firm focuses on capturing carbon emissions before reaching

the atmosphere directly. Carbon Engineering was founded in 2009 in Calgary before relocating to Squamish, employing about 142 in 2021. It focuses on capturing carbon from the air and storing it underground or converting it to a carbon-neutral fuel. Both companies have received substantial funding and joined with energy MNCs in operating pilot plants in Canada and the United States.

18 Langford, Wood, and Jacobson, *The Evolution and Structure of the Vancouver Wireless Cluster.*

19 Rees, "Interregional Collaboration and Innovation in Vancouver's Emerging High-tech Cluster," Langford, Wood, and Jacobson, *The Evolution and Structure of the Vancouver Wireless Cluster.*

20 BC Stats, *Profile of the British Columbia High Technology Sector 2020 Edition* (Victoria: Prepared for Ministry of Jobs, Recovery and Innovation, 2021, by Dan Schrier), 104–5, uses a broad definition of telecommunications that appears to include (if not precisely stated) wired and wireless telecommunications carriers, satellite communications, telecommunications resellers (including firms providing video entertainment services in facilities operated by others), various data-processing firms, and firms engaged in internet broadcasting and web search portals.

21 Rees, "Collaboration, Innovation and Regional Networks"; Rees, "Interregional Collaboration and Innovation."

22 When AbCellera began in 2012, it had six employees, and its growth was not reported at the time the UBC website was recorded.

23 S. Silcoff, "B.C. Heart Device Firm Kardium Founded by Creo Executives Raises $115-Million from Fidelity, T. Rowe Price Ahead of Going Public"; T. Orton, "Long Road to Commercialization about to Pay Off for BC's Kardium," *Technology*, March 7, 2018, https://www.biv.com/news/technology/long-road-commercialization-about-pay-bcs-kardium-8252175.

24 G. Hoekstra, "BC's 'World-Class' Biotech Sector Plays Key Role in Developing COVID-19 Treatments and Vaccines," *Vancouver Sun*, May 7, 2021, https://vancouversun.com/news/b-c-s-world-class-biotech-sector-plays-key-role-in-developing-covid-19-treatments-and-vaccines. In addition to Stemcell Technologies and AbCellera Biologics, this article refers to Acuitus Therapeutics, Starfish Medical, Precision NanoSystems, and SaNOtize.

25 M. Gilding, J. Brennecke, V. Bunton, D. Lusher, P.L. Molloy, and A. Codoreanu, "Network Failure: Biotechnology Firms, Clusters and Collaborations Far from the World Superclusters," *Research Policy* 49 (2020): 1–17.

26 The material costs of the Quill suture were found to be six times more than standard sutures but marginally offset by an 11 percent reduction in wound closure times, reported as of "questionable clinical importance" in J.M. Gililland, L.A. Anderson, G. Sun, A. Jill, P.A.C. Erickson, and C.L. Peters, "Perioperative Closure-Related Complication Rates and Cost Analysis of Barbed Suture for Closure in TKA," *Clinical Orthopaedics and Related Research* 470 (2012): 125–29 (quotation on 125).

27 L. Hon, "B.C. Biotech on Life Support," *BC Business*, September 5, 2011, www.bcbusiness.ca/industries/general/bc-biotech-on-life-support.

28 S. Silicoff, "Vancouver Looks to Join the Global Big Leagues of Modern Medicine," https://www.theglobeandmail.com/business/article-vancouver-biotech-startups-medicine-pharmaceuticals/ *Globe and Mail*, March 9, 2024

29 Silicoff, "Vancouver Looks to Join the Global Big Leagues of Modern Medicine."
30 Silicoff, "Vancouver Looks to Join the Global Big Leagues of Modern Medicine."
31 Department of Trade and Industry (UK), *House of Commons Science and Technology Report – Third Report* (London: Department of Trade and Industry, 2003).
32 J.N.H. Britton, D.-G. Tremblay, and R. Smith, "Contrasts in Clustering: The Example of Canadian New Media," *European Planning Studies* 17 (2009): 211–34.
33 Barnes and Hutton, "Situating the New Economy"; Coe, "A Hybrid Agglomeration?"; Barnes and Coe, "Vancouver as Media Cluster."
34 For a historical perspective, see D.J. Duffy, *Motion Picture Production in British Columbia 1941–65*, n.d., https://staff.royalbcmuseum.bc.ca/wp-content/uploads/2016/11/Motion-Picture-Production-in-BC-Duffy-1986.pdf.
35 Barnes and Coe, "Vancouver as Media Cluster."
36 In brief, symbolic learning uses symbols to represent and give greater meaning to concepts.
37 R. Hayter and J. Patchell, *Economic Geography: An Institutional Approach* (Toronto: Oxford University Press, 2016), 247–48.
38 The "B movie" category is determined mainly by budget and often includes low-budget sci-fi, not just horror, movies.
39 Since located in Squamish, which makes sense for this type of industry, the workforce that it is trying to attract, and the lifestyle that Squamish now offers. It is located on Howe Sound, north of Lion's Bay, just outside Metro Vancouver's official boundary (see Figure 1.2) but strongly connected in terms of commuting.
40 K. Chan, "BC's Film Industry Generated over $3.4 Billion for the Local Economy Last Year," *Venture Vancouver*, July 17, 2018, https://dailyhive.com/vancouver/bc-film-industry-economy-2017-2018-statistics.
41 MPC had a major facility in Yaletown, which at one time employed 800 staff, closing down in December 2019. MPC had won an Academy Award for the visual effects in *Life of Pi* and was responsible for major live action remakes, including *The Jungle Book* and *The Lion King*.
42 Barnes and Coe, "Vancouver as Media Cluster."
43 S. Bröring, "Developing Innovation Strategies for Convergence – Is 'Open Innovation' Imperative?," *International Journal of Technology Management* 49 (2010): 272–94.
44 Life Sciences British Columbia, *Growing British Columbia's Bioeconomy* (Vancouver: Business in Vancouver, 2013), 10.
45 An illustration of the challenge facing nutraceuticals is the "combination of compound efficacy" – in this case being able to demonstrate that the product rescues cholesterol in the consumer – with taste, visual appeal, cost, and the requirement to "do no harm" in a consumer environment in which dosage is uncontrolled. In contrast, the efficacy and safety of pharmaceutical products are linked explicitly to dosage, with taste and visual appeal largely irrelevant and consumer demand less sensitive to cost.
46 Information obtained by Kevin Rees in an interview with the company in 2019.
47 Life Sciences British Columbia, *BC Life Sciences Update 2021: Building on a Foundation of Innovation* (Vancouver: Greater Vancouver Board of Trade, 2021), 10. Earlier reports make similar comments.

48 Wireless 2000 illustrates a failure to realize potential convergent technology to develop new products. The company was founded by Efraim Gavrilovch in 2003 after he had moved from Toronto in 1997 to apply wireless technologies to medical devices, including those monitoring vital signs in patients. Patents were issued, clinical trials were held, and products were approved and manufactured – but by 2005 the US-based Optex had acquired control of the tracking devices used in products such as the Apple iPhone 11. Wireless 2000 employed six engineers and a technician in Vancouver when it closed, and Gavrilovich relocated to Quebec.

49 The range of organizational collaborations created by converging technologies, even in small projects, is illustrated by Lignol, which developed connections within Metro Vancouver with FPInnovations (various branches), UBC's Faculty of Forestry, and massive model rendering expertise at SFU (and it networked with the University of Victoria's Genome BC Proteomics Centre).

Chapter 5: Deepening Institutional Support for Metro Vancouver High Tech

1 Agglomeration economies conventionally distinguish between localization and urbanization economies of scale. The former develop around particular industries and in recent years typically have been discussed as clustering economies. The latter reflect the benefits of cities available to all industries. Agglomeration diseconomies of scale similarly distinguish between urban and localization types. In this chapter, we focus on cluster qua localization economies.

2 Textbooks on regional economics and economic geography routinely discuss the agglomeration economies and diseconomies. For a research elaboration, see A. Potts and H.D. Watts, "Evolutionary Agglomeration Theory: Increasing Returns, Diminishing Returns, and the Industry Life Cycle," *Journal of Economic Geography* 11 (2010): 1–39.

3 Across Canada as elsewhere in recent decades, policies favouring the spatial concentration of economic activities generally have been labelled "cluster policies." In this regard, Porter's studies have been influential. See R.E. Porter, *The Competitive Advantage of Nations* (New York: Free Press, 1990).

4 The same rationale occurs when firms prefer to "buy" from external suppliers rather than "make" policies in which goods and services are provided internally.

5 Cluster (localization) external economies, or agglomeration economies in general, imply unit cost advantages for businesses but are hard to measure quantitatively because they are multifaceted, often subjective, and can be countered by agglomeration diseconomies. See R. Hayter, *The Dynamics of Industrial Location* (Chichester, UK: Wiley, 1997).

6 On the related idea of institutional thickness, and difficulties in its precise definition, see A. Amin and N. Thrift, "Globalisation, Institutional Thickness and the Local Economy," in *The New Urban Context*, ed. P. Healey, S. Cameron, S. Davoudi, S. Graham, and A. Madani-Pour (Chichester, UK: Wiley, 1994), 93–108.

7 Porter, *The Competitive Advantage of Nations*; M.E. Porter and W.M. Emmons, "Institutions for Collaboration, Overview," *Harvard Business Review*, January 2003, 703–46.

8 R. Bennett, "Business Associations, Their Potential Contributions to Government Policy and the Growth of Small and Medium Sized Enterprises," *Environment and Planning C* 17 (1999): 593–608. For a Canadian reference, see A. Kingsbury and R. Hayter, "Business Associations and Local Development: The Okanagan Wine Industry's Response to NAFTA," *Geoforum* 37 (2006): 596–609.

9 Supported by a $40.5 million grant from the BC government, the Great Northern Way Campus opened in 2007 as a joint initiative of UBC, SFU, BCIT, and Emily Carr to establish an MA program in digital media. It moved to a new building in 2021 with about 100 students.

10 In 2020, UBC had almost 59,000 students in Metro Vancouver, and SFU had around 37,000 students. BCIT, with its vocational focus, is the next largest tertiary educational organization, with a budget in 2020 of around $346 million and a student population of 40,000. Other community colleges that have become universities typically have budgets in the $150–$200 million range and student populations in the 12,000–20,000 range.

11 K. Bruland and D. Mowery, "Innovation through Time," in *The Oxford Handbook of Innovation*, ed. J. Fagerberg and D. Mowery (Oxford: Oxford University Press, 2006), 349–79.

12 G. Gunasekara, "Reframing the Role of Universities in the Development of Regional Innovation Systems," *Journal of Technology Transfer* 31 (2006): 101–13; H. Etzkowitz, *The Triple Helix: University-Industry-Government Innovation in Action* (London: Routledge, 2006); A. Varga, ed., *Universities, Knowledge Transfer and Regional Development: Geography, Entrepreneurship and Policy* (Cheltenham, UK: Edward Elgar, 2009).

13 See uilo.ubc.ca. This website details its organization and systematically lists all UBC spinoffs since the 1980s, along with feature stories.

14 See the SFU Innovates website, https://www.sfu.ca/research/km-innovation/innovation. For the four pillars underlying SFU Innovates, this website documents their mandates and main types of support. Information on individual spinoffs is sporadic.

15 In 2023, SFU opened a smart manufacturing hub at its Surrey campus, the first in western Canada, as a highly sophisticated training system that will help to promote collaboration with industry. SFU, "SFU Opens State-of-the-Art Smart Manufacturing Hub in Surrey," *SFU News*, June 22, 2023, https://www.sfu.ca/sfunews/stories/2023/06/sfu-opens-state-of-the-art-smart-manufacturing-hub-in-surrey.html.

16 UBC's UILO has records of supporting 114 inventions between 1964 and 1984. Greg Wheeler, Technology Transfer Manager, UBC, personal communication, May 25, 2023. On the Moli Energy story, see Case Study 2.1. On John MacDonald, see "Engineer John S. MacDonald Took Canadian Technology into Orbit," obituary, *Globe and Mail*, January 16, 2020, https://www.theglobeandmail.com/canada/article-engineer-john-s-macdonald-took-canadian-technology-into-orbit/; also Case Study 3.4.

17 For the full range of services provided by UBC's UILO and SFU Innovates, consult their websites. Note that these organizations also liaise with governments and non-profits as well as businesses.

18 SFU Intellectual Property Policy web page, https://www.sfu.ca/technology-licensing/ip-policy.html.
19 Canada Foundation for Innovation, *Commercialization Report*, third annual report (n.p.: Canada Foundation for Innovation, 2004).
20 C. Wilson, "SFU's Impact," March 26, 2018, https://www.cwilson.com/sfus-impact/. Clark Wilson provides legal advice to SFU Innovates. This news release also notes that SFU has assisted with eighty or so "social innovation ventures."
21 Canada Foundation for Innovation, *Commercialization Report*.
22 UBC's UILO website, uilo.ubc.ca. For SFU, see B.P. Clayman and J.A. Holbrook, "The Survival of University Spin-Offs and Their Relevance to Regional Development," SFU: Centre for Research Policy on Science and Technology, circa 2003, https://www.innovation.ca/sites/default/files/pdf/clayman1.pdf, accessed June 2018.
23 See M. Gilding, J. Brennecke, V. Bunton, D. Lusher, P.L. Molloy, and A. Codoreanu, "Network Failure: Biotechnology Firms, Clusters and Collaborations Far from the World Superclusters," *Research Policy* 49 (2020): 103902, doi:10.1016/j.respol.2019.103902. This study of Australia's biotechnology (globally peripheral) clusters emphasizes the severe problems in bringing biotech products to markets and resonates with the Metro Vancouver case.
24 In April 2022, UBC's UILO provided some information on impacts of its largest spinoffs. Regarding the two largest, QLT had lifetime sales of $4.1 billion, and Westport Innovations employed over 1,000 people and had lifetime sales of over $2.1 billion (see Appendix 1). The third largest in lifetime revenues, pioneered by Professor David Lowe, developed the Scale Invariant Feature Transform, a sophisticated mapping detection algorithm, apparently had relatively small local employment impacts. For the other twelve companies listed, lifetime sales varied from $35 million to $700 million, and some had been acquired by outside interests.
25 For example, TIR Systems, which pioneered LED lighting based on the research and patents of Dr. Lorne Whitehead, established a facility in Burnaby in 1978 and was acquired by the Netherlands MNC Philips in 2007. Once employing 200, there were 35 employees as of 2021. As another example, Dr. Murray Goldberg's WebCT innovation for online learning was introduced in 1995 and sold to Universal Learning Technology of Boston in 1999.
26 Simon Fraser University, "Vehicles Designed to Drive Underwater Research," April 9, 1997, http://www.sfu.ca/mediapr/releases/features/1997/april1997/underwater.htm.
27 Simon Fraser University, "Scientists to Gain from Inside View of Fuel Cells," SFU Engaging the World, October 25, 2013, https://www.sfu.ca/mechatronics/news/archives/2013/scientists-to-gain-from-inside-of-fuel-cells/.
28 The Times Higher Education impact rankings involve more than 1,000 institutions around the world in seventeen categories. In category nine, "Industry, Innovation and Infrastructure," designed to capture industry innovation and spinoffs et cetera, UBC was tied for first in 2022 and within the top seven on three other categories related to sustainability issues. Meanwhile, according to the (less well-known) rankings of the World Universities with Real Impact, in 2022 SFU was ranked first for the "Entrepreneurial Spirit" category and overall was ranked eighteenth in the world for innovation.

29 R. Brown, "Mission Impossible? Entrepreneurial Universities and Peripheral Regional Innovation Systems," *Industry and Innovation* 23 (2016): 1–17.

30 N. Reif, "Series A, B and C Funding: How Seed Funding Works," *Investopedia*, December 22, 2023, https://www.investopedia.com/articles/personal-finance/102015/series-b-c-funding-what-it-all-means-and-how-it-works.asp#:~:text=Series%20A%2C%20B%2C%20and%20C%20are%20funding%20rounds%20that%20generally,each%20separate%20fund%2Draising%20occurrences.

31 T-Net, "Chinook Therapeutics," *T-Net*, August 21, 2020, https://www.bctechnology.com/news/2020/8/21/vancouver-based-chinook-therapeutics-closes-major-$106-million-financing-to-advance-precision-medicines-for-kidney-disease.

32 T. Orton, "B.C.'s Stable of Unicorns Expands Rapidly," *Business in Vancouver*, April 30, 2021, https://www.biv.com/news/technology/bcs-stable-unicorns-expands-rapidly-2021-8264130.

33 D. Castle, "British Columbia: The Pacific Economy," in *Ideas, Institutions and Interests: The Drivers of Canadian Provincial Science, Technology, and Innovation Policy*, ed. P.W.B. Phillips and D. Castle (Toronto: University of Toronto Press, 2022), 307–29.

34 The (right-wing) Social Credit formed governments from 1951 to 1973 and from 1976 to 1991; the (centrist) Liberals from 2001 to 2016; and the (left-wing) NDP from 1973 to 1976, 1992 to 2001, and since 2016.

35 The BC government's announcement of Bombardier's plans to build railcars in Burnaby can also be noted; see *CBC News*, "Burnaby Home to New Bombardier Plant," January 18, 2009, https://www.cbc.ca/news/business/burnaby-home-to-new-bombardier-plant-1.179924. This post reported that the new plant would have 900 jobs, starting with an order for fifty railcars with further investment in BC businesses. Nothing happened.

36 R. Hayter and T.G. Gunton, "Discovery Park Policy: A Regional Planning Perspective," in *Topics in Cartography and Physical and Human Geography*, ed. N.M. Waters, BC Geographical Series No. 40 (Vancouver: Tantalus Press, 1984), 27–42.

37 The policy confusion, anger, and protests of the time are captured in R.C. Allen and G. Rosenbluth, eds., *Restraining the Economy* (Vancouver: New Star Books, 1986). The Social Credit Party sooned disappeared, becoming relabelled as the Liberal Party.

38 See the *BC Cancer Research Report 2021*, https://www.bccrc.ca/sites/bccrc.ca/files/2022-12/2021_ResearchReport_Final_web.pdf.

39 Creative BC publishes annual impact statements online.

40 T. Crawford, "New $701 Million Biotech Campus for Clinical Trials Planned for Vancouver," *Vancouver Sun*, May 24, 2023, https://www.vancouversun.com/news/local-news/new-701-million-biotech-campus-vancouver. The BC government will provide $75 million and the federal government $225 million (see Table 5.5).

41 A. Coyne, "The Productivity Puzzle: How Could We Be Doing So Poorly? We Do Everything Right!" *Globe and Mail*, March 23, 2024, https://www.theglobeandmail.com/opinion/article-the-productivity-puzzle-how-could-we-be-doing-so-poorly-we-did/.

42 Castle, "British Columbia," 325, argues that the BC government is now taking a leadership role in developing innovation capacity.

43 Pharma Boardroom, "Interview: David Main – CEO and President, Aquinox Phar-
    maceuticals Canada," 2018, https://pharmaboardroom.com/interviews/interview
    -david-main-ceo-and-president-aquinox-pharmaceuticals-canada/.
44 Castle, "British Columbia: The Pacific Economy."
45 D. Naylor and S. T. Toope, "Untangling the Great Policy Mess of Canada's Innova-
    tion Problem," *Globe and Mail*, October 27, 2023, https://www.theglobeandmail.
    com/business/commentary/article-canada-innovation-research-funding
    -economy/. J.P. Chauvet, L. Weir, B. Alarie, and N. Janssen, "Here's How Canada Can
    Fix its Research-and-Development Tax Credit System," *Globe and Mail*, February 1,
    2024, https://www.theglobeandmail.com/business/commentary/article-heres-how
    -canada-can-fix-its-research-and-development-tax-credit/.
46 Jim Balsillie, "An Outdated Myth About Business Investment is Hurting the Can-
    adian Economy," *National Post*, January 13, 2024, https://nationalpost.com/opinion/
    an-outdated-myth-about-business-investment-is-hurting-the-canadian-economy;
    Breznitz, "Innovation in Real Places."
47 H. Bathelt, A. Malmberg, and P. Maskell, "Clusters and Knowledge: Local Buzz,
    Global Pipelines and the Process of Knowledge Creation," *Progress in Human
    Geography* 28 (2004): 31–56.
48 C. Freeman, "Continental, National and Sub-National Innovation Systems," in
    Systems of Innovation: Essays in Evolutionary Economics, ed. C. Freeman (Chelten-
    ham, UK: Edward Elgar, 2008), 106–41; P. Cooke, "Regional Innovation Systems,
    Clusters, and the Knowledge Economy," *Industrial and Corporate Change* 10 (2001):
    945–74; B.T. Asheim and M. Gertler, "The Geography of Innovation: Regional
    Innovation Systems," in *The Oxford Handbook of Innovation*, ed. J. Fagerberg, D.
    Mowery, and R. Nelson(Oxford: Oxford University Press, 2006), 291–317; B.
    Asheim, H. Lawton Smith, and C. Oughton, "Regional Innovation Systems: Theory,
    Empirics and Policy," *Regional Studies* 45 (2011): 875–91.

Chapter 6: Lifestyle Innovators, West Coast Style

1 S. Zukin, *Landscapes of Power* (Berkeley: University of California Press, 1993); S.
   Zukin, "Urban Lifestyles: Diversity and Standardisation in Spaces of Consumption,"
   Urban Studies 35 (1998): 825–39.
2 R. Florida, *The Rise of the Creative Class* (New York: Basic Books, 2002).
3 G.F. Mulligan and J.I. Carruthers, "Amenities, Quality of Life and Regional Development," in *Investigating Quality of Life: Theory, Methods and Empirical Research:
   Social Indicators Research,* ed. R.W. Marans and R. Stimson, Series 45 (Heidelberg:
   Springer Science Business Media B.V., 2011), Chapter 5. Note that amenities are
   often portrayed as a supply-side locational condition that varies across space, but
   their translation as business opportunities is often driven by local demands.
4 A.J. Scott, *A World in Emergence – Cities and Regions in the 21st Century* (Cheltenham, UK: Edward Elgar, 2012). Scott expresses the dynamics of leading cities in
   terms of "cognitive-cultural capitalism," a perspective that resonates with Florida's
   creative city concepts.
5 P. Bourdieu, *Distinction: A Social Critique of the Judgment of Taste* (Cambridge,
   MA: Harvard University Press, 1984).

6 J. Shortridge, "Keeping Tabs on Kansas: Reflections of Regionally Based Field Study,"*Journal of Geography* 21 (1996): 45–59.

7 A.J. Scott, "Creative Cities: Conceptual Issues and Policy Questions," *Journal of Urban Affairs* 28 (2006): 1–17.

8 H. Molotch, "Places and Product," *International Journal of Urban and Regional Research* 26 (2002): 665–88 (quotation on 668).

9 M.E. Porter, "Location, Competition, and Economic Development: Local Clusters in a Global Economy," *Economic Development Quarterly* 14 (2000): 15–34.

10 C. Wilson, *Little Black Stretchy Pants* (Vancouver: Time Is Tight Communications, 2018).

11 T.G. Gunton, "Natural Resources and Regional Development," *Economic Geography* 79 (2003): 67–94; R. Hayter and T. Barnes, "Innis' Staple Theory, Exports, and Recession: British Columbia 1981–86," *Economic Geography* 66 (1990): 156–73.

12 Environmental analytics are discussed in R. Hayter and J. Patchell, *Economic Geography: An Institutional Approach* (Toronto: Oxford University Press, 2016), 435–38; the leaders of the firm, Tony Lea and Michael J. Weiss, introduce the nature of the geodemographic industry.

13 Strategy Staff, "Special Report: Distinctive but Part of the Mainstream," *Strategy,* September 4, 1995, https://strategyonline.ca/1995/09/04/11080-19950904.

14 T. O'Reilly, "Live and Let Buy: Where You Live Dictates What You Purchase. Under the Influence," *CBC Radio,* March 10, 2016, https://www.cbc.ca/listen/live-radio/ 1-70-under-the-influence. He notes, for example, that per capita consumption of luxury cars is 42 percent higher in British Columbia than the national average and higher than in New York, where purchases of luxury watches are significantly above the national (US) average. Also see T. O'Reilly, "Geography as Branding: An Encore Presentation," *CBC Radio,* June 27, 2015, https://www.cbc.ca/listen/live-radio/ 1-70-under-the-influence.

15 More than a century ago, Veblen proposed that consumers' decisions were determined not by the rational utilitarian logic implied by consumer sovereignty but by social conditions and expectations. Thus his famous identification of the "conspicuous consumption" of luxury goods and services by members of the emerging "leisure class," motivated not by any functional need but merely by the desire to flaunt their wealth. Indeed, "Veblen effects or goods" occur when, contrary to conventional demand theory, higher prices stimulate purchases of prestige goods perceived to enhance status. He further argued that the upper classes exercised a powerful influence on consumption through what he called "status emulation," in which consumers of lower social strata sought to increase their own status and self-worth by following the trends set by the strata above them. A tendency to copy the behaviour of peers ("bandwagon effects"), a preference for goods that can be appreciated only by cultural elites ("snob effects"), and a preference for simpler, more austere lifestyles ("countersnobbery effects") further indicate how consumption is socialized. The idiom "keeping up with the Joneses" is a variant of bandwagon effects that stresses the desire of people to consume goods similar to those of neighbours or friends. See T. Veblen, *The Theory of the Leisure Class: An Economic Study of Institution* (New York: Macmillan, 1899).

16 J. Sutherland, "Everything Cool Comes from Vancouver," *Globe and Mail, Report on Business,* November 24, 2016, 50–55, https://www.theglobeandmail.com/report-on-business/rob-magazine/sorry-toronto-everything-cool-comes-from-vancouver/article32955661/.

17 Sutherland, "Everything Cool Comes from Vancouver," 52.

18 Sutherland, "Everything Cool Comes from Vancouver," 53.

19 See L. Beasley, *Vancouverism* (Vancouver: UBC Press, 2019).

20 Vancouver Economic Commission, "Performance Apparel and Fashion," in *Vancouver Economy Report* (Spring 2022), 11–14.

21 Beyond apparel and fashion, other innovative lifestyle companies can be noted, such as Clearly Contacts and Saje Natural Wellness. Clearly Contacts was founded in 2000 in Vancouver as an internet retailer by local entrepreneurs (Roger and Michaela Hardy) and Derek Cardigan, the designer. It acquired companies around the world, and revenue reached $143 million by 2013. Saje was founded in North Vancouver in 1992 by Jean-Pierre and Kate Ross Leblanc, expanded across Canada and the United States, and employed 1,500 in fifty-seven stores in 2019.

22 The seedbed hypothesis is introduced in Chapter 2.

23 Wilson, *Little Black Stretchy Pants,* 90.

24 S.R. Robertson, "The Resurrection of MEC: Inside the Beleaguered Retailer's Bid for a Comeback," *Globe and Mail,* April 17, 2021, https://www.theglobeandmail.com/business/article-the-resurrection-of-mec-inside-the-beleaguered-retailers-bid-for-a/.

25 R. Nair, "MEC to Be Acquired by Private U.S. Investment Firm," *CBC News,* September 14, 2020, https://www.cbc.ca/news/business/mec-acquired-private-investment-firm-1.5723934.

26 Ebner, "Canadian Footwear Company Fluevog."

27 Ebner, "Canadian Footwear Company Fluevog."

28 Canadian Press, "Lululemon Promises 2,600 New Jobs for Vancouver after Exemption from Some Immigration Rules," *Vancouver Sun,* May 25, 2023, https://vancouversun.com/business/lululemon-promises-2600-new-jobs-for-vancouver-after-exemption-from-some-immigration-rules.

29 www.arcteryx.com.

30 Mustang Survival (1967), Delta Kayaks (1985), and Northern Surf (2004) are innovative SMEs supporting recreational water uses. Mustang Survival started in Vancouver's Gastown, is now located in Burnaby, and pioneered insulated life preserver and jacket clothing for cold weather use by fishers, sailors, and others. It is a leading supplier of water survival gear and in 1995 supplied NASA astronauts. In 2013, its 400 employees in locations in Burnaby, Bellingham, West Virginia, and Maryland were acquired by a US firm.

31 "John Mitchell Raises Toast to BC's Craft Breweries in Parting Message," What's Brewing, June 17, 2019, https://www.whatsbrewing.ca/2019/06/john-mitchell-salute/. See also J. Wiebe, *Craft Beer Revolution: The Insider's Guide to B.C. Breweries* (Madeira Park, BC: Douglas and McIntyre, 2013).

32 The opening of Metro Vancouver's first craft breweries during the early 1980s followed a seventeen-week lockout at the province's main breweries operated by

Labatt, Molson, and Carling O'Keefe during 1978 that led to consumer complaints, likely a factor in the provincial government's subsequent support for microbreweries.

33 Earls and the Cactus Club competed amicably until 2019, when, following a court dispute, the former took control of the latter. B. Lindsay, "Restaurant War Shatters 3 Decades of Peace between Cactus Club and Earls," *CBC News,* July 13, 2019, https://www.cbc.ca/news/canada/british-columbia/cactus-club-earls-joey -restaurant-war-1.5210465.

34 R. Mangelsdorf, "Remembering John Mitchell: A Look at the Legacy of the Grand-father of Canadian Craft Beer," *Growler,* September 4, 2019, https://bc.thegrowler. ca/features/remembering-john-mitchell-a-look-at-the-legacy-of-the-grandfather -of-canadian-craft-beer/. As this requiem notes, Mitchell was much helped by Appleton, a master brewer who had been living in the remote town of Edgewood in southeastern British Columbia. Appleton has reflected on his career in craft brewing in F. Appleton, *Brewing Revolution: Pioneering the Craft Beer Movement* (Victoria: Harbour Publishing, 2016).

35 A. Findlay, "BC's First Class Micro Breweries," *BC Business,* October 2, 2006, https:// www.bcbusiness.ca/industries/general/bcs-first-class-micro-breweries/; D. Fumano, "Hops Bounce Back in BC, Thanks to Craft Beer," *Province,* September 8, 2015, https://www.timescolonist.com/bc-news/hops-bounce-back-in-bc-thanks-to -craft-beer-4626584.

36 R. Campbell, *Sit Down and Drink Your Beers: Regulating Vancouver's Beer Parlours 1925– 1954* (Toronto: University of Toronto Press, 2001). This book emphasizes the culture of control organized by the Liquor Control Board on behalf of the govern-ment, still intact in 1980 by supporting the domination of the beer industry by the big three of Labatt, Molson, and Carling O'Keefe. Beer was sold cold, had similar alcohol content, was fizzy, and tasted similar; the main differences were the labels and bottle caps. Traditionally, beer drinking often took place in huge barn-like pubs where customers had to sit and were basically all served the same drink.

37 C.S. Mendes, "Red Tape Peeling Off Craft Breweries," *BC Business,* June 11, 2013, https://www.bcbusiness.ca/industries/general/red-tape-peeling-off-craft -breweries/; R. Mangelsdorf, "B.C.'s Booze Blues: As Craft Beer Booms, Can Our Liquor Laws Keep Up?," *The Growler,* October 27, 2017, https://bc.thegrowler.ca/ features/b-c-s-booze-blues-as-craft-beer-booms-can-our-liquor-laws-keep-up/. Some privatization of wine stores began in 1988.

38 M. Fawcett, "How Cactus Club Turned One Funky Restaurant into a Growing National Chain," *Canadian Business,* October 6, 2016; T. Wilson, "The Keg's Founder Built a Legacy," *Globe and Mail,* October 15, 2014, https://www.theglobeandmail. com/report-on-business/small-business/sb-marketing/the-kegs-founder-built-a -legacy/article21088882/.

39 Across British Columbia, the number of craft breweries increased from 54 in 2010 to 125 in 2017, with 77 located in Metro Vancouver.

40 A listing is provided in "Discover all 73 craft breweries in Vancouver, British Col-umbia," https://www.breweriesnearby.com/city/vancouver-bc (accessed January 2024).

41 Mitchell urged a return to wooden keg beer making, a 100 percent barley mash, and the use of whole cone hops, whereas craft brewing has incorporated the traditional

practice of double fermentation (involving stainless steel casks or tanks rather than wooden barrels) and forgoing the forced carbonation often used in large-scale beer making. Craft brewing is further distinguished by experimentation with the traditional mixes of barley (and wheat) malts and hops along with many other ingredients (lime, lemon, blackberries, orange peel, chocolate, etc.).

42 In British Columbia, microbreweries are defined by the British Columbia Liquor Distribution Board as producing less than 15,000 hectolitres per year, whereas regional breweries produce between 15,000 and 350,000 hectolitres per year.

43 Spinnakers had four distinct offerings from its opening day, including two flagship beers, Piper's Pale Ale and Hermann's Dark Lager. Subsequently, with regulations well established, new craft breweries typically have opened with a range of offerings, sometimes with food options, with several allowing customers to bring their own food. As Spinnakers first revealed, craft breweries need to combine achieving the MES with the economies of scope necessary to produce not one beer but a range of beers. These options need to be appealing to remain attractive to a sufficient number of customers over time. Mass production alternatives are always going to be cheaper. The problems of achieving profitability at start-up were evident at both Horseshoe Bay Brewery and Granville Island Brewing. At the former, Mitchell brewed one type of beer from second-hand (former dairy processing) equipment, but this experiment proved to be uneconomic, closing in 1985 (although reopening again soon afterward). The operation kept going with five new beers released by 2005 before being acquired in 2006. Meanwhile, at Granville Island, the focus on lager beer required extra brewing time, with supplies hard to replenish.

44 A. Findlay, "BC's First Class Micro Breweries," *BC Business*, October 2, 2006.

45 V. Mathews and R.M. Picton, "Intoxifying Gentrification: Brew Pubs and the Geography of Post-Industrial Heritage," *Urban Geography* 35 (2014): 337 56.

46 S.M. Schnell, "Deliberate Identities: Becoming Local America in a Global Age," *Cultural Geography* 30 (2013): 55–89; D. Eberts, "Neolocalism and the Branding and Marketing of Place by Canadian Microbreweries," in *The Geography of Beer: Regions, Environment, and Societies*, ed. M. Patterson and N. Hoelst-Pullen (New York: Springer, 2014), 189–99.

47 "Steamworks: Our Story," https://steamworks.co.uk/about/.

48 For example, Port Moody's celebrated Yellow Dog Brewery offers Shake a Paw, Chase My Tail, and Play Dead with no reference to its location.

49 Schnell, "Deliberate Identities."

50 Similarly, one of British Columbia's earliest craft brewers, Okanagan Springs of Vernon, was acquired in 1996 by Sleeman Brewing, Canada's third largest brewer, itself purchased by Sapporo of Japan in 2006, and Howe Sound Brewery in Squamish was acquired by the Viaggio Hospitality Group in 2021.

51 R. Mangelsdorf, "Beer Today, Gone Tomorrow: Remembering BC's Defunct Craft Breweries," *Vancouver Courier*, July 13, 2019, https://www.vancouverisawesome. com/courier-archive/living/beer-today-gone-tomorrow-remembering-bcs -defunct-craft-breweries-3103270. For example, John Mitchell's first Horseshoe Bay Brewery was closed in 1985, only to be reopened and modernized, operating until 1999, when it permanently closed. As another Mitchell-influenced venture, Shaftsbury Brewing relocated to Delta to obtain a lower-cost space; it was acquired by

Sleeman Brewing and moved to Vernon as part of the Okanagan Springs Brewery before being acquired by a Kelowna firm. Granville Island Brewing also changed ownership, first acquired in 2006 by Andrew Peller, a wine firm based in Kelowna that renovated the facility and expanded in Kelowna, before becoming a subsidiary of Molson, a global beer giant, in 2009. Vern Lambourne, the original brewmaster, was retained until 2015, and the brewery continued to develop and produce small craft beers with the main brewing done at Molson's established brewery. With respect to other ownership changes, Steel Toad opened in 2014 in Vancouver's Olympic Village but never did well and was acquired by the Tap and Barrel group in 2018. On the North Shore, Avalon Brewing experienced a rather tortuous history since 2004, and Sailor Hagar's pioneering craft brewery has contracted out its brands since 2003.

52 The Keg organizes its meat supplies separately in western and central Canada. In both cases, there is a strong emphasis on quality control.

53 J. St. Denis, "We've Made a Mistake: Earls Reverses Decision on U.S.-Only Beef," *Vancouver Business,* May 4, 2016, https://www.biv.com/news/hospitality-marketing -tourism/weve-made-mistake-earls-reverses-decision-us-only-8246184.

54 D. Fumano, "Hops Bounce Back in BC, Thanks to Craft Beer," *Province,* September 8, 2015; G. Luymes, "Could B.C. Hops Growers Mirror Wine Industry Success? With Use of Genomics They Hope So," *Vancouver Sun,* July 31, https:// vancouversun.com/business/local-business/bc-hops-growers-use-genomics -in-hunt-for-new-varieties.

55 Fumano, "Hops Bounce Back in BC."

56 D. Ryan, "How One Man Founded Canada's Craft Beer Industry Right Here in B.C.," *Vancouver Sun,* July 6, 2022, https://vancouversun.com/news/local-news/how-one -man-founded-canadas-craft-beer-industry-right-here-in-bc.

Chapter 7: Metro Vancouver on the Thin Edge of Innovation, and Associated Conundrums

1 D. Breznitz and M. Murphree, *Run of the Red Queen: Government, Innovation, Globalization, and Economic Growth in China* (New Haven, CT: Yale University Press, 2011).

2 A. Agrawal and J. Cockburn, "The Anchor Tenant Hypothesis: Exploring the Role of Large, Local, R&D-Intensive Firms in Regional Innovation Systems," *International Journal of Industrial Organization* 21 (2003): 1227–53; M.P. Feldman, "The Character of Innovative Places: Entrepreneurial Strategy, Economic Development, and Prosperity," *Small Business Economics* 43 (2014): 9–20.

3 D. Castle, "British Columbia: The Pacific Economy," in *Ideas, Institutions, and Interests: The Drivers of Canadian Provincial Science, Technology, and Innovation Policy,* ed. P.W.B. Phillips and D. Castle (Toronto: University of Toronto Press, 2022), Chapter 14.

4 The development of vanadium flow (big) batteries can be added to this list. D. Penner, "Future of Renewable Energy Looks Like a Giant Battery as Vancouver Company Scales Up Production," *Vancouver Sun,* June 9, 2023, https://vancouver sun.com/news/local-news/vancouver-company-bets-on-utility-sized -batteries-for-renewable-energy.

5 B.J. Asheim, "Smart Specialisation, Innovation Policy and Regional Innovation Systems: What about New Path Development in Less Innovative Regions?," *Innovation: The European Journal of Social Science Research* 32 (2019): 8–25.

6 An interesting counterfactual question is whether the same increasing population of firms among fewer specializations in Metro Vancouver high tech would have led to strong self-reliance and a better chance of core company emergence.

7 Castle, "British Columbia."

8 Third-party, truly independent assessments of federal and provincial government policies are rare; government bureaucracies routinely publicize the success of their programs by simple counts or lists of recipients and likely overstate incremental effects and significant benefits.

9 In this regard, a recent survey by University of Waterloo engineering graduates almost certainly resonates with the situation at UBC and SFU in Metro Vancouver. See Software Engineering Class, "Software Engineering 2020 Class Profile," Waterloo, June 2020, https://uw-se-2020-class-profile.github.io/profile.pdf.

10 Vancouver 2020, *A Bright Green Future*, produced by the Green Action Team, 2020, https://vancouver.ca/files/cov/bright-green-future.pdf.

11 With respect to the first theme, a green economy, Vancouver 2020, *A Bright Green Future*, discusses green business and jobs, climate leadership, and green buildings as combined efforts to reduce reliance on fossil fuels. The second theme is greener communities, and the third is human health.

12 P. Gurstein and T. Hutton, *Planning on the Edge: Vancouver and the Challenges of Reconciliation, Social Justice and Sustainable Development* (Vancouver: UBC Press, 2019).

13 E.J. Malecki, "Economic Competitiveness and Regional Development Dynamics," in *Handbook of Regions and Competitiveness*, ed. R. Huggins and P. Thompson (Cheltenham, UK: Edward Elgar, 2017), 136–52.

14 D. Penner, "Microsoft Executive Promotes Virtual Reality 'Super Cluster' for Vancouver," *Vancouver Sun*, November 2, 2017, http://vancouversun.com/news/local-news/microsoft-executive-promotes-virtual-reality-super-cluster-for-vancouver.

15 At the federal level, the government's decision in 2023 to pay Volkswagen $16–$17 billion to establish a battery assembly factory in Ontario seems to be questionable, even appalling, on straightforward economic criteria. It also seems to have been made without much thought to how it can support new mineral developments or new energy sources or contribute to an overall innovation policy for Canada.

16 "The Global Power City Index 2022," Institute for Urban Strategies, The Mori Memorial Foundation, 1, https://mori-m-foundation.or.jp/english/ius2/gpci2/index.shtml. This study details the rankings of all forty-eight cities studied, both in overall terms and for each of the six dimensions according to the various indicators used. As might be expected, London, New York, Paris, and Tokyo dominate the rankings.

17 The GPIC is based on data collected for seventy indicators for each of the cities. Basically, scores or points are assigned to the indicators (and dimensions) and summed up to provide a comprehensive ranking. The methodology has been developed by an expert panel of urban scholars and, if judgmental, is the most rigorous, systematic ranking of global cities yet developed.

18 For the GPCI study, Vancouver refers to Vancouver itself. However, several indicators are also derived from data taken across the metropolitan region.
19 D. Todd, "Is Vancouver Narcissistic? A Global Ranking Suggests Some Humility is in Order," *Vancouver Sun,* January 5, 2022, https://vancouversun.com/opinion/columnists/is-vancouver-narcissistic-a-global-ranking-suggests-some-humility-is-in-order.
20 C. Freeman and F. Louçã, *As Time Goes By: From the Industrial Revolution to the Information Revolution* (Oxford: Oxford University Press, 2001).
21 J. Patchell, "Kaleidoscope Economies: The Processes of Cooperation, Competition and Control," *Annals of the Association of American Geographers* 86 (1996): 481–506.
22 P. Sunley, R. Martin, and P. Tyler, "Cities in Transition: Problems, Processes and Policies," *Cambridge Journal of Regions, Economy and Society* 10 (2017): 383–90.

Selected Bibliography

Adams, S.B. 2011. "Growing Where You Are Planted: Exogenous Firms and the Seeding of Silicon Valley." *Research Policy* 40: 368–79.

Affolderbach, J., Hayter, R., and Clapp, R. 2012. "Environmental Bargaining and Boundary Organizations: Remapping British Columbia's Great Bear Rainforest." *Annals of the Association of American Geographers* 102: 1391–440.

Aggrawal, A., and Cockburn, I. 2003. "The Anchor Tenant Hypothesis: Exploring the Role of Large, Local, R&D-intensive Firms in Regional Innovations Systems." *International Journal of Industrial Organization* 21: 1227–253.

Allen, R.C., and Rosenbluth, G. (eds.). 1986. *Restraining the Economy*. Vancouver: New Star Books.

Andreasen, E. 2020. "B.C. Mass Timber Is Ready for Global Prime Time." *Vancouver Sun*, September 1.

Amin, A., and Thrift, N. 1994. "Globalisation, Institutional Thickness and the Local Economy." In *The New Urban Context*, ed. P. Healey, S. Cameron, S. Davouidi, S. Graham, and A. Madinpur, 91–108. Chichester: Wiley.

Appleton, F. 2016. *Brewing Revolution: Pioneering the Craft Beer Movement*. Madeira Park, BC: Harbour Publishing.

Asheim, B., and Gertler, M.S. 2005. "The Geography of Innovation: Regional Innovation Systems." In *The Oxford Handbook of Innovation*, ed. J. Fagerberg, D. Mowery, and R. Nelson, 291–317. Oxford: Oxford University Press.

–, Lawton Smith, H., and Oughton, C. 2011. "Regional Innovation Systems: Theory, Empirics and Policy." *Regional Studies* 45: 875–91.

Asheim, B.J. 2019. "Smart Specialisation, Innovation Policy and Regional Innovation Systems: What About New Path Development in Less Innovative Regions?" *Innovation: The European Journal of Social Science Research* 32: 8–25.

Audretsch, D.R. 1995. *Innovation and Industry Evolution*. Cambridge: MIT Press.

–, Keilbach, M., and Lehmann, E.E. 2006. *Entrepreneurship and Economic Growth*. Oxford: Oxford University Press.

–, and Feldman, M.P. 2004. "Knowledge Spillovers and the Geography of Innovation." In *Handbook of Urban and Regional Economics, Vol 4 Cities and Geography*, ed. J.V. Henderson and J-F Thisse. Amsterdam: Elsevier.

Ballard. 2019. *Our History*, https://www.ballard.com/our-company.

Barnes, T.J. 1987. "Homo Economicus, Physical Metaphors and Universal Models in Economic Geography." *The Canadian Geographer* 31: 299–308.

–, and Hayter, R. 2005. "No Greek-letter Writing: Local Models of Resource Economies." *Growth and Change* 36: 453–70.

Barnes, T., Edgington, D.W., Denike, K.G., and McGee, T.G. 1992. "Vancouver, the Province and the Pacific Rim." In *Vancouver and Its Region*, ed. G. Wynn and T. Oke, 171–99. Vancouver: UBC Press.

Barnes, T., and Hutton, T. 2009. "Situating the New Economy: Contingencies of Regeneration and Dislocation in Vancouver's Inner City." *Urban Studies* 46: 1247–269.

–. 2016. "Vancouver and the New Economy of Culture and Innovation." In *Growing Urban Economies: Innovation, Creativity and Governance in Canadian City-Regions*, ed. D. Wolfe and M. Gertler, 109–38. Toronto: University of Toronto Press.

Bathelt, H., Malmberg, A., and Maskell, P. 2004. "Clusters and Knowledge: Local Buzz, Global Pipelines and the Process of Knowledge Creation." *Progress in Human Geography* 28: 31–56.

BC Cancer Agency, http://www.bccancer.bc.ca, accessed April 5, 2023.

BC Stats. 1996. *The British Columbia High Technology Sector 1988–1995*. Victoria: Information, Science and Technology Agency, Government of British Columbia.

Beasley, L. 2019. *Vancouverism*. Vancouver: UBC Press.

Beaudry, C., and Schiffauerova, A. 2009. "Who's Right, Marshall or Jacobs? The Localization Versus Urbanization Debate." *Research Policy* 38: 318–37.

Bell, D. 1974. *The Coming of Post-industrial Society: A Venture in Social Forecasting*. New York: Heinemann.

Benneth, P. Coenen, L., Moodyson, J., and Asheim, B. 2009. "Exploring the Multiple Roles of Lund University in Strengthening the Scania Regional Innovation System: Towards Institutional Learning?" *European Planning Studies* 17: 1645–664.

Bennett, R.J. 1999. "Business Associations: Their Potential Contribution to Government Policy and the Growth of Small and Medium-Sized Enterprises." *Environment and Planning C: Government and Policy* 17: 593–608. https://doi.org/10.1068/c170593.

Binkley, C.S. 1993. "Creating a Knowledge-based Forest Sector." *Forestry Chronicle* 69: 294–99.

–. 1997. "A Crossroad in the Forest: The Path to a Sustainable Forest Sector in BC." *BC Studies* 113: 39–61.

Bonaccorsi, A. 2017. "Addressing the Disenchantment: Universities and Regional Development in Peripheral Regions." *Journal of Economic Policy* 20: 293–320.

Boschma, R. 2005. "Proximity and Innovation: A Critical Assessment." *Regional Studies* 39: 61–74.

–. 2021. "Designing Smart Specialization Policy: Relatedness, Unrelatedness or What?" *Papers in Evolutionary Economic Geography* 21.28. Utrech University, Department of Human Geography and Spatial Planning.

–, and Martin, R. (eds.). 2010. *The Handbook of Evolutionary Economic Geography.* Cheltenham: Edward Elgar.

Bourdieu, P. 1984. *Distinction: A Social Critique of the Judgment of Taste.* Cambridge, MA: Harvard University Press.

Brethour, P. 2002. "The Decline of Vancouver's Pivotal Corp Shows the Perils of Partnering with Microsoft." *Globe and Mail,* April 1.

Breznitz, D. 2021. *Innovation in Real Places: Strategies for Prosperity in an Unforgiving World.* New York: Oxford University Press.

–, and Murphree, M. 2012. "Shaking Grounds: Technology Standards in China." Working draft, accessed January 2022.

Bridge, G., Bouzarovski, S., Bradshaw, M., and Eyre, N. 2013. "Geographies of Energy Transition: Space, Place and the Low-carbon Economy." *Energy Policy* 53: 331–40.

British Columbia. 2009. *Generating More Value from our Forests: A Vision and Action Plan for Further Manufacturing.* Victoria: Ministry of Forests.

British Columbia Innovation Council. 2008. *Ballard's Fuel Cell Project: Next Stop – Changing the World.* Burnaby.

Britton, J.N.H. 2004. "High Technology Localization and Extra-regional Networks." *Entrepreneurship and Regional Development* 16: 369–90

–, and Gilmour. J.M. 1978. *The Weakest Link: A Technological Perspective on Canadian Underdevelopment. Ottawa.* Science Council of Canada, Background Study 22.

–, Tremblay, D-G., and Smith, R. 2009. "Contrasts in Clustering: The Example of Canadian New Media." *European Planning Studies* 17: 211–34.

Brock Commons Tallwood House, nd. *Think Wood,* https://www.thinkwood.com/construction-projects/brock-commons-tallwood-house, accessed August 10, 2020.

Bröring, S. 2010. "Developing Innovation Strategies for Convergence – Is 'Open Innovation' Imperative?" *International Journal of Technology Management* 49: 272–94.

Brown, R. 2016. "Mission Impossible? Entrepreneurial Universities and Peripheral Regional Innovation Systems." *Industry and Innovation* 23: 189–205.

Buckley, P.J., and Casson, M.C. 1976. *The Future of the Multinational Enterprise.* London: Macmillan.

Bruland, K., and Mowery, D. 2006. "Innovation through Time." In *The Oxford Handbook of Innovation,* ed. J. Fagerberg and D. Mowery, 349–79. Oxford: Oxford University Press.

Campbell, R.A. 2001. *Sit Down and Drink Your Beer.* Toronto: University of Toronto Press.

Canada Foundation for Innovation. 2004. "Commercialization Report. Third Annual Report." https://www.innovation.ca/sites/default/files/2021-09/CFI-Annual-report-2003-2004.pdf, accessed April 5, 2023.

Canadian Forest Service. 2003. *Secondary Wood Manufacturing in BC.* Forest Renewal B.C. Victoria: Ministry of Forests.

Canadian Human Computer Communications Society. 2016. "Canadian Digital Media Pioneer Award: Don Mattrick, 2016." https://graphicsinterface.org/awards/cdmp/don-mattrick/.

Cantwell, Dunning, J.N.H., and Lundan, S.M. 2010. "An Evolutionary Approach to Understanding International Business Activity: The Co-evolution of MNEs and the Institutional Environment." *Journal of International Business Studies* 41: 567–86.

Castle, D. 2022. "British Columbia: The Pacific Economy." In *Ideas, Institutions, and Interests: The Drivers of Canadian Provincial Science, Technology, and Innovation Policy*, ed. P.W.B. Phillips and D. Castle. Toronto: University of Toronto.

Caves, R.E. 1971. "International Corporations: The Industrial Economics of Foreign Investment." *Economica* 38: 1–27.

CBC News. 1999. "Burnaby Home to New Bombardier Plant." https://www.cbc.ca/news/business/burnaby-home-to-new-bombardier-plant-1.179924, accessed April 5, 2023.

Chan, K. 2017. "Facebook to Open New Major Downtown Vancouver Office on Burrard Street." https://dailyhive.com/vancouver/facebook-vancouver-office-200-burrard-street.

Chandler, A.D. 1962. *Strategy and Structure: Chapters in the History of American Industrial Enterprise*. New York: Doubleday.

Cheung, C. 2020. "Inside the 'Growth Machine' that Made Vancouver World-Class Unaffordable." https://thetyee.ca/Analysis/2020/02/13/Gov-Real-Estate-Vancouver-Housing-Unaffordable.

Church, M. 2019. "Leading the Masses: Structurlam Expands Okanagan Mass Timber Operation." *Canadian Forest Industries*. http://www.woodbusiness.ca/leading-the-masses-structurlam-expands-okanagan-mass-timber-operation.

Clague, J., and Turner, B. 2003. *Vancouver: City on the Edge*. Vancouver: Tricouni Press.

Clark-Jones, M. 1987. *A Staple State: Canadian Industrial Resources in Cold War*. Toronto: University of Toronto Press.

Clapp, A. 1998. "The Resource Cycle in Forestry and Fishing." *Canadian Geographer* 42: 129–44.

–, Hayter, R., Affolderbach, J., and Flores, L.G. 2016. "Institutional Thickening and Innovation: Reflections on the Remapping of the Great Bear Rainforest." *Transactions of the Institute of British Geographers* 41: 244–57. https://doi.org/10.1111/tran.12119.

Clayman, B.P., and Holbrook, J.A. 2003. "The Survival of University Spin-Offs and Their Relevance to Regional Development." SFU: Centre for Research Policy on Science and Technology. https://www.innovation.ca/sites/default/files/pdf/clayman1.pdf, accessed June 2018.

Coe, N.M. 2000a. "The View From Out West: Embeddedness, Inter-personal Relations and the Development of an Indigenous Film Industry in Vancouver." *Geoforum* 31: 391–407.

–. 2000b. "On Location: American Capital and the Local Labour Market in Vancouver's Film Industry." *International Journal of Urban and Regional Research* 24: 79–94.

–. 2001. "A Hybrid Agglomeration? The Development of a Satellite-Marshallian Industrial District in Vancouver's Film Industry." *Urban Studies* 38: 1753–777.

Cooke, P. 2001. "Regional Innovation Systems, Clusters, and the Knowledge Economy." *Industrial and Corporate Change* 10: 945–74.

Creative BC. https://www.creativebc.com, accessed April 5, 2023.

Davidoff, T., Akaabre, P.B., and Jones, C. 2022. "Policy Forum: The Prevalence of Low Income Tax Payments among Owners of Expensive Homes in Vancouver and Toronto." *Canadian Tax Journal* 70: 843–59.

Dosi, G., Freeman, C., Nelson, R.R., Silverberg, R., and Soete, L. (eds.). 1988. *Technical Change and Economic Theory*. London: Pinter.

Drache, D. (ed.). 1995. *Staples, Markets and Cultural Change: Selected Essays, Harold A Innis*. Montreal and Kingston: McGill-Queen's Press.

Duggain, E. 2014. "International Visual Effects Firm Makes Vancouver Its First Anchor in North America." *Vancouver Sun,* November 11.

–. 2019. "Amazon to Take over Entire Former Canada Post Office Building in Downtown Vancouver." *Vancouver Sun,* December 10. https://vancouversun.com/business/commercial-real-estate-amazon-to-take-over-entire-former-canada-post-building.

Dunning, J.H. 1988. *Explaining International Production*. London: Unwin Hyman.

Eberts. D. 2014. "Neolocalism and the Branding and Marketing of Place by Canadian Microbreweries." In *The Geography of Beer: Regions, Environment, and Societies,* ed. M. Patterson and N. Hoelst-Pullen, 189–99. New York: Springer.

Ebner, D. 2018. "Canadian Footwear Company Fluevog Prepares for Life Without Founder." *Globe and Mail,* March 18. https://www.theglobeandmail.com/report-on-business/small-business/canadian-footwear-company-fluevog-prepares-for-life-without-founder/article38298110, accessed April, 5 2023.

Economist Intelligence Unit. 2022. "The Global Liveability Index." *Economist,* June 2022.

Edenhoffer, K., and Hayter, R. 2013. "Restructuring on a Vertiginous Plateau: The Evolutionary Trajectories of British Columbia's Forest Industries 1980–2010." *Geoforum* 44: 139–51.

Eder, J. 2019. "Innovation in the Periphery: A Critical Survey and Research Agenda." *International Regional Science Review* 42: 119–46.

Engel, J.S. 2015. "Global Clusters of Innovation: Lessons from Silicon Valley." *California Management Review* 57: 36–66.

–, and del-Palacio, I. 2011. "Global Clusters of Innovation: The Case of Israel and Silicon Valley." *California Management Review* 53: 27–49.

Etzkowitz, H., 2008. *The Triple Helix: University-Industry-Government Innovation in Action*. London: Routledge.

Evans. P. 2022. "Big Tech Hiring Cements Canada's Status as Silicon Valley North – but There Is a Catch." *CBC News,* April 24. www.cbc.ca/news/business/canada-tech-sector-boom-1.6425879.

Evenden, L. (ed.). 1974. *Vancouver: Western Metropolis*. Western Geographical Series, Vol. 16. Victoria: University of Victoria.

Fast, P.A., and Jackson, R. 2017. "Brock Commons: A Case Study in Tall Timber."

Fawcett, M. 2016. "How Cactus Club Turned One Funky Restaurant into a Growing National Chain." *Canadian Business.* https://archive.canadianbusiness.com/lists -and-rankings/best-managed-companies/cactus-club/, accessed April 5, 2023.

Feldman, M.P. 2014. "The Character of Innovative Places: Entrepreneurial Strategy, Economic Development, and Prosperity." *Small Business Economics* 43: 9–20.

Findlay, A. 2006. "BC's First Class Micro Breweries." *BC Business,* October 2. https:// www.bcbusiness.ca/bcs-first-class-micro-breweries, accessed April 5, 2023.

Finlayson, J., and Peacock, K. 2020. "Opinion: Export of Services Plays a Strong Growing Role in B.C. Economy." *Business in Vancouver,* June 15.

F.L.C. Reed and Associates. 1974. *Canada's Reserve Timber Supply.* Prepared for the Department of Industry, Trade and Commerce, Ottawa.

Fletcher, T. 2019. "B.C.'s Engineered Wood Leadership Many Years in the Making." https://www.campbellrivermorror.com/business/b-c-s-engineered-wood -construction-leadership-years-in-the-making/, accessed August 10 2020.

Florida, R. 2002. *The Rise of the Creative Class.* New York: Basic Books.

–, and Smith, D.F. 1993. "Venture Capital Formation, Investment and Regional Industrialization." *Annals of the Association of American Geographers* 83: 434–51.

Fralic, S. 2021. "Vancouver, Once Heaven, Now Merely a Mess Choking Itself to Death." *Vancouver Sun,* May 16.

Freeman, C. 2008. "Continental, National and Sub-National Innovation Systems – Complementarity and Economic Growth." In *Systems of Innovation: Essays in Evolutionary Economics,* ed. C. Freeman, 106–41. Cheltenham: Edward Elgar.

–, and Louçã, F. 2001. *As Time Goes By: From the Industrial Revolution to the Information Revolution.* Oxford: Oxford University Press.

Fritsch, M., and Wyrwich, M. 2021. "Is Innovation (Increasingly) Concentrated in Large Cities? An International Comparison." *Research Policy* 50: 4–32.

Frome, A. 2005. "A Sawmill Icon." *The Logging and Sawmill Journal,* February.

Fumano, Dan. 2015. "Hops Bounce Back in BC, Thanks to Craft Beer." *Times-Colonist,* September 8. https://www.timescolonist.com/bc-news/hops-bounce -back-in-bc-thanks-to-craft-beer-4626584, accessed April 5, 2023.

Gainor, C. 2020. Engineer John S. "MacDonald Took Canadian Technology into Orbit." *Globe and Mail,* January 16. https://www.theglobeandmail.com/canada/ article-engineer-john-s-macdonald-took-canadian-technology-into-orbit/, accessed April 5, 2023.

Galbraith, J.K. 1967. *The New Industrial Estate.* Houghton Mifflin, Boston, MA.

Gibbon, A. 2000. "Greenbacks Flow to BC Tech Sector." *Globe and Mail,* January 10 (updated March 23, 2018). https://www.theglobeandmail.com/report-on-business/ rob-magazine/greenbacks-flow-to-bc-tech-sector/article4158645/.

Gilani, H.R., Kozack, R.A., and Innes, J.L. 2016. "The State of Innovation in the British Columbia Value-added Wood Products Sector: The Example of Chain of Custody Certification." *Canadian Journal of Forest Research* 46: 1067–75.

Gill, A.M., and Williams, P.W. 2011. "Rethinking Resort Growth: Understanding Evolving Governance Strategies in Whistler, British Columbia." *Journal of Sustainable Tourism* 19: 629–48.

Givetash, L. 2016. "Wood Tower at the University of British Columbia a Game-Changer for Construction." *Vancouver Sun,* June 13.

Global Power City Index. 2022. https://mori-m-foundation.or.jp/english/ius2/gpci2/index.shtml.

Golding, M., Brennecke, J., Bunton, V., Lusher, D., Molloy, P.L., and Codoreanu, A. 2020. "Network Failure: Biotechnology Firms, Clusters and Collaborations Far From the World Superclusters." *Research Policy* 49: 1–17.

Gordon, J. 2020. "Solving Puzzles in the Canadian Housing Market: Foreign Ownership and Decoupling in Toronto and Vancouver." *Housing Studies.* https://doi.org/10.1080/02673037.2020.1842340.

Granovetter, M.S. 1973. "The Strength of Weak Ties." *American Journal of Sociology* 78: 1360–80.

Grass, E., and Hayter, R. 1989. "Employment Change During Recession: The Experience of Forest pPoduct Manufacturing Plants in British Columbia, 1981–1985." *The Canadian Geographer* 33: 240–52.

Gray, M., Golob, E., and Markusen, A. 1996. "Big Firms, Long Arms, Wide Shoulders: The Hub and Spoke Industrial District in the Seattle Region." *Regional Studies* 30: 651–66.

Gunasekara, C. 2006. "Reframing the Role of Universities in the Development of Regional Innovation Systems." *Journal of Technology Transfer* 31: 101–13.

Gunton, T. 2009. "Natural Resources and Regional Development: An Assessment of Dependency and Comparative Advantage Paradigms." *Economic Geography* 79: 67–94. https://doi.org/10.1111/j.1944-8287.2003.tb00202.x.

Gurstein, P., and Hutton, T. 2019. *Planning on the Edge: Vancouver and the Challenges of Reconciliation, Social Justice, and Sustainable Development.* Vancouver: UBC Press.

Haley, D., and Leitch, J. 1992. *The Structure and Product Mix of the Solid Wood Products Sector.* Prepared for the British Columbia Forest Resources Commission.

Hamilton, W. 2014. "It's Glory Days for Heavy Wood Timber in British Columbia." *Resource Works.* https://www.resourceworks.com/-it-s-glory-days-for-heavy-wood-timber-in-british-columbia.

Hanna, R., Hayter, R., and Clapp, A. 2017. "Threshold Firms: Innovation, Design and Collaboration in British Columbia's Forest Economy." *Growth and Change* 48: 700–18. https://doi.org/10.1111/grow.12210.

Hardwick, W. 1963. *Geography of the Forest Industry in British Columbia.* Occasional Papers in Geography No. 5. Vancouver: Canadian Association of Geographers, British Columbia Division.

Hardwick, W.G. 1974. *Vancouver.* Don Mills: Collier-MacMillan Canada.

Hayter, R. 1976. "Corporate Strategies and Industrial Change in the Canadian Forest Product Industries." *Geographical Review* 66: 209–28.

–. 1982. "Research and Development in the Canadian Forest Product Sector – Another Weak Link?" *The Canadian Geographer* 26: 256–62.

–. 1988. *Technology Policy Perspectives and the Canadian Forest Product Industries.* Background Study No.56, Science Council of Canada, Ottawa, 1988.

–. 1992. "International Trade Relations and Regional Industrial Adjustment: Implications of the 1980s' North American Softwood Lumber Dispute for British Columbia." *Environment and Planning A* 24, 153–70.

–. 2000. *Flexible Crossroads: The Restructuring of British Columbia's Forest Economy.* Vancouver: UBC Press.

–. 2003. "'The War in the Woods': Post-Fordist Restructuring, Globalization and the Contested Remapping of British Columbia's Forest Economy." *Annals of the Association of American* Geographers 93: 706–29. https://doi.org/10.1111/1467-8306. 9303010.

–. 2008. "Environmental Economic Geography in Institutional Perspective." *Geography Compass* 3: 831–50. http://www.blackwell-compass.com/subject/geography/ article.

–, and Barnes, T. 1990. "Innis' Staple Theory, Exports and Recession: British Columbia 1981–86." *Economic Geography* 66: 156–73.

–, and Barnes, T. 1992. "Labour Market Segmentation, Flexibility and Recession: A British Columbian Case Study." *Environment and Planning C* 10: 333–53.

–, and Barnes, T. 1997. "The Restructuring of British Columbia's Coastal Forest Sector: Flexibility Perspectives." In *Troubles in the Rainforest: British Columbia's Forest Economy in Transition*, ed. T. Barnes and R. Hayter, 181–202. Victoria: Western Geographical Series.

–, and Clapp, A. 2020. "Towards a Collaborative (Public-Private) Partnership Approach to Research and Development in Canada's Forest Sector: An Innovation Systems Perspective." *Forest Policy and Economics* 113. https://doi.org/10.1016/ j.forpol.2020.102119.

–, and Edenhoffer, K. 2016. "Shakeouts, Shakeins and Industry Population Dynamics: British Columbia's Forest Industries 1980–2008." *Growth and Change* 47: 497–519.

–, and Edgington, D.F. 1999. "'Getting Tough' and 'Getting Smart': Politics of the North American-Japan Wood Products Trade." *Environment and Planning C: Government and Policy* 17: 319–44.

–, and Gunton, T.G. 1984. "Discovery Park Policy: A Regional Planning Perspective. In *Topics in Cartography and Physical and Human Geography,* ed. N.M. Waters. *B.C. Geographical Series No. 40*, 27–42. Vancouver: Tantalus Press.

–, and Patchell, J. 2016. *Economic Geography: An Institutional Approach.* Don Mills, Ontario: Oxford University Press.

–, Patchell, J., and Rees, K.G. 1999. "Business Segmentation and Location Revisited: Innovation and the Terra Incognita of Large Firms." *Regional Studies* 33: 425–42.

Hoekstra, G. 2021. "BC's 'World-Class' Biotech Sector Plays Key Role in Developing COVID-19 Treatments and Vaccines." *Vancouver Sun.* May 7.

Hon, L. 2011. "B.C. Biotech on Life Support." *BC Business*, September 5.

Howlett, M., Rayner, J., Tollefson, C., 2009. "From Government to Governance in Forest Planning? Lessons from the Case of the British Columbia Great Bear Rainforest Initiative." *Forest Policy Econ.* 11: 383–91.

Huggins, R., and Thompson, P. 2017. "Introducing Regional Competitiveness and Development: Contemporary Theories and Perspectives." In *Handbook of Regions and Competitiveness*, ed. R. Huggins and P. Thompson, 1–31. Cheltenham: Edward Elgar.

Hunt, E., 2018. "Plyscraper City: Tokyo to Build 350m Tower Made of Wood." *The Guardian*, February 16.

Hurley, A.K. 2017. "The Weird, Wooden Future of Skyscrapers." *The Atlantic*, December.

Hutton, T. 2004. "Post-industrialism, Post-modernism and the Reproduction of Vancouver's Central Area: Re-theorising the 21st Century." *Urban Studies* 41: 1953–1982.

Hymer, S.H. 1960. *The International Operations of National Firms: A Study of Direct Foreign Investment.* Cambridge, MA, MIT Press.

Innovation Canada. 2005. *Case 2: Ballard Power Systems.* Ottawa. https://web. archive.org/20051217125101/http://www.innovation.gc.ca/gol/innovation/site. nsf/en/in04204.htm.

Jaganmohan, M. 2021 "Global R&D Spending by Key Fuel Cell Companies 2021." January 29 2021.

Jang, B. 2020. "Chasing the Hydrogen Dream: Ballard in Quest to Transform Long-Haul Transportation." *Globe and Mail,* Dec 4.

Jarratt. E. 2020. "New Lessons from the Epic Story of Moli Energy, the Canadian Pioneer of Rechargeable Lithium Battery Technology." Electric Autonomy Weekly, April. https://electricautonomy.ca/2020/09/18/moli-energy-lithium-battery-technolgy/.

Johansson, J., and Valhne, J.E. 1977. "The Internationalization Process of the Firm – A Model of Knowledge Development and Increasing Foreign Market Commitments." *Journal of International Business Studies* 88, 23–32.

Johnson, W. 2021. "Meet Rivian, the $808 EV Maker with Offices in Yaletown." *Vancouver Tec Journal*, October 18. www.vantechjournal.com/p/rivian-vancouver?s=r.

Kay, J. 2021. "RIP PLC: The Rise of the Ghost Corporation." *Prospect,* March 3. www. prospectmagazine.co.uk/ideas/economics/37397/rip-plc-the-rise-of-the-ghost-corporation.

Kenney, M., and Patton, D. 2006. "The Coevolution of Technologies and Institutions: Silicon Valley as the Iconic High-technology Cluster." In *Cluster Genesis: Technology-based Industrial Development,* ed. P. Braunerhjelm and M.P. Feldman, 38–60. Oxford: Oxford University Press.

Kingsbury, A., and Hayter, R. 2006. "Business Associations and Local Development: The Okanagan Wine Industry's Response to NAFTA." *Geoforum* 37: 596–609. https://doi.org/10.1016/j.geoforum.2005.12.001.

Kirkwood, E. 2019. "Tile Expands to Canada, Opens Engineering Hub in Vancouver." *Betakit,* May 29. https://betakit.com/tile-expands-to-canada-opens-engineering-hub-in-vancouver/.

Kitching, H. 2022. "Is Timber the Future for Highrise Buildings? Lakehead Researchers Develop Patent to Help Make It Happen." *CBC News,* May 3.

Klepper, S., and J. Miller. 1995. "Entry, Exit, and Shakeouts in the United States in New Manufactured Products." *International Journal of Industrial Organization* 13: 567–91.

–, and Simmons, S. 2005. "Industry Shakeouts and Technological Change." *International Journal of Industrial Organization* 23: 23–43.

Koppel, T. 2001. *Powering the Future.* Cheltenham: Wiley.

Kozak, R., and Mannes, T. 2005. "Towards a Value Focused Forest Sector in British Columbia." *BC Forum on Forest Economics and Policy Issues Brief: IB 05-01.* http://conservation economics.com/pdf_pubs/issue_brief/IB050_ValueFocused Forestry.pdf.

KPMG. 2018. "BC Technology Report Card: From Growth to Scale."

KPMG. 2020. "BC Technology Report Card: Tackling the Scale-up Challenge."

Krashinsky Robertson, Susan. 2021. "The Resurrection of MEC: Inside the Beleaguered Retailer's Bid for a Comeback." *Globe and Mail*, April 17. https://www.theglobeandmail.com/business/article-the-resurrection-of-mec-inside-the-beleaguered-retailers-bid-for-a/, accessed April 5 2023.

Kuhn, R.L. 1985. *To Flourish Among Giants.* London: John Wiley.

Langford, C.H., Wood, J.R., and Jacobson, A. 2004. "The Evolution and Structure of the Vancouver Wireless Cluster: Growth and Loss of Core Firms." https://www.researchgate.net/publication/265533886_The_evolution_and_structure_of_the_Vancouver_wireless_cluster_Growth_and_loss_of_core_firms.

Lawrance, J., and Miller, S. 1995. *Defining the High Technology / Knowledge Sector in British Columbia.* Victoria: BC Stats.

–. 1996. *The British Columbia High Technology Sector, 1988–1994.* Victoria: BC Stats.

Levy, D 2016. "ORNL Researchers Invent Tougher Plastic with 50% Renewable Content." https://www.ornl.gov/news/ornl-researchers-invent-tougher-plastic-50-percent-renewable-content, accessed May 14, 2018.

Ley, D. 1980. "Liberal Ideology and the Post-industrial City." *Annals of the Association of American Geographers* 83: 272–30.

–. 2017. "Global China and the Making of Vancouver's Residential Property Market." *International Journal of Housing Policy* 1: 17–34.

–. 2021. "A Regional Growth Ecology: A Great Wall of Capital and a Metropolitan Housing Market." *Urban Studies* 58: 297–315.

–. 2023. *Housing Booms in Gateway Cities.* Chichester: Wiley

–, and Hutton, T. 1987. "Vancouver's Corporate Complex and Producer Services Sector: Linkage and Divergence within a Provincial Staple Economy." *Regional Studies* 21: 413–24.

Lindsay, B. 2019. "Restaurant War Shatters 3 Decades of Peace Between Cactus Club and Earls." *CBC News,* July 13. https://www.cbc.ca/news/canada/british-columbia/cactus-club-earls-joey-restaurant-war-1.5210465, accessed April 5, 2023.

Littlemore, R. 2015. "Vancouver's High Tech Makeover." *Globe and Mail,* March 26. https://www.theglobeandmail.com/report-on-business/rob-magazine/vancouvers-high-tech-makeover/article23614007/.

Lundvall, B.-Å. (ed.). 1992. *National Systems of Innovation: Towards a Theory of Innovation and Interactive Learning.* London: Anthem Press.

Malecki, E.J. 2017. "Economic Competitiveness and Regional Development Dynamics." In R. Huggins and P. Thompson, ed., *Handbook of Regions and Competitiveness,* 136–52. Cheltenham: Edward Elgar.

Malmberg, A., and Maskell, P. 2006. "The Elusive Concept of Localization Economies, Towards a Knowledge-based Theory of Spatial Clustering." *Environment
and Planning A* 34: 429–49.

Mangelsdorf, R. 2017. "B.C.'s Booze Blues: As Craft Beer Booms, Can Our Liquor
Laws Keep Up." *BC Business*, October 27. https://bc.thegrowler.ca/features/b-c-s
-booze-blues-as-craft-beer-booms-can-our-liquor-laws-keep-up/. Accessed April
5, 2023.

–. 2019. "Beer Today, Gone Tomorrow: Remembering BC's Defunct Craft Breweries." *Vancouver Is Awesome*, July 13.

–. 2019. "Remembering John Mitchell: A Look at the Legacy of the Grandfather of
Canadian Craft Beer." *The Growler*, September 4. https://bc.thegrowler.ca/features/
remembering-john-mitchell-a-look-at-the-legacy-of-the-grandfather-of-canadian
-craft-beer/, accessed April 5, 2023.

Manninen, H. 2014. *Long-term Outlook for Engineered Wood Products in Europe*.
European Forestry Institute Technical Report 91.

Manning, S. 2013. "New Silicon Valleys or a New Species? Commoditization of
Knowledge Work and the Rise of Knowledge Service Clusters." *Research Policy* 42:
379–90.

Marchak, P. 1983. *Green Gold: The Forest Industry in British Columbia*. Vancouver:
UBC Press.

–, Aycock, S., and Herbert, D. 1999. *Falldown: Forest Policy in British Columbia*.
Vancouver: Ecotrust Canada.

Markusen, A. 1985. *Profit Cycles, Oligopoly and Regional Development*. Cambridge,
MA: MIT Press.

–. 1996. "Sticky Places in Slippery Space: A Typology of Industrial Districts." *Economic Geography* 72: 293–313.

Marshall, H., Southward, F.A., and Taylor, K.W. 1936. *Canadian-American Industry:
A Study in International Investment*. Toronto: Ryerson.

Martin, R., Sunley, P., and Tyler, P. 2015. "Local Growth Evolution: Recession, Resilience and Recovery." *Cambridge Journal of Regions, Economy and Society* 8: 141–48.

Massey, D., and Wield, D. 2003. *High-tech Fantasies: Science Parks in Society, Science
and Space*. Routledge.

Mathews, V., and Picton, R.M. 2014. "Intoxifying Gentrification: Brew Pubs and the
Geography of Post-industrial Heritage." *Urban Geography* 35: 337–56.

McCrank, J. 2009. "Nanotechnology Applications in the Forest Sector." *Natural
Resources Canada*, Canadian Forest Service, Ottawa.

McCullough, M. 2012. "Creo: The Digitization Printing Company That Could Have
Saved Kodak." *Canadian Business*. https://canadianbusiness.com/article/71121
--creo-the-digitization-printing-company-that-could-have-saved-kodak.

McGovern, P.D. 1961. "Industrial Development in the Vancouver Area." *Economic
Geography* 37: 189–206.

Mclhenney, K., and Hayter, R. 2014. "Sustaining Jobs and Environment? The Wood
Industry in Vancouver-Metro, British Columbia." *Local Environments* 19: 605–25.
http://dx.doi.org/10.1080/13549839.2013.854755.

McWilliams, J. 1991. *Profile of the B.C. Wood Products Value-added Sector.* FRDA Report. Vancouver: Forintek Canada.

Mendes, C. 2013. "Red Tape Peeling Off Craft Breweries." *BC Business,* June 11, https://www.bcbusiness.ca/red-tape-peeling-off-craft-breweries, accessed April 5, 2023.

M'Gonigle, M., and Parfitt, B. 1994. *Forestopia.* Madeira Park, BC: Harbour Publishing.

Michailova, S., and Mustaffa, Z. 2012. "Subsidiary Knowledge Flows in Multinational Corporations: Research Accomplishments, Gaps and Opportunities." *Journal of World Business* 47: 383–96.

Molotch, H. 2002. "Places and Product." *International Journal of Urban and Regional Research.* 26: 665–88.

Monte, Carlo D. 2016. "Industry Innovation: A Canadian Perspective." In *Presentation: PwC 29th Annual Global Forest, Paper and Packaging Industry Conference.* Vancouver, May 4. https://www.pwc.com/ca/en/industries/forest-paper.../29th-fpp-conference.html.

Mulligan, G.F., and Carruthers, J.I. 2011. "Amenities, Quality of Life, and Regional Development." In *Investigating Quality of Urban Life: Theory, Methods, and Empirical Research,* ed. R. Marans and R. Stimson, 107–33. Berlin: Springer.

Munro, J. and Gill, W. 2006. "The Alaska Cruise Industry." In *Cruise Ship Tourism,* ed. R.K. Dowling, 145–60. CAB eBooks.

Nakamura, H. 1990. *New Mid-sized Firm Theory* (in Japanese). Tokyo Keizai Shinpansha, Tokyo.

Nelson, R. 1988. "Institutions Supporting Technical Change in the United States." In *Technical Change and Economic Theory,* ed. G. Dosi, C. Freeman, R.R. Nelson, G. Silverberg, and L. Soete, 312–39. New York: Pinter.

– (ed.). 1993. *National Innovation Systems: A Comparative Analysis.* Oxford: Oxford University Press.

Nighbor, D. 2016. "Fpinnovations Needs Renewed Government Funding to Help Turn Trees into Airplane Parts." *Vancouver Sun,* November 4. https://vancouversun.com/opinion-turning-trees-into-airplane-parts.

Oinas, P., and Malecki, E.J. 2002. "The Evolution of Technologies in Time and Space: From National and Regional to Spatial Innovation Systems." *International Regional Science Review* 25: 102–31.

Olds, K. 2001. *Globalization and Urban Change: Capital, Culture and Pacific Rim Mega-Projects.* Oxford: Oxford University Press.

O'Reilly, T. 2019. "Live and Let Buy: Where You Live Dictates What You Purchase." *Under the Influence Series,* CBC, aired October 7.

Orton, T. 2018. "Long Road to Commercialization About to Pay Off for BC's Kardium." *Technology,* March 7 (accessed March 2019).

–. 2019a. "Consumer Electronics Firm Tile Taps Vancouver as New Engineering Hub." *Business in Vancouver,* May 29.

–. 2019b. "Big Tech Expansion in Vancouver a 'Magnet for U.S. Firms." *Business in Vancouver,* June 20. https://big-tech-expansion-vancouver-magnet-us-firms.

–. 2021. "B.C.'s Stable of Unicorns Expands Rapidly." *Business in Vancouver,* April 30, https://biv.com/article/2021/04/bcs-stable-unicorns-expands-rapidly-2021, accessed April 5, 2023.

Palmer, V. 2021. "B.C. Forest Companies Expanding at a Rapid Pace, but Not at Home." *Vancouver Sun,* December 1.

Parfitt, B. 2010. *After the Windfall: Plotting a New Course for BC Beyond the SLA.* Vancouver: Canadian Centre for Policy Alternatives.

–. 2017. "Raw Logs and Lost Jobs: How the BC Government Has Sacrificed Forest Communities." *Tyee,* February 27.

–. 2022. "BC's Chief Forester Jumps to Multinational Wood Pellet Corporation." *Tyee,* April 7.

–. 2023. "How Monster Mills Ate BC's Timber Jobs." *Tyee,* March 6.

Patchell, J. 1993a. "From Production Systems to Learning Systems: Lessons from Japan." *Environment and Planning A* 25: 797–81.

–. 1993b. "Composing Robot Production Systems: Japan as a Flexible Manufacturing System." *Environment and Planning A* 25: 923–44.

–. 1996. "Kaleidoscope Economies: The Processes of Cooperation, Competition and Control." *Annals of the Association of American Geographers* 86: 481–506.

Peacock, K. 2022. "A Brief Primer on BC's Export Base." May 12. https://bcbc.cominsights-and-opinions/a-brief-primer-on-b-c-s-export-base.

Pearse, P.H. 1976. *Timber Rights and Forest Policy in British Columbia: Report of the Royal Commission on Forest Resources.* Victoria: Queen's Printer.

Peltoniemi, M. 2011. "Reviewing Industry Life Cycle Theory. Avenues for Further Research." *International Journal of Management Reviews* 13: 349–75.

Penner, D. 2014. "Prince George Centre Opens as Towering Experience in All-Wood Construction Sector." *Vancouver Sun,* November 18.

–. 2017. "Microsoft Executive Promotes Virtual Reality 'Super Cluster' for Vancouver." *Vancouver Sun,* November 2, accessed April 1, 2020.

–. 2021. "New Bentall Tower to Be Focal Point of Timber in Vancouver's Concrete Jungle." *Vancouver Sun,* September 23.

–. 2019. "Japanese Giant Fujitso Picks Vancouver for Global Artificial Intelligence HQ." *Vancouver Sun,* July 9.

Perkins. S. 2016. "How to Make Window 'Glass' from Wood." In *Science News for Students.* https://www.sciencenews-for-students.org/article/how-to-make-window-glass-wood.

Pike, A., Rodríguez, A., and Tomaney, J. 2017. *Local and Regional Development.* London: Routledge.

Porter, Michael. E. 1990. *The Competitive Advantage of Nations.* New York: Free Press.

Potter, A., and Watts, H.D. 2010. "Evolutionary Agglomeration Theory: Increasing Returns, Diminishing Returns, and the Industry Life Cycle." *Journal of Economic Geography* 11: 417–55.

PricewaterhouseCoopers. nd. *British Columbia TechMap™ 1997, 2003 and 2013.* Maps provided directly by PwC.

Proctor, J. 2016. "Deal of the Century: Expo 86 Land Purchase Changed Vancouver." *CBC News,* May 4.

Punter, J. 2003. *The Vancouver Achievement: Urban Planning and Design.* Vancouver: UBC Press.

Rabbiosi, L., and Santangelo, G.D. 2013. "Parent Company Benefits From Reverse Knowledge Transfer: The Role of the Liability of Newness in MNEs." *Journal of World Business* 48: 160–70.

Rees, K.G. 1999. "Innovation in the Periphery: Networks or Fragments in the High Technology Industries of Greater Vancouver." Ph.D. Thesis, Department of Geography, Simon Fraser University.

–. 2004. "Collaboration, Innovation and Regional Networks: Evidence from the Medical Biotechnology of Greater Vancouver." In *Proximity, Distance and Diversity: Issues on Economic Interaction and Local Development,* ed. A. Lagendijk and P. Oinas. London: Ashgate.

–. 2005. "Interregional Collaboration and Innovation in Vancouver's Emerging High-Tech Cluster." *Tidjschrift voor Economicshe en Social Geografie* 96: 298–312.

–, and Hayter, R. 1996. "Flexible Specialization, Uncertainty and the Firm: Enterprise Strategies and Structures in the Wood Remanufacturing Industry of the Vancouver Metropolitan Area, British Columbia." *Canadian Geographer* 40: 203–19.

Reif, N. 2023. "Series A, B and C Funding: How Seed Funding Works." *Investopedia,* June 5. https://www.investopedia.com/articles/personal-finance/102015/series-b-c-funding-what-it-all-means-and-how-it-works.asp, accessed April 5 2023.

Reiffenstein. T., Hayter, R., and Edgington, D.W. 2002. "Crossing Cultures, Learning to Export: Making Houses in British Columbia for Export in Japan." *Economic Geography* 78: 195–220.

Richardson, K. 2016. "Attracting and Retaining Foreign Highly Skilled Staff in Times of Global Crisis: A Case Study of Vancouver, British Columbia's Biotechnology Sector." *Population, Space and Place* 22: 428–40.

Rigby, D. 2012. "The Geography of Knowledge Relatedness and Technological Diversification in US cities." *Papers in Evolutionary Economic Geography* 1218. Utrech University, Department of Human Geography and Spatial Planning.

Rodríguez-Pose, A., and Fitjar, R.D. 2013. "Buzz, Archipelago Economies and the Future of Intermediate and Peripheral Areas in a Spiky World." *European Planning Studies* 21: 355–72.

–, and Griffiths, J. 2021. "Developing Intermediate Cities." *Regional Science Policy and Practice* 13: 441–56.

Rugman, A.M., and Verbeke, A. 2001. "Subsidiary Specific Advantages in Multinational Enterprises." *Strategic Management Journal* 22: 237–35.

Samsung. 2017. "News: Samsung Research & Development Centre Vancouver." December 19. https://dailyhive.com/vancouver/samsung-research-development-centre-vancouver.

Saxanian, A. 1981. "The Genesis of Silicon Valley." *Built Environment* 9: 7–17.

–. 1994. *Regional Advantage: Culture and Competition in Silicon Valley and Route 128.* Cambridge, MA: Harvard University Press.

Schell, S.M. 2013. "Deliberate Identities: Becoming Local America in a Global Age." *Cultural Geography* 30: 55–89.

Schumpeter, J. 1943. *Capitalism, Socialism and Democracy.* New York: Harper.

Schwindt, R., and Heaps, T. 1996. *Chopping up the Money Tree: The Distribution of*

Wealth from British Columbia's Forests. Vancouver: David Suzuki Foundation.

Scott, A.J. 2006. "Creative Cities: Conceptual Issues and Policy Questions." *Journal of Urban Affairs* 28: 1–17.

–. 2012. *A World in Emergence – Cities and Regions in the 21st Century.* Cheltenham: Edward Elgar.

SFU Feature. 1997. "Vehicles Designed to Drive Underwater Research," April 9.

SFU Intellectual Property Policy. 2023. http://www.sfu.ca/policies/gazette/research/r30-03.html, accessed April 5, 2023.

Shaw, R. 2018. "Housing Revenues Help Balance B.C. Budget Again, but Downtown Looms." *Vancouver Sun,* August 28.

Shortridge, J. 1996. "Keeping Tabs on Kansas: Reflections of Regionally Based Field Study." *Journal of Geography,* 21: 45–59.

Silcoff, S. 2021. "B.C. Heart Device Firm Kardium Founded by Creo Executives Raises $115-Million from Fidelity, T. Rowe Price Ahead of Going Public." *Globe and Mail,* January 29.

Silverwood, A. 2017. "Weyerhaeuser Uses Strong Scraps." *Canadian Forest Industries,* October 17.

Simon H. 1992. "Lessons from Germany's Midsized Giants" *Harvard Business Review* 70: 115–23.

Smith, C. 2022. "The B.C. Economy and the Broadway Plan: Sn Explainer." *Georgia Strait,* May 9.

Sonn, J.W., and Lee, D. 2012. "Revisiting the Branch Plant Syndrome: Review of Literature on Foreign Direct Investment and Regional Development in Western advanced economies." *International Journal of Urban Sciences* 16: 243–59.

St. Denis, J. 2016. "Earls Reverses Decision on U.S.-only Beef." *Alaska Highway News,* May 4. https://www.alaskahighwaynews.ca/local-business/earls-reverses-decision-on-us-only-beef-3492752, accessed April 5, 2023.

Start-up Genome. 2019. "Global Startup Ecosystem Report 2019." https://startupgenome.com/reports/global-startup-ecosystem-report-2019, accessed September 2020.

Strategy Staff. 1995. "Special Report: Marketing in Vancouver: Distinctive but Part of the Mainstream." https://strategyonline.ca/1995/09/04/11080-19950904, September 4. Accessed April 6, 2023.

Steed, G.P.F. 1973. "Intrametropolitan Manufacturing: Spatial distribution and Location Dynamics in Greater Vancouver." *The Canadian Geographer* 17: 235–58.

–. 1982. *Threshold Firms: Backing Canada's Winners. Science Council of Canada.* Ottawa: Ministry of Supply and Services.

–, and Genova, D. 1983. "Ottawa's Technology-oriented Complex." *Canadian Geographer* 27: 262–78.

Storper, M. 1995. "The Resurgence of Regional Economies, Ten Years Later: The Region as a Nexus of Untraded Interdependencies." *European and Urban Regional Studies* 2: 191–221.

Sunley, P. Martin, R., and Tyler, P. 2017. "Cities in Transition: Problems, Processes and Policies." *Cambridge Journal of Regions, Economy and Society* 10: 383–90.

Sutherland, J. 2016. "Everything Cool Comes from Vancouver." *Globe and Mail,* 50–55. Updated November 12, 2017.

Synder, J. 2020. "Unclear Intellectual Property Rules Put Canada at Risk Amid Higher Threat of Foreign Takeovers." *National Post,* June 15.

Tajusu, N., and Shiraki, T. 2017. "Tougher Than Steel: Japan Looks to Wood Pulp to Make Lighter Auto Parts." https://www.reuters.com/article/technology/tougher -than-steel-japan-looks-to-wood-pulp-to-make-lighter-auto-parts-idUSKCN 1AU2FQ/.

Taylor, T. 2011. "Ballard Power and the Quest for Profitability." *BC Business,* May 2. https://www.bcbusiness.ca/ballard-power-and-the-quest-for-profitability, accessed April 5, 2023.

Todd, D. 2020. "Hidden Foreign Ownership Helps Explain Metro Vancouver's 'Decoupling' of House Prices, Incomes." *Vancouver Sun,* December 4.

–. 2022. "Is Vancouver Narcissistic? A Global Ranking Suggests Some Humility Is in Order." *Vancouver Sun,* January 5.

–. 2023. "How Global Liveability Rankings Cursed Vancouver." *Vancouver Sun,* March 2.

Travers, O.R. 1993. "Forest Policy: Rhetoric and Reality." In *Touch Wood: BC Forests at the Crossroads,* ed. K. Drushka, B. Nixon, and R. Travers, 171–224. Madeira Park, BC: Harbour Publishing.

University of British Columbia University. Industry Liaison Office, 2023. https:// uilo.ubc.ca, accessed April 5.

Varga, A. 2009. *Universities, Knowledge Transfer and Regional Development.* Cheltenham: Edward Elgar.

Veblen, T. 1899. *The Theory of the Leisure Class.* London: Macmillan.

Wang, Y., and Chung-Sok, S. 2009. "Towards a Re-conceptualization of Firm Internationalization: Heterogeneous Process, Subsidiary Roles and Knowledge Flow." *Journal of International Management* 15: 447–59.

Watkins, M. 1963. "A Staple Theory of Economic Growth." *Canadian Journal of Economic and Political Science* 29: 141–48.

Wei, P. 2017. "Silicon Valley 150 Rankings of the Top 150 Public Tech Companies in The Bay Area." https://www.mercurynews.com/2017/05/01/sv150-top-10-the -best-and-worst-performances, accessed February 2, 2018.

Williams, L. 2018. "The Wood Fibre Solution to the World's Plastic Problem." *Eureka,* June 13. https://eureka.eu.com/innovation/wood-fibre-plastic.

Wilson, C. 2018. *Little Black Stretchy Pants.* Time is Tight Communications.

Wilson, J. 1998. *Talk and Log: Wilderness Politics in British Columbia 1965–96.* Vancouver: UBC Press.

Wilson, T. 2014. "The Keg's Founder Built a Legacy." *Globe and Mail,* October 15. https://www.theglobeandmail.com/report-on-business/small-business/sb -marketing/the-kegs-founder-built-a-legacy/article21088882/, accessed April 5, 2023.

Woodbridge Associates. 2009. "Opportunity BC 2020." *BC's Forest Industry:*

Moving from a Volume Focus to a Value Perspective. Report prepared for the Business Council of BC.

Woodin, H. 2017. "B.C. Budget 2017: Government Plans for a Lower Housing Market." *Real Estate,* February 21. https://biv.com/article/2017/02/bc-budget-2017-government-plans-slower-housing-market.

Wynn, G. 1992. "The Rise of Vancouver." In *Vancouver and Region,* ed. G. Wynn and T. Oke, 69–148. Vancouver: UBC Press.

Young, I. 2021. "Vancouver Became a Byword for Money Laundering, Fuelled by Chinese Cash. Can It Flip the Script?" *South China Morning Post,* December 21.

Zukin, S. 1993. *Landscapes of Power: from Detroit to Disney World.* Berkeley: University of California Press.

–. 1998. "Urban Lifestyles: Diversity and Standardisation in Spaces of Consumption." *Urban Studies* 35: 825–39.

Index

Note: "(f)" after a page number indicates a photograph or map; "(t)" after a page number indicates a table.

Printed and bound by CPI Group (UK) Ltd, Croydon, CR0 4YY

Set in Segoe and Warnock by Artegraphica Design Co.

Copy editor: Dallas Harrison

Cartographer: Eric Leinberger

Cover designer: Martyn Schmoll

Authorized Representative:

Easy Access System Europe

Mustamäe tee 50, 10621 Tallinn, Estonia

gpsr.requests@easproject.com

Printed and bound by CPI Group (UK) Ltd, Croydon, CR0 4YY

23/04/2025

14660942-0003